REAL ESTATE
APPRAISAL

2ND EDITION, 2ND PRINTING

ASHLEY CROWN SYSTEMS, INC.

ROY K. BOTTGER • ERIC SHARKEY

This publication is designed to provide accurate and current information regarding the subject matter covered. The principles and conclusions presented are subject to local, state and federal laws and regulations, court cases and revisions of same. If legal advice or other expert assistance is required, the reader is urged to consult a competent professional in the field.

Real Estate Publisher
Leigh Conway

Academic Information Analyst
Laura King

Writer
Sue Carlson

Senior Technical Writer
Nicole Thome

Graphic Designer
Susan Mackessy Richmond

©2013 by Ashley Crown Systems, Inc., a division of Allied Business Schools, Inc.
2nd Edition, 2nd Printing

Published by
Ashley Crown Systems, Inc.
22952 Alcalde Drive
Laguna Hills, California 92653

Printed in the United States of America

ISBN: 978-0934772-39-6

TABLE OF CONTENTS

PREFACE

Appraisal plays a crucial role in hundreds of thousands of real estate transactions every year. Appraisers rely on their knowledge of real estate and economics to determine the property values for their clients—from lenders to lawyers. *Real Estate Appraisal* introduces the beginner to the key concepts of the real estate appraisal profession.

Real Estate Appraisal combines theoretical concepts with practical examples to produce a concise, accurate, and easy-to-understand text. Each unit begins with learning objectives to help the student identify the most important information. Relevant forms, data charts, and illustrations abound throughout the units, making the text visually appealing. Units conclude with summary and review questions that not only test comprehension, but also reinforce knowledge. Answers and detailed explanations are provided at the end of each unit.

Real Estate Appraisal has been written and organized to meet the licensing requirements as established by the Appraiser Qualifications Board of the Appraisal Foundation. This text explores all the required subtopics of basic appraisal principles and procedures and provides students with a comprehensive overview of appraisal fundamentals and general real estate principles.

The concepts and techniques provided in *Real Estate Appraisal* are useful for students in any field of real estate, but naturally focus on the individual who is seeking state licensure in real estate appraisal.

ABOUT THE AUTHORS

ROY K. BOTTGER

Roy Bottger has over twenty years of experience in California real estate appraisal, and has published several articles on real estate in national publications. As an expert real estate witness, he has performed forensic appraisals for legal litigation on construction defects, condemnation, and other stigmatized properties.

Mr. Bottger has a Bachelor of Science Degree in Business Administration with a real estate emphasis from San Diego State University. He is currently a California Certified General Real Estate Appraiser and AQB Certified USPAP instructor.

ERIC T. SHARKEY

Eric Sharkey is a licensed appraiser and a certified instructor for the California Bureau for Private Postsecondary and Vocational Education. He has a Bachelor of Arts Degree in English from Seattle University. Mr. Sharkey has personally assisted many students in attaining their appraisal licenses in California, Washington, Louisiana, and Virginia.

The Appraisal Profession

Unit 1

INTRODUCTION

The most frequently asked question in real estate is probably, "How much do you think my property is worth?" Anyone in the real estate industry is likely to be asked this question by friends and family.

Most homeowners know, within a range, the value of their home. Without realizing it, they often use some of the same techniques as a professional appraiser.

> Example: Joe and Mary know the selling price of their neighbors' house and the selling price of the house down the street. Based on amenities, location, and condition, they have added to—or subtracted from—those selling prices, to come up with an accurate value for their own house.

This text will examine the appraisal process and the methods used to develop an opinion of the market value of property so that you can answer when a client asks the question, "How much do you think my property is worth?"

Learning Objectives

After reading this unit, you should be able to:

- choose the appropriate definitions for appraiser and appraisal.
- differentiate among value, cost, and price.
- recall the different appraisal boards.
- recognize FIRREA and the reason for its enactment.
- distinguish the differences between license levels.
- identify the parts of the Dodd-Frank Act, passed in response to the financial crisis of 2008, that affect the appraisal profession.

DEFINITION OF APPRAISAL

An **appraisal** is an unbiased opinion of a specific property's value on a given date. An **appraiser** is a person who is expected to value property in a competent, objective, and impartial manner. An appraiser usually gives his or her opinion of value in a written statement called an **appraisal report**. It is the conclusion of the appraiser's research and analysis of all relevant data regarding the subject property.

The majority of appraisals are performed for companies involved in real estate financing. Almost everyone who purchases a single-family residence takes out a loan to cover the majority of the cost of the house. Lenders need to be sure that the value of the real estate being used as collateral is sufficient to cover the amount of the loan. **Collateral** is property pledged to secure a loan. Lenders can take ownership of the property if the debt is not paid.

With over eight million sales of single-family residences in the last year, there are plenty of opportunities for appraisers. In fact, appraisals are used in a wide variety of situations.

Appraisals are usually required whenever property is bought, sold, refinanced, assessed, taxed, condemned, insured, or mortgaged. They may be required for divorce settlements, when business partnerships are dissolved, or when property is listed as a business asset.

Not only are appraisals required for different reasons, appraisals can also look at different time periods. Most appraisals are used to develop an opinion of a property's current value, but there are other possibilities.

Appraisal Assignment

Past   Present   *Future*

The value of a house destroyed by fire is an example of retrospective appraisal.

Retrospective appraisals are ones that look at the value of a property at a point of time in the past.

For example, a retrospective appraisal could be used for insurance purposes to find the value of a house that has since burned down.

A prospective appraisal looks at the value of a property at a future point of time.

Example: A lender who is providing a construction loan might ask an appraiser to determine if houses should be built for sale in a particular area. Part of the appraiser's work would be to value the houses as if they were finished.

Definition of Value

Value is defined as the monetary worth of property, goods, or services to buyers and sellers at a given time. It is important to note that people create value. Value is not built into an item. An item is valuable because people perceive it has worth.

Depending on the purpose of the appraisal, appraisers are asked to find different types of value. The focus of most real estate appraisal assignments is developing an opinion of the market value of a specified property. **Market value** is usually defined as the most probable price a property would bring in normal market conditions.

Remember that the price or cost of a property is not always the same as its value. **Price** is the amount of money requested or paid for a property. To an appraiser, **cost** is the amount of money it takes to build a structure.

The Appraiser's Role

In real estate transactions, an objective, third-party opinion is often needed to develop an opinion of the market value of real property. The professional appraiser, because of training, experience, and ethics, is responsible for giving clients an objective opinion of value, reached without bias. An appraiser has a serious responsibility to be correct in evaluating data and not to allow other factors to influence evaluation of a property. The appraiser must remember to be a neutral party, responding only to the forces affecting value and not to people with special interests who might want to influence his or her judgment.

APPRAISER REGULATION

Appraisal services have been a part of the real estate industry for a very long time. Over time, real estate appraisal has become its own structured industry as professional associations have developed and national standards and laws have been created to regulate the industry.

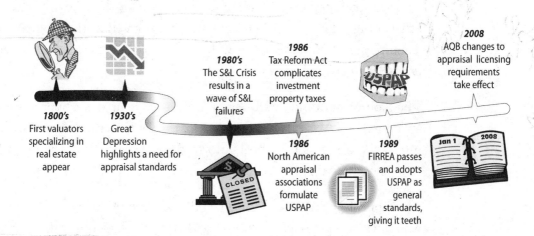

1800's
First valuators specializing in real estate appear

1930's
Great Depression highlights a need for appraisal standards

1980's
The S&L Crisis results in a wave of S&L failures

1986
North American appraisal associations formulate USPAP

1986
Tax Reform Act complicates investment property taxes

1989
FIRREA passes and adopts USPAP as general standards, giving it teeth

2008
AQB changes to appraisal licensing requirements take effect

Professional Associations

Individuals and firms first began specializing in real estate valuation during the 1800s. Their services were connected primarily with brokerage and insurance underwriting at that time. Chaos in the economy during the era of the Great Depression in the 1930s highlighted the need for professionalism and standards for regulating real estate appraisers. During that time, the first formally organized groups of professional appraisers appeared.

Appraisers with membership in these groups educated themselves through classes and written materials, with the more experienced members teaching the newer appraisers. The associations offered designations or titles for different levels of expertise, and their members were bound to a code of ethics regulating professional behavior.

In 1986, the major North American-based appraisal associations formulated a set of written standards defining the ethical and competent behavior for appraisers. The stated purpose for these standards was to promote and maintain a high level of public trust and confidence in professional appraisal practice. This document was called the **Uniform Standards of Professional Appraisal Practice** (USPAP).

The Appraisal Foundation

The Appraisal Foundation (TAF) includes the Appraiser Qualifications Board, the Appraiser Standards Board, and the Appraisal Practices Board.

The **Appraiser Qualifications Board** (AQB) is an independent board of The Appraisal Foundation. It is made up of at least five practicing appraisers who are appointed by TAF's Board of Trustees for three-year terms. Among other things, the AQB establishes the minimum education, experience, and examination requirements an individual must meet in order to become a licensed or certified appraiser.

The **Appraisal Standards Board** (ASB) is made up of six appraisers who are appointed by TAF's Board of Trustees for three-year terms. The ASB develops, interprets, and amends the Uniform Standards of Professional Appraisal Practice (USPAP).

The **Appraisal Practices Board** (APB) is composed of five to seven members who can serve up to eight years on the Board. It will identify and issue opinions on Recognized Valuation Methods and Techniques, which may apply to all disciplines within the appraisal profession.

Since TAF is a private entity, neither TAF nor its Boards have any legal authority of their own.

FINANCIAL CRISES AND REGULATORY REFORMS

Every financial crisis seems to be followed by Congressional reforms and new regulations, which are designed to prevent future financial meltdowns. Within the last 25 years, financial institutions have been part of two such fiascos—the Savings & Loan Crisis in the late 1980s and the Housing Bubble and Financial Crisis of the late 2000s. In part, both of these were caused primarily by unsound real estate lending practices.

Savings & Loan Crisis of the Late 1980s - FIRREA

The **Savings and Loan Crisis** (S&L Crisis) of the 1980s was a wave of savings and loan failures caused by mismanagement, failed speculation, and, in some cases, fraud. The **Tax Reform Act of 1986** also caused problems when it changed the tax implications associated with many investment properties. These things, along with other economic issues at the time, combined to cause serious adverse economic consequences. When the economy declined, many property owners defaulted on their loans resulting in huge losses for lenders.

The causes and consequences of these problems have been examined, and it has been found that in a large percentage of cases, the loans that were defaulted on had been based on inflated real estate values. In some cases, this overvaluation was due to appraiser incompetence. In

other cases, it appraisers yielded to pressure from lenders or developers to manufacture values high enough to make the loan work.

All of this led to the realization that credible appraisal reports, performed by ethical and competent appraisers, are necessary to the country's economic well-being. Since only a small portion of practicing appraisers had memberships in the generally recognized appraisal organizations at that time, most appraisers were not bound to any one set of qualifications, standards, or ethics rules. This deficiency in the real estate appraisal industry that needed to be addressed.

Financial Institutions Reform, Recovery, and Enforcement Act of 1989

As a response to the Savings & Loan crisis, Congress passed the **Financial Institutions Reform, Recovery, and Enforcement Act** (also known as FIRREA or the "S&L Bailout Bill") in 1989.

Title XI of FIRREA empowered federal mortgage regulators to adopt USPAP as the generally recognized standards of practice in the appraisal profession.

FIRREA required all states to establish agencies to license and certify real property appraisers. In addition, FIRREA required that federally related transactions with a transaction value greater than $250,000 be performed by a licensed or certified appraiser. If the transaction is a business loan, a licensed or certified appraiser must be used if the transaction value is greater than $1 million. A **federally related transaction** is any real estate-related financial transaction which a federal financial institution's regulatory agency engages in, contracts for, or regulates, and which requires the services of an appraiser. The **transaction value** is either the loan amount or the market value of the property involved.

Since lending institutions are federally regulated and because the financial world is so interconnected, almost every real estate-related financial transaction ends up being federally related, so this limitation is almost universal. Some states have stricter legislation that requires an appraisal license or certification regardless of transaction value. Regulations change periodically, so individuals pursuing an appraisal license should check with their state's agency to find the most current requirements.

Appraisal Subcommittee

FIRREA also established the **Appraisal Subcommittee (ASC)**, which among other things, maintains the official registry of state licensed and certified appraisers, oversees the appraiser regulatory programs established by the States, and monitors operations of The Appraisal Foundation.

The purpose of the Appraisal Subcommittee is to ensure that real estate appraisers are sufficiently trained and tested since real estate appraisers play such an important role in the economy. This helps to guarantee that appraisals are competently performed and that they are based on unbiased, independent judgment.

State Agencies

In response to FIRREA's mandate, all states have set up real estate appraiser licensing and regulatory agencies. These agencies issue licenses or certifications based upon the appraiser's education, experience, and qualifications. The state agencies are the ones who enforce compliance with USPAP. They receive and investigate complaints against licensees and administer discipline where appropriate.

Check The Appraisal Foundation's website for a current list of all the state agencies and their contact information at www.appraisalfoundation.org.

License Classifications

Although appraisal licensing and certification is regulated by each state, FIRREA gave the Appraiser Qualifications Board (AQB) authority to establish the minimum education, experience, and examination requirements that an appraiser must meet in order to obtain a state certification.

There are four levels of real property appraiser classifications, although some states do not have the appraiser trainee license level.

1. Appraiser Trainee Classification
2. Residential Licensed Appraiser Classification
3. Certified Residential Appraiser Classification
4. Certified General Appraiser Classification

The following details are the AQB recommended minimum requirements for licensure for each classification. Some states have chosen to adopt stricter policies. Please check with your local state licensing board before pursuing your license.

Trainee Classification

In most states, to qualify for the Appraiser Trainee Classification, an applicant must successfully complete 75 hours of qualifying education covering the modules in the Required Core Curriculum. Although a state examination and experience are not required by the AQB for this classification, a few states do require an exam, or experience, or both.

Trainees must work under the direct supervision of certified residential or general appraisers in good standing. Trainees may have more than one supervising appraiser, but a supervising appraiser can supervise no more than three trainees at one time. A trainee may appraise any property that the supervising certified appraiser is permitted and qualified to appraise.

Appraiser trainees must maintain an appraisal log jointly with the supervising appraiser. The log must show the date of the report and the type and address of the property. Trainees must describe the work performed and the number of actual hours worked. Supervising appraisers must describe the scope of their review, write their certification number, and sign the log. A trainee, who has more than one supervising appraiser, must maintain a separate appraisal log for each supervising appraiser.

Licensed Classification

To qualify to take the Licensed Residential Appraiser Examination, a person must successfully complete 150 hours of qualifying education and have 2,000 hours of experience. The 2,000 hours of experience must be obtained in no fewer than 12 months.

A Licensed Appraiser may accept assignments to appraise non-complex 1-4 residential units with a transaction value less than $1,000,000 and complex 1-4 residential units with a transaction value less than $250,000, without any supervision. A Licensed Residential Real Property Appraiser can appraise properties that are more complex or with higher transaction values, but any such assignment requires the supervision of a certified appraiser who is qualified to appraise those property types.

Certified Residential Classification

To qualify to take the Certified Residential Appraiser Examination, a person must meet the college course, Required Core Curriculum, and experience requirements.

The applicant must have an Associate degree, or higher, from an accredited college or university. In lieu of the Associate degree, the person may have successfully passed 21 semester credit hours in selected subjects. Additionally, the applicant must complete the 200 hours of qualifying education covering the modules in the Required Core Curriculum for the classification sought. The appraiser must obtain 2,500 hours of experience in no fewer than 30 months.

A Certified Residential appraiser may accept assignments to appraise 1-4 residential units without regard to value or complexity. However, this does not include the appraisal of subdivisions.

Certified General Classification

As the highest level of license, a Certified General appraiser may accept assignments to appraise all types of real property.

To be eligible to take the Certified General Real Property Appraiser Examination, a person must meet the college course, Required Core Curriculum, and experience requirements.

The applicant must either have a Bachelor degree, or higher, from an accredited college or university have successfully passed 30 college-level semester hours in selected subjects. Furthermore, the applicant must complete 300 hours of qualifying education covering the modules in the Required Core Curriculum for the classification sought. The appraiser must also obtain 3,000 hours of experience in no fewer than 30 months. At least 1,500 of the hours must be in non-residential appraisal work.

EDUCATION, EXPERIENCE, EXAMINATION, AND CONTINUING EDUCATION REQUIREMENTS

	Trainee License No changes.	Residential License See italicized requirements.	Certified Residential See italicized requirements.	Certified General See italicized requirements.
Scope	Must be directly supervised by a state certified appraiser. May appraise any property that the supervising appraiser is permitted to appraise.	May appraise any non-complex 1-4 unit residential property with a transaction value of less than $1 million and complex 1-4 unit residential property less than $250,000.	May appraise any 1-4 unit residential properties. *May supervise up to 3 trainees.*	May appraise any property. *May supervise up to 3 trainees.*
Education	*75 hours* (including 15 hours of USPAP).	*150 hours* (including 15 hours of USPAP).	*200 hours* (including 15 hours of USPAP). An associate degree or 21 units in specified college courses.	*300 hours* (including 15 hours of USPAP). A bachelor degree or 30 units in specified college courses.
Experience	None required.	2000 hours *during at least one year.*	2,500 hours *during at least two-and-a-half years.*	3,000 hours during at least two-and-a-half years *including at least 1,500 hours of non-residential appraisal work.*
Exam	None required.	Licensed Real Property Appraiser Examination	Certified Residential Real Property Appraiser Examination	Certified General Real Property Appraiser Examination
Continuing Education*	14 hours per year including 7 hours of USPAP once every two years.	14 hours per year including 7 hours of USPAP once every two years.	14 hours per year including 7 hours of USPAP once every two years.	14 hours per year including 7 hours of USPAP once every two years.

*Some states have stricter Continuing Education requirements.

Housing Bubble and Financial Crisis of the Late 2000s – Dodd-Frank Act

The rise in the housing prices since 2000 was described by *The Economist* magazine as the "biggest bubble in history". The perfect storm of record low interest rates, abandonment of mortgage underwriting standards, subprime loans, and out-right mortgage fraud combined to create this housing bubble that burst in 2006.

The plunge in home sales led to a huge increase in foreclosures of subprime mortgages. By 2007, many subprime lenders filed for chapter-11 bankruptcy or closed. Even large mortgage lenders, such as Countrywide Financial, and investment banks, such as Bear Sterns, were not immune to the meltdown. By the summer of 2008, the overleveraged financial institutions were in a state of chaos and reported billions of dollars in losses that caused some to fail and others to survive only with government help. The 2008 financial crisis led to the deepest recession since the 1930s.

Dodd-Frank Act

Once again, the government's solution to the disintegration of the housing market and financial crisis was more regulation—the **Dodd-Frank Wall Street Reform and Consumer Protection Act** of 2010 (Dodd-Frank Act). The Dodd-Frank Act made sweeping changes to financial regulatory agencies and affects almost every aspect of the nation's financial services industry. It creates new agencies and changes others, amends the Federal Reserve Act, promotes transparency, and establishes rigorous standards and supervision to protect consumers, investors, and businesses. Its goal is to end taxpayer bailouts of financial institutions and to eliminate the loopholes that led to the economic recession. Because it is so far reaching, the legislation will certainly have unintended consequences not yet even envisioned.

Of the sixteen titles of the Dodd-Frank Act, Title XIV-Mortgage Reform and Anti-Predatory Lending Act (Reform Act) has direct impact on the appraisal industry. The Reform Act has eight subtitles dealing with various aspects of the mortgage process.

However, Subtitle F of the Reform Act addresses a variety of appraisal and valuation issues. For example, it requires that appraisers are independent and have no interest in the underlying transaction. It allows use of an automated valuation model (AVM) but prohibits a broker price opinion (BPO) as the primary valuation tool in connection with valuation of a primary residence. Appraisals for high-risk mortgages must include a visit to the interior of the property. The Reform Act also addresses appraisal management companies (AMC) which are widely used by financial service institutions. It requires that the fee paid to appraisers and the administration fee charged by appraisal management companies both be set forth on the closing statement, commonly referred to as the HUD-1.

Subtitle F Provisions that Impact Appraisers

- Appraisal independence requirements
- Conflicts of interest defined and prohibited
- Mandatory reporting of appraisers who violate the Uniform Standards of Professional Appraisal Practice (USPAP)
- Customary and reasonable appraisal fees
- Borrowers entitled to copies of all appraisals and valuations
- Sunset of the Home Valuation Code of Conduct (HVCC)

SUMMARY

An **appraisal** is an unbiased opinion of a specific property's value on a given date. An **appraiser** is a person who is expected to value property in a competent, objective, and impartial manner. An appraiser gives his or her opinion of value in a written statement called an **appraisal report**. The majority of appraisals are performed for companies involved in real estate financing. The focus of most real estate appraisal assignments is developing an opinion of the market value of a specified property. **Market value** is usually defined as the most probable price a property would bring in normal market conditions.

Appraisal services have been a part of the real estate industry for a very long time. In 1986, the major North American-based appraisal associations formulated a set of written standards defining the ethical and competent behavior for appraisers called the **Uniform Standards of Professional Appraisal Practice (USPAP)**. They also founded a private, non-profit organization called **The Appraisal Foundation (TAF)**. The Appraisal Foundation includes the **Appraiser Qualifications Board (AQB)**, the **Appraiser Standards Board (ASB)**, and the **Appraisal Practices Board (APB)**.

Within the last 25 years, financial institutions have been part of two devastating financial crises—the Savings & Loan Crisis in the late 1980s and the Housing Bubble and Financial Crisis of the late 2000s. Each of these financial fiascos led to reforms and new regulations of the appraisal industry.

The **Financial Institutions Reform, Recovery, and Enforcement Act** (FIRREA) of 1989 enforces a set of standards and ethics on the real estate appraisal profession. FIRREA require all states to set up real estate appraiser licensing and regulatory agencies. These state agencies issue licenses or certifications based upon the appraiser's education, experience, and qualifications, and they enforce compliance with USPAP.

The **Dodd-Frank Wall Street Reform and Consumer Protection Act** of 2010 (Dodd-Frank Act). The Dodd-Frank Act made sweeping changes to financial regulatory agencies and affects almost every aspect of the nation's financial services industry. Of the sixteen titles of the Dodd-Frank Act, Title XIV-Mortgage Reform and Anti-Predatory Lending Act (Reform Act) has direct impact on the appraisal industry. Subtitle F of the Reform Act addresses a variety of appraisal and valuation issues.

UNIT 1 REVIEW

Matching Exercise

Instructions: Write the letter of the matching term on the blank line before its definition, and then check your response with the Answer Key that immediately follows the Multiple Choice Questions.

Terms

A. APB

B. appraisal report

C. Appraisal Standards Board

D. Appraisal Subcommittee

E. appraiser

F. AQB

G. BPO

H. Certified General appraiser

I. Certified Residential appraiser

J. collateral

K. federally related transaction

L. FIRREA

M. Licensed Appraiser

N. market value

O. price

P. retrospective appraisals

Q. S&L Crisis

R. Subtitle F

S. transaction value

T. USPAP

Definitions

1. ___E___ Person who is expected to value property in a competent, objective, and impartial manner.

2. ___B___ Written statement in which an appraiser gives his or her opinion of value.

3. ___J___ Property pledged to secure a loan.

4. ___P___ Appraisal that looks at the value of a property at a point of time in the past.

5. ___N___ Most probable price a property would bring in normal market conditions.

6. ___O___ Amount of money paid for a property.

7. ___T___ Set of written standards defining ethical and competent behavior on the part of appraisers.

AQB. Aprzr Qualifications Board

8. _~~W~~ F_   Board that establishes the minimum education, experience, and examination requirements an individual must meet in order to become a licensed or certified appraiser.

Aprzl Standards Board

9. _~~W~~ C_   Board that develops, interprets, and amends the Uniform Standards of Professional Appraisal Practice.

APB - Aprzl practices Board

10. _A_   Board that issues opinions on Recognized Valuation Methods and Techniques.

S&L Crisis

11. _Q_   Wave of savings and loan failures in the 1980s caused by mismanagement, failed speculation, and, in some cases, fraud.

FIRREA

12. _L_   Law that empowered federal mortgage regulators to adopt USPAP as the generally recognized standards of practice in the appraisal profession.

Federally related transaction

13. _K_   Any real estate-related financial transaction that a federal financial institutions regulatory agency engages in, contracts for, or regulates and which requires the services of an appraiser.

transaction value

14. _S_   Either the loan amount or the market value of the property involved.

Aprzl Subcommittee

15. _D_   Agency created by FIRREA that maintains the official registry of appraisers and oversees the state agencies and The Appraisal Foundation.

Licensed Aprzr

16. _M_   Appraiser who may only accept assignments to appraise non-complex 1-4 residential units with a transaction value less than $1,000,000 and complex 1-4 residential units with a transaction value less than $250,000, without any supervision.

Cert. Res. Aprzr

17. _I_   Appraiser who may accept assignments to appraise 1-4 residential units without regard to value or complexity.

Cert. Gen. Aprzr

18. _H_   Appraiser who may accept assignments to appraise all types of real property.

Subtitle F

19. _R (All)_   Part of the Dodd-Frank Act, Title XIV-Mortgage Reform and Anti-Predatory Lending Act that addresses a variety of appraisal and valuation issues.

BPO

20. _G_   Reform Act allows use of an (AVM) but prohibits a _____ as the primary valuation tool in connection with valuation of a primary residence.

Multiple Choice Questions

Instructions: Circle your choice, and then check your response with the Answer Key that immediately follows the Multiple Choice Questions.

1. An appraisal is:
   a. a person who values property in a competent, objective, and impartial manner.
   b. a biased estimation of value.
   c. an unbiased opinion of value.
   d. a written statement depicting the appraiser's opinion.

2. Why do lenders usually use the services of an appraiser?
   a. To ensure that the property value is high enough to cover the loan amount
   b. Because of a legal contract between The Appraisal Foundation and Fannie Mae
   c. For income tax reasons
   d. None of the above

3. A prospective appraisal looks at the:
   a. amount of money paid for a property.
   b. value of a property as if additional modifications had already been completed.
   c. value of a property at a point of time in the past.
   d. value of a property at a future point in time.

4. The money, labor, and material are the _____ to build a property.
   a. collateral
   b. cost
   c. price
   d. value

5. Which is NOT part of The Appraisal Foundation?
   a. Appraisal Qualifications Board
   b. Appraisal Subcommittee — oversees the Apez Foundation
   c. Appraisal Standards Board
   d. Appraisal Practices Board

6. In the late 1980s, appraisers' overvaluation of real estate led to the:
   a. Great Depression.
   b. Savings and Loan Crisis.
   c. Tax Reform Act of 1986.
   d. formation of TAF.

7. The purpose of the Appraisal Subcommittee is to:
   a. develop, publish, interpret, and amend USPAP.
   b. establish the minimum education, experience, and examination requirements for appraisers.
   c. ensure that real estate appraisers are sufficiently trained and tested.
   d. promote and maintain a high level of public trust and confidence in professional appraisal practice.

8. Which of the following is NOT a license classification?
   a. Trainee License
   b. Residential License
   c. Certified Trainee
   d. Certified Residential

9. Under the current requirements, how many hours of experience are needed to obtain a trainee license?
   a. 2,000 hours
   b. 3,000 hours
   c. At least two years
   d. No experience is required.

10. Which of the following laws is a direct result of the housing bubble and financial meltdown of the late 2000s?
    a. FIRREA
    b. Gramm-Leach-Bliley Act
    c. Home Mortgage Disclosure Act
    d. Dodd-Frank Act

UNIT 1 ANSWER KEY

Answers – Matching

1. E	6. O	11. Q	16. M
2. B	7. T	12. L	17. I
3. J	8. F	13. K	18. H
4. P	9. C	14. S	19. R
5. N	10. A	15. D	20. G

Answers – Multiple Choice

1. **(c)** An appraisal is an unbiased opinion of a specific property's value on a given date. An appraiser is a person who is expected to value property in a competent, objective, and impartial manner. **Page 2**

2. **(a)** Lenders need to be sure that the value of the real estate being used as collateral for a loan is enough to cover the amount of the loan and thus protect investors. **Page 2**

3. **(d)** A prospective appraisal looks at the value of a property at a future point in time. **Page 4**

4. **(b)** Cost represents expenses in money, labor, material, or sacrifices in acquiring or producing something. Remember that the cost or price of a property is not always the same as its value. **Page 4**

5. **(b)** The Appraisal Foundation (TAF) includes the Appraiser Qualifications Board, the Appraiser Standards Board, and the Appraisal Practices Board. **Page 6**

6. **(b)** In examining the causes and consequences of the S& Loan Crisis, many of the loans that defaulted were based on inflated real estate values. **Page 7**

7. **(c)** The purpose of the Appraisal Subcommittee is to ensure that real estate appraisers are sufficiently trained and tested since real estate appraisers play such an important role in the economy. **Page 8**

8. **(c)** There are four levels of real property appraiser classifications—Trainee License, Residential License, Certified Residential, and Certified General. However, some states do not have the appraiser trainee licensee level. No states have a "certified trainee" level. **Page 9**

9. **(d)** Although each state may vary somewhat in what is required for different license levels, no state that has a trainee license requires experience in order to obtain that license. **Page 9**

10.   **(d)**   Once again, the government's solution to the disintegration of the housing market and financial crisis was more regulation—the Dodd-Frank Wall Street Reform and Consumer Protection Act of 2010 (Dodd-Frank Act). The Home Mortgage Disclosure Act was passed in 1975, FIRREA was passed in 1989, and the Gramm-Leach-Bliley Act was passed in 1999. **Page 12**

Real Property Concepts & Characteristics

Unit 2 √

INTRODUCTION

When starting on an appraisal, it is critical for the real estate appraiser to know what exactly he or she is appraising. The appraiser must know what is included in the appraisal and how to describe it. This unit introduces the definitions of real property and personal property and the three types of legal descriptions the appraiser will encounter.

Learning Objectives

After reading this unit, you should be able to:

- recall the bundle of rights included in property ownership.
- differentiate personal property from real property.
- identify the components of real property.
- recognize land and its attachments as components of real property.
- recall typical appurtenances to land.
- identify the different types of legal descriptions and their use.

PROPERTY

Property is anything that may be owned and gained lawfully. The word property refers more to the rights that the owner has in property than to the fact that the property is owned. Property rights are known as the bundle of rights. The **bundle of rights** consists of all legal rights that are attached to the ownership of physical property.

The bundle of rights includes the right to use, possess, transfer, encumber, and enjoy property. This bundle of rights safeguards the owner's rights to the property. An owner may choose to sell or give away one of the rights and keep the rest. For example, under a lease agreement, an owner may give away the right of use for a certain time to a tenant. However, if one of these rights is affected, control of the property is diminished.

Property can be real or personal and anything that is not real property is personal property. Each type of property has unique features that distinguish one from the other.

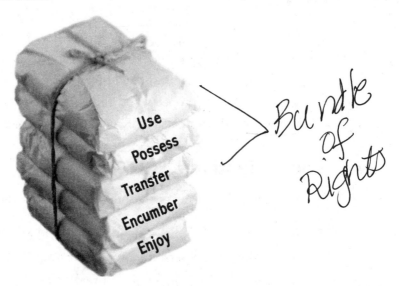

Personal Property

Personal property refers to those items that are not permanently attached to land and are usually moveable and portable. Essentially, personal property is everything other than real property and is often referred to as movable property. Personal property can also be referred to as **personalty or chattel**.

Personal property can be transferred or sold using a bill of sale and may be pledged as security for a loan. Some examples of personal property include cash, negotiable instruments, securities, royalties, goods, emblements, intangible assets, cars, boats, airplanes, bank accounts, wages, furniture, equipment, mineral rights, insurance policies, jewelry, and patents.

Personal property also some growing things such as crops. Personal property and real property and can change from one to the other.

> Example: A tree is real property until it is cut as timber, at which time it becomes the personal property of whoever cut it. If that timber is milled into lumber, sold and used to build a house, it becomes real property. Over time, the house ages and deteriorates. When it is torn down and hauled away as scrap lumber, it becomes personal property once again.

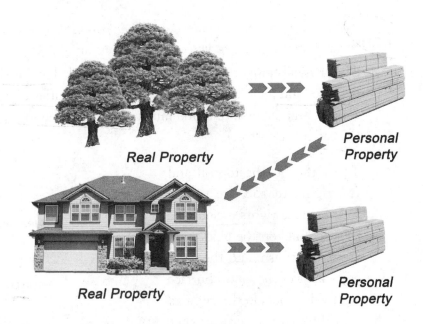

Real Property

Personal Property

Real Property

Personal Property

In the sale of real estate, the personal property goes with the seller rather than staying with the real property belonging to the buyer. The appraiser must identify which items are considered personal property, since personal property does not contribute any value to the real property being appraised.

Real Property

The terms real property and real estate are often used interchangeably. At one time, the term **real estate** was used to describe the physical object owned—the land. Real property was used to describe the rights gained by owning the land. This distinction is not commonly used anymore.

Real property is immovable and is usually transferred or sold by a deed. Anything that is not real property is personal property. When real property is sold, anything that has become attached to it goes to the buyer as part of the sale unless other arrangements have been made.

The components of real property include the land, anything permanently attached to the land, anything appurtenant to the land, or anything immovable by law.

Land

The physical component of real property is land. Land is three-dimensional because **land** includes the surface, limited quantities of airspace above the surface, and the materials and minerals beneath the surface to the center of the earth (subsurface).

The surface is the topsoil and the rights to the use of the soil. **Surface rights** include the right to build on the land, grow crops, hunt, fish, and the basic enjoyment of the land. Surface rights also include the right to drill through the surface when subsurface rights are involved.

A good illustration of this concept is an inverted pyramid with the tip at the center of the earth and its base extending out into the sky above the property to a reasonable height.

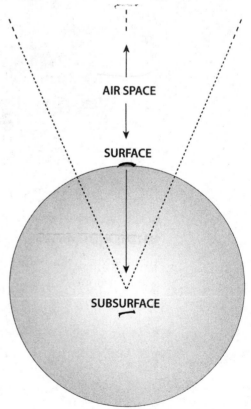

AIR SPACE

SURFACE

SUBSURFACE

Attachments to the Land

Items permanently attached to the land are real property and belong to the owner. These items include natural attachments, improvements, and fixtures.

Natural Attachments

Real property includes natural attachments. Natural attachments are growing plants attached by their roots, such as trees, shrubs, and flowers. The two types of natural attachments are *fructus naturales* and *fructus industriales*.

Fructus naturales are naturally occurring plant growth, such as grasses, trees, and shrubs and are considered part of the real property. Therefore, when a home is sold, the planted trees and landscaping are real property and are included in the sale.

Fructus industriales are annual crops produced by human labor, such as fruits, nuts, vegetables, and grains. The main difference between cultivated plants and wild plants is that cultivated plants are considered personal property even before they are harvested. Emblements are a specific type of *fructus industriales*. **Emblements** are annual crops cultivated by tenant farmers and sharecroppers. If a large tract of farmland is being sold, it is important to have a written agreement stating who will retain ownership of the crops that are growing in the field. The emblements rule does not apply to ornamental trees, rose bushes, or any other type of perennial growth.

Improvements

Improvements, such as houses, garages, fences, swimming pools, or anything resting on the land to become permanent are owned as a part of the land.

Fixtures

A **fixture** is anything that is permanently attached to real property by man or by nature. It also includes anything permanently attached to the fixture, such as the door to a cabinet. When real property is sold, the buyer may assume that all fixtures will remain with the property, unless there is a written agreement to the contrary.

If there is a dispute, there are five tests used to determine if property is considered a fixture or personal property. The tests are agreement of the parties, method of attachment, adaptation, intent of the parties, and the relationship of the parties.

Agreement of the Parties

When there has been a clear agreement between the parties in a dispute about fixtures, the courts will apply this test to determine who is in the right.

Method of Attachment

The next criterion to consider is whether a piece of property is attached. Most believe this to be the overruling factor, but the first and primary factor is whether an agreement exists between the parties. If the buyers and sellers have not agreed that a particular item is included in a sale, the next step is to look at the method of attachment.

> Example: A chandelier wired into the electrical system becomes a fixture, or real property. It would be included in the sale of the house as something attached or affixed to the land unless the sellers specifically mentioned they wanted to take it with them.

Adaptation

The test of adaptation considers whether an item materially affects the use of the property as intended in the contract. Was the item made specifically for the property? For example, have the drapes been custom-made for the windows? Has the carpet been cut especially to fit the rooms? Is the stove built into the counter? If so, each has become a fixture and has lost its status as personal property.

Intention

If apparent, either in writing or by the actions of either party involved, intention is considered the most important test of a fixture.

> Example: Renter Bob wired special cosmetic lights into the bathroom wall, telling the landlord he intended the lights to remain his personal property. Bob said he would repair the wall when he moved and would take the lights with him. This was a clear case of Bob's intention to keep the lights as his personal property. A fixture may remain personal property if all parties are informed. Intention should always be put in writing.

Relationship of the Parties

In a dispute about fixtures, when there is no convincing evidence of the right of one party, courts will look at whether the parties are landlord-tenant, lender-borrower, or buyer-seller. The court then makes a decision based on the relationship of the parties in the case. Usually the court will favor the tenant over the landlord, the lender over the borrower, and the buyer over the seller.

Exception - Trade Fixtures

Trade fixtures are considered personal property not real property. **Trade fixtures** are fixtures that are attached to real estate by a tenant, usually to conduct a trade or business from a commercial property. They include items of personal property, such as shelves, cash registers, room partitions, or wall mirrors, used to conduct a business. Tenants retain ownership of the items as personal property when they vacate the premises, but are responsible for repairing any damage that results from placing or removing the trade fixtures.

Appurtenances

An **appurtenance** is anything belonging to a particular piece of land that is used for its benefit. Appurtenances to real property pass to the new owner when title transfers, whether or not they are mentioned in the deed. However, most deeds describe the property being transferred and then state that the property is being transferred "together with all appurtenances". Typical appurtenances include air rights, water rights, support rights, subsurface rights, easements, and rights-of-way.

Air Rights

Air rights are the rights an owner of real property has to the air space above the property to a reasonable height. As real property, air rights can be sold, leased, or encumbered separately from the land.

Air rights can be severed or restricted under certain circumstances. The United States Code §40110 allows reasonable use of the airspace above real property as a public highway for the navigation of airplanes, satellites, and spacecraft. Often the height of telecommunication towers, water tanks, power line poles, and signs is restricted near airports or in areas where there could be over flight of aircraft.

Additionally, there may be restrictions on the placement of trees or other tall structures that would either block a neighbor's view or dramatically impair the amount of sunlight that would otherwise naturally occur on a neighbor's property.

Water Rights

Water in its natural state on the surface of the land or underground is real property. If it is taken and bottled, then it becomes personal property. In addition, certain **water rights** that go with the land are considered real property. The owner of

property bordering a stream or river has **riparian rights**, which include the rights of irrigation, swimming, boating, and fishing among others. Owners of land bordering a lake possess **littoral rights.** Littoral property owners generally own to the average low water mark or the edge of the lake. The boundary line of land touching the ocean is the ordinary high-tide mark.

Support Rights

A property owner has the right to have his or her property naturally upheld by the soil beneath and by the adjoining properties. Neighboring property owners not only have the obligation to avoid trespasses onto their neighbor's land. They also owe an affirmative duty to provide surrounding properties (or, in some cases, different estates on the surface if the ownership in question is underground) support from landslides and cave-ins. The two kinds of support that neighboring property owners owe each other are lateral support and subjacent support.

Lateral support is the absolute right of the property owner to have his or her land held in place from the sides (laterally) by adjoining land so that it will not fall away. The owner of the adjoining land cannot change the land in such a way that it weakens or causes the support to collapse causing slippage, cave-in, or landslide.

Subjacent support is the absolute right of the property owner to have his or her land supported from beneath its surface. The owner of the land below the surface cannot alter it in a way that weakens the subjacent support of the adjoining property. Someone excavating below ground or removing minerals, oil, or gas owes the surface owner subjacent support.

Subsurface Rights

Subsurface rights are the rights to the natural resources, such as minerals, oil, and gas below the surface. Minerals are owned as real property. However, oil and gas are considered **migratory minerals** and may not be owned until taken from the ground, at which time they become the personal property of whoever removed them. The rights to the minerals, oil, and gas can be sold or leased separately.

Easements

An **easement** is a right, privilege, or interest limited to a specific purpose which one party has in the land of another. Common examples include easements for the purposes of access to adjoining land and access to public utility equipment and services. Easements are discussed in detail in the next unit.

Rights of Way

A **right of way** is a legal right to pass over another person's land. A public right of way is a designated area, such as a sidewalk, footpath, bridleway, bike path, or any alley street, or road that is dedicated to public use.

Anything Immovable by Law

Some items are considered immovable by law and must be sold with the property. Established trees are an example of this. A seller may not sell the property and exclude the orange grove from the sale. The seller may have sold the crop resulting from the trees as personal property. However, the actual trees are real property and may not be excluded from the sale.

LEGAL DESCRIPTIONS

Once the appraiser has identified the real estate and property rights included in the appraisal, the next step is to describe it accurately—typically with a legal description. A **legal description** is a written description of a particular parcel of land that identifies it as precisely as possible. A street address is an informal reference and is not sufficient for a legal description. It only tells you how to find a property, but does not tell you the boundaries of the property.

Today, a legal description is required before a deed can be recorded to transfer title to a new owner. Appraisers include the legal description in the appraisal report, and it is a critical part of identifying the subject property.

The three common ways to describe property are metes and bounds, Public Land Survey System, and the recorded plat system. The Public Land Survey System describes more land (in surface area) in the United States than any other method. However, when based on the number of properties, the recorded plat method is the most frequently used method to describe land.

Real estate appraisers are not required to be an expert in any of the three land-description methods. However, they find it helpful to be adequately informed about which method is used for the type of property they most frequently appraise.

Methods of Land Description	
Method	**Typical Use**
Metes and Bounds	Irregular parcels of land
Public Land Survey System	Rural, undeveloped areas
Recorded Plat System	Urban areas, cities

Metes and Bounds

The **metes and bounds** description is the oldest method used to describe real property. **Metes** mean measurements in length (measured in feet) from one monument to another. **Bounds** refer to the direction. The direction of the boundary lines are given in degrees ($^\circ$), minutes ('), and seconds (").

A metes and bounds description measures the dimensions of the property using direction and distance between landmarks and monuments. A **landmark** is a geographic feature, such as a large rock, an old tree, a fork in a creek, or the intersection of two roads. A landmark may also refer to a monument (Washington Monument), prominent building (the White House), or structure (Statue of Liberty). **Monuments** used by surveyors are man-made objects, such as stakes or iron posts. Both landmarks and monuments are used as a point of reference to establish the boundaries of the property, locate its corners, or identify the point at which the boundary changes direction.

Land that is irregular in shape or cannot be described using other methods may have a metés and bounds description. In a metes and bounds description almost every tract of land has a different shape and size. A metes and bounds description is often lengthy, because it must identify each line and angle.

A metes-and-bounds description starts at a well-marked **point of beginning** (POB), and—following the boundaries of the land—measures the distances between landmarks, then returns to the beginning.

Example: Description of an uneven, hilly parcel of land with an avocado grove in Vista, California:

Beginning at the intersection of the east line of Buena Creek Road and the south line of Cleveland Trail; thence east along the south line of Cleveland Trail 300 feet; thence south 657.5 feet to the center line of Buena Creek; thence northwesterly along the center line of Buena Creek to its intersection with the east line of Buena Creek Road; thence north 325 feet along the east line of Buena Creek Road to the place of beginning.

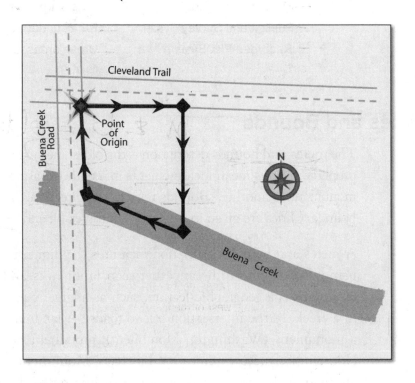

Public Land Survey System

By the late 19th century, the U.S. government had established a system of land description for new territories, states, and other public lands. It was known as the U.S. Government Section and Township Survey or the rectangular survey system. Currently, it is known as the **Public Land Survey System (PLSS)**.

When a survey is done using the PLSS, all its distances and bearings are measured from two imaginary lines that are at right angles to each other. These two lines, from which the measurements are made, are the **principal meridians**, which run north and south, and the **base lines** that run east and west. Both are located by reference to degrees of longitude and latitude. The intersection of principal meridian and base lines creates grids, which form the basis for surveying and measuring all the lands within the territory that they control.

After establishing a starting point at the intersection of a chosen principal meridian and baseline, the government surveyors drew imaginary vertical lines called **range lines** every six miles east and west of the meridian to form columns called **ranges**. Each range was numbered either east or west of the principal meridian.

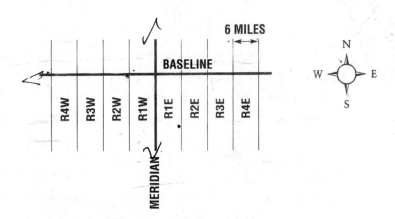

Example: The first range east of the meridian was called Range 1 East (R1E), and the first range west of the meridian was called Range 1 West (R1W).

Imaginary **township lines** were drawn every six miles north and south of the baseline to form a horizontal row or **tier of townships**. Then these rows were numbered according to their distance from the baseline.

Example: The first row of townships north of the baseline was called Township 1 North (T1N) and the first row of townships south of the baseline was called Township 1 South (T1S).

Thus, a grid of squares, called **townships**, appears. Each township is six miles by six miles (36 square miles). Each township is described by its location, relative to the intersection of the baseline and meridian.

Example: A township in California in the fourth tier north of the baseline and in the third range west of the meridian—with "T" for township and "R" for range—would be described as follows: T4N, R3W, San Bernardino Baseline and Meridian. The way to locate T4N, R3W is to start at the intersection of the baseline and meridian and count up—or north—four rows and then count to the left—or west—three rows.

Within a township, there are 36 sections—each measuring one mile by one mile. The sections are numbered, starting with section 1 in the northeast corner, and continuing in a snake-like manner to section 36 in the southeast corner. Each section is one mile by one mile and contains 640 acres.

A section may then be divided further into quarter sections containing 160 acres each, and then divided into smaller and smaller parcels. These parcels are identified by their compass direction (NE, SE, NW, and SW). Armed with this knowledge, a student may locate any size parcel, no matter how large or small, by simply dividing the section.

Using the PLSS, a particular piece of property could be described as the Northeast quarter of the Southeast quarter of section 22, Township 1 North, Range 1 East. It is normally expressed as a legal description in abbreviated form: NE 1/4 of the SE 1/4 of section 22, T1N, R1E. The quickest way to calculate the acreage contained within this description is to multiply the fractions by 640 acres (acres within a section). $1/4 \times 1/4 \times 640 = 40$ acres.

When ranges and tiers of townships intersect, a township is formed. Townships are further divided into 36 sections, each measuring one square mile or 640 acres.
Sections may then be divided into any number of smaller parcels.

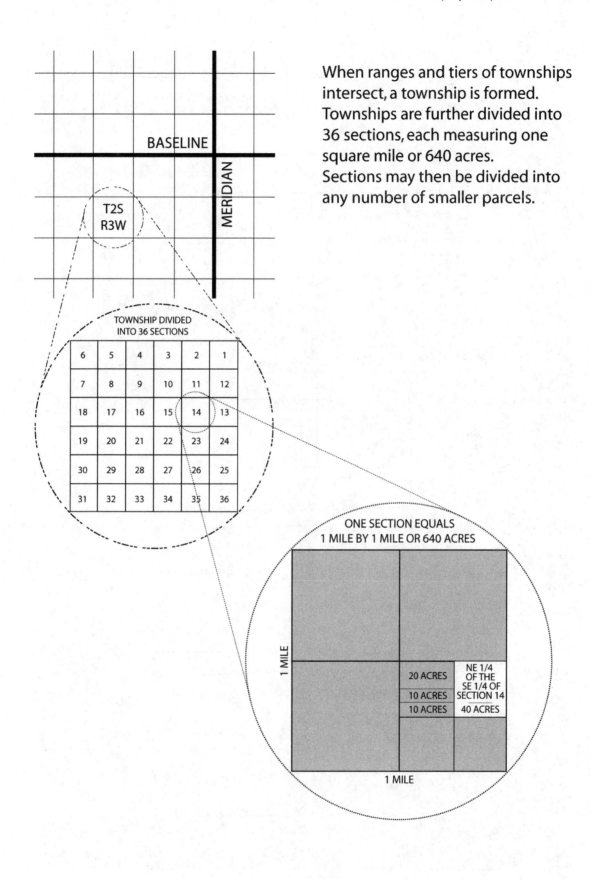

BASELINE

MERIDIAN

T2S
R3W

TOWNSHIP DIVIDED
INTO 36 SECTIONS

6	5	4	3	2	1
7	8	9	10	11	12
18	17	16	15	14	13
19	20	21	22	23	24
30	29	28	27	26	25
31	32	33	34	35	36

ONE SECTION EQUALS
1 MILE BY 1 MILE OR 640 ACRES

1 MILE

1 MILE

20 ACRES

10 ACRES

10 ACRES

NE 1/4
OF THE
SE 1/4 OF
SECTION 14

40 ACRES

20 ACRES

10 ACRES

10 ACRES

NE 1/4
OF THE
SE 1/4 OF
SECTION 14
———
40 ACRES

Recorded Plat System

The **recorded plat system** describes property by identifying the registered lot and the block on a recorded subdivision plat or survey. The recorded plat system is also called the **lot and block system** or **subdivision map system**. It is the most convenient and easily understood method of land description and is most common for metropolitan use.

A **plat** is a subdivision map filed with the county recorder's office that shows the location and boundaries (lot and block number) of individual parcels of land (lots), street right-of-way, subdivision name, and easements. Lots and blocks are assigned numbers or letters. A **lot** is a single parcel of land that will be sold within a subdivision to a buyer. A **block** is a contiguous group of lots, which are generally bounded by man-made features, such as streets or natural features, such as creeks.

When developers divide parcels of land into lots, they prepare and record a **subdivision map** or **plat map**. The subdivision map, showing the location and boundaries of each new lot in the subdivision, must be recorded in the county recorder's office. After the subdivision map has been filed or recorded, it is public record and is available to anyone. Each lot in a subdivision is identified by number, as is the block in which it is located; each lot and block is in a referenced tract. Recorded map descriptions of land are most likely to be found in cities where developers have planned communities and commercial growth areas.

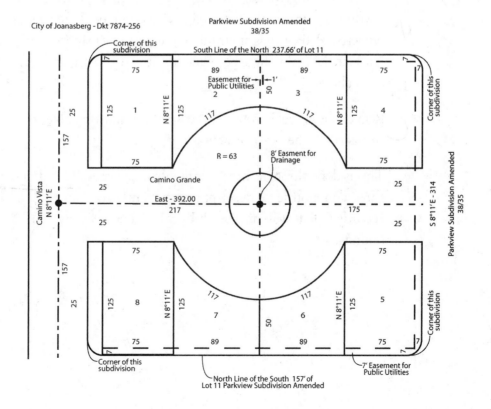

This type of legal description refers to the recorded map. A lot, block, and tract description might read something like this: Lot 5 of block B of Lake Forest Estates, Tract 4312, as recorded November 18, 1955, in Book 17 of Maps, Page 211, official records of Anywhere County.

SUMMARY

In common law, the word property refers more to the rights that the owner has in property than to the fact that the property is owned. Property rights are known as the bundle of rights. The **bundle of rights** consists of all legal rights that are attached to the ownership of property, which include the right to possess, use, enjoy, and dispose of property.

Anything that may be owned and gained lawfully is known as **property.** Property can be real or personal. **Personal property** refers to those items that are not permanently attached to land and are usually moveable and portable. **Real property** is the land and the bundle of rights inherent with its ownership. **Land** includes both the land and anything attached to it by nature from the center of the earth into the sky above the property. The components of land include air rights, surface rights, subsurface rights, water rights, and support rights.

Items permanently attached to the land are real property and belong to the owner. **Improvements,** such as houses, garages, fences, swimming pools, or anything resting on the land to become permanent are owned as a part of the property. A **fixture** is anything that is permanently attached to real property. It also includes anything permanently attached to the fixture, such as the door to a cabinet.

Before valuing real property, the appraiser must be able to identify correctly the land that he or she is appraising.

This is done through three commonly used types of **legal descriptions**. The three common legal descriptions currently used in the United States are **recorded plat system**, the **Public Land Survey System**, and **metes and bounds.**

UNIT 2 REVIEW

Matching Exercise

Instructions: Write the letter of the matching term on the blank line before its definition, and then check your response with the Answer Key that immediately follows the Multiple Choice Questions.

Terms

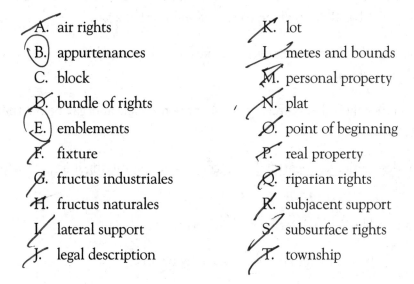

A. air rights
B. appurtenances
C. block
D. bundle of rights
E. emblements
F. fixture
G. fructus industriales
H. fructus naturales
I. lateral support
J. legal description

K. lot
L. metes and bounds
M. personal property
N. plat
O. point of beginning
P. real property
Q. riparian rights
R. subjacent support
S. subsurface rights
T. township

Definitions

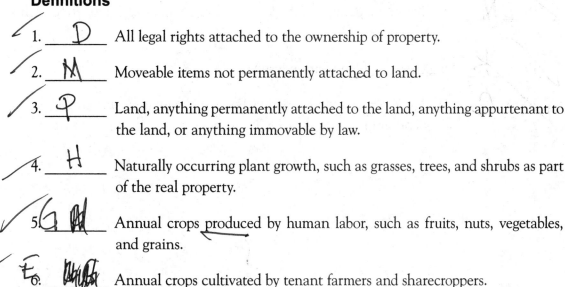

1. __D__ All legal rights attached to the ownership of property.

2. __M__ Moveable items not permanently attached to land.

3. __P__ Land, anything permanently attached to the land, anything appurtenant to the land, or anything immovable by law.

4. __H__ Naturally occurring plant growth, such as grasses, trees, and shrubs as part of the real property.

5. __G__ Annual crops produced by human labor, such as fruits, nuts, vegetables, and grains.

6. __E__ Annual crops cultivated by tenant farmers and sharecroppers.

7. __F__ Anything permanently attached to real property.

8. _____A_____ Rights to the air space above the property.

9. _____B_____ All rights, privileges, and improvements that belong to and pass with the transfer of the property, but that are not necessarily a part of the actual property.

10. _____Q_____ Right of an owner of property bordering a surface water source to use the water.

11. _____I_____ Landowners' right to have their land in its natural condition held in place from the sides by adjoining land so that it will not fall away.

12. _____R_____ Absolute right of the property owner to have his or her land supported from beneath its surface.

13. _____S_____ Rights to the natural resources, such as minerals, oil, and gas below the surface.

14. _____J_____ Written description of a particular parcel of land identifying it as precisely as possible.

15. _____L_____ Oldest method used to describe real property.

16. _____O_____ Point from which a metes and bounds survey begins.

17. _____T_____ Grid of square, each six miles by six miles (36 square miles).

18. _____N_____ Subdivision map showing the location and boundaries of lots, street rights-of-way, project name, and easements.

19. _____K_____ Single parcel of land within a subdivision.

20. _____C_____ Contiguous group of lots generally bounded by man-made features, such as streets or natural features, such as creeks.

Multiple Choice Questions

Instructions: Circle your choice, and then check your response with the Answer Key that immediately follows the Multiple Choice Questions.

1. Tom and Sarah decided to sell their home. Which of the bundle of rights gives them the right to sell their property?
   - a. Right of enjoyment
   - b. Right of possession
   - c. Right of transfer
   - d. Right to use.

2. Real property includes four things. These components are:
   - a. the land, anything immovable by law, the airspace, anything permanently attached to the land.
   - b. anything permanently attached to the land, anything appurtenant to the land, the land, the airspace.
   - c. anything appurtenant to the land, the land, the airspace, anything immovable by law.
   - d. the land, anything permanently attached to the land, anything appurtenant to the land, and anything immovable by law.

3. What is the commonality of air rights, surface rights, and subsurface rights?
   - a. Bundle of rights
   - b. Contracts
   - c. Land
   - d. Personal property

4. Of the following, which is NOT considered permanently attached and is NOT real property?
   - a. Ranch style, 3-bedroom, 2-bath home
   - b. A crop of wheat ready to be harvested
   - c. Wild red raspberry bushes
   - d. A recently installed skylight on the roof of a cottage

5. A tree purchased at a nursery and then planted in a backyard is NOT considered:
   - a. real property.
   - b. immovable by law.
   - c. chattel.
   - d. a fixture.

6. A commercial walnut grove is sold one week before the harvest. What happens to the walnut crop?
    a. The new owner takes possession.
    b. The previous owner retains possession.
    c. It is up to a court to decide.
    d. The new owner must split the proceeds from this crop with the seller.

7. Teresa rents a condominium to three college kids. While tenants, they install a custom sprinkler system in the lawn and garden. There is no agreement. When they move out the sprinklers are:
    a. Teresa's because of the sprinklers' method of attachment.
    b. the tenants' unless specified in writing.
    c. the tenants' because of the sprinkler's adaptation.
    d. Teresa's because of the relationship of the parties.

8. The Bakers purchased a 40-acre parcel with the following legal description in the deed—the SW1/4 of the S1/2 of the E1/2 of Section 27 in T7S, R8E. Which type of legal description is this?
    a. Lot and block system
    b. Metes and bounds system
    c. Public Land Survey System
    d. Recorded plat system

9. The following legal description is an example of which system?

    Starting from the south west corner of Smith Street and Barney Avenue, traveling north 158 yards, thence north easterly for 91 yards until the great pine tree, thence directly south 167 yards to the south east corner of Smith Street and Westin Lane, thence along the southern border of Smith Street to the point of beginning.
    a. Lot and block system
    b. Metes and bounds system
    c. Public Land Survey System
    d. Recorded plat system

10. While appraising in a metropolitan area, which type of legal description is an appraiser most likely to encounter?
    a. Public Land Survey System
    b. Metes and bounds system
    c. Benchmark survey system
    d. Recorded plat system

UNIT 2 ANSWER KEY

Answers – Matching

1. D	6. E	11. I	16. O
2. M	7. F	12. R	17. T
3. P	8. A	13. S	18. N
4. H	9. B	14. J	19. K
5. G	10. Q	15. L	20. C

Answers – Multiple Choice

1. **(c)** The right of transfer gives an owner of property the right to dispose of the property in any way permitted by law, including transferring ownership of the property by gift, sale, or trade. **Page 22**

2. **(d)** Real property includes four things: the land, anything permanently attached to the land, anything appurtenant to the land, and anything immovable by law. Airspace is a part of the land, and the land is part of real property. However, choice d. is the most correct. **Page 24**

3. **(c)** Land is three-dimensional because land includes the surface, limited quantities of airspace above the surface, and the materials and minerals beneath the surface to the center of the earth. **Page 24**

4. **(b)** The wheat crop is fructus industriales and is personal property. The ranch style home is an improvement and is real property. The raspberry bushes are fructus naturales and are real property. The skylight is a permanently installed fixture on the roof of the cottage, which is an improvement. **Page 25**

5. **(c)** Any growing thing attached by roots (trees, shrubs, and flowers) are real property and established trees are considered immovable by law. By definition, a fixture is real property that used to be personal property. When the nursery sold the tree sapling, it was personal property at that time, but became a fixture once it was planted. **Page 25**

6. **(b)** Crops ready for harvest are emblements and are personal property. **Page 25**

7. **(a)** The sprinklers are permanently attached and custom-made for the property. There is no expressed intention or clear agreement that the tenants would take the sprinklers, so they are real property. When tenants move out, they take personal property with them. Real property remains with the landlord. **Page 26**

8. **(c)** This is an example of the Public Land Survey System legal description. **Page 34**

9. **(b)** A metes and bounds description of land delineates boundaries and measures distances between landmarks like trees, boulders, creeks, fences, etc. This method describes the dimensions of the property as measured by distance and direction. **Page 31**

10. **(d)** The recorded plat system (lot and block system) and is most common system used in metropolitan areas. **Page 37**

Legal Considerations in Appraisal

Unit 3 ✓

INTRODUCTION

Owning real estate is considered a basic right in our culture, and each owner of real estate acquires certain rights along with property ownership. In fact, ownership of real estate is legally described in terms of these rights and not in terms of what is owned.

Historically, the question has been, "Who owns this property, and what is their interest in it?" To appraise property, the appraiser must know the ways property may be owned, what kind of ownership may be taken, how ownership is measured, how long ownership lasts, and how much is owned. This unit answers these questions about titles and estates.

Learning Objectives

After reading this unit, you should be able to:

- distinguish between freehold estates and less-than-freehold estates.
- recognize financial and non-financial encumbrances.
- identify different forms of ownership.
- recall the ways that ownership can be transferred.
- identify the recording process and the effect and priority of recording.
- classify contracts and recall how to interpret and discharge contracts.

INTERESTS IN REAL PROPERTY

After identifying the property, the appraiser determines what type of interest is being appraised. An **interest** includes any of the various rights, privileges, powers, and immunities with respect to any kind of property, including real property. The extent of ownership or interest in property determines the rights that go along with the property. Rights affect value because they set the limits within which the property may be used, so the appraiser must know the ownership interest owned in order to develop an opinion of its value under that type of ownership.

> Example: If Joe is leasing property from Sally, his interest in the property is described as a partial interest because he does not have all the rights that typically go along with ownership of property. In Joe's case, he has the right to use the property, but he does not have the right to sell it.

Real property interests can be categorized as possessory and non-possessory interests. A **possessory interest** means the present right to physically occupy land and to exclude others from that same land. A **non-possessory interest** is one that cannot presently be exercised today but which may or will become possessory in the future or under appropriate circumstances.

Another way to categorize ownership interests is present and future interest. A **present interest** in land is one that can be exercised by the owner today. A **future interest** is one that cannot be exercised today, but which might be exercised in the future. Present interests are usually possessory and future interests, because they cannot be exercised today, are non-possessory interests. However, they can be bought, sold, and transferred as if they were possessory.

Estates

Estates are POSSESSORY INTERESTS in real property. An **estate** is an interest that is (or may become) possessory and that can be measured in terms of duration. Ownership of the estate is measured by its duration—indefinite or definite. An estate with indefinite duration or that is measured by the length of someone's life is classified as a **freehold estate**. Whereas, an estate with a fixed or determinable duration is classified as a **nonfreehold estate**.

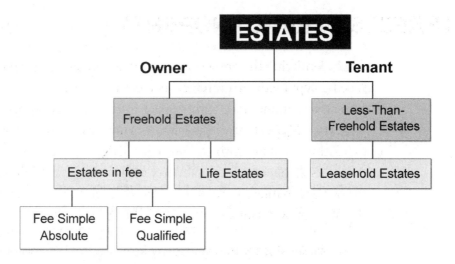

Freehold Estates

A **freehold estate** is an estate of indefinite duration. It is the most complete form of ownership and includes the most rights. The types of freehold estates are fee estates and life estates.

Fee Simple Estates

A **fee simple estate**, sometimes known as a **fee simple** or **estate in fee**, is the most complete form of ownership. This is the most common type of estate that is transferred in a normal real estate transaction. It is known as an estate of inheritance or a **perpetual estate** because an owner may dispose of it in his or her lifetime or after death by will.

A **fee simple absolute** is a freehold that includes all the rights to sell, exclude others, finance, and do any other thing with real property that the law allows. If the deed by which someone acquires property shows no restrictions on ownership and none can be found in past transactions, then the title is an unencumbered fee simple absolute.

> Example: Paul buys a parcel of land from Sally. The deed by which he acquires the property from her has no restrictions on his use of the land. The title search performed by the title company before he pays her for the land shows no restrictions imposed by any previous owners. Therefore, at the conclusion of his transaction with Sally, Paul has a fee simple absolute.

A property owner may impose qualifications, conditions, or restrictions when transferring title to property by deed or written agreement. These freehold estates with property conditions or restrictions are known as **fee simple defeasible** estates or defeasible fees.

If a condition in the granting of title were so restrictive that it limited the use of the property and caused it to be less desirable in the marketplace, such a condition would have an impact on value and would have to be taken into consideration by the appraiser.

Life Estates

A **life estate** is a present interest that gives its owner (the **life tenant**) a possessory interest for the length of a measuring life. The **measuring life** is usually the grantee's life—but it does not have to be. It can even be created on the life of a designated person who has no interest in the property as the measuring life—known as **pur autre vie**.

Since a life estate is a type of freehold estate, the life tenant has all the rights that go with fee ownership except disposing of the estate by will. Remember, the life estate is tied to a designated life and when that party dies, the estate goes to either the person in reversion or the person in remainder or the heirs.

Life estate holders must pay the taxes and maintain the property. They may collect all rents and keep all profits for the duration of the life estate. They may encumber the property or dispose of it in any way except by will. Any interest the life estate holders may create in the property—extending beyond the life of the person used to measure the estate—will become invalid when that designated person dies.

Types of life estates include estate in reversion, estate in remainder, and grant reserving a life estate. This type of ownership arrangement presents an unusual appraisal problem. The estate will endure for an indefinite amount of time, so the time period has to be estimated using actuarial tables, based on the age and life expectancy of the designated persons. The value of the estate then has to be estimated based on capitalization or comparison, and reconciled with its expected duration.

Estate in Reversion

An **estate in reversion** is a life estate in which the property owner (grantor) retains a future right to the property after the life tenant's death (or the death of a designated person). The grantor has a reversionary interest.

Example: Amy conveys a property to her friend Bob for life. Bob has the use of the property for the rest of his life. The property will revert to Amy (or her heirs) upon Bob's death. If Amy dies before Bob, Amy's heirs will inherit the property.

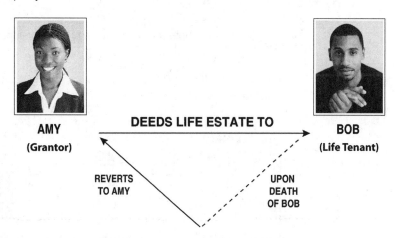

Estate in Remainder

Instead of keeping a reversionary interest, the grantor can identify someone to receive the property when the life tenant dies. That interest is known as a remainder and the person who owns the estate in remainder is the **remainderman**. A **remainder** is a future interest that takes effect upon the expiration of a life estate when the life tenant dies.

Example: Greg conveys a parcel of land to his friend Linda Smith for life, with a remainder to Charles Baker. Linda is the life tenant and Charles is the remainderman. Charles has no present right to enter the property or to use it.

Upon Linda's death, the remainder interest and the life estate are merged. Charles or his heirs will own the complete fee simple interest that Greg "divided" into a life estate and a remainder in the original transaction.

Grant Reserving a Life Estate

The grant reserving a life estate is probably the most commonly used life estate. In this type of life estate, the grantor sells the property but reserves the right to live on the property until his or her death.

> Example: An elderly couple sells their property to a developer reserving the right to live on the property until their death. At that time, the developer will be able to take possession of the property. This is called a grant reserving a life estate.

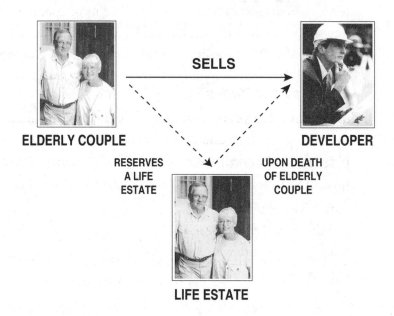

ELDERLY COUPLE   SELLS   DEVELOPER

RESERVES A LIFE ESTATE   UPON DEATH OF ELDERLY COUPLE

LIFE ESTATE

Nonfreehold Estates

A **nonfreehold estate** is also known as a **less-than-freehold estate** or a **leasehold**, which is a tenant's possessory estate in land or premises. It is created by a lease or other agreement (written or unwritten) that gives temporary rights in a real property estate to the renter or tenant. The owner of the leased property is called the **lessor**, and the tenant is called the **lessee**.

A lease creates two types of estates. The owner's fee estate becomes a **leased fee estate** and the tenant owns a **leasehold estate**. The owner of the leased fee estate (the lessor) maintains the rights to take out a loan on the property and to sell it or give it away. The owner of the leasehold estate (the lessee) has exclusive possession and use of the rented property for a fixed period of time. During any leasehold, the lessor has a **reversionary interest** because at the end of the lessee's term, the property reverts to the lessor.

Types of Leaseholds

The four basic tenancies (leaseholds) differ in how they are initiated, how they are terminated, and in the relationship between the lessor and lessee during the term of each tenancy.

Periodic Tenancy

A **periodic tenancy** (estate from period-to-period) refers to a leasehold interest that is for an indefinite time. The duration of the tenancy is determined by the term or frequency of rent payment. The most common version of a periodic tenancy is the month-to-month tenancy, which requires 30 days notice to quit. It automatically renews itself unless terminated by the owner or tenant.

Tenancy for Years

A **tenancy for years** lease has a fixed term and definite end date. It is sometimes called an estate for years and is what most people in everyday usage mean when they refer to having a lease. A tenancy for years does not actually have to be for a term of years, but refers to any rental of property with a specific beginning and ending date.

Since the end date is mutually agreed upon, notice to terminate is not required. The tenancy terminates automatically at the end of the specified rental period. During the term of a lease, the owner cannot end the tenancy without cause, such as the tenant not paying rent on time.

Tenancy at Sufferance

A **tenancy at sufferance** is often referred to as a **holdover tenancy**. It typically occurs when the tenant's original lease expires and there is no agreement for an extension or the conversion of that lease to a month-to-month tenancy. If the tenant does not leave, the owner must commence eviction proceedings to remove the tenant.

Tenancy at Will

When there is no written agreement between the owner and tenant, the tenancy is known as a **tenancy at will**. A tenancy at will has no specified term and often no rent is paid or the rent is offset by some form of service. The tenancy may be ended by the unilateral decision of either party.

> Example: Laura allows Tim to live in a house that she owns in exchange for his maintaining the property and making repairs. Tim has a tenancy at will because he moved onto the premises with the permission of the lessor, his tenancy is for an indefinite time, and he is not required to pay Laura rent on a periodic basis.

NONFREEHOLD ESTATES				
	Periodic Tenancy	**Tenancy for Years**	**Tenancy at Will**	**Tenancy at Sufferance**
Creation	Agreement or by accepting rent at end of lease term	Oral or written agreement	Take possession while negotiating lease	Remain in possession at end of term
Duration	Indefinite	Definite	No duration	None
Term	Indefinite	Fixed term	No specified term	None
Termination	30-day notice or per lease terms	Automatic termination at end of lease	30-day notice	No notice

Lease Provisions

Through a lease agreement, the owner temporarily transfers certain rights to the tenant, and the tenant compensates the owner.

Methods of compensation to the owner are varied and flexible. A lease may be set up as a gross lease or a net lease. A **gross lease** means that the tenant pays a fixed amount of rent, and the owner pays all the expenses of ownership, such as maintenance, insurance, taxes, and assessments. This is the type of lease typically used with residential property. A **net lease** means that the tenant pays rent plus at least some of the ownership expenses.

Another issue to be decided is how to determine the amount of the rent. The most basic form of payment is a flat monthly rent. However, when renting commercial property, like a strip mall, the owner wants to maximize his or her income from the property. If the tenant is doing extremely well in business, part of that success can be attributed to the location and facilities provided by the owner. In a **percentage lease**, the tenant pays a minimum monthly amount plus a percentage of the gross receipts from the business. The amount over the minimum that the tenant pays is called **overage rent**. Another alternative is to establish a **graduated lease** that contains an **escalator clause** that allows for increases in rent based on increases in the consumer price index or some other economic indicator. Establishing a pattern of increases like this makes sense, because the tenant can afford to pay. If the owner tries to increase the rent regardless of the well being of the tenant, that could be the last straw and force the tenant out.

Encumbrances

Encumbrances are NON-POSSESSORY INTERESTS in real estate. An **encumbrance** is an interest in real property that is held by someone who is not the owner. Anything that burdens or affects the use or the title of the property is an encumbrance. Real estate professionals must make inquiries regarding any encumbrances on the property, such as easements, because they can inhibit use or transferability. Because encumbrances are so commonplace, most buyers purchase encumbered property, i.e. burdened with some type of easement or lien. Encumbrances fall into two categories—financial encumbrances and non-financial encumbrances.

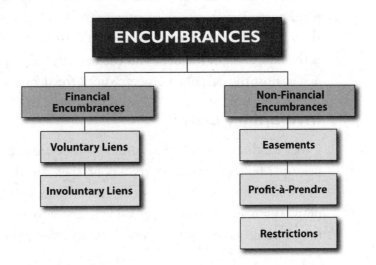

Financial Encumbrances

A **financial encumbrance** is one that affects the title to property. A financial encumbrance that creates a legal obligation to pay is known as a **lien**. A lien uses real property as security for the payment of a debt.

Liens may be specific or general. A **specific lien** is one that is placed against a certain property, such as a mechanic's lien, deed of trust, and property tax lien. A **general lien** affects all property of the owner, such as a judgment lien or federal or state income tax liens.

Additionally, liens are classified as voluntary or involuntary.

Voluntary Liens

An owner may choose to borrow money, using the property as security for the loan, creating a **voluntary lien**. A voluntary lien does not have to be recorded, but if it is not recorded, then other parties (such as purchasers and lenders) may not be bound by it.

Security instruments are the most common voluntary liens. A **security instrument** is a legal document that is given by the borrower to hypothecate (pledge) real property to the lender as collateral for a loan. Although the lender retains a security interest in the property, the borrower retains right of possession as long as payments are made according to the loan agreement. If the borrower does not make payments per the agreement, he or she loses the rights of possession and ownership.

Deeds of trust and mortgages are the most common types of security instruments used in real estate financing. A **deed of trust** involves three parties—the borrower (**trustor**), the lender (**beneficiary**), and a neutral third party (**trustee**). A **mortgage** involves two parties—the **mortgagor** (borrower) and the **mortgagee** (lender). In both cases, the promissory note is the obligation of the debt and the deed of trust or mortgage is a voluntary lien against the described property until the debt is repaid.

Involuntary Liens

Other kinds of liens are involuntary—they are used to collect money from debtors who have real property among their assets. If an owner fails to pay taxes, assessments, or other debts, a lien may be placed against his or her property without permission, creating an **involuntary lien**. Typical involuntary liens include judgment liens, tax liens, and mechanic's liens.

Judgment

A **judgment** is the final determination by the court of the rights of the parties in a lawsuit. A judgment does not automatically create a lien. A summary of the court decision, known as an **abstract of judgment**, must be recorded with the county recorder. When the abstract of judgment is recorded, it creates a public, involuntary, general lien on all non-exempt property owned or acquired by the judgment debtor in the county in which the abstract is filed. The court may force a sale of the property to satisfy the judgment by issuing a writ of execution. The sale is called an **execution sale**. If the judgment debtor pays off the lien or reaches an agreement with the judgment creditor, the judgment creditor will record a document known as a **notice of satisfaction of judgment** acknowledging payment of the judgment. When recorded, it expunges the lien against the debtor's real property.

Writ of Attachment

A **writ of attachment** is used by the court to hold the real or personal property of a defendant as security for a possible judgment pending the outcome of a lawsuit. An attachment is an, involuntary, specific lien.

Lis Pendens

A **lis pendens** (also called a pendency of action) is a recorded notice that indicates pending litigation affecting the title on a property. It acts as notice to prospective lenders or buyers that title to the property is disputed. It does not actually prevent anyone from buying the property, but it warns parties that they could be involved in a lawsuit if they do.

Tax Liens

A **tax lien** is an involuntary, financial encumbrance placed upon property as a claim for payment of a tax liability. Tax liens are levied by local, state, and federal government agencies. Tax liens can attach to any property owned by the taxpayer or acquired after the lien is placed. They continue until the tax liability is satisfied or becomes unenforceable.

Property Tax Liens

When a property tax is assessed against a property, a property tax lien for that amount is placed on the property. This type of lien is superior to all other liens and cannot be cleared by a foreclosure. Since tax liens are superior to any other lien, the property can be sold at a public auction, which in turn, dissolves all other liens, except for property tax liens and special assessments.

Special Assessments

Special assessments are levied against property owners to pay for local improvements, such as underground utilities, street repair, or water projects. Payment for the projects is obtained through a special form of borrowing called **bonds**. The money borrowed through the bond is secured by the special assessment, which becomes a lien against real property. Assessments are collected annually in the same way as property taxes until all of the borrowed funds have been repaid.

Mechanic's Liens

A **mechanic's lien** is a statutory lien that secures payment for labor or materials supplied in improving, repairing, or maintaining real property. Mechanics include contractors, subcontractors, laborers, materialmen, architects, and other parties who improve a specific parcel of real property. Mechanic's liens are involuntary, specific liens.

Non-Financial Encumbrances

A **non-financial encumbrance** is one that affects the physical use or condition of the property, such as easements, profit-à-prendres, and restrictions.

Easements

An **easement** an interest owned by one person in the land of another person. An easement allows its owner to use or, in some cases, to prevent the use of, the land burdened by the easement. Easement rights are often created for the benefit of the owner of adjoining land. The holder of an easement can use it only for the purpose intended and may not exclude anyone else from using it. There are many ways to establish and terminate easements; however, the important thing for appraisers to determine is what impact easements have on value.

The two kinds of easements are appurtenant easements and easements in gross.

Appurtenant Easements

An **appurtenant easement** is an easement that is connected to a particular property and is transferred along with that property. An appurtenant easement has a dominant and a servient tenement. The **dominant tenement** is the land receiving the benefit of the easement. The **servient tenement** is encumbered by the easement and the land is being used by someone other than the owner.

An appurtenant easement automatically goes with the sale of the dominant tenement and is said to "run with the land". The typical appurtenant easement is the right to cross over the land of the servient tenement to get to the land of the dominant tenement as with a driveway or a path to a river or lake.

Appurtenant easements are characterized as affirmative or negative. An **affirmative easement** is one that requires the owner of the servient estate to do something to benefit the dominant estate. An easement is called a **negative easement** if it prohibits a property owner from doing something on his or her estate because of the effect it would have on the dominant estate.

Easement in Gross

An **easement in gross** is a personal right of one person (or company) to use land owned by another. Unlike an appurtenant easement, there is only a servient tenement burdened by the easement, but no dominant tenement. Easements in gross are the most common type of easement. These are typically owned by utility companies.

Types of Easements

An easement can be under, over, or on the property of another. An easement can be underground (for example, a pipeline easement enjoyed by a utility company) or it can be overhead (for example, a power line easement enjoyed by a private electric company). Alternatively, it can be on the surface (a road easement held by one person over land owned by another). In some instances, an easement can encompass the entire property but only remove one right, as in a conservation easement.

Underground Easements. Underground easements lie below the surface of the ground. They include pipeline easements of all types, such as storm drainage, sewer, water, and underground conduits for electrical cable. Some underground easements would restrict the use of the surface for residential purposes. For example, the existence of an underground easement for a pipeline running diagonally across a backyard would restrict the building of a swimming pool.

Overhead Easements. Power line easements are the most common type of overhead easement. Depending on the placement of the overhead easement, use of the surface property could be restricted. For example, an easement for a power line that diagonally crossed the backyard of

a home possibly could restrict planting trees or constructing a swimming pool.

Another type of overhead easement would be an avigation easement. An **avigation easement** is an easement over private property near an airport that limits the height of structures and trees in order to keep the takeoff and landing paths of airports clear.

Surface Easements. Road easements are the most common type of surface easement. Easements for roads, flood control channels, drainage ditches, or other purposes that use the land surface are generally valued at 100% of fee value of the area occupied by the easement. The land surface is usually the most usable portion of the property.

Conservation Easement. A **conservation easement** is an interest in real property voluntarily conveyed by the owner of the property to qualified nonprofit organizations. Its purpose is to preserve land in its natural, scenic, agricultural, historical, forested, or open-space condition. Since the conservation easement creates

open space, the underlying property owner is left with limited uses.

Encroachments

An **encroachment** is the intrusion into, under, or over the property of another without that person's permission. An encroachment is not an easement; it is considered a nuisance as well as a trespass. No one legally may build a structure such as a fence, wall, driveway, or roof, so that it extends over the lot line into adjacent property owned by another.

This unauthorized intrusion on the adjoining land can limit its use and reduce it in size and value. The property owner has a certain time period (determined by local laws) in which to take legal action to have the neighbor remove the unauthorized encroachment. After that time period, the encroachment can become a permanent prescriptive easement.

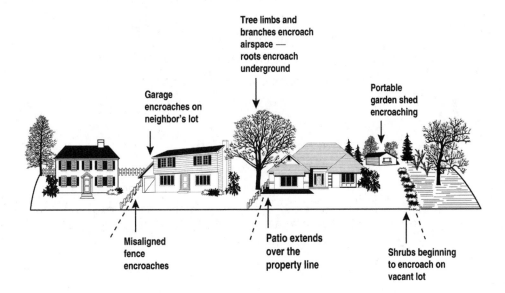

Tree limbs and branches encroach airspace — roots encroach underground

Garage encroaches on neighbor's lot

Portable garden shed encroaching

Misaligned fence encroaches

Patio extends over the property line

Shrubs beginning to encroach on vacant lot

Profit-à-Prendres

A **profit-à-prendre** is the right to enter another's land to remove soil or substances of the soil (water, minerals, timber, fruit, game, or other resource). An example would be the right to harvest timber on land owned by someone else. It differs from an easement because an easement only gives the right to use the land, whereas, a profit-à-prendre gives the right to remove the soil or products of the soil. A profit-à-prendre can last indefinitely. If an owner grants a profit-à-prendre to someone and then sells the property, the new owner will still have to abide by the terms of the profit-à-prendre. The profit holder can sell, lease, give away, or bequeath the profit-à-prendre to someone else.

Private Restrictions

A **restriction** placed by a private owner, a developer, or the government, is a limitation placed on the use of the property. They are usually placed on property to assure that land use is consistent and uniform within a certain area.

Private restrictions may be included in a deed as a condition of the grant or be created by a separate contract between property owners.

> An example of a deed restriction is the reservation of mineral rights by a previous owner. This type of restriction must be carefully reviewed because it can include the right of surface entry. The holder of the mineral rights can mine for those minerals at any time without regard to any improvements on the property. That situation would make building on the property extremely difficult.

Private restrictions are voluntarily accepted by the purchaser of property subject to these restrictions, because, unlike governmental restrictions, the purchaser can choose to avoid them by buying elsewhere.

Usually restrictions are covenants or conditions.

> A **covenant** is a promise to do or not do certain things. The penalty for a breach of a covenant is usually money damages or a court order forcing compliance with the covenant. An example of a covenant might be that the tenant agrees to make some repairs, or that a property may be used only for a specific purpose.

> A **condition** is a limitation imposed by a grantor in a deed that can cause the ownership of the property to revert to the grantor who imposes the condition if the condition is not satisfied. Conditions actually lessen or diminish the estate that a purchaser obtains in acquiring title to property.

Appraisers must take into account any restrictions present that make an impact on the property's value.

Public Restrictions

All land in the United States is subject to various obligations and public restrictions imposed by federal, state, and local governments. **Public restrictions** on use of real property are those associated with government intervention. Within any region, federal and state environmental regulations affect the way in which it is developed. County and city agencies regulate and enforce building codes, health codes, and safety codes. Local zoning ordinances control the areas in which housing and businesses are located. Homeowners who want to add a pool in their yard must secure a permit for the pool addition and for most remodeling projects. Builders must apply for building permits from the local government, and business owners must acquire business licenses before they open their doors to the public.

Planning

Most cities and counties have a general or comprehensive plan to control land use and growth within their boundaries.

The **general plan** is the starting point for land use and determines the physical development of the city or county. Development regulations (zoning, subdivision, and other controls) must be consistent with the general plan. A general plan includes land use maps and land use elements that address the city's or county's overall goals with respect to growth. The land use element of the general plan lists use classifications, such as agricultural, commercial, industrial, or residential. Each land use element is tied to a map that shows the designation of every parcel in the city or county. Broad areas of a given community might have the same general plan classifications, but different parcels within the same general plan classification might have different zoning.

> Example: A given parcel's zoning must be consistent with the general plan category for that parcel. Thus, if two parcels each had a general plan classification of residential, one of those parcels could be zoned for apartment buildings and the other for single-family homes, but neither could be zoned for industrial use.

Zoning

Zoning—the earliest of all modern land-use tools—is the foundation of contemporary planning. The purpose of zoning is to locate particular land uses where they are most appropriate, considering public utilities, road access, and the established development pattern.

Like the general plan, a zoning ordinance divides a city or county into different geographic **zones**, identifying what uses can and cannot be made on each parcel. A typical zoning code will first contain a list of different **zoning districts**, which are all of the possible classifications that might be given to any particular parcel of land. For ease of reference, these are identified by a one-, two-, or three-letter designation (or sometimes a combination of letters and numbers).

Typical Zoning Symbols

A – Agriculture

C – Commercial

R1 – Single-Family Home

R2 – Duplex

R3 – Multiple Residential Units

PD – Planned Development

M – Manufacturing

P – Public Uses

Remember, many zoning codes are similar but jurisdictions may not use exactly the same zoning restrictions even if the terms they use are identical. Do not assume, therefore, that a parcel with the designation SR in one city or county has the same meaning as the same classification in another city or county. Many cities and counties now have their entire local codes online. Sometimes they are linked to the land use maps or to a list by the assessor's parcel number for that community, so that the general zoning definitions and, even the zoning for individual parcels, can be obtained.

Zoning ordinances often list **size restrictions** applicable to each parcel with a given category. Examples of those restrictions include height limits, setbacks, and the minimum lot size. **Height limits** state how tall the buildings can be above the average grade. **Setbacks** limit how close a structure can be built to neighboring property lines. The **minimum lot size** limits how small the parcels can be if the property were subdivided. If the minimum lot size in the SR zone in the example above were a half-acre, a two-acre parcel could be subdivided into no more than four resulting lots.

Special Types of Zoning

- **Aesthetic zoning** regulates the appearance of buildings in the area. For example, aesthetic-zoning laws may require that new buildings conform to specific types of architecture.

- **Historic zoning** helps protect historic buildings within a specified area referred to as a historic district. Within historic districts, cities typically provide incentives for meeting requirements that are additional to the existing zoning rules for that area.

- **Cumulative zoning** allows so-called higher uses (residential) to exist in lower use zones (industrial), but not vice versa.

- **Bulk zoning** controls density and prevents overcrowding. Bulk zoning regulates setbacks, building height, and percentage of open area.

- **Incentive zoning** is more flexible than traditional zoning laws. It allows a developer to exceed the limitations set by a zoning law if the developer agrees to fulfill conditions specified in the law. For example, the developer may be allowed to exceed height limits by a specified amount in exchange for providing open spaces adjacent to the building.

Land Uses – Permitted and Conditional

Each zoning district lists the allowed uses—permitted uses and conditional uses. **Permitted uses** meet the current use requirements within the district. **Conditional uses** do not meet the current use requirements; however, a conditional use may be allowed by obtaining a special permit. A **conditional-use permit** or **special-use permit** allows a land use that may be incompatible with other uses existing in the zone. The use is allowed as long as the project owner complies with the conditions specified in the permit. If the owner does not comply with the conditions, the permit may be revoked. A conditional-use permit runs with the land and its provisions still apply even if there is a change in ownership. Any uses that are not listed as either allowed or conditional are presumptively **prohibited uses** by the zoning code.

Changes in zoning may be initiated by a single property owner, developer, or government entity. A person who wants to use his or her property in a way that does not meet the current use regulations may be able to obtain an exception to the zoning ordinances. Typical exceptions include nonconforming use, variance, or rezoning.

Nonconforming Use. If a city or county changes the zoning of a parcel so that the existing uses are no longer allowed by the new zoning, those existing activities are known as **nonconforming use**. Nonconforming uses that existed prior to the adoption of the current zoning that were lawful when established are normally allowed to continue indefinitely.

> Example: If farmland is rezoned for residential use, all new structures must conform to the new zoning and be for residential use. Existing farms are now nonconforming properties. However, they may continue to operate because a grandfather clause allows an owner to continue to use structures that are now nonconforming within the new zoning laws.

Variances. A **variance** is a local land use decision allowing a use that is not strictly in compliance with local zoning or building regulations. The city or county will typically only allow the variance under unique circumstances.

> Example: Donna owns a parcel that is unusually long and thin. She wants to build a house on the property, but the local zoning code requires a ten-foot setback between the exterior of a structure and any property line. The only house that Donna could build on her parcel given those restrictions would be exceedingly long and thin.

Because her parcel is so narrow, Donna applies for a variance from the conditions of the zoning code. She asks the city planning commission to allow her to construct her house with only a five-foot setback from each of the two property lines. Her house will still be relatively long compared to its depth, but it will at least allow her to have more interior space. The commission agrees, finding that the strict application of the code to Donna's parcel would be unfair because she cannot build a conventionally sized house on the property as the owners of most other nearby parcels could.

Rezoning. **Rezoning** is converting the use of a property from one zoning category to another. When an entire area is rezoned, commonly zoning is changed from a high-density use to a lower-density use, such as from residential to conservation. This is called **downzoning**. Sometimes developers ask for higher density, such as changing from low-density residential (R-1) to high-density (R-3) in order to build condominiums. Rezoning an area can create nonconforming uses.

If only one property (rather than the entire area) is rezoned, it might constitute spot zoning. **Spot zoning** occurs when a public entity makes the decision to change the zoning for a single parcel without considering the larger planning context.

OWNERSHIP OF REAL PROPERTY

All property has an owner, whether the government, a private institution, or an individual. **Title** is the evidence that the owner of land is in lawful possession; it is the proof of ownership. **Tenancy** refers to a mode or method of ownership or holding title to property.

Separate ownership and ownership of an undivided interest are two ways a person or other entity can take title to or own real estate. An **undivided ownership interest** is an interest held under the same title by two or more people, whether their rights are equal or unequal in value or quantity. Undivided interests include fractional ownership interests, common interest developments, and timeshares.

Separate Ownership

Separate ownership means ownership by one person or one entity, such as a corporation. Property owned by one person or entity is known as sole and separate ownership or **ownership in severalty.** With separate ownership, the ownership rights are "severed" from everyone else. When a person obtains title to property in severalty, the description of that person's status on the deed is often "an unmarried man" or "an unmarried woman."

Fractional Ownership Interests

When two or more persons or entities own property at the same time with undivided use, **fractional ownership interests** are created because each owner has a fraction of the whole. The owner of a fractional interest has less control over a property than if he or she owned the entire property and cannot unilaterally make decisions regarding the property. Fractional interest ownership includes concurrent ownership and business ownership.

Concurrent Ownership

Concurrent ownership, or co-ownership, refers to the ownership of real property by more than one person. Types of concurrent ownership include tenancy in common, joint tenancy, and marital property (community property or tenancy by the entirety).

Tenancy in Common

A **tenancy in common** exists when two or more persons are owners of an undivided interest in a single estate. **Undivided interest** means that, although their ownership interests are not necessarily equal (one party may have one-half interest, one-fourth interest, etc.), they each have the right to use the whole property. None of the owners may exclude any co-owner from the property, nor claim any portion of the property for exclusive use.

Example: Arthur, Frank, and Charles purchase a parcel of land. The deed conveying the property to them from Greg, the seller, states that he is conveying, "To Arthur, Frank, and Charles." Because no other form of concurrent ownership is specified, they hold title as tenants in common. Each of the three co-owners has an undivided one-third interest in the property.

Whenever there are co-owners and some other form of ownership is not mentioned specifically, title is assumed to be a tenancy in common.

Joint Tenancy

When two or more parties own real property as co-owners, with the right of survivorship, it is called **joint tenancy**. The **right of survivorship** means that if one of the joint tenants dies, the surviving joint tenant automatically becomes sole owner of the property. Due to the right of survivorship, a joint tenant may not will his or her share as can be done in a tenancy in common. The deceased's share becomes the property of the co-tenant without becoming involved in probate. In addition, the surviving joint tenant is not liable to creditors of the deceased who hold liens on the joint tenancy property.

Joint tenancy is characterized by four unities—time, title, interest, and possession. This means all joint tenants must take title at the same time, with each tenant receiving equal interest in the property with the right of possession. If any one of the unities is missing, a tenancy in common is created.

Four Unities of Joint Tenancy
1. **Unity of time** (created among all owners at the same time)
2. **Unity of title** (acquired on the same deed or will)
3. **Unity of interest** (equal as between or among all joint tenants)
4. **Unity of possession** (rights of use are co-equal)

Co-owners may sell their interest, give it away, or borrow money against it, without consent of the other joint tenants. However, all four unities must occur to have a joint tenancy, so joint tenancy is terminated when any one of the four unities ends. Joint tenancy can be terminated by sale, gift or by mutual agreement. A joint tenancy is not severed if a lien is put against the interest of one of the co-owners. However, a foreclosure on the lien would sever that interest from the joint tenancy.

Example: Dan, Robin, and Sam own a parcel together in joint tenancy. As a result, each one owns a one-third undivided share. One day, Robin dies. At the moment of Robin's death, Dan and Sam succeed to the ownership of her share. Dan and Sam are now the owners of a one-half undivided share as joint tenants. Their interests still share the four unities, except that, with Robin's death, they are the only members of the original joint tenancy.

Marital Property

Married people may have a special status as property owners. Forms of marital property ownership vary from state-to-state. The two most common forms are community property and tenancy by the entirety. When determining the ownership interest, appraisers must consider marital property ownership.

Community Property

Nine states—Arizona, California, Idaho, Louisiana, Nevada, New Mexico, Texas, Washington, and Wisconsin—use the community property system to determine the interest of a husband and wife in property acquired during marriage.

In these states, property is classified as separate property or community property. **Separate property** is property either spouse owned before marriage and property either spouse acquires by gift or inheritance during marriage. **Community property** is all other property acquired by either spouse during a valid marriage.  Community property has one unity—equal interest—with each spouse owning 50%.

Each spouse's income is also considered community property, unless it is income derived from separate property. Income derived from separate property must be kept separate, or it becomes community property. If separate income is used to purchase property, that property is also separate property.

Community property cannot be sold or encumbered by only one of the partners. Either spouse may lease community property for up to one year. Both husband and wife must accept and sign any contract for the transfer of community property to a new owner.

Either husband or wife may buy real or personal property without the consent of the other, and both spouses are bound by the contract made by either one. This does not apply if the new property is bought specifically as separate property, with funds from a separate property account.

When title is taken as community property, either party may will one-half of the community property. Upon the death of the husband or wife, the court determines the status of property—either community property or separate property. Then the property is distributed according to the terms of the will or by intestate succession, if there is no will.

Tenancy by the Entirety

Tenancy by the entirety is another form of marital ownership in which each spouse has an undivided interest in the entire property and the right of survivorship. Tenancy by the entirety is used in Alaska, Arkansas, Delaware, Florida, Hawaii, Indiana, Kentucky, Maryland, Massachusetts, Michigan, Mississippi, Missouri, New Jersey, New York, North Carolina, Ohio, Oklahoma, Oregon, Pennsylvania, Tennessee, Vermont, Virginia, Wyoming, and the District of Columbia.

Like community property, property owned by spouses as tenants by the entirety cannot be sold or encumbered by only one of the partners. In fact, any document relating to property held in a tenancy by the entirety must be signed by both spouses. Because of the right of survivorship, upon the death of one of the spouses, the deceased spouse's interest in the property devolves to the surviving spouse, and not to other heirs of the deceased spouse.

Business Ownership

A business entity can own real property in many different ways. Real estate appraisers must be aware of the different types of entities, especially if a party in the transaction involves a business. The most common types of business entities include the sole proprietorship, partnership, corporation, and limited-liability company.

Sole Proprietorship

A **sole proprietorship** exists when a single individual files with the state and then operates a business with no other owners. This single owner owns all assets and assumes all liabilities. The business can be sold or terminated at the owner's will. The owner is personally liable for all debts without separation. If the owner decides to operate under a different type of name, such as Best Bakery, then the owner would have to file an Assumed Name Certificate or a DBA—**doing business as** certificate with the county clerk. The advantage to the owner of a DBA is that the transfer of ownership during a sale is easier and the new owner can take over without changing the name.

Partnership

A **partnership** is one form of business organization. Partnerships are normally created among natural persons, but other entities, such as unincorporated associations or corporations, can also be parties to a partnership. Like any enterprise conducting business under a fictitious name, a partnership must register its partnership name in the county where its principal place of business is located, showing the full names and residences of all of the partners. Unlike a corporation, which is legally deemed a "person" for various purposes, a partnership does not reflect a different legal "personality" from the partners. Typically, partnerships are formed as general partnerships or limited partnerships.

Corporation

A **corporation** is a legal entity, which has a separate legal identity from its owners or members. A corporation is viewed as a legal person (has rights) and not a natural person (has body). Because a corporation is viewed as a legal person, a corporation can buy and sell real property, bind itself to a contract, and pay taxes. The corporation structure offers protection to the business owners' (stockholders) personal assets from debts and liabilities relating to the operation of the corporation. As a legal entity, the corporation has inherent rights and obligations.

S-corporations and limited liability companies are other variations of a corporation. An **S-corporation** is a business entity that operates as a corporation, has the tax advantages of a partnership, and passes along any profits or losses through to shareholders. A **limited liability company (LLC)** is a business entity that combines the tax advantages of a partnership and the limited liability of a corporation, but does not require any advanced financial reporting or the complicated structuring that a corporation normally requires.

Common Interest Developments

A **common interest development** (CID) is a development involving a combination of individually owned lots or units coupled with common area parcels or spaces. Common interest developments include planned developments, condominium projects, cooperatives, and community apartment projects. Each of these projects is similar because they combine the individual ownership of private dwellings with an interest in common with other owners. The interest in common may be through membership in an association. In CIDs, the common areas are owned either in common by the owners as in condominiums or by an association as in planned developments. A common interest development is also called a common interest community (CIC) or a community interest development (CID).

All CIDs are similar in that they allow individual owners the use of common property and facilities and provide for a system of self-governance through some type of homeowners' association. Membership in the association is automatic. When a person buys a lot, home, or condominium in a CID, he or she automatically becomes a member of the association.

The most important difference in CIDs is their legal structure, e.g. planned developments, condominiums, cooperatives, and community apartment projects. Each type confers specific ownership rights—from fee ownership of the unit including the underlying lot to ownership of stock with a proprietary lease giving its owner an exclusive right to occupy an apartment.

Planned Development

A **planned development**, or planned unit development (PUD), is another form of common ownership. A PUD is a community of clustered single-family detached residences, townhouses, garden apartments, and other types of residences, with ample open space, community recreational facilities, and sometimes local shopping and employment centers.

Planned development owners have fee title to their separately owned dwelling along with the lot underneath it. They do not directly own the common areas. The common areas are owned and managed by a homeowners' association to which the owner belongs.

Note: For financing purposes, both Fannie Mae and Freddie Mac consider property as a planned unit development (PUD) if the development that has common property and improvements that are owned and maintained by a homeowners' association for the benefit and use of the individual PUD units. In addition, there is an automatic and non-severable membership in the Homeowner's Association and there are mandatory dues. However, Zoning is not a basis for classifying a project or subdivision as a PUD.

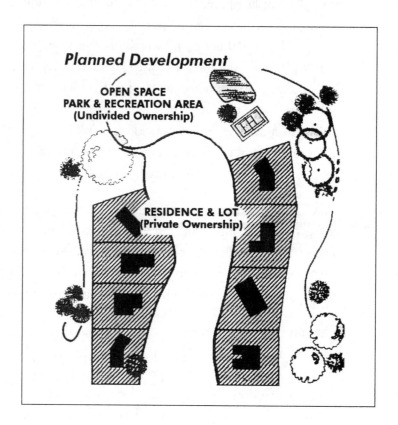

Condominium

A **condominium** consists of a separate fee interest in airspace and everything contained within (the unit), plus an undivided interest in all common or public areas of the development. The underlying land and virtually all of the rest of the structure that houses the condominium unit, along with any common ground, lawns, recreational facilities, and the like are owned in tenancy in common with other owners in the development.

Unit owners each have a deed, they each obtain separate financing, and they each pay the property taxes for their unit but have no interests in the land beneath their unit.

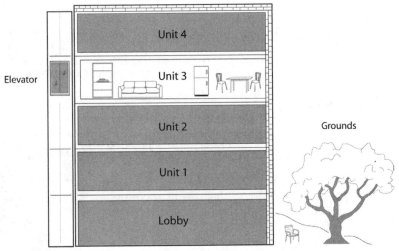

Residential Condominium

Cooperative

A **cooperative** (stock cooperative) is different from most other ways of owning real property because a corporation holds title to all of the real property of the cooperative. Co-op owners do not have fee ownership in their unit and do not receive a deed. Instead, they purchase stock in the corporation that owns the property. The shares of stock give the co-op owners the exclusive right to occupy a particular unit under a **proprietary lease**. When a unit is sold, the proprietary lease is assigned to the buyer along with the seller's stock certificate.

The cooperative differs from a condominium in that any charges or debts attached to any units can become the obligation of the other units or shareholders. Another difference is that approval must be received from the other shareholders before a unit can be sold, rented, gifted, or leased or any other similar action can be taken.

Community Apartment Projects

A **community apartment project** is a development in which an undivided interest in land is coupled with the right of exclusive occupancy of any apartment located in the project. Purchasers generally receive a leasehold interest for a specific unit in the community apartment. Community apartment projects are typically operated, maintained, and controlled by a governing board elected by the owners of the fractional interests.

Timeshares

A **timeshare** is the common ownership of a single piece of property by an association of people with each owner having the exclusive right to occupy a unit for a specified period each year. Timeshare ownerships, which are also known as **interval ownerships**, are usually for specific blocks of time per year. The blocks of time in each timeshare sell for different amounts. Purchasers may pay a premium for certain times of the year, view, exposure, or other amenities. For example, if the timeshare is located in a ski resort, time blocks will sell for a premium during the winter months and possibly at a discount during the summer months. The time blocks are usually for one or two weeks, which can be a fixed week or floating.

TRANSFER OF OWNERSHIP

The act of transferring or conveying property to another—voluntarily or involuntarily—is called **alienation**. Real estate can be conveyed by transfer, will, succession, occupancy, and accession. Beginning real estate appraisers almost invariably deal with properties that are being conveyed by transfer. Therefore, this text will focus on transfer rather than on all of the ways to convey property.

Property is acquired by **transfer** when, by an act of the parties or of law, title is transferred from one person to another by means of a written document. Real property is most commonly transferred from one person to another by a

voluntary transfer, such as the sale of a home. **Involuntary alienation** is the transfer of property against the wishes of the owner. Title may be transferred involuntarily by operation of law, government action, adverse possession, or even by physical changes in the land itself.

Deeds

The most common method of transferring real property is with a deed. A **deed** is a written instrument that is used to transfer title to real property from one person to another. The parties involved in deed are the grantor and grantee. The **grantor** is the person conveying the property, and the **grantee** is the person receiving the property or to whom it is being conveyed. A deed must satisfy certain requirements in order to be legally binding.

Various types of deeds are used throughout the United States; however, the deeds commonly used for private grants include warranty deeds, grant deeds, quitclaim deeds, and gift deeds.

Warranty Deed

In some states, the general warranty deed is the most frequently used instrument to transfer title. A **warranty deed** is a document containing five implied warranties from the grantor to the grantee. The five basic implied warranties are covenant of seisin, covenant against encumbrances, covenant of quiet enjoyment, covenant of further assurance, and covenant of warranty forever. The grantor also promises to deed any rights he or she might acquire to the property after conveying it to the grantee. This is called **after-acquired title**, which means any benefits that come to the property after a sale must follow the sale and accrue to the new owner.

Grant Deed

The **grant deed** is another frequently used instrument to transfer title. A grant deed contains two implied warranties by the grantor. One is that the grantor has not already conveyed title to any other person, and the other is that the estate is free from encumbrances other than those disclosed by the grantor. A grant deed conveys both whatever title the grantor has at the time of the conveyance and after-acquired title.

Quitclaim Deed

Unlike a warranty deed or a grant deed, a **quitclaim deed** has no warranties. The grantor of a quitclaim transfers any interest the grantor may have at the time the deed is signed. It is often used to clear a cloud on the title or any condition that affects the clear title of real property or minor defect in the chain of title that needs to be removed. A quitclaim deed is frequently used to transfer interests between husband and wife or to terminate an easement. If a buyer defaults on a loan carried back by the seller, the fastest way to clear title would be for the defaulting buyer to sign a quitclaim deed to the seller.

Gift Deed

A **gift deed** is used to make a gift of property to a grantee, usually a close friend or relative. The consideration in a gift deed is called **love and affection**.

Operation of Law

Sometimes property is transferred by the **operation of law** or **court action**. It is usually an involuntary transfer involving foreclosure or is the result of a judgment or some other lien against the title. Frequently, courts establish legal title regardless of the desires of the record owners.

Foreclosure

Foreclosure is the legal procedure lenders use to terminate the trustor or mortgagor's rights, title, and interest in real property by selling the property and using the sale proceeds to satisfy the liens of creditors. The two methods of foreclosure are non-judicial foreclosure (trustee's sale) and judicial foreclosure.

Partition Action

A **partition action** is a court proceeding to settle a dispute between co-owners (joint tenants or tenants in common) about dividing their interests in real property. A partition action may be available to terminate the interest of one co-owner (a partial interest) or to terminate the entire ownership through physical division or sale. The court can physically divide either the property or the money derived from its sale.

His   Hers

Quiet Title Action

A quiet title action is a court proceeding to establish an individual's right to ownership of real property against one or more adverse claimants. It is used to clear a cloud on the title of real property, such as titles based on adverse possession or the seller's title under a forfeited, recorded land contract.

Tax Sale

A **tax sale** is the forced sale of real property (usually via an auction) by a taxing authority (usually the county) to satisfy delinquent taxes along with any penalties and costs. Persons who buy such property receive a **tax deed**.

Execution Sale

An **execution sale** is a forced sale of property under a **writ of execution** with the proceeds used to satisfy a money judgment. A sheriff's deed is given to a buyer when property is sold through court action in order to satisfy a judgment for money or foreclosure of a mortgage. A **sheriff's deed**, as the name implies, is issued by the sheriff of the county where real property is located when the property goes through a sheriff's sale to satisfy a civil court judgment against the property owner.

Eminent Domain

Eminent domain is the power of the government to take private property for public use after paying just compensation to the owner. **Just compensation** is fair and reasonable payment due to a private property owner when his or her property is condemned under eminent domain.

The traditional understanding of a "public use" was that the government could condemn land for such things as roads, schools, hospitals, or military bases because the needs of the larger community outweighed the desire of one property owner to hold onto a specific parcel of land. Over time, however, the notion of what is a "public" use expanded to include such things as elimination of "blighted" areas through urban redevelopment. Local governments would use the condemnation power to acquire dilapidated buildings in city centers to construct public housing. Over time, this expanded to include the idea of using condemnation to acquire even unblighted land merely to provide economic stimulus.

Condemnation is the process by which the government acquires private property for public use, under its right of eminent domain. The condemnation process starts with an appraisal performed on behalf of the government agency acquiring the property. The owner is contacted by the agency and notified of the impending acquisition as well as the price to be paid based on the appraisal. If the property owner feels the price to be inadequate, he or she is entitled to obtain an independent appraisal and challenge the offer in court.

Inverse condemnation is the process in which a private party can argue that activity by a public entity has effectively caused a "taking". The government entity is forced to pay just compensation if the property value or use has been diminished by a public entity.

Example: If part of a farmer's land is flooded because the Army Corps of Engineers altered the course of a stream that bordered the farm, the farmer could sue for inverse condemnation since part of the farm has been effectively taken without just compensation.

IMPORTANCE OF RECORDING

Recording permits, rather than requires, documents that affect title to real property to be filed. Whenever an interest in real property is transferred voluntarily or involuntarily, the new owner should record the transfer instrument to protect his or her legal interests.

Recording Process

After acknowledgment, any instrument affecting the title to—or possession of—real property may be recorded. In fact, a deed must be acknowledged before it can be recorded. **Acknowledgment** is a formal declaration before a notary public or certain public officials, by the person (grantor) who signed (executed) the instrument (deed) that he or she in fact did execute (sign) the document. Acknowledgment acts as a safeguard against forgery and once acknowledged, a document is accepted as *prima facie* (on its face) evidence in court. Acknowledgement is necessary before recording any instrument or judgment affecting the title to real property. A deed does not have to be acknowledged to be valid; but, must be acknowledged to be recorded.

To be valid, documents must be recorded by the county recorder in the county within which the property is located. When the recorder receives a document to be filed, he or she marks the original document as "filed for record," stamps it with the proper time and date of recording, and returns to the person who requested the recording. The instrument to be recorded is copied into the proper index, and filed in alphabetical order, under the names of the parties.

Effect of Recording

The purpose of recording is to protect subsequent purchasers and lien creditors against prior unrecorded interests.

Recording any conveyance pertaining to real property (deed or lien) gives constructive notice of its contents to subsequent purchasers and mortgagees. **Constructive notice** is imputed by law, which means that everyone is presumed to have knowledge about a particular recorded document, because it can be looked up in the public records. Conversely, if a person has direct, express information about the ownership interest of a property, it is called **actual notice**. Actual notice is a fact, such as seeing the grant deed or knowing that a person inherited a property by will. Actual notice deals with facts a person actually knows; whereas, constructive notice deals with things a reasonably prudent person should know or investigate and discover.

In addition, recording a deed protects the chain of title. The **chain of title** is a sequential record of changes in ownership showing the connection from one owner to the next. A complete chain of title is desirable whenever property is transferred and is required by title insurance companies if they are writing a policy on a property.

Priorities in Recording

Recording laws are meant to protect citizens against fraud and to give others notification of property ownership. Whether it is a grant deed, trust deed or some other evidence of a lien or encumbrance, the priority is determined by the date stamped in the upper right-hand corner of the document by the county recorder. **Priority** means the order in which deeds are recorded. To obtain priority through recording, a buyer must be a good faith purchaser and record the deed first. The first valid deed that is recorded determines the owner, unless that person had either actual or constructive notice of the rights of others prior to recording. For this reason, it is important that recording be done immediately.

Some instruments are not affected by the priority of recording rule. For example, tax liens and mechanic's liens take priority even though they are recorded after a deed.

CONTRACTS

A **contract** is a legally enforceable agreement made by competent parties, to perform or not perform a certain act.

Classification of Contracts

Contracts may be classified as express or implied, bilateral or unilateral, and executory or executed.

Express or Implied Contracts

In an **express contract**, the parties declare the terms of the agreement and put their intentions in words, either orally or in writing. An example of an express contract is a lease or rental agreement in which the landlord agrees to allow the tenant to live on the property and the tenant agrees to pay rent in return.

When a contract is implied, the agreement is demonstrated by conduct rather than by words. For example, when a person goes into a restaurant and orders food, it creates an **implied contract**. By showing a desire to use a service, it is implied that the person will pay for the service.

Bilateral or Unilateral Contracts

Contracts are classified as bilateral (two-sided) or unilateral (one-sided).

Bilateral Contracts

A **bilateral contract** is an agreement in which each party promises to perform an act in exchange for the other party's promise to perform his or her part of the agreement. The mutual promises made by the parties are the actual consideration that supports a bilateral contract—not the underlying things of value or other action or performance to which the promises relate. An example might be a promise from a would-be pilot to pay $2,500 for flying lessons, and a return promise from the instructor to teach him or her to fly.

Unilateral Contracts

A **unilateral contract** is a contract in which a party promises to perform without the expectation that the other party will perform. The second party is not obligated to act, but if he or she does, the first party must keep his or her promise.

A reward, such as the finder's fee is one of the most common kinds of offers for a unilateral contract. Someone who offers a reward does not want the offeree to "agree" to the terms of the offer; he or she seeks the performance of an act that meets the terms of the offer.

> Example: A neighbor who is missing a pet may post signs offering a reward for the return of the pet. If the pet is returned, the neighbor is required to pay the promised reward.

Thus, the consideration for a unilateral contract is the PERFORMANCE of whatever act constitutes acceptance of the offer, whether providing information leading to the return of a lost pet—or the introduction of the eventual buyer of a parcel of property to the seller.

A typical unilateral contract sometimes encountered in the real estate business is an open listing. An open listing would denote that a parcel of real property is for sale for which no broker is formally representing the seller.

Executory or Executed Contract

A contract may be executory or executed.

A contract that remains to be performed by one or both parties is referred to as an **executory contract**. An example of an executory contract is a contract that has not yet closed or a contract that has not been signed by both parties.

In an **executed contract**, all parties have performed according to the agreement. Performance may be as simple as signing the document, but a typical real estate contract requires much more than signatures. An **executed contract** is a sales agreement that has been signed by all parties involved in the transaction.

Elements of a Valid Contract

In order for a contract to be legally binding and enforceable, there are four requirements: (1) legally competent parties, (2) mutual consent between the parties, (3) lawful object, and (4) sufficient consideration. Some people describe five elements that must exist in order for a valid contract to exist. The five elements are legally competent parties, an offer, an acceptance, a lawful object, and consideration. In essence, "mutual consent" is separated into two parts—offer and acceptance.

Legally Competent Parties

Parties entering into a contract must be legally capable of contracting or competent. All persons are capable of contracting, except minors, persons of unsound mind, and persons deprived of civil rights."

Mutual Consent (Offer and Acceptance)

In a valid contract, all parties must mutually agree. **Mutual consent** (or mutual assent) is sometimes called a "**meeting of the minds**." It is an offer by one party and acceptance by the other party. Both parties must genuinely consent to the contract.

An **offer** shows the contractual intent of the **offeror**, or the person making the offer, to enter into a contract. That offer must be communicated to the **offeree**, the person to whom the offer is being made, and the offer must be definite and certain in its terms.

An **acceptance** is an unqualified agreement to the terms of an offer. The offeree must agree to every item of the offer for the acceptance to be complete. Acceptance of an offer must be communicated to the offeror, in the manner specified, before a contract becomes binding between the parties. The seller may rescind an offer prior to acceptance. Silence is not considered to be acceptance.

If the original terms change in any way in the acceptance, the offer becomes a **counteroffer**, and the first offer terminates. The person making the original offer is no longer bound by that offer, and may or may not accept the counteroffer. The counteroffer becomes a new offer, made by the original offeree.

Lawful Object

Even though the parties are capable, and mutually agreeable, the object of the contract still must be lawful. A contract requiring the performance of an illegal act would not be valid, nor would one where the consideration was stolen. An example in real estate would be someone attempting to sell a piece of property that he or she does not own and has no reasonable expectation to own prior to the closing date.

The contract also must be legal in its formation and operation. For example, a note bearing an interest rate in excess of that allowed by law would be void. Contracts contrary to good morals and general public policy are also unenforceable.

Consideration

Legally, all contracts require sufficient consideration or payment. Consideration may be a promise for a promise, money for a promise, money for property, or goods for services. Legally, every contract must have acceptable consideration. Terms that denote **acceptable consideration** include valuable, adequate, good, or sufficient consideration. Forbearance, or forgiving a debt or obligation, or giving up an interest or a right, qualifies as valuable consideration. Gifts, such as real property based solely on love and affection, are good consideration. These gifts meet the legal requirement that consideration be present in a contract.

Void and Voidable Contracts

Two terms that sometimes confuse newcomers to the area of contract law are void and voidable. In one sense, they do not really describe two different kinds of contracts, because a "void contract" is really a contradiction in terms. On the other hand, the concept of voidable contracts provides one party, but not both, with the right to set aside a contract.

Void Contracts

The term **void contract** is an oxymoron. It refers to a "contract" that is not really a contract at all. If two parties have entered into what they believe to be a contract but it is either lacking an element or violates the law, then what they believe to be a contract is not, in fact, a contract. If an agreement is void, then there is no contract and the court will not enforce it.

Such a contract is sometimes referred to as a "void contract" in order to distinguish it from a **valid contract**, which is a contract that has all required elements and is therefore binding and enforceable. An **unenforceable contract** is valid, but for some reason cannot be proved by one or both of the parties. For example, an oral agreement that should have been in writing because of the statute of frauds is unenforceable.

Voidable Contracts

A **voidable contract** is a contract that is valid and enforceable on its face, but may be rejected by one or more of the parties. A voidable contract is not unlawful under all circumstances.

> Example: A contract with a minor is considered voidable and can be disaffirmed by the minor. However, it is valid until the minor disaffirms it. Until that party exercises its right to disaffirm the contract, it is presumptively valid and can be performed by either party.

When creating a contract, mutual consent must be genuine, which means that an offer and acceptance must be genuine and freely made by all parties. Genuine assent does not exist if there is fraud, misrepresentation, mistake, duress, menace, or undue influence involved in reaching an agreement. A contract is also voidable if one party was acting under duress.

Interpreting Contracts

A written contract may prevent misunderstandings once it has been signed. However, disputes may still arise about how certain terms or phrases in the agreement are to be interpreted. The law has a number of principles and rules regarding the interpretation of contracts.

Statute of Frauds

The **statute of frauds**, a law in every state, requires that certain contracts be in writing to prevent fraud in the sale of land or an interest in land. Included in this are offers, acceptances, loan assumptions, land contracts, deeds, escrows, and options to purchase. Trust deeds, promissory notes, and leases for more than one year must also be in writing to be enforceable.

Parol- Evidence Rule

Another rule relating to the interpretation of contracts is known as the parol-evidence rule. **Parol evidence** refers to the oral discussions that precede the parties' reduction of those discussions into a written agreement. When two parties make oral promises to each other, and then write and sign a contract promising something different, the written contract will be considered the valid one.

The **parol-evidence rule** relates to when such oral promises can and when they cannot, be considered by a court when it interprets a contract. Occasionally a contract is ambiguous or vague. Under these circumstances, a judge might allow prior agreements to be entered into evidence in order to clarify the contract that is under dispute.

Preprinted Forms

Often, the question arises as to whether or not changes can be made to a preprinted form. If the parties involved want to make handwritten changes and initial them, those changes control the document.

General Rules for Using Preprinted Forms
- Specific information takes precedence over general information
- Typed clauses and insertions take precedence over the preprinted material
- Handwritten clauses and insertions take precedence over the typed and preprinted material

Discharge of Contracts

Discharging a contract refers to the cancellation or termination of a contract. Typically, contracts are terminated through performance. Seller's performance would be to sell the property. Buyer's performance would be to purchase the property. However, there are many other ways to discharge or terminate a contract.

Discharge of Contracts

- Performance
- Mutual rescission
- Cancellation
- Release
- Revocation
- Assignment
- Novation
- Accord and satisfaction
- Breach

SUMMARY

After identifying the property, the appraiser determines what type of interest is being appraised and extent of property ownership. Real property interests can be categorized as **possessory** and **non-possessory** interests.

Estates are possessory interests in real property. An **estate** is an interest that is (or may become) possessory and that can be measured in terms of duration. Ownership of the estate is measured by its duration—indefinite or definite. An estate with indefinite duration or that is measured by the length of someone's life is classified as a freehold estate. Whereas, an estate with a fixed or determinable duration is classified as a **leasehold estate**.

Encumbrances are non-possessory interests in real estate. Encumbrances fall into two categories—financial encumbrances and non-financial encumbrances. A **financial encumbrance** is one that affects the title to property, such as a lien. A **non-financial encumbrance** is one that affects the physical use or condition of the property, such as easements, profit-à-prendres, and restrictions.

Property ownership can be separate or fractional. **Fractional interest ownership** includes concurrent ownership and business ownership. Types of **concurrent ownership** include tenancy in common, joint tenancy, and marital property (community property or tenancy by the entirety).

Real estate can be conveyed by transfer, will, succession, occupancy, and accession. The most common method of transferring real property is with a deed. Deeds are acknowledged and recorded in order to protect the chain of title and make it clear who rightfully owns the property.

In real estate, as with any type of contract, contracts must have legally competent parties, mutual consent between the parties (offer and acceptance), lawful object, and sufficient consideration in order to be valid. Most real estate contracts must also be in writing to be enforceable under the **statute of frauds**.

Trust.

UNIT 3 REVIEW

Matching Exercise

Instructions: Write the letter of the matching term on the blank line before its definition, and then check your response with the Answer Key that immediately follows the Multiple Choice Questions.

Terms

A.	appurtenant easement	U.	leasehold
B.	community property	V.	life estate
C.	condemnation	W.	mortgage
D.	condition	X.	non-financial encumbrance
E.	condominium	Y.	non-possessory interest
F.	corporation	Z.	partition action
G.	easement in gross	AA.	periodic tenancy
H.	encroachment	BB.	permitted uses
I.	encumbrance	CC.	planned development
J.	estate	DD.	possessory interest
K.	estate in reversion	EE.	priority
L.	fee simple estate	FF.	profit-à-prendre
M.	financial encumbrance	GG.	setbacks
N.	foreclosure	HH.	statute of frauds
O.	freehold estate	II.	tax lien
P.	general plan	JJ.	tenancy by the entirety
Q.	involuntary lien	KK.	tenancy for years
R.	joint tenancy	LL.	tenancy in common
S.	judgment	MM.	undivided ownership
T.	leased fee estate	NN.	variance

Definitions

1. _____ Present right to physically occupy land and to exclude others from that same land.

2. _____ Interest that cannot presently be exercised today but which may or will become possessory in the future or under appropriate circumstances.

3. _____ Possessory interest in real property that can be measured in terms of duration.

4. _____ Estate of indefinite duration.

5. _____ Most complete form of ownership.

6. _____ Present interest that gives its owner a possessory interest for the length of a measuring life.

7. _____ Life estate in which the grantor retains a future right to the property after the life tenant's death.

8. _____ Tenant's possessory estate in land or premises.

9. _____ Property owner's interest under a lease.

10. _____ Leasehold interest that is for an indefinite time.

11. _____ Leasehold interest with a fixed term and definite end date.

12. _____ Interest in real property that is held by someone who is not the owner.

13. _____ Encumbrance that affects the title to property.

14. _____ Common security instrument used in real estate financing.

15. _____ Lien placed against property without the owner's permission.

16. _____ Final determination by the court of the rights of the parties in a lawsuit.

17. _____ Involuntary, financial encumbrance placed upon property as a claim for payment levied by local, state, and federal government agencies.

18. _____ Encumbrance that affects the physical use or condition of the property.

19. _____ Easement that is connected to a particular property and is transferred along with that property.

20. _____ Personal right of one person (or company) to use land owned by another.

21. _____ Intrusion into, under, or over the property of another without that person's permission.

22. _____ Right to enter another's land to remove soil or substances of the soil.

23. _____ Limitation imposed by a grantor in a deed that can cause the ownership of the property to revert to the grantor.

24. _____ Starting point for land use and determines the physical development of the city or county.

25. _____ Restrictions that limit how close a structure can be built to neighboring property lines.

26. _____ Uses that meet the current use requirements within the district.

27. _____ Land use decision allowing a use that is not strictly in compliance with local zoning or building regulations.

28. _____ Interest held under the same title by two or more people, whether their rights are equal or unequal in value or quantity.

29. _____ Ownership interest created when two or more persons are owners of an undivided interest in a single estate.

30. _____ Ownership interest created when two or more parties own real property as co-owners, with the right of survivorship.

31. _____ Marital ownership in which one-half of the property can be willed.

32. _____ Marital ownership in which each spouse has an undivided interest in the entire property and the right of survivorship.

33. _____ Legal entity, which has a separate legal identity from its owners or members.

34. _____ Type of ownership in which owners have fee title to their separately owned dwelling along with the lot underneath it with no direct ownership of the common areas.

35. _____ Type of ownership in which owners have a separate fee interest in airspace and everything contained within (the unit), plus an undivided interest in all common or public areas of the development.

36. _____ Legal procedure lenders use to terminate the trustor or mortgagor's rights, title, and interest in real property by selling the property and using the sale proceeds to satisfy the liens of creditors.

37. _____ Court proceeding to settle a dispute between co-owners about dividing their interests in real property.

38. _____ Legal process by which the government acquires private property for public use, under its right of eminent domain.

39. _____ Order in which deeds are recorded.

40. _____ Law that requires that certain contracts be in writing to prevent fraud in the sale of land or an interest in land.

Multiple Choice Questions

Instructions: Circle your choice, and then check your response with the Answer Key that immediately follows the Multiple Choice Questions.

1. The present right to physically occupy land and to exclude others from that same land is known as a:
    a. future interest.
    b. possessory interest.
    c. non-possessory interest.
    d. potential interest

2. All of the following would be considered a possessory interest in real property, except a(n):
    a. fee simple.
    b. grant reserving an estate.
    c. specific lien.
    d. periodic tenancy.

3. An owner who can dispose of his or her estate by will, owns which type of estate?
    a. Perpetual estate
    b. Reversion estate
    c. Life estate
    d. Estate intestate

4. Sam deeds his property to his first wife, Susan, with the condition that after his second wife, Elizabeth, dies, the property title will pass to his daughter, Nancy. What type of estate does Susan possess?

    a. Fee simple qualified

    b. Life estate

    c. Less-than-freehold estate

    d. Estate at will

5. Sam deeds his property to his first wife, Susan, with the condition that after his second wife, Elizabeth, dies, the property title will pass to his daughter, Nancy. What type of estate does Nancy have?

    a. Estate in reversion

    b. Estate in remainder

    c. Less-than-freehold estate

    d. Estate at will

6. Which type of estate does a tenant possess?

    a. Freehold

    b. Fee simple

    c. Less-than-freehold

    d. Life

7. Who has exclusive possession and use of the rented property?

    a. Lessor

    b. Lessee

    c. Leasehold

    d. Leased Fee

8. Tom has a tenancy for years for 18 months that ends on July 31. If Tom's lease expires and there is no agreement for an extension or the conversion of that lease to a month-to-month tenancy, which type of leasehold will Tom have?

    a. Tenancy for years

    b. Tenancy at sufferance

    c. Periodic tenancy

    d. Tenancy at will

9. An interest in real property that is held by someone who is NOT the owner is known as an:

    a. encumbrance.

    b. encroachment.

    c. escheat.

    d. estate at sufferance.

10. A mortgage is an example of:

    a. an encumbrance.

    b. a specific lien.

    c. a voluntary lien.

    d. all of the above.

11. The commonality of judgment liens, tax liens, and mechanic's liens is that they are all:

    a. easements.

    b. encroachments.

    c. involuntary liens.

    d. non-financial encumbrances.

12. Easement and restrictions are examples of:

    a. financial encumbrances.

    b. non-financial encumbrances.

    c. liens.

    d. possessory estates.

13. Which term is not associated with easements?

    a. Appurtenant

    b. Dominant

    c. Encroachment

    d. Servient

14. Because of how the street access is set up, Bob's driveway must cross over Kate's property. Which of the following describes this scenario?

    a. Bob is the dominant tenement.

    b. Bob is the servient tenement.

    c. Kate is the dominant tenement.

    d. Kate has a negative appurtenant.

15. A cable company has an easement permitting it to install wiring for digital cable and broadband internet services. What kind of easement is this?

    a. Avigation easement

    b. Easement in gross

    c. Negative easement

    d. Prescriptive easement

16. Easements for roads, flood control channels, and drainage ditches are:

    a. avigation easements.

    b. conservation easements.

    c. prescriptive easements.

    d. surface easements.

17. Eva deeds her house to Mary with the provision that Mary keeps the garden planted with roses. This is an example of a:

    a. life estate.

    b. condition.

    c. private restriction.

    d. public restriction.

18. Most cities and counties control land use and growth within their boundaries. Which of the following is considered the starting point for planning and land use?

    a. General plan

    b. Restrictions

    c. Subdivision regulations

    d. Zoning

19. A city requires that all buildings in its downtown retail district be Spanish-style stucco with red tile roofs. This is an example of:

    a. incentive zoning.

    b. aesthetic zoning.

    c. visual zoning.

    d. reverse condemnation.

20. Donna owns a convenience store in a district that was rezoned for residential use. Donna's convenience store would be a:

    a. non-conforming use.

    b. variance.

    c. conditional use.

    d. spot zone.

21. Which type of ownership is not considered an undivided ownership interest?

    a. Fractional ownership interests
    b. Common interest developments
    c. Ownership in severalty
    d. Timeshares

22. Frank purchased an investment property with Kate and John. He and the other owners have the nonexclusive right to the use and occupancy of the property. Since no specific type of ownership was mentioned in the deed, what type of ownership is this?

    a. Joint tenancy
    b. Severalty ownership
    c. Tenancy in partnership
    d. Tenancy in common

23. Bill, Bob, and Ben take joint tenancy of a vacation house. Bill sells his share to Jack after 3 years. Which of the following is true?

    a. Bill, Bob, and Jack are joint tenants.
    b. Bob, Ben, and Jack are joint tenants.
    c. Bob and Ben are joint tenants with Jack as a tenant in common.
    d. Bob, Ben, and Jack are tenants in common.

24. Which type of concurrent ownership includes the right of one owner to will his or her interest?

    a. Ownership in severalty
    b. Joint tenancy
    c. Tenancy in common
    d. Tenancy by the entirety

25. Janice owned a flower store for four years before she married Ron. After she married, she purchased another store with proceeds from her original store.

    a. The flower stores are both considered separate property.
    b. The flower stores are both considered community property.
    c. The original flower store is separate property, and the new one is community property.
    d. The original flower store is community property, and the new one is separate property.

26. A common interest development is a development involving a combination of individually owned lots or units coupled with common area parcels or spaces. CIDs do NOT include:

    a. condominium projects.

    b. cooperatives.

    c. planned unit developments.

    d. timeshares.

27. Which type of undivided ownership is also known as an interval ownership?

    a. Fractional ownership interests

    b. Community apartment project

    c. Planned unit developments

    d. Timeshares

28. Which type of deed has no warranty whatsoever?

    a. Quitclaim deed

    b. Warranty deed

    c. Grant deed

    d. Deed of reconveyance

29. Each of the following is most likely an involuntary alienation, except:

    a. condemnation.

    b. foreclosure.

    c. partition action.

    d. quitclaim deed.

30. Of the following, which is NOT essential to create a valid contract?

    a. Legally competent parties

    b. Mutual consent between the parties

    c. Sufficient consideration

    d. Unlawful object

UNIT 3 ANSWER KEY

Answers – Matching

1. DD	11. KK	21. H	31. B
2. Y	12. I	22. FF	32. JJ
3. J	13. M	23. D	33. F
4. O	14. W	24. P	34. CC
5. L	15. Q	25. GG	35. E
6. V	16. S	26. BB	36. N
7. K	17. II	27. NN	37. Z
8. U	18. X	28. MM	38. C
9. T	19. A	29. LL	39. EE
10. AA	20. G	30. R	40. HH

Answers – Multiple Choice

1. **(b)** Real property interests can be categorized as possessory or non-possessory interests and as present or future. **Page 46**

2. **(c)** Estates are possessory interests in real property. Choices (a), (b), and (d) are types of estates. Encumbrances are non-possessory interests in real estate. A specific lien is an encumbrance. **Page 46**

3. **(a)** A fee simple estate is sometimes known as a fee simple, estate in fee, or perpetual estate because an owner may dispose of it in his or her lifetime or after death by will. **Page 47**

4. **(b)** A life estate is a present interest that gives its owner (the life tenant) a possessory interest for the length of a measuring life. In this question, the person with the measuring life is Elizabeth. **Page 48**

5. **(b)** The grantor (Sam) can identify someone to receive the property when Elizabeth, who has the measuring life, dies. That interest is known as an estate in remainder and the person who owns the estate in remainder is the remainderman. **Page 49**

6. **(c)** A tenant's possessory estate in land or premises is known as a nonfreehold estate, a less-than-freehold estate, or leasehold. **Page 50**

7. **(b)** The owner of the leasehold estate (the lessee) has exclusive possession and use of the rented property for a fixed period. **Page 50**

8. **(b)** A tenancy at sufferance (holdover tenancy) occurs when the tenant's original lease expires and there is no agreement for an extension or the conversion of that lease to a month-to-month tenancy. **Page 51**

9. **(a)** An encumbrance is an interest in real property that is held by someone who is not the owner. **Page 53**

10. **(d)** Any lien is considered an encumbrance. A specific lien is one that is placed against a certain property, such as a trust deed or mortgage. Trust deeds and mortgages are also voluntary liens. **Page 53**

11. **(c)** Typical involuntary liens include judgment liens, tax liens, and mechanic's liens. They are financial encumbrances. **Page 54**

12. **(b)** A non-financial encumbrance is one that affects the physical use or condition of the property, such as easements, profit-à-prendres, and restrictions. **Page 56**

13. **(c)** An appurtenant easement is an easement that is connected to a particular property and is transferred along with that property. An appurtenant easement has a dominant and a servient tenement. An encroachment is the intrusion into, under, or over the property of another without that person's permission. An encroachment is not an easement; it is considered a nuisance as well as a trespass. **Page 56**

14. **(a)** The dominant tenement is the land (Bob) receiving the benefit of the easement. The servient tenement is the land (Kate) encumbered by the easement and the land is being used by someone other than the owner.. **Page 56**

15. **(b)** Easements not appurtenant to a specific parcel are known as easements in gross. Typically, these are owned by utility companies. **Page 57**

16. **(d)** Easements for roads, flood control channels, drainage ditches are common types of surface easements. **Page 58**

17. **(c)** A restriction is a limitation placed on the use of the property. It is not a condition because nothing states that the property will revert to Eva or her heirs if Mary fails to plant roses in the garden. **Page 60**

18. **(a)** Most cities and counties have a general or comprehensive plan to control land use and growth within their boundaries. The general plan is the starting point for land use and determines the physical development of the city or county. Development regulations (zoning, subdivision, and other controls) must be consistent with the general plan. **Page 61**

19. **(b)** Aesthetic zoning is zoning that is used to regulate the appearance of buildings in the area. **Page 63**

20. **(a)** If a city or county changes the zoning of a parcel so that the existing uses are no longer allowed by the new zoning, those existing activities are known as nonconforming use. Nonconforming uses that existed prior to the adoption of the current zoning that were lawful when established are normally allowed to continue indefinitely. **Page 64**

21. **(c)**   Separate ownership and ownership of an undivided interest are two ways a person or other entity can take title to or own real estate. An undivided ownership interest is an interest held under the same title by two or more people, whether their rights ar equal or unequal in value or quantity. Undivided interests include fractional ownership interests, common interest developments, and timeshares. **Page 65**

22. **(d)**   Whenever there are co-owners and some other form of ownership is not mentioned specifically, title is assumed to be a tenancy in common. **Pages 66-67**

23. **(c)**   A joint tenant may sever his or her interest in the joint tenancy by selling it. The new co-owner would become a tenant in common with the remaining joint tenants. **Page 67**

24. **(c)**   Tenancy in common allows a tenant to will his or her share. Due to the right of survivorship, neither joint tenancy nor tenancy by the entirety, allow ownership interests to be willed. Ownership in severalty is not concurrent ownership. **Page 69**

25. **(a)**   Income derived from separate property is considered separate income. If separate income is used to purchase property, that property is also separate property. **Page 68**

26. **(d)**   A common interest development (CID) is a development involving a combination of individually owned lots or units coupled with common area parcels or spaces. Common interest developments include planned developments, condominium projects, cooperatives, and community apartment projects. **Page 71**

27. **(d)**   Timeshare ownerships are also known as interval ownerships. **Page 74**

28. **(a)**   A quitclaim deed contains no warranties and transfers any interest the grantor may have at the time the deed is signed. **Page 76**

29. **(d)**   A quitclaim deed is often used to clear a cloud on the title or to transfer interests between husband and wife. The other choices are examples of an involuntary transfer through operation of law or court action. **Page 76**

30. **(d)**   A valid contract is a contract that has all required elements and is therefore binding and enforceable. In order for a contract to be legally binding and enforceable, there are four requirements: (1) legally competent parties, (2) mutual consent between the parties, (3) lawful object, and (4) sufficient consideration. **Page 83**

Value & Economic Principles

Unit 4

INTRODUCTION

What is value? Most people have a general understanding of value and could explain it adequately, but the idea of value is a multifaceted and vague concept.

Four elements combine to create value, but many other dynamics influence value on a local, regional, and national level. There are also different types of value, each of which has its own particular meaning and particular context. Being familiar with these factors and different types of value, as well as when a certain type is appropriate for an assignment, is a major responsibility of an appraiser.

Value and economic principles are interrelated. In order to perform the function of estimating value accurately, the appraiser also needs to have an understanding of the basic foundational economic principles applicable in the valuation of real estate.

Learning Objectives

After reading this unit, you should be able to:

- identify value and recognize the elements that create it.
- recall the factors that influence value.
- identify the different types of value.
- recognize the principles of valuation.
- name the stages of the neighborhood life cycle.
- name the four agents of production.

WHAT IS VALUE?

The concept of value affects all areas of the real estate industry. Property value considerations are at the core of real estate activity and are of critical importance. A synonym of "value" is the word "worth". When appraisers indicate the value of property, they are usually indicating an estimate of its monetary worth. **Value** has been defined as the monetary worth of a property, good, or service to buyers and sellers at a given time. Similarly, the Uniform Standards of Professional Appraisal Practice (USPAP) define value as the monetary relationship between properties and those who buy, sell, or use those properties. It is important to note that people create value. Value is not built into an item. An item is valuable because people perceive it has worth.

Though the term value is often used imprecisely in everyday conversation, it has a very specific meaning in appraisal. Appraisers develop an opinion of the value of a property. More precisely, the majority of appraisal assignments entail developing an opinion of the market value of a property. The price of buying a property or the cost of a building is often considered as an indicator of value. However, there can be large differences between the price, the cost, and the market value of a property. Be careful not to confuse value with the related concepts of price and cost.

Price

USPAP defines **price** as "the amount asked, offered, or paid for a property". Once stated, price is a fact. A price, once finalized, represents the amount a particular purchaser agrees to pay and a particular seller agrees to accept under the circumstances surrounding their transaction. The price paid for a property may or may not relate to the value that might be ascribed to that property by others.

The term price usually refers to a sale or transaction price and implies an exchange. When thinking of the concept of price, realize it applies to "exchange". In other words, sellers are willing to exchange their property for money (or its equivalent). On the other hand, buyers are willing to exchange their money (or its equivalent) for property.

Cost

USPAP defines **cost** as "the amount required to create, produce, or obtain a property". As used by appraisers, cost applies to production. Cost is the total dollar expenditure to develop an improvement and applies to either reproduction of an identical improvement or replacement with a functional equivalent.

> **Review**
>
> **Value:** The worth of a property, good, or service to buyers and sellers at a given time.
>
> **Price:** The amount asked, offered, or paid for a property.
>
> **Cost:** The amount of money it takes to build a structure.

FOUR ELEMENTS THAT CREATE VALUE

For real property to have value, four elements must be present: (1) the property must be in demand, (2) it must have usefulness or utility, (3) there must be a degree of scarcity, and (4) it must be possible to transfer it legally in title or use.

Demand

Demand is desire or ability to purchase a commodity. For real property to have value, it must be in demand. People have to want to own or use the property for some reason.

However, wanting a property is not enough by itself. The market participants must have purchasing power. This creates what is known as **effective demand**, which is desire coupled with the ability to satisfy the desire. Desire that is not backed by purchasing power creates a demand that is impotent and makes no impact in the financial marketplace.

Utility

Utility is the ability or power of an item to perform a service or meet a need. For real property to have value, it must have a distinct usefulness—there has to be a distinct utility for the land to contribute to value. The utility of property can be affected by many factors  including the location of the property, the physical attributes of the property, and government regulations such as zoning and environmental restrictions. These are only a few of the factors that can affect the utility or usefulness of a property.

Added amenities may increase the utility or desirability of a property, so they often result in a higher value. The amenities may be off-site improvements that impact the value of the subject property, such as schools, parks, pools, lakes, theaters, stores, transportation facilities, or amusement parks. Alternatively, the amenities may be within the subject's property lines such as a swimming pool, a view, or a covered patio.

Scarcity

The term **scarcity** refers not just to a shortage of an item, but a shortage of an item relative to the demand for that item. Some items fill significant needs—air for instance. It is so essential that life could not survive without it, so there is definitely a huge demand for air! Air, however, does not have value measurable in terms of money because it is so overwhelmingly abundant. In order to have monetary value, an item has to be scarce.

Land itself is finite in supply—there is only a certain amount. However, although the supply of land does not change, the supply of a particular type of property changes as buildings are constructed or destroyed. In the realm of real estate, there must be a relative scarcity of property for its value to increase. As an example, a house in the desert is relatively inexpensive. This is partly because desert land is not scarce. There are many thousands of similar acres available, all in the same area. In comparison, coastal land is much scarcer and, consequently, a house built on that land is more valuable. When scarcity combines with the other three elements (demand, utility, and transferability), value is enhanced immensely.

Transferability

Transferability refers to the ability to transfer ownership of an item from one person, or entity, to another. This includes both possession and control. Even if the other elements that create value (demand, utility, and scarcity) are present, an item will not reach its full value if there is no way effectively to transfer ownership.

> Example: A stolen car definitely has utility. The car may even be scarce, and there may be plenty of demand for it. However, the problem is transferability. There is no legal way to transfer ownership of the car, so its value is negatively affected.

It is important to note that, in real estate, transferability does not have anything to do with physical mobility. Instead, transferability refers to the rights associated with ownership. The use or ownership of land must have the capability to be legally transferred, because a property that does not have a marketable title cannot be transferred, which dramatically affects its value.

> **Review – Elements to Create Demand**
>
> **Mnemonic – "DUST"**
> - Demand
> - Utility
> - Scarcity
> - Transferability

FACTORS IMPACTING VALUE

In addition to the four elements that create value, other factors impact value, both positively and negatively. These factors are classified according to their source—physical and environmental, economic, governmental, and social. However, there are hundreds of possible influences on real estate value, and they do not always fit neatly within one particular category. Following is a partial list of factors that influence value. You will be able to add to this list as you gain experience and discover local factors that influence real estate value in your area.

Physical Characteristics and Environmental Forces

Many physical characteristics of land and property have a definite influence on value. Physical characteristics and environmental forces include the property's location, the surrounding climate, its topography and soil composition, the size and shape of the property, and the ease of navigation. These physical characteristics or environmental forces can exert major effects on values. Some of the physical characteristics can be changed, some can be worked around, and others are unchangeable. The expense of alteration must always be taken into consideration.

Location

People who sell real estate say there are three factors to consider—location, location, and location. Unlike other types of assets, land cannot be moved, so its location has an impact on its value. In fact, location may be the most important factor influencing value, particularly because it has such an effect on the usefulness of the property.

> Example: Commercial properties that are located on a corner benefit from more exposure, whereas the value of residential corner lots may be negatively affected due to the lack of privacy.

And as was discussed earlier, certain locations are scarcer and may be more valuable. A house located right by the beach will be worth more than that same house would be if it were located in the desert.

In addition, width of streets, traffic congestion, and condition of pavement affect the value of properties fronting on those streets. The term **front foot** defines the width of a property along a street or other boundary. It is most widely used as a measurement for properties located on beaches and lakeshores.

Another locational attribute that may affect a property is its exposure. The south and west sides of business streets are usually preferred by shopkeepers because customers will seek the shady side of the street, and window displays will not be damaged by the sun. The

north and east sides are less desirable. Even if the lot is in a good location, a building's **orientation** on the lot in relation to exposure to the sun, prevailing wind, traffic, and accessibility from the street can dramatically affect value as well.

Climate

Climate is an obvious factor and plays an enormous role in the overall value of a property. Climatic conditions including snowfall, rainfall, humidity, temperature, topography, soil conditions, and prevailing winds are items of consideration that can promote, or hinder areas.

Anyone who has lived in harsh and frigid climates has noticed there are certain benefits to a more temperate climate. In fact, in the most extreme climates, population is generally sparse. Demand is much greater in areas with better climates. These conditions spell out benefits, and these benefits are measurable in the marketplace.

Climate must also be matched to the intended use of the property. If land is to be used as a ski resort, temperature and precipitation must be ideal to maximize the number of days there will be snow. Then, the value of such a property will also be impacted by other factors, such as accessibility and topography.

Topography and Soil

Topography affects both the desirability of the land and its development. The nature and desirability of areas around the country are impacted by features such as rivers, lakes, streams, oceans, mountains, valleys, forests, meadows, prairies, and deserts. In developing a property, construction costs will be affected by the terrain and soil conditions. Limited irregularity in the contour is best for residential property. In many areas, all of the land is flat. Other areas are mountainous, hilly, or somewhere in between.

The characteristics of the soil at a given site can also have a direct impact on value, depending on the intended use of the land. Unproductive soil will have a negative impact on the value of farmland, but the same characteristic will have no impact on industrial land.

Land is not completely usable if it does not have full drainage capacity. Whether intended for residential, industrial, or commercial use, it is essential that there is no standing water on the land. If the appraiser inspects a property and no standing water is present on the land, he or she could detect evidence of a drainage problem by looking for water lines on any structures on the land. Correcting the problem can be expensive, and an appraiser would have to consult with the appropriate experts to find out the cost to cure such a problem.

On the other hand, land without access to water is probably not worth much in any marketplace. Water sustains life. Humans need it to inhabit land. Animals must have it to survive. Crops cannot be grown without water. Industrial and manufacturing processes cannot take place without the use of water.

Terrain and soil can limit an appraiser during the appraisal process. When appraising a single-family residence, the appraiser may find that the subject property is situated on approximately an acre of land, 100% usable.

Example: While the appraiser searches for comparable sales on approximately the same size lot, he or she visits one of the comparable sales, and discovers that the lot is indeed approximately an acre, but only about 30% of it is usable. The remaining 70% is rocky slope. These two parcels are not comparable; and if used, would require a significant adjustment.

Size and Shape

The size of the land must be accepted as is, unless an adjacent parcel could be acquired. The use of a property may be determined by the width and depth of the land. Some parcels of land are simply too small to be put to the desired use and must be put to a lesser use, generating a lesser value. If adjacent parcels can be obtained, the process of **assemblage** may occur. By putting several smaller, less valuable parcels together into one ownership interest, the value of the combined parcels may increase.

The shape of the parcel also has significant influence on its usefulness and therefore, its value. Irregular-shaped lots are more difficult and expensive to develop. A 10-foot wide acre of land running parallel to a highway is certainly less valuable than another acre that is square, and suitable for the construction of a single-family residence.

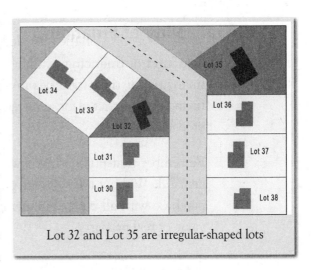

Lot 32 and Lot 35 are irregular-shaped lots

Transportation

The availability and ease of transportation is an important factor that affects real estate value. It is typically classified as an environmental force, but it is a good example of a factor that interweaves all four categories: physical, economic, social, and governmental.

Airports, freeways, railroads, and waterways used for navigation all have influences over surrounding areas and as such affect values. Similarly, if a parcel is conveniently accessible by road, it generally will have greater value than if it is in a remote location accessible only by a dirt road. The impact that accessibility has on the property value will depend on the property's intended use.

Economic Influences

Real estate values, price levels, and sales activity are directly influenced by the economic activity and economic well-being of both the country as a whole and the local real estate market. Some economic forces that influence value are the availability of money and credit, interest rates, industrial and commercial trends, employment trends, wage levels, price levels, regional and community economic base, new development, and rental and price patterns. Appraisers should be aware of the economic forces influencing value.

Availability of Financing

The kind of financing available impacts property values. A full array of financing for the properties in the area gives buyers purchasing power. If financing is restricted for some reason, it is more difficult for buyers to purchase property.

Remember that purchasing power is one of the elements essential to actual demand. Without the ability to purchase, houses are not sold. Very few buyers purchase with all cash. Financing is extremely important in supporting the value of real property.

Interest Rate

Related to financing is the prevailing interest rate. If a loan program is available, but the interest rate is prohibitive, the effect is the same as if financing were not obtainable. The interest rate determines the quality of the financing and the purchasing power of the buyers in the marketplace.

Interest rates, of course, are largely a function of government policy, inflation rate, and supply of funds in relation to demand. Local factors such as risk, however, can affect local interest rates. If an area were viewed by the lender to present a higher risk factor due to social or economic characteristics, interest rates could increase.

Inflation

Inflation in the economy or just in the regional or local real estate market can cause an apparent increase in value. **Unearned increment** is the term used in real estate appraisal to indicate an increase in value that was not the result of anything the owner did. Both inflation and appreciation would be categorized this way, and it can be difficult to distinguish between the two.

Employment and Wage Levels

Sources of employment are an important factor affecting the economic health of an area. Jobs may be offered from private enterprise, government sources, or military installations. The availability of good, high-paying jobs in an area can have a positive effect on the property values in the area. Wage levels provided by the employment in the area should be sufficient to support a family and buy a house.

Another important factor to keep in mind is whether employment in the area is dependent upon a single industry or even a single company. If this is the case, the risk of eventual economic obsolescence is higher than if the majority of employment were spread over several industries.

Business Climate

The presence of shopping areas, offices and medical suites as well as financial, wholesale, industrial, and other consumer-friendly businesses is important to establishing value.

The presence of a college or university can have a significant impact in a local community. A major state university could have 25,000 students. The number of employees to operate such a university also will be in the thousands, creating further impact. The area surrounding the college will have many rental units that are in constant demand and numerous businesses providing a variety of needed products and services. The economic influence in the local area is significant, and will be reflected in the data from the local marketplace.

Most major urban centers have a blighted area that depresses property values in the blighted areas as well as properties on the outskirts or areas. A **blighted area** is a section of the inner city, where the majority of buildings are run down. It creates a cycle in which the decrepit atmosphere repels business and industry. In turn, the lack of this incoming business and industry further hastens the decline of the area. Only a large-scale revitalization of the area can reverse the process.

Natural Resources

Natural resources have an effect on property value. Although this is a physical characteristic, natural resources typically have an economic impact. They can make the difference in the economic viability of an area. In fact, they can be the primary source of wealth for the area, with industry and employment centering on them.

Political or Government Regulations

Governmental, political, and legal activity significantly affect the value of real estate. On the national level, tax policy, government loan-guarantee programs, and environmental regulations are among the most influential political forces that can influence real estate value. At the state and local level, zoning and health regulations, building codes, health codes, rent controls, redevelopment districts, first-time homebuyer assistance programs, and public services such as police and fire protection are among the things significantly impacting real estate values. Appraisers must take special care to identify, examine, and analyze the potential influence governmental activity has on property values.

Taxes

Federal, state, and local taxes can impact real estate values. High income taxes result in less money available for real estate purchases. Capital gains taxes and allowable depreciation schedules particularly impact real estate investors. If city taxes and other local fees are prohibitively high, developers and businesses may go elsewhere. Other cities, where fees are not as high, may offer a greater opportunity for development and profit.

Federal Financing

FHA and VA loans are federal programs permitting a very low down payment or no down payment. This facilitates purchasing power and increases the number of potential buyers for housing. This makes home ownership an attainable goal for more buyers. When these programs are not available in an area, conventional financing is the alternative. Since conventional financing requires a much higher down payment, this would eliminate some otherwise qualified buyers from the marketplace and decrease the effective demand.

Environmental Restrictions

Government organizations like the Environmental Protection Agency (EPA) as well as private groups like the Sierra Club and Greenpeace have combined to create a strong voice of concern about the environment. In many regions of the country, habitats are protected for endangered species, restricting the development of lands for commercial purposes.

Case Study – Wall Street Journal, August 14, 2009
"It's Fish Versus Farmers in the San Joaquin Valley"

"Crops rot and people stand in line for food while the EPA engineers a drought. Today the San Joaquin Valley is being transformed into a dust bowl. Hundreds of thousands of acres are fallow, while almond and plum trees are being left to die in the scorching sun. Tens of thousands of people have been tossed out of work—the town of Mendota alone has an unemployment rate of about 40%—and the lines for food donations stretch down streets."

Sometimes protective decrees prevent all development of land. In areas where a housing shortage exists, the balance of supply and demand makes supply even shorter. This condition raises the values of existing housing and makes the building of new housing even more expensive. In other areas, the economy is so depressed that supply exceeds demand and housing prices plummet.

Every environmental regulation, whether well intentioned or not, often results in a negative economic effect on a given area.

Building Restrictions and Zoning

The Planning Commission and the City Council can slow growth and determine the direction of growth by imposing certain zoning regulations. By consulting the general plan of any city or county, zoning and zoning changes for all parcels can be observed, and growth patterns and trends can be determined. Building restrictions and zoning ordinances also affect utility, which is the ability to use the property for the purpose intended.

Building codes pertain to the structures that will be placed on land; their main purpose is to provide minimum standards to protect the environment, and the lives of occupants and the public. The local building code will deal with the issues of fire safety, building materials, heating, plumbing, gas and electrical systems, and energy efficiency. Building codes should be effective in promoting the public welfare in the ways intended. This enhances the desirability of the community by providing buildings that are safe and compatible with environmental needs. This, in turn, enhances value of individual properties and the community in general. However, a building department that is unreasonable can be a detriment to the normal growth and development of a community.

A city or county government may impose a moratorium on development, water accessibility, utilities, or anything deemed necessary at a given time. The purpose of a moratorium is to place a temporary restriction on development in a particular area. This is done by not allowing certain utilities to be installed, not allowing new water hookups, or not issuing building permits. Without the necessary element, development cannot occur in that area. Growth is stopped temporarily, and if demand for housing continues in the area, the value of the limited supply will increase.

Public Services

Public services like police and fire protection, schools, hospitals, and city parks, pools and other recreational facilities can add appeal and value to a community. To most families, quality schools are probably the most important government-provided service, and families may go to great lengths to live in a specific school district.

Social Ideals and Standards

In each local real estate market, the number of people and their characteristics, lifestyles, standards, and preferences will influence the real estate values in that market.

Population Trends

Birthrates, mortality rates, and migration to and from an area are all social influences on value. When there is an increase in the population in an area,  there is a corresponding increase in the needs of that population. It naturally follows that the more people there are in an area, the more need for housing. The balance of supply and demand has a great impact on value.

This information can be determined for any given time frame: past, present and future. Present time frame will be most useful for knowing present value, but future trends are important to understand as well.

Family Characteristics

Over the last several decades, changes in marriage rates, divorce rates, typical family size, and average household age have impacted the demand for real estate of different types. Not only does family size have an impact on the necessary house size, but also what is important to the people who comprise a particular marketplace can have an effect on property values. Young and growing families may seek good schools, where older couples whose children have grown up and moved out may seek smaller homes that are easy to maintain.

Other Social Factors

Other societal changes can also impact real estate values. For example, many people work from home, so space and appropriate wiring for home offices are important. Other people have created media rooms where they can enjoy all the entertainment that technology offers.

Tastes change dramatically over time as well. Avocado green appliances and acoustic ceilings are out; stainless steel and crown molding are in. These trends are constantly changing, and a "dated" look will affect a home's value.

A **stigma** is a lingering effect in the minds of people regarding the desirability or usefulness of a property. The property is regarded as tainted in some way; and if the property is regarded as tainted in a given marketplace, it is tainted in that marketplace. A home in which a notorious murder occurred most likely will carry a stigma with it, at least for a generation and possibly longer, depending on the population turnover in that neighborhood.

TYPES OF VALUE

In a dictionary, you can find numerous definitions of value that each have to do with a specific context. In real estate appraisal, value is the monetary worth of a property in a given marketplace at a given time. It is not what an owner would like to think he or she can obtain. It is what owners actually can obtain based on objectively reading the marketplace.

Appraisers will encounter several types of value and it is important to understand that different definitions of value produce different estimates of value.

Market Value

The overwhelming majority of appraisals performed are concerned with estimating the market value of a property. The concept of market value is extremely important in appraising real property. Loans are granted and capital is invested based on a professional opinion of market value. Real estate taxes, litigation, and legislation also reflect a concern for market value.

Both Fannie Mae and Freddie Mac use the following definition of market value.

> **Market value** is the most probable price that a property should bring in a competitive and open market under all conditions requisite to a fair sale, the buyer and seller, each acting prudently, knowledgeably and assuming the price is not affected by undue stimulus.

Implicit in this definition are the consummation of a sale as of a specified date and the passing of title from seller to buyer under the following conditions:

(1) buyer and seller are typically motivated,

(2) both parties are well informed or well advised, each one acting in what he considers his or her own best interest,

(3) a reasonable time is allowed for exposure in the open market,

(4) payment is made in terms of cash in U.S. dollars or in terms of financial arrangements comparable thereto, and

(5) the price represents the normal consideration for the property sold unaffected by special or creative financing or sales concessions granted by anyone associated with the sale.

USPAP uses the following definition for market value.

> **"Market value** is a type of value, stated as an opinion, that presumes the transfer of a property (i.e., a right of ownership or a bundle of such rights), as of a certain date, under specific conditions set forth in the definition of the term identified by the appraiser as applicable in an appraisal."

USPAP goes on further to say: "Forming an opinion of market value is the purpose of many real property appraisal assignments, particularly when the client's intended use includes more than one intended user. The conditions included in market value definitions establish market perspectives for development of the opinion."

Categories of Conditions in Market Value Definition

1. Relationship, knowledge, and motivation of the seller and buyer

2. Terms of sale

3. Conditions of sale

USPAP cautions "appraisers to identify the exact definition of market value, and its authority, applicable in each appraisal completed for the purpose of market value."

Remember, the USPAP definition is intended for illustrative purposes only and should not be cited as a recognized source within an appraisal report. The definition of market value being used in an appraisal assignment must be clearly understood and communicated. Recognize that definitions of market value may vary slightly from jurisdiction to jurisdiction, as well as from client to client.

Understanding market value eliminates the consideration of any comparable sales in an appraisal that do not meet these qualifications.

> Example: A foreclosure sale would mean the seller is under duress and does not have the luxury of a reasonable time for exposure in the marketplace. Such a sale would not be an arm's-length transaction and would not meet the definition of market value. An **arm's-length transaction** refers to a transaction in which all parties involved are knowledgeable, acting in their own self-interest and are under no undue influence or pressure from other parties.

Rather than being eliminated because of a distress sale, some sales need to be eliminated if they sold for more because the buyer based the purchase on emotional or subjective reasons. In this instance, value is in the eyes of the beholder—not the market.

> Example: Grandparents want to buy a property with a large yard where they can entertain their grandchildren. They found the perfect property listed for $200,000. Unfortunately, there were other offers on the property. Rather than lose the property, they offer $230,000, which is accepted. At this time and for their purposes, there is more value in buying the property than to try to find another property. To them, the property is worth more than $200,000. Theirs is a subjective decision. It does not equate with the marketplace, but it is, nonetheless, very real to them.

Investment Value

Investment value is the value of an income-producing property to a specific investor based on his or her investment requirements. In contrast to market value, investment value is value to an individual, not necessarily value in the marketplace. This value may be different from market value, reflecting the unique needs and intended use of the investor.

> Example: Bill is an investor who has purchased three of the four storefronts in a strip mall. He leases the storefronts to tenants, and he has determined that it would be more beneficial to own four contiguous storefronts than three out of the four would, so he wants to acquire the fourth property. If an individual buyer wanted to purchase the fourth storefront, that buyer would probably not be willing to pay as much for it as Bill would. The property would not be as valuable to someone who did not own the adjacent properties. This example illustrates that investment value is specific to a particular investor and that investment value can be higher than market value.

Value-in-Use

Value-in-use (use value) is the value a specific property has for a specific use. Value-in-use represents the value of an income-producing property to its current owner. In estimating use value, the appraiser focuses on the value the real estate contributes to the enterprise of which it is a part, without regard to the property's highest and best use or the monetary amount that might be realized from its sale.

For example, a building may have attributes that benefit an existing tenant who uses the building for a special purpose or to create a unique product with limited demand in the market. These attributes may not be needed or wanted by a new tenant. It also occurs with agricultural land. For example, farmland is often suitable for development. Sometimes, people want to know the worth of the property as farmland and as if it were developed into another use. Though this property may be significantly more valuable if developed commercially, it still has value as farmland.

Assessed Value

Assessed value applies in ad valorem taxation and is the value of a property as it appears in the tax assessor's office. Assessed value may not conform to market value, but it is usually calculated in relation to a market value base. A percentage is applied to this value to determine the amount of property tax the owner will pay. Different jurisdictions have different methods and formulas for determining assessed value. These are guided by law. Some jurisdictions apply mass appraisal formulas to numerous properties. In other areas, the purchase price of the property at the time of acquisition determines assessed value.

From time to time, assessed value will be adjusted. This is also dictated by law and policy within the local jurisdiction. In most areas, assessed value has no relationship to market value, which fluctuates freely with the market. Assessed value will be determined as of a particular time, and probably will adjust more slowly. Only appraisers employed by the tax assessor's office will work to determine assessed value.

Insurable Value

Insurable value is the value of an asset as determined by the estimated cost of replacing it. Insurable value (replacement value) is important to insurance companies and property owners alike. If improvements have been lost to fire, flood, wind or other natural disasters, the amount of money required to replace them needs to be determined. Finding this value requires expert knowledge of the cost approach to appraising, and the appraiser should be familiar with all methods of estimating building costs and pricing building components.

Going Concern Value

Going concern value is the value of an entire business operation. As such, it applies only to a business that is currently operating. It is based on capitalizing the net income produced by that business. Like any other income-producing entity, a business has value because it has the capacity to produce. If the business were to cease operation, it would still have value because of the capital assets it owns, but it would not have going concern value.

In a situation when a business has ceased operations, the capital assets could be sold or liquidated, usually at a fraction of their value to a going concern. A business as a going concern is valuable because the value of the capitalized income is greater than the liquidation value and because a prospective owner can look to the future and anticipate continued years of operation. The appraisal of businesses as a going concern is a specialized area of appraisal, and experience must be gained to perform competently.

Salvage and Scrap Value

Salvage value is the estimated value that an asset will realize upon its sale at the end of its useful life. **Scrap value** is the estimated value for a property that is sold primarily for its components.

Example: Often older properties have unique building components that are highly prized by collectors or are desired for use in other structures. Those building components, such as windows, fireplace mantles, stairways, banisters, unique plumbing and lighting fixtures, and building materials are often salvaged from an older structure for use elsewhere.

Liquidation Value

Liquidation value is the value of a property that has to be sold immediately by a seller who is under extreme compulsion to sell. It precludes the element of a reasonable time of exposure in the marketplace that is included in the definition of market value. Circumstances arise when an owner must sell immediately. With no time to list and sell through normal channels, the property owner may call a company or investor who will perform quickly with cash, but will require a substantial discount on the price.

Liquidation value can be determined by first estimating market value. Then, by observing distressed sales in the marketplace, the appraiser calculates how much below market value these prices are and applies that discount to the subject's market value. This valuation is not common in the residential appraiser's daily practice but a client may request it.

Other Types of Value

We can see that there are many types of value, each involving unique circumstances, and requiring specific definitions. Other types of value that are used in appraisal include loan value, book value, condemnation value, easement value, extrinsic value, contract value, corner value, front-foot value, square-foot value, advertising value, cash value, interim value, nuisance value, and the like. This indicates how complex the value concept is, and how specific the appraiser must be in understanding exactly what type of value is sought.

PRINCIPLES OF VALUATION

Appraisal is based on several basic principles of economic theory. These theories attempt to explain the market behavior that influences value. Even though the principles are interrelated, their relative importance varies depending upon other factors affecting the property being appraised. A working knowledge of the principles of valuation is indispensable to becoming a competent appraiser.

Principle of Supply and Demand

Like all other marketable commodities, real estate is affected by supply and demand. The law of **supply and demand** is almost universally recognized as being the first step in how market prices are determined. In order to understand the principle of supply and demand, both concepts need to be understood.

In referring to real estate, **supply** refers to the total amount of a given type of property for sale or lease, at various prices, at any given point in time. Land itself is finite in supply – there is only a certain amount. However, although the supply of land does not change, the supply of a particular type of property changes as buildings are constructed or destroyed. As market conditions change or as properties become more or less available for various reasons, supply fluctuates.

Demand refers to the desire and ability to acquire goods and services through purchase or lease. When speaking of real estate, this is refined to include the total amount of a type of real estate that is desired for acquisition, through purchase or lease, at various prices. The price range is an important factor since demand must be accompanied by purchasing power. If a beautiful, 10 million-dollar home is constructed in a middle-class neighborhood, everyone will like it, but if no one can afford to buy it, there is no real demand.

Increasing supply or decreasing demand will reduce the price in the market. Reducing supply or increasing demand will raise the price in the market. When appraising real property, the appraiser cannot avoid the influence of the principle of supply and demand.

Principle of Substitution

The principle of substitution is the foundation for all of the appraisal process. **Substitution** states that the market value of a property is affected by the cost of obtaining an equally desirable and valuable property as a substitute. Simply put, an owner cannot expect to sell his or her property for more than someone would ordinarily pay for a similar property under similar conditions. Given the choice of two like properties with similar utility and amenities, a buyer will naturally gravitate to the less expensive one. Similarly, a landlord cannot expect to rent property for more than someone would pay to rent a similar place.

In this regard, the principle of substitution is the basis for all three approaches to value and is found most prominently in the sales comparison analysis when using comparables sales. Comparable properties are chosen on the basis of their overall similarity to the subject. For purposes of analysis, they are considered substitutes for the property being appraised. In the cost approach, appraisers use the principle of substitution for reproduction estimates of like properties as well as finding comparable land. Finally, in the income capitalization approach, substitution is utilized when determining capitalization rates and gross rent multipliers.

Principle of Competition

Competition tends to bring supply and demand back into balance. Competition is fundamental to the dynamics of supply and demand in a free enterprise, open market economy. Competition among properties leads to a continual shift in availability of different kinds of properties.

When supply is less than demand, buyers compete with each other to purchase properties.

> Example: When two or more prospective buyers are competing to obtain a particular property, the one giving the most attractive offer to a seller is the one most likely to prevail. In this case, buyers are in competition with one another to obtain a property.

When supply is more than demand, sellers must compete with each other to attract buyers to their properties.

Example: In order to attract prospective buyers, a seller must price his or her property competitively with other comparable offerings. The seller must balance the desire to attract buyers with the desire to obtain the most favorable sales agreement possible. In this case, the seller is in competition with other sellers offering similar properties.

This also holds true for landlords and prospective tenants. In order to lease their properties, landlords have to offer properties and rates that are competitive with similar lease offerings. Prospective tenants, similar to buyers, must compete with other prospective tenants in order to obtain the property they desire.

In the same way, properties also compete with one another. Amenities, physical characteristics, and location serve to make a property more, or less, desirable. Property owners will often upgrade properties in order to attract more prospective buyers or tenants.

Principle of Change

The **principle of change** states that the continuing effects of economic, social, and governmental forces on the property and its environment result in continuous changes in market value. Change may occur rapidly or proceed very slowly over time. Rapid changes may be caused by natural disasters, plant closings, new construction, or governmental action. Slower change may be the gradual change in land use over years from primarily residential to commercial in nature. This kind of change may be almost imperceptible from one year to the next.

Some changes are internal to a property, whereas others are external. Physical, functional, or locational factors may combine to bring about change to a property as well. Room additions, remodeling and the addition of upgrades are examples of positive changes internal to a property. Rezoning of an area by the local governing agency, the building of a new regional mall nearby, or the closing of a nearby military base are examples of external changes.

All these changes affect property values. Though not all changes are detrimental to a property, they are inevitable. It is the appraiser's responsibility to research and identify these changes, and consider these changes when formulating his or her opinions and conclusions.

Neighborhood Lifecycle

Cities and neighborhoods are always changing, and individual homes within those neighborhoods reflect that change. An appraiser must be aware of trends that affect the value of real estate.

Neighborhoods start out as young, dynamic areas, and eventually disintegrate over the years. All improved real property experiences a four-stage **neighborhood life cycle**. The four stages, although not always distinct, can best be described as development, stability, decline, and revitalization.

Life-Cycle Stages

Development (Growth). Development is initially the stage when the subdivision is being built. The infrastructure is established, trees are planted, and the houses are constructed. Established values may increase.

Stability. Stability is usually an extended period of time when the amenities are enjoyed and used by families. During this time, we could expect that the values gradually will be on the rise.

Decline. Old age and decline eventually come. The properties are not as desirable as they once were. The neighborhood is not as appealing. There may be newer subdivisions nearby that are preferred in the marketplace. Construction styles may have changed, and property values may suffer from functional obsolescence. Social and economic factors may have combined to cause a loss in value.

Revitalization. Growth and decline is normal in all areas, and often it can be reversed just as it reaches the last stages. For example, when a lovely neighborhood grows to be old and worn out, young families may choose to move in and completely restore the process of change by starting the life cycle of the neighborhood all over again with revitalization.

Neighborhood Life Cycle
The house on the left has been refurbished. The house in the
center is in the beginning stages of renovation. The house
on the right is currently being repainted.

Principle of Anticipation

The principle of **anticipation** anticipates the future benefits that are to be derived from the property. Probable future benefits to be derived from a property will increase its value. An appraiser estimates the present worth of future benefits when he or she assigns a value based on anticipated returns.

> Example: The purchaser of a home has the perception he or she will be able to enjoy the use of that home in the future. They are anticipating the future benefits they are purchasing. Similarly, the buyer of a commercial property might be anticipating the future income, as well as possible tax benefits, associated with property ownership.

Often, nearby off-site improvements will have an effect on value. Schools, freeways, roads, parks, utilities, airports, and commercial developments are just of few of the many off-site improvements that may affect the value of a particular property. In many cases, the off-site improvements are only in the planning stages at the time of the appraisal, but anticipation is already having an effect upon the value for the subject property. USPAP requires the appraiser to "analyze the effect on value, if any, of anticipated public or private improvements, located on or off the site, to the extent that market actions reflect such anticipated improvements as of the effective appraisal date".

The principle of anticipation applies not only to positive future benefits but to anticipated negative future influences as well.

Example: A property might be located in a small town where the major employer indicated its operation would permanently close in the near future. In response to this news, property values would decrease due to anticipation. Similarly, a home in a presently quiet location could lose value if it is located next to the vacant field where the new extension of the interstate freeway is to be built.

It is important that appraisers stay fully informed of local community affairs as well as local economic trends in order to analyze accurately the effect of anticipation in the subject property's market.

Principle of Balance

The principle of **balance** states that equilibrium is reached when complementary uses of neighboring property permit maximum value for individual properties and the neighborhood. A careful mix of varying land use creates value. Over-improvement or under-improvement will cause imbalance.

An example of balance could be the construction of a strip commercial center located near a primarily residential neighborhood. Though these two uses are dissimilar, they are compatible since residents of the homes surrounding the strip center frequent the stores located in that center. By extension, the people who work in that center live close by in the surrounding residential neighborhood.

Agents of Production

Production, which is the ability to create wealth, can be used to measure real estate value. For any production—residential, agricultural, industrial, or commercial—to be profitable, four basic agents must be in proper proportion. The four **agents of production** are labor, management, capital, and land. Labor has first claim on returns from production, management is second, capital is third, and the last to be satisfied is land.

Labor includes wages and all payrolls except management. In addition, it includes all operating expenses (usually paid monthly), which generally represent a form of labor, maintenance, repairs, electricity, gas, water, rubbish removal, and supplies.

Management includes all charges for coordinating the enterprise. The entrepreneur who started the business manages smaller enterprises. In larger enterprises, salaried management personnel have replaced the entrepreneur.

Capital covers the costs of constructing the necessary buildings and providing equipment. It includes amortization of loans to pay for capital expenditures. Amortization, of course, includes return of money borrowed (principal) and return on money borrowed (interest). Capital also includes reserves for future depreciation of capital improvements. Fixed expenses of insurance and

taxes also are included. Insurance is generally a protection against capital loss; the major tax assessments are against capital improvements (structure and fixed equipment). Taxes and insurance are usually payable either annually or semi-annually.

Whatever return is left after full satisfaction and payment of the other three agents in production is imputable to the **land**. This residual, if properly interpreted, can be used as a basis for determining the value of the land. This process occurs in the land residual method of income approach to value and in the land residual approach to site valuation, discussed later in the course.

Principle of Surplus Productivity

Surplus productivity is the net real property income after the costs of labor, capital, and management have been paid. Labor, capital, and management are all expenses of ownership. Once these ownership expenses have been paid, any remaining surplus is attributable to land and is the investor's return on the use of the land (otherwise known as land rent). Land rent is the basis for residual land valuation techniques discussed later.

Principle of Contribution

The principle of **contribution** is the concept that the worth of a particular component is calculated in terms of its contribution to the value of the whole property, or its worth is calculated as the amount that its absence would detract from the value of the whole.

This principle is based on the premise that the value of a component part, whether it is added to land or building, is only equal to what it adds to the overall value of the property regardless of the actual cost of the improvement.

> Example: Although a home is worth more if it has a pool, the actual cost of adding a pool is higher than the expected increase in value. A new family room, however, generally increases the value of the house by more than the cost to build. The principle of contribution must be kept in mind by homeowners who want to remodel in some way. Before making any changes, the homeowner should try to determine if the changes would contribute enough to the property's value to justify the costs.

Increasing and Decreasing Returns

The theory of **increasing and decreasing returns** states that successive increments of one or more agents of production added to fixed amounts of other agents will enhance income, in dollars, benefits, or amenities, at an increasing rate until a maximum return is reached. Then, income will decrease until the increment to value becomes increasingly less than the value of the added agent or agents.

Increasing returns applies when additional investment in a property adds a reasonable return on that investment. At a certain point, maximum value will be reached. At this point, decreasing returns apply; continued investment will yield less and less return.

> Example: Imagine an older office building in an aging commercial district. In order to perpetually maintain the value of the building, certain upgrades must be considered, things like repainting, reroofing, upgrading of fixtures; eventually, the entire edifice may have to be remodeled to conform to whichever style is popular at that time. Eventually, though, no matter how much money the owners sink into the office building, it will have outlived its usefulness and further investment will not provide enough return to be worth the investment. It will have evolved from an investment that provides increasing returns to one that provides decreasing returns. At that point, demolition and reconstruction is oftentimes the most economically feasible option.

Principle of Conformity

The principle of **conformity** states that the more the form, manner, and character of structures are in harmony with one another, the more valuable each of those structures is. A home's maximum value is realized when surrounding land uses are compatible and nearby homes are similar in design and size. This similarity is called conformity, and it upholds neighborhood values. Where there are mixed types of homes, unstable real estate values may occur.

Progression

The theory of **progression** states that the value of an inferior property is enhanced by its association with better properties of the same type. A lesser-valued property will be worth more because of the presence of greater-valued properties nearby.

> Example: Joe purchased a 20-year old condominium in excellent condition and in a very good neighborhood. Not long after his purchase, developers put in a brand new high-end high-rise condominium complex adjacent to his property. As a result, the value of his property rose dramatically and immediately. In addition, having a brand-new modern-styled structure in the area encouraged the various local neighborhood associations to revitalize their strip mall edifices and public streets, contributing to an overall better looking neighborhood. As a result, property values in the entire area rose.

Regression

The opposite of progression, **regression** states that the value of a superior property is adversely affected by its association with an inferior property of the same type. A higher-valued property will be worth less because of the presence of lower-valued properties nearby.

Although constructing a new housing complex in an aging neighborhood elevates the surrounding property values, the surrounding, older properties can prevent the new complex from realizing its highest potential value.

Principle of Opportunity Cost

The principle of **opportunity cost** recognizes another type of competition— one that occurs between industries. Investors have many options in choosing where to put their investment dollars. For any investor, real estate is one of the many investment alternatives available, but it is not the only investment alternative. Whenever one investment is chosen, other options are not chosen. **Opportunity cost** is the profit lost on an investment you were unable to make because the money was already invested in something else.

> Example: If $10,000 is invested in a real estate investment, that $10,000 is not available to be invested in the stock market. If the investor receives a return of 6% on the real estate investment, but could have received a return of 9% by investing in the stock market, the opportunity cost is the 3% (9% - 6%) "lost."

Opportunity costs are often used in real estate appraisal analysis when estimating rates of return that are necessary to attract investment. Appraisers consider alternative investments in selecting a rate of return for a property being appraised. This affects the final estimate of value for that property.

SUMMARY

Property value considerations are at the core of real estate activity and are of critical importance. Understanding **value** includes determining which definition of value is appropriate for each assignment.

Appraisers must also be familiar with the various forces that create and influence value. The four elements—**demand, utility, scarcity, and transferability**—must be present in order for something to have any value. When value does exist for an item, there are **physical, economic, political, and social forces** that impact and shape value further.

There are numerous principles of valuation that, depending on how they are applied and analyzed, will affect the appraiser's overall analysis.

Typically, appraisers will be estimating **market value,** but there will be occasions when an appraiser must determine one of a number of other varieties of value. These include investment value, value-in-use, assessed value, insurable value, going concern value, salvage value, and liquidation value, to name a few.

Appraisal is based on several basic principles of economic theory. As these factors interact, property values will increase or decrease in response. The law of **supply and demand** is almost universally recognized as being the first step in how market prices are determined. The principle of substitution is the foundation for all of the appraisal process. **Substitution** states that the market value of a property is affected by the cost of obtaining an equally desirable and valuable property as a substitute. **Competition** tends to bring supply and demand back into balance. The **principle of change** states that the continuing effects of economic, social, and governmental forces on the property and its environment result in continuous changes in market value. All improved real property experiences a four-stage **neighborhood life cycle**. The four stages, although not always distinct, can best be described as development, stability, decline, and revitalization. The principle of **anticipation** anticipates the future benefits that are to be derived from the property. The principle of **balance** states that equilibrium is reached when complementary uses of neighboring property permit maximum value for individual properties and the neighborhood. Production can be used to measure real estate value. The four **agents of production** are labor, management, capital, and land. **Surplus productivity** is the net real property income after the costs of labor, capital, and management have been paid. The principle of **contribution** purports that the worth of a particular component is calculated in terms of its contribution to the value of the whole property. The principle of **conformity** states that the more the form, manner, and character of structures are in harmony with one another, the more valuable each of those structures is. **Opportunity cost** is the profit lost on an investment you were unable to make because the money was already invested in something else.

UNIT 4 REVIEW

Matching Exercise

Instructions: Write the letter of the matching term on the blank line before its definition, and then check your response with the Answer Key that immediately follows the Multiple Choice Questions.

Terms

A. agents of production

B. anticipation

C. assemblage

D. assessed value

E. blighted area

F. conformity

G. contribution

H. cost

I. effective demand

J. investment value

K. liquidation value

L. market value

M. neighborhood lifecycle

N. price

O. regression

P. substitution

Q. supply

R. supply and demand

S. unearned increment

T. value

Definitions

1. _____ Monetary worth of a property, good, or service to buyers and sellers at a given time.

2. _____ Amount asked, offered, or paid for a property.

3. _____ Amount required to create, produce, or obtain a property.

4. _____ Desire coupled with the ability to satisfy the desire.

5. _____ Process of obtaining and combining parcels to create a larger, more valuable parcel.

6. _____ Increase in value that is not the result of anything the owner did.

7. _____ Section of the inner city, where the majority of buildings are run down.

8. _____ Transaction in which all parties involved are knowledgeable, acting in their own self-interest and are under no undue influence or pressure from other parties.

9. _____ Value of an income-producing property to a specific investor based on his or her investment requirements.

10. _____ Value of a property as it appears in the tax assessor's office.

11. _____ Value of a property that has to be sold immediately by a seller who is under extreme compulsion to sell.

12. _____ Principle considered the first step in how market prices are determined.

13. _____ Total amount of a given type of property for sale or lease, at various prices, at any given point in time.

14. _____ Principle that affirms that the maximum value of a property tends to be set by the cost of acquiring an equally desirable and valuable alternate property.

15. _____ Growth, Stability, Decline, and Revitalization

16. _____ Principle that expresses that value is created by the expectation of future benefits.

17. _____ Land, labor, capital, and management

18. _____ Worth of a particular component is calculated in terms of its contribution to the value of the whole property, or as the amount that its absence would detract from the value of the whole.

19. _____ Structures are more valuable if they are similar in form, manner, and character to other structures in the neighborhood.

20. _____ Principle that states that the value of a superior property is adversely affected by its association with an inferior property of the same type.

Multiple Choice Questions

Instructions: Circle your choice, and then check your response with the Answer Key that immediately follows the Multiple Choice Questions.

1. In real estate, the term "worth" is synonymous with which of the following terms?
   a. Value
   b. Price
   c. Cost
   d. All of the above

2. Donna sold her house to her son for $250,000. Similar properties in the area are selling for $325,000. $250,000 is representative of this property's:
   a. value.
   b. price.
   c. cost.
   d. going concern value.

3. If a 3 bedroom/2 bath house cost $200,000 to build last year and recently sold for $250,000, what is its value?
   a. $200,000
   b. $250,000
   c. $300,000
   d. Depends on what the property would bring in the current fair and open market.

4. What are the four elements that create value?
   a. Transferability, utility, scarcity, and discount
   b. Demand, utility, substitution, and transferability
   c. Demand, uniformity, scarcity, and transferability
   d. Transferability, demand, scarcity, and utility

5. What is the difference between demand and effective demand?
   a. Demand is the desire or ability to purchase a commodity; effective demand is the desire and ability.
   b. Demand is the desire and ability to purchase a commodity; effective demand is the desire or ability.
   c. There can be no demand without effective demand.
   d. There is no difference.

6. A lot that previously supported a gas station is contaminated because of its prior use. Which of the four elements that creates value does this property most likely lack?

    a. Demand
    b. Utility
    c. Scarcity
    d. Transferability

7. A lakefront property is currently on the market for $850,000. It has 2,500 square feet and the lot is 50 feet deep. What is the cost per front foot?

    a. $1,700
    b. $17,000
    c. $340
    d. $3,400

8. Which exposure orientation would a street front retailer prefer?

    a. South and east
    b. North and east
    c. North and west
    d. South and west

9. A major corporation purchases several waterfront commercial lots with the plan of demolishing the current structures and erecting a large retail complex. This is known as:

    a. an arm's-length transaction.
    b. anticipation.
    c. assemblage.
    d. conformity.

10. Tom purchases a home in the first phase of development. By the time the home is prepared for occupation, Tom's property value has risen by 35%. This is an example of:

    a. progression.
    b. regression.
    c. unearned increment.
    d. opportunity cost.

11. Diana is a real estate agent who has been trying to sell the old Green place on Elm Street for several years. Even though it is on the market under value, the property will not sell because the local townspeople are convinced it is haunted. What term describes this property?

    a. Stigma

    b. Utility

    c. Effective demand

    d. Scarcity

12. In a typical appraisal assignment, which type of value is of greatest importance to an appraiser?

    a. Market value

    b. Appraisal value

    c. Value in use

    d. Effective value

13. Which of the following is an example of an arm's-length transaction?

    a. Parent sells family home to child for $25.00.

    b. Wealthy eccentric must have the neighboring lot and overpays.

    c. Seller does not notify buyer of known property stigma.

    d. None of the above.

14. Which one of the following statements is most correct?

    a. When supply is high and demand is high, then value tends to be high.

    b. When supply is low and demand is high, then value tends to be high.

    c. When supply and demand are in equilibrium, then value tends to be high.

    d. When supply is high and demand low, then value tends to be high.

15. Which principle of valuation is the underlying principle of all approaches to value?

    a. Substitution

    b. Supply and demand

    c. Competition

    d. Contribution

16. What are the four stages of the neighborhood lifecycle?

    a. Growth, stability, demand, and revitalization

    b. Regression, growth, stability, and decline

    c. Decline, revitalization, growth, and stability

    d. Scarcity, decline, revitalization, and growth

17. Which of the following is one of the four agents of production?
    a. Management
    b. Demand
    c. Supply
    d. Value

18. Chet bought a cabin in the mountains for $45,000. He repaired the furnace, redecorated the interior, and repainted the exterior. All of this work totaled just over $7,000. When he tried to resell it, the best offer he got for his cabin was $48,500. Which principle of valuation does this scenario exemplify?
    a. Opportunity cost
    b. Competition
    c. Regression
    d. Contribution

19. Dan is presented with Investment A and Investment B, both very attractive. Dan can only afford to invest in one and chooses Investment B. One year later, he learns that Investment A yielded 80% more profit than the investment he chose. Dan is a victim of:
    a. substitution.
    b. opportunity cost.
    c. unearned increment.
    d. regression.

20. Bob purchased adjacent lots in a suburban area where the typical house is a 3 bedroom/2 bath under 2000 square feet. Bob intends to combine the lots and build a 7 bedroom/6 bath Spanish style mansion. Which principle of valuation is Bob disregarding?
    a. Principle of progression
    b. Principle of regression
    c. Principle of conformity
    d. Principle of surplus productivity

UNIT 4 ANSWER KEY

Answers – Matching

1. T	6. S	11. K	16. B
2. N	7. E	12. R	17. A
3. H	8. L	13. Q	18. G
4. I	9. J	14. P	19. F
5. C	10. D	15. M	20. O

Answers – Multiple Choice

1. **(a)** When appraisers indicate the value of property, they are usually indicating an estimate of its monetary worth. **Page 102**

2. **(b)** Price is the amount a purchaser agrees to pay and a seller agrees to accept under the circumstances surrounding their transaction. **Page 102**

3. **(d)** By definition, value is the price an object or service would bring in a fair, open market. **Page 103**

4. **(d)** The four elements that create value are demand, utility, scarcity, and transferability. **Page 103**

5. **(a)** Demand is the desire OR the ability to purchase a commodity. Effective demand implies possession of both. **Page 103**

6. **(b)** While this particular property may be missing other elements that create value, from the information provided, its utility is negatively impacted by the contamination. **Page 104**

7. **(b)** A lot that contains 2,500 square feet and is 50 feet deep has a width of 50 feet. (2,500 square feet ÷ 50 feet = 50 feet). Front foot is the width of a property along a street or other boundary, and is most widely used as a measurement for properties located on beaches and lakeshores. $850,000 ÷ 50 feet = $17,000. **Page 106**

8. **(d)** The south and west sides of business streets are usually preferred by shopkeepers because customers will seek the shady side of the street and window displays will not be damaged by the sun. **Page 107**

9. **(c)** Assemblage is the act of putting several smaller, less valuable parcels together under one ownership interest so that the value of the combined parcels may increase. **Page 109**

10. **(c)**   An unearned increment is a term used in real estate appraisal to indicate that an increase in value was not the result of anything the owner did. Factors like inflation, in the economy or just in the regional or local real estate market, can cause an increase in value. **Page 110**

11. **(a)**   A stigma is a lingering effect in the minds of people regarding the desirability or usefulness of a property, whether real or imagined. **Page 116**

12. **(a)**   The overwhelming majority of appraisals performed are concerned with estimating the market value of a property, which is the same as its value in exchange. **Page 116**

13. **(d)**   An arm's-length transaction refers to a transaction where all parties involved are knowledgeable, acting in their own self-interest, and are under no undue influence or pressure from other parties. **Page 118**

14. **(b)**   Increasing supply or decreasing demand will reduce the price in the market. Reducing supply or increasing demand will raise the price in the market. **Page 122**

15. **(a)**   The principle of substitution is the foundation for all of the appraisal process. **Page 123**

16. **(c)**   Property goes through four distinct changes called a neighborhood lifecycle: Growth, Stability, Decline, and Revitalization. **Page 125**

17. **(a)**   The four agents of production (land, labor, capital, and management) may be increased in varying amounts to increase the value and/or income attributable to a property. **Page 127**

18. **(d)**   The principle of contribution is the concept that the worth of a particular component is calculated in terms of its contribution to the value of the whole property, or as the amount that its absence would detract from the value of the whole. **Page 129**

19. **(b)**   Opportunity cost is the highest valued alternative investment that was NOT chosen. **Page 131**

20. **(c)**   Progression and regression only affect properties of the same type. Leonard's mansion is clearly defiant of the principle of conformity, which holds that when land uses are compatible and homes are similar in design and size, the maximum value is realized. **Page 130**

Real Estate Markets & Analysis

Unit 5

INTRODUCTION

In the last unit, we discussed value, the factors that create value, the forces that influence value, and numerous economic principles that affect value. However, before appraisers can develop an opinion of the value of a particular property, they must understand how the primary and secondary mortgage markets contribute to financing real estate transactions and the characteristics that make the real estate market unique.

A **market** may be defined as trade in a specified commodity. Markets work by bringing interested buyers and sellers together and making it easier to complete transactions. Markets exist for virtually every known commodity and service; however, this unit focuses on mortgage and real estate markets.

Learning Objectives

After reading this unit, you should be able to:

- identify the role of money and policies that affect its availability.
- recognize and differentiate between the participants of the primary and secondary mortgage markets.
- identify the characteristics, purpose, type of amortization, government backing, and underwriting criteria of real estate loans.
- recall the finance instruments used for real estate loans.
- select the characteristics of a real estate market.
- recognize the purpose and elements of a real estate market analysis.

THE ROLE OF MONEY

Purchasing power is influenced by the availability of money. Most people must borrow money to purchase properties, so they go to banks (or other sources of available funds) that lend money. Since money is a commodity to be purchased and sold, money has a price. That price is interest. **Interest** is the charge for the use of money.

A synonym for money is capital. **Capital** consists of equity (one's own money) and debt (borrowed money). **Equity** is an owner's financial interest in real or personal property at a specific moment in time. **Debt** is a dollar amount that is borrowed from another party, usually under specific terms.

In real estate, equity is the difference between what a property is worth and what the owner owes against that property. At purchase, the equity is equal to the amount of the down payment. If the property is encumbered with a loan, the equity is the difference between the appraised market value of the property and the balance of any outstanding loans.

> Example: Robert purchased his home 3 years ago for $150,000 with a 10% down payment. At that time, his equity was $15,000 and the debt was $135,000. After making payments for 3 years, the mortgage is $130,000 and the current market value of his home is $175,000. Therefore, his equity in the property is $45,000.

The amount of money in the economy at any given time is a function of both supply and demand. As a result, the availability of funds to purchase real estate has a direct impact upon the demand for real property.

> Example: The availability of funds used for loans to purchase real estate also affects the interest rate charged for those loans. The greater the availability of capital to finance real estate, the lower the interest rate. Conversely, if capital is scarce, the interest rates will be higher. Since financing has such a dramatic impact upon real estate markets, appraisers need to be aware of factors influencing this aspect of real estate transactions.

The availability of funds for financing real estate, and thus the ability of buyers to buy real estate, is heavily tied to monetary and fiscal policies. The **monetary policy** influences the cost and availability of credit to promote economic growth, full employment, and price stability. It works by affecting demand across the economy. The **fiscal policy** is the government policy on taxes and government spending and affects supply. The Federal Reserve System is responsible for the monetary policy and the U.S. Treasury is responsible for the fiscal policy. Appraisers need to be aware of the actions of the Federal Reserve and the Treasury in order to identify trends.

The Federal Reserve System

The **Federal Reserve System** has the greatest effect upon the availability of money in the economy. Regulating the money supply is one of the most significant roles of the Federal Reserve. The supply of money in an economy greatly affects the availability of credit in that economy. Since the real estate market relies so heavily upon credit, the actions of the Federal Reserve have a significant effect upon real estate markets.

The **Federal Reserve System** (the Fed) is the central bank of the United States. It is an independent banking system designed to manage money and credit and to promote orderly growth in the economy. Although it operates within the general structure of the government, it operates independently from the government.

The Fed is a major player in the supply of money. The Fed implements monetary policy through its control over the fed funds rate, reserve requirements, discount rate, and open market operations.

The **fed funds rate** is the rate at which depository institutions trade balances at the Federal Reserve.

Reserve requirements refer to a certain percentage of each deposit in a bank that must be set aside as a reserve. The Fed increases or decreases the amount of money in circulation by raising or lowering reserve requirements for member banks. When the Fed requires a larger reserve, the banks have less to lend, so interest rates increase while borrowing and spending decrease. If the Fed lowers the reserve requirement, the banks have more money to lend, interest rates may decrease, and borrowing and spending increase.

The **discount rate** is the interest rate that is charged by the Federal Reserve to its member banks for borrowing money. A decrease in the discount rate allows more bank borrowing from the Fed. Bank borrowing increases money available for lending to the consumer. Raising the discount rate results in less borrowing from the Fed. The decrease in bank borrowing reduces the amount of money available for lending to the consumer.

Open market operations refer to the purchases and sales of U.S. Government and federal agency securities. When the Fed buys securities, the banks have more money to lend. When it sells securities, the amount of money in the economy is reduced. This causes a slowing of economic growth. The open market operations process is the most flexible and widely used technique for expanding or slowing the economy.

U.S. Department of the Treasury

The U.S. Department of the Treasury was created in 1789 to manage the government finances and formulate broad fiscal policies that have general significance for the economy. The government uses fiscal policy to regulate the total level of economic activity within a nation. Examples of fiscal policy include setting the level of government expenditures and the level of taxation.

THE MORTGAGE MARKETS

At the center of nearly all real estate transactions is some type of financing. Without an understanding of how real property is financed, real estate professionals will find themselves out of a job. The real estate lending industry is comprised of two distinct markets—the primary mortgage market and the secondary mortgage market. The purpose of the mortgage markets is to create a continuous flow of money to borrowers.

Primary Mortgage Market

The **primary mortgage market** is the market in which mortgage originators provide loans to borrowers. Participants in the primary mortgage market include commercial banks, thrifts, mortgage bankers, and other lenders. Sources of capital for purchasing real estate are categorized as equity investors or debt investors.

Equity Investors

An **equity investor** is a person or entity that invests money in a business and in return receives part ownership of the business. Typically, equity investors actively operate the investment, have an ownership interest in the property, and assume a relatively higher risk. Trusts, partnerships, joint ventures, syndications, pension funds, and life insurance companies are sources for equity financing.

Trusts

A **trust** is a legal arrangement in which an individual (**trustor**) gives fiduciary control of property to a person or institution (**trustee**) for the benefit of beneficiaries. **Fiduciary** means that those controlling the trust act for the benefit of others and have a standard of care that is higher than what is typically found throughout the rest of society. Trusts can be temporary, conditional, or permanent in nature. In a trust, title to and control of property is placed in the hands of a party called the trustee. The trustee acts to benefit and protect the interests of the person(s) called the **beneficiary**. Individual investors, as well as groups of investors employ trusts as an investment strategy in order to reap the benefits while avoiding the liabilities of ownership.

Relatively small groups of investors pool their assets in order to acquire larger properties and have successfully used Real Estate Investment Trusts (REITs). REITs give their investors freedom from personal liability and the shares of publically traded REITs are readily transferable. The trustee oversees management of the real estate.

Partnerships

Partnerships are arrangements in which two or more partners jointly own an asset and share in the profits or losses. General and limited partnerships are common ways for individuals to pool their funds with others to acquire properties.

In a **general partnership**, all partners have a proportionate share in the gains and losses associated with the property. However, the individual partners also have full responsibility for all liabilities of the partnership. The fact that general partners have full responsibility is one of the disadvantages to this kind of arrangement.

A **limited partnership** is an arrangement consisting of general and limited partners. The general partners have an active role in that they manage investment and assume full liability. The limited partners have a passive role and their liability is limited only to the amount of capital invested.

Joint Ventures

Joint ventures (JVs) are a contractual agreement joining two or more entities on a temporary basis for a specific project. Joint ventures usually form as a partnership to purchase or develop large projects. The partnership typically has one entity providing management expertise and a financial institution providing the bulk of the capital needed.

Syndications

Syndications are used to raise real estate equity capital. A **syndication** is a public or private partnership that pools funds to purchase and develop projects. Private syndications are small and relatively free of government regulation. Public syndications tend to be large and are subject to federal rules and regulations. Syndications are often set up and promoted by a general partner who advertises the investment opportunity and assumes full financial responsibility. Other investors buy shares in the syndication and are limited partners. Syndication agreements are written to offer an unequal distribution of tax benefits as an enticement to investors.

Life Insurance Companies

Through their sale of policies, life insurance companies accumulate large amounts of capital. They often invest in real estate both as equity investors and as mortgage lenders. Financial managers within these companies look for investment opportunities offering growth in the value of their investment as well as protection against inflation.

Pension Funds

Private and government pension funds are major equity investors in real estate. Employers and employees contribute funds to pension funds with the anticipation of paying retirement income to the employee upon retirement. Pension funds are usually under the control of a trustee obligated to invest the funds prudently for the benefit of the employees. In order to ensure the growth of these funds, the trustee actively seeks investments offering growth potential and safety. The amount of money controlled by pension funds is extremely large (over $1 trillion) which consequently has a significant effect upon real estate markets.

Debt Investors

A **debt investor** is a person or entity that lends money to a business and in return receives interest from the loan. Debt investors have a relatively passive role in the operation and management of the real estate. They usually do not participate in the management nor the gains or losses associated with buying and selling real estate. These sources of capital seek conservative investments, with relatively little risk, that produce income and repayment of principal with a high degree of certainty. These sources invest in debt and expect a priority claim on the property used to secure the debt. Though these organizations are thought of as lenders, they are investors since they are investing their funds into loans with the expectation of earning a return on (interest) and a return of (principal) their investment. Banks, savings and loans, commercial banks, credit unions, thrifts, and life insurance companies are examples of debt investors. Since appraisers receive so much of their business from these capital sources, they should be familiar with how they operate.

Savings & Loans

Savings & loan associations, also known as thrifts or S&Ls, are either federal or state-chartered financial institutions that take deposits from individuals with which they fund loans and pay dividends to investors. They have been the traditional source of capital for home loans. Thrifts are required by law to make a certain percentage of their loans as home mortgages.

Banks

Since deregulation in the 1980s, the distinction between S&Ls and commercial banks has blurred. Commercial banks have traditionally been the largest source of loans to small business and have historically specialized in short-term loans. Today they offer a variety of long-term real estate loans. Among other things, they offer mortgages and consumer loans, credit cards, and deposit products including savings accounts and certificates of deposit (CDs). They also offer checking accounts for individuals and businesses. Because of deregulation, banks now offer such products as insurance, mutual funds, and Individual Retirement Accounts (IRAs). Many banks also offer trust services, asset management, and estate planning as well.

Credit Unions

Credit unions are nonprofit, cooperative financial organizations of individuals having a common bond. They are formed by large organizations and companies for the benefit of their members or employees. They accept deposits from members, pay interest in the form of dividends on deposits, and use their funds mainly for consumer installment loans. Credit unions often offer higher interest rates on deposits and have a tendency to offer lower rates on the loans they make. When a person makes a deposit to a credit union, he or she becomes a member of that credit union because his or her deposit is considered partial ownership in that credit union.

Mortgage Bankers

A **mortgage banker** is a direct lender that lends its own money, whose principal business is the origination and funding of loans secured by real property. Once a loan is originated, lenders have a choice. Either they can hold the mortgage in their own portfolios or they can sell the mortgages to secondary market participants. About half of all new single-family mortgages originated today are sold to secondary market participants. When lenders sell their mortgages, they replenish their funds allowing them to make more loans to homebuyers.

Mortgage brokers do not fund loans themselves. Instead, they originate loans with the intention of brokering them to lending institutions. Mortgage brokers find the borrower, process the application, and submit the loan package to a lender who ultimately makes the loan. Mortgage brokers are paid a commission by the lender based upon the loan amount.

Private Investors

In addition, real estate loans are made by private individuals. When interest rates are high or credit is difficult to obtain, sellers personally may offer to finance a part of the sale as a way to facilitate the transaction. In these cases, the financing is tied to a particular property and the sale price is usually higher because of the private financing. When it is offered, it is often for a shorter term than other kinds of real estate financing. It often has a balloon payment that requires the buyer to refinance the loan.

In most instances though, private investors actively seek to make real estate loans. Usually working through mortgage brokers, private investors make loans that traditional lenders refuse to lend on, such as damaged homes, atypical construction, or unique properties. Often financing from private investors is above the market rate for conventional financing and usually comes with shorter loan terms.

Secondary Mortgage Market

In contrast to the primary mortgage market, in which lending institutions make mortgage loans directly to borrowers, participants in the secondary mortgage market do not originate loans. The **secondary mortgage market** can be seen as a resale marketplace by purchasing loans from lenders and channeling liquidity into the primary market.

There major participants in the secondary mortgage market are the Federal National Mortgage Association (Fannie Mae), the Federal Home Loan Mortgage Corporation (Freddie Mac), the Government National Mortgage Association (Ginnie Mae), and the Federal Agricultural Mortgage Corporation, (Farmer Mac).

Government-Sponsored Enterprises

Both Fannie Mae and Freddie Mac are congressionally chartered, shareholder-owned corporations commonly known as government-sponsored enterprises (GSEs). **Government-sponsored enterprises (GSEs)** are financial services corporations created by the United States Congress. Their purpose is to increase the availability and reduce the cost of credit to the residential finance, agriculture, and education sectors of the economy. Fannie Mae and Freddie Mac only buy conforming loans to hold in their own portfolios or to issue securities for sale to investors. Each year the limit of the size of a conforming loan is set, which is based on the October-to-October changes in mean home price. Fannie Mae and Freddie Mac are the largest sources of housing finance in the United States.

HUD regulated both Fannie Mae and Freddie Mac from 1968 and 1989, respectively, until September 2008 when they were placed under the conservatorship of the Federal Housing Finance Agency. The **Federal Housing Finance Agency** (FHFA) is an independent agency that was established by the Federal Housing Finance Reform Act of 2007 to regulate the GSEs.

Federal National Mortgage Association

The Federal National Mortgage Association (**Fannie Mae**) was created by Congress in 1938 to bolster the housing industry in the aftermath of the Great Depression. Initially, it was authorized to buy and sell FHA-insured loans from lenders, but its role was expanded to add VA-guaranteed loans in 1944 and conventional mortgages in 1972. In 1968, the Federal National Mortgage Association was divided into two entities—Fannie Mae and Ginnie Mae. Fannie Mae became a stockholder company that operated with private capital on a self-sustaining basis, but Ginnie Mae remained a government agency.

Federal Home Loan Mortgage Corporation

The Federal Home Loan Mortgage Corporation (**Freddie Mac**) is a stockholder-owned corporation charted by Congress in 1970 to stabilize the mortgage markets and support homeownership and affordable rental housing. Freddie Mac stock is traded on the OTC Bulletin Board under FMCC.

Government National Mortgage Association

The Government National Mortgage Association (**Ginnie Mae**) was created in 1968 as a government owned corporation within the Department of Housing and Urban Development (HUD). Its purpose was—and is—to serve low-to moderate-income homebuyers. Ginnie Mae does not buy or sell loans or issue mortgage-backed securities (MBS). It guarantees investors the timely payment of principal and interest on MBS backed by federally insured or guaranteed loans—mainly loans insured by FHA or guaranteed by the VA.

Mortgage-backed securities (MBS) are pools of mortgages used as collateral for the issuance of securities in the secondary market. MBS are commonly referred to as **pass-through securities** because the principal and interest of the underlying loans are passed through to investors. Ginnie Mae MBS are fully modified pass-through securities guaranteed by the full faith and credit of the United States government.

Federal Agricultural Mortgage Corporation

The Federal Agricultural Mortgage Corporation (**Farmer Mac**) is a federally chartered, stockholder-owned organization created by the U.S. Congress in 1988 to attract capital for financing agricultural and rural properties. It is primarily designed to benefit farmers and ranchers by maintaining a dependable and competitive supply of mortgage credit.

Like the other secondary-market participants, Farmer Mac purchases qualified loans from lenders thereby replenishing their source of capital to make new loans. It sells securities to investors backed by the mortgages it purchases. Farmer Mac also guarantees timely payment of principal and interest on securities backed by guaranteed portions of farm ownership and farm-operating loans as well as rural business and community-development loans. Though much smaller than Fannie Mae, Freddie Mac, and Ginnie Mae, it provides a much-needed secondary market for loans on rural properties, farms and ranches.

Real Estate Loans

As we have seen, lenders originate real estate loans in the primary market and then sell them in the secondary market to increase their liquidity and ability to make more loans. This section presents an overview of real estate loans.

Real estate loans can be classified in several ways. One of the most obvious ways to classify loans is by their purpose—purchase, refinance, or cash out. Lenders also classify loans by the type of amortization—fixed-rate, ARM, or

GPM. Any mortgage product other than a 30-year, fixed-rate mortgage is called a **nontraditional mortgage product**. Another classification is by type of loan—conventional and government-backed.

Purpose of the Loan

Lenders offer a variety of loans to help people purchase a property, refinance an existing loan, or get cash out of a property. For example, loan products are available to assist first-time homebuyers who only have a small down payment, and to retired individuals who want to draw on the equity in their home. In order to select the appropriate type of loan, a lender must know the purpose of the loan.

Is the loan to purchase a home or investment property? This is important because loans that are used to purchase owner-occupied properties have different underwriting guidelines than those used to finance investment properties. A loan that is used to purchase property is called a **purchase money loan**. It is used strictly for financing the purchase of real property.

A borrower might refinance an existing loan. **Refinancing** replaces the old loan with a new one. A person may refinance to reduce the interest rate, lower monthly payments, or change from an adjustable-rate to a fixed-rate loan.

If the borrower wants cash to make home repairs, pay for college tuition, pay off high-interest credit card debt, or take a vacation, he or she can get a cash-out refinance. **Cash-out refinancing** involves refinancing the loan for a larger amount than the current loan. Any loan used to take cash out of a property is a **hard money loan**. Hard money loans draw on the equity in property. This type of loan includes home equity loans, home equity lines-of-credit, and swing loans.

> Example: Homeowner Pat owes $90,000 on a house valued at $180,000 and wants $30,000 to add a family room. Pat can refinance the loan for $120,000, pay off the existing loan, and have $30,000 to add the family room.

Cash-out refinancing is not the same as a home equity loan. Cash-out refinancing replaces an existing loan with a new one. A home equity loan is a second loan against the equity in the property.

Type of Amortization

Loan products differ based on the terms of the loan, which include the amount borrowed, interest rate, length of the loan, and amortization. **Amortization** is the liquidation of a financial obligation on an installment basis. An amortization schedule details each payment, displays the specific amount applied to interest and principal, and shows the remaining principal balance after each payment.

A **fully amortized loan** is fully repaid at maturity by periodic reduction of the principal. When a loan is fully amortized, the payments the borrower makes are equal over the duration of the loan. Any mortgage other than a 30-year, fully amortized, fixed-rate mortgage is a nontraditional mortgage.

A **partially amortized loan** has a repayment schedule that is not sufficient to pay off the loan over its term. This type of loan calls for regular, periodic payments of principal and interest for a specified period. At maturity, the remaining unpaid principal balance is due as a balloon payment. A **balloon payment** is substantially larger than any other payment and repays the debt in full.

A **straight loan** is not amortized. The borrower only makes periodic interest payments during the term of the loan. The entire principal balance is due in one lump sum upon maturity. These loans are also called interest-only loans. This type of loan is not commonly offered by institutional lenders but may be offered by a seller or a private lender to a buyer.

Amortization is the basis for how a loan will be repaid. The type of amortization influences changes in repayment terms during the life of the loan. The most common amortization types include fixed-rate loans, adjustable-rate mortgages (ARM), hybrid loans, and graduated payment mortgages (GPM).

Fixed-Rate Loans

A **fixed-rate loan** has two distinct features—fixed interest for the life of the loan and level payments. The level payments of principal and interest are structured to repay the debt completely by the end of the loan term.

A **traditional 30-year fixed-rate loan** offers low monthly payments while providing for a never-changing monthly payment schedule. A typical 30-year, fixed-rate loan takes 22.5 years of level payments to pay half of the original loan amount. In fact, any mortgage product other than a 30-year, fixed-rate mortgage is called a **nontraditional mortgage product**.

Adjustable-Rate Loans

When a fixed-rate loan is impractical for the borrower, a nontraditional mortgage product, such as an ARM product may meet the borrower's specific financial situation. An adjustable-rate loan or **adjustable-rate mortgage (ARM)** is a loan with an interest rate that adjusts in accordance with a movable economic index. The interest rate on the loan varies upward or downward over the term of the loan depending on money market conditions and the agreed upon index. The interest rate on the ARM only changes if the chosen index changes. The borrower's payment stays the same for a specified time (for example, one year or two years) depending on the borrower's agreement with the lender. At the agreed upon time, the rate adjusts according to the current index rate.

Basic Features of ARMs

Initial Interest Rate and Payment. Many adjustable-rate loans (ARMs) have a low introductory rate or start rate, sometimes as much as 5.0% below the current market rate of a fixed-rate loan. This start rate is usually good for 1 month to as long as 10 years. As a rule, the lower the start rate, the shorter the time before the lender makes the first adjustment to the loan.

Adjustment Period. The period between rate changes.

Interest Rate. The **interest rate** is made up of two parts: the index and the margin. The interest rate is determined by the current rate of the chosen index. Then, a margin, which might be anywhere from 1 to 3 percentage points, is added to the initial interest rate.

> The **index** is a publicly published number that is used as the basis for adjusting the interest rates of adjustable-rate mortgages. The most common indices, or indexes, are the Constant Maturity Treasury (CMT), the 11th District Cost of Funds Index (COFI), the London Inter Bank Offering Rates (LIBOR), Certificate of Deposit Index (CODI), and the Bank Prime Loan (Prime Rate).
>
> The lender adds the **margin** (a few percentage points) to the index to determine the interest rate that a borrower pays.

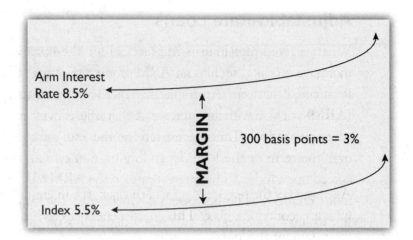

Margins on loans range from 1.75% to 3.5%, depending on the index and the total amount financed in relation to the property value. When the margin is added to the index, the result is known as the **fully indexed rate** on the loan.

> Example: The current index value is 5.5% and the loan has a margin of 2.5%. Therefore, the fully indexed rate is 8.0%.

Caps. Caps regulate how much the interest rate or payment can increase in a given period.

Interest Rate Caps. The two interest rate caps are periodic adjustment caps and lifetime caps. The **periodic adjustment cap** limits the amount the interest rate can adjust up or down from one adjustment period to the next after the first adjustment. The **lifetime cap** is the maximum interest rate that may be charged over the life of the loan.

Payment Caps. In addition to interest-rate caps, some ARMs have payment caps. A **payment cap** restricts a payment from increasing more than a specified percentage above the prior year's payment amount. These loans reduce payment shock in a rising interest rate market, but can also lead to negative amortization. **Negative amortization** is an increase in the principal balance caused by low monthly payments that do not pay all the interest due on the loan. This deferred interest is added to the principal on the loan. In some instances, the borrower can owe more than the amount of the original loan. Typically, the payment caps range between 5.0% and 8.0%. If a loan has a 6.0% payment cap and the borrower's monthly payment is $1,000, the payment cannot increase more than $60 regardless of the actual interest rate increase.

Hybrid Loans

A **hybrid loan** combines the features of a fixed-rate loan with those of an adjustable-rate loan. The fixed-rate feature gives the borrower some security with fixed payments in the initial term of the loan. The adjustable-rate feature is that the initial interest rates on these loans are typically lower than a fixed-rate loan. Initially, a fixed interest rate exists for a period of 3, 5, 7, or 10 years.

At the end of the fixed-rate term of the loan, the interest rate adjusts periodically with an economic index. This adjustment period begins on what is called the reset date for the loan.

Hybrid ARMs are often advertised as 3/1, 5/1, 7/1, or 10/1 ARMs. These loans are a mix (hybrid) of a fixed-rate period and an adjustable-rate period. The interest rate is fixed for the first few years of these loans, for example, for 5 years in a 5/1 ARM. After that, the rate may adjust annually (the 1 in the 5/1 example) until the loan is paid off.

> ### 3/1, 5/1, 7/1, 10/1 ARMs
>
> - The first number describes the initial period for the fixed interest-rate.
> - The second number tells how often the rate will adjust after the initial period.

Graduated Payment Mortgage Loans

A **graduated payment mortgage (GPM)** is a fixed-rate loan with initial payments that are lower than the later payments. The difference between the lower initial payment and the required amortized payment is added to the unpaid principal balance. The lower qualifying rate of the GPM helps borrowers maximize their purchasing power.

Unlike an ARM, GPMs are fixed-rate loans and have a fixed payment schedule. With a GPM, the payments are usually fixed for 1 year at a time. Each year for 5 years, the payments graduate from 7.5% to 12.5% of the previous year's payment.

Because of the graduated payments and fixed interest rate, GPMs have scheduled **negative amortization**. The higher the note rate, the larger the negative amortization becomes.

Types of Loans

Loans can be classified as conventional or government-backed. Some lenders specialize in only conventional conforming loans, whereas, full service lenders offer a wide selection of loan programs including conventional loans, non-conforming loans, and government-backed loans.

Conventional Loans

The majority of loans originated for 1-to-4 unit residential properties are conventional loans. A **conventional loan** is any loan without government insurance or guarantees. The basic protection for a lender making conventional loans is the borrower's **equity** in the property. A low down payment will mean greater risk for the lender and a higher interest charged to the borrower. If the borrower has less than a 20% down payment, lenders usually require private mortgage insurance. **Private mortgage insurance (PMI)** is extra insurance that lenders require from most homebuyers who obtain conventional loans that are more than 80% of their new home's value.

Lenders who originate conventional loans set their own lending policies and underwriting standards on loans they keep. For these loans, the lenders are only subject to federal and state regulatory agencies. Lenders can establish the types of loans they originate and the types of acceptable properties. They determine acceptable borrower qualifications, maximum loan limits, loan-to-value ratios, and loan fees.

Conventional loans may be conforming or non-conforming.

Conforming Loans

Conforming loans have terms and conditions that follow the guidelines set forth by Fannie Mae and Freddie Mac. These loans are called "A" paper loans, or prime loans, and can be made to purchase or refinance homes (1-4 residential units).

Fannie Mae and Freddie Mac guidelines determine which properties are suitable, set maximum loan limits, and set debt-to-income ratios for conforming loans. Fannie Mae and Freddie Mac announce new loan limits every year. This limit is reviewed annually and, if needed, modified to reflect changes in the national average price for single-family homes.

Non Conforming Loans

A **non-conforming loan** is a loan that does not meet the Fannie Mae or Freddie Mac lending guidelines. This can be due to the type of property being financed or because the borrower's income is difficult to verify. Loans that exceed the maximum loan amount are called jumbo loans. Sometimes, subprime loans are an option for borrowers whose creditworthiness does not meet the guidelines.

Jumbo Loans

A **jumbo loan** exceeds the maximum conforming loan limit set by Fannie Mae and Freddie Mac. Because jumbo loans are bought and sold on a much smaller scale, these loans usually carry a higher interest rate and have additional underwriting requirements.

Sub Prime Loans

Loans that do not meet the borrower credit requirements of Fannie Mae and Freddie Mac are called **subprime loans** or "B" paper and "C" paper loans as opposed to "A" paper conforming loans. The purpose of "B" and "C" paper loans is to offer financing to applicants who do not currently qualify for conforming "A" paper financing. Subprime loans are offered to borrowers who may have recently filed for bankruptcy or foreclosure, or have late payments on their credit reports.

Borrowers in the subprime category include those who have low credit scores or no credit score, income that is difficult or impossible to verify, an excessively high debt-to-income ratio, or a combination of these factors. Other factors, such as the purpose of the loan and the property type, may require the borrower to secure a subprime loan.

> Example: Alice is qualified to purchase a single-family home under standard Fannie Mae guidelines. However, she may have to use a subprime loan to finance the purchase of a non-owner occupied fourplex.

Government-Backed Loans

Government-backed loans are just that—loans with some type of government backing. Federal agencies that participate in real estate financing include the Federal Housing Administration (FHA), the Department of Veterans

Affairs (VA), and the United States Department of Agriculture (USDA) FMHA Loan Program. Together, they make it possible for people to buy homes they would never be able to afford to purchase. The main difference between the programs is that only an eligible veteran may obtain a VA loan. The programs were created to assist people in buying homes when conventional loan programs do not fit their needs. Regulations change from time to time. Be sure to check current information on loan programs at their respective websites.

Federal Housing Administration

The **Federal Housing Administration (FHA)** is a federal government agency that insures private home loans for financing homes and/or home repairs. Created by Congress in 1934, the FHA became part of the Department of Housing and Urban Development (HUD) in 1965.

Originally created to stabilize the mortgage market, the FHA caused some of the greatest changes in the housing industry in the 20th century. It forever changed home mortgage lending by insuring long-term, amortized loans; implementing standardized loan instruments, creating standards for qualifying borrowers; and by establishing minimum property and construction standards for residential properties.

Mutual Mortgage Insurance

The FHA does NOT make loans. It insures loans to protect the lenders who make the loans. On loans with less than a 20% down payment, the lender is protected in case of foreclosure by **mutual mortgage insurance (MMI)**. The borrower pays the mutual mortgage insurance premiums to the FHA Mutual Mortgage Insurance Fund. Money placed into the fund is used to pay lenders in the event of loss resulting from foreclosure. As long as FHA guidelines are used when the loan is financed, the FHA will pay the lender up to the established limit of the insurance upon default and foreclosure.

Property Appraisal

The value of the property is the lender's best assurance that it will recover the money it lends. Therefore, the FHA requires an appraisal of the property, which is used to determine the market value and acceptability of the property for FHA mortgage insurance purposes. The FHA loan amount that is approved is based on the appraised value of the property or the sales price, whichever is lowest.

Appraisals are performed for the use and benefit of HUD and the lenders involved in FHA transactions, not the borrower. The FHA allows only FHA-approved, licensed appraisers to perform the appraisals because they must check for required FHA items to confirm that the property does not contain any health or safety issues. Appraisers are reprimanded if they do not use FHA appraisal guidelines when preparing appraisals for FHA loans. Additionally, an appraiser who intentionally misrepresents the value on FHA loan appraisals, which subsequently cause a loss, could be fined and face legal action.

FHA-approved appraisers use the standardized Fannie Mae appraisal reporting forms. The appraisal reporting form used depends on the type of property that is being appraised.

Uniform Residential Appraisal Report. This report form is designed to report an appraisal of a one-unit property or a one-unit property with an accessory unit, including a unit in a planned development (PD).

Individual Condominium Unit Appraisal Report. This report form is designed to report an appraisal of a unit in a condominium project or a condominium unit in a planned development (PD).

Manufactured Home Appraisal Report. This report form is designed to report an appraisal of a one-unit manufactured home, including a manufactured home in a planned development (PD).

Small Residential Income Property Appraisal. This report form is designed to report an appraisal of a two-to-four unit property, including a two-to-four unit property in a planned development (PD).

Department of Veterans Affairs

The United States **Department of Veterans Affairs (VA)** was created in 1989 to replace its predecessor, the Veterans Administration, which was established in 1930. It is a government-run military veteran benefit system with the responsibility of administering programs of veterans' benefits for veterans, their families, and survivors.

The VA does not make loans. It guarantees loans made by approved lenders, much like the FHA. Only lenders who are VA-approved lenders can make VA loans. Veterans may not need to make a down payment. Instead of the down payment from the borrower, lenders receive a **certificate of guaranty** from the VA. The VA's guaranty on the loan protects the lender against loss if payments are not made. The amount of guaranty on the loan depends on the amount of the loan and if the veteran previously used some of his or her entitlement. The **entitlement** is the maximum guaranty that the VA will provide for the veteran's home loan.

Before lenders accept an application for a VA-guaranteed loan, they must be sure that the VA has determined that the applicant is eligible. The VA evaluates each applicant to see if the applicant meets the eligibility criteria established by law. The **Certificate of Eligibility** (COE) is important because the lender may rely on it as proof that a veteran is eligible for a VA home loan. The most important item on the COE is the amount of the entitlement, because the VA's guaranty on the loan generally cannot exceed the amount of the entitlement.

USDA Guaranteed Loan Program

Rural property is property located in the outlying region of an urban center. Obtaining financing for rural property can be a challenge, because most traditional lenders do not specialize in these types of properties.

A source of financing for rural properties is the United States Department of Agriculture (USDA). A **USDA Guaranteed Loan** is Government insured 100% purchase loan for properties in rural areas. Under the USDA loan program, the Housing and Community Facilities Programs guarantees loans made by private-sector lenders.

Under the terms of the program, an individual or family may borrow up to 100% of the appraised value of the home, which eliminates the need for a down payment. Mortgages are 30-year fixed rate at market interest rates. Loans may include funds for closing costs, the guarantee fee, legal fees, title services, and other prepaid items, if the appraised value is higher than sales price.

Underwriting Criteria

Underwriting is the practice of analyzing the degree of risk involved in a real estate loan. Lenders consider many criteria and follow underwriting guidelines to determine whether the borrower has the ability and willingness to repay the debt and if the property to be pledged as collateral is adequate security for the debt. **Underwriting guidelines** are principles lenders use to evaluate the risk of making real estate loans. The guidelines are just that—guidelines. They are flexible and vary according to loan program.

During the underwriting process, underwriters use loan-to-value ratios, debt-to-income ratios, creditworthiness of the borrower, and the suitability of the collateral.

Loan-to-Value Ratios

Evaluating the loan-to-value ratio (LTV) is probably the most important aspect of the underwriting process. The **loan-to-value ratio (LTV)** is the relationship between the loan (amount borrowed) and the value of the property.

> Example: If the property in question is valued at $100,000 and the loan amount requested is $80,000, the loan-to-value ratio is 80%.

The loan amount is determined by the value of the property and the borrower's personal financial condition. To estimate the value of the property, the lender asks a real estate appraiser to give an opinion about its value. The appraiser's opinion can be an important factor in determining if the borrower qualifies for the loan size he or she wants.

Lenders usually lend borrowers up to a certain percentage of the appraised value of the property, such as 80 or 90%, and expect the down payment to cover the difference. The **down payment** is the initial equity the borrower has in the property. If the appraisal is below the asking price of the home, the down payment the borrower plans to make and the amount the lender is willing to lend may not be enough to cover the purchase price. In that case, the lender may suggest a larger down payment to make up the difference between the price of the house and its appraised value.

There is a distinct relationship between borrower equity and loan default. Borrowers with a sizable down payment are less likely to default. In one 5-year period for loans purchased by Freddie Mac, borrowers who put down 5% to 9% were 5 times more likely to enter foreclosure than those who made down payments of 20% or more.

Example: Freddie Mac found that borrowers with both smaller down payments (collateral) AND risky credit profiles have a higher probability of default than borrowers who have only one of these two risk factors.

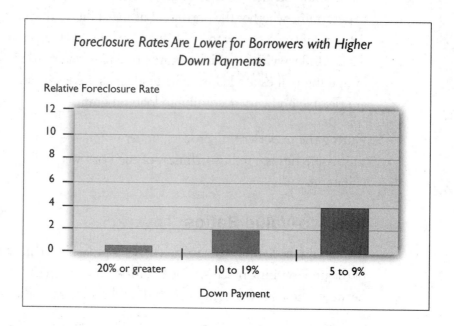

Larger down payments lower the LTV ratio on the loan and reduce risk to the lender. The risk to the lender is the risk that the borrower will default on loan payments, thereby causing the property to go into foreclosure. In that event, the lender either receives the property at the foreclosure sale or receives a deficient amount at the sale. A **deficiency** occurs when the amount for which the property sells is less than the total amount due to the lender. Neither is desirable from the point of view of the lender or investor. Therefore, it is important for the underwriter to determine if the LTV falls within the guidelines for that particular loan.

Debt-to-Income Ratios

A lender calculates the maximum loan amount for which a borrower qualifies. To determine the borrower's ability to repay the loan, the underwriter uses debt-to-income ratios to calculate the risk that the borrower will default. The **debt-to-income ratio (DTI)** is simply the percentage of a borrower's monthly gross income that is used to pay his or her monthly debts.

> ### Common DTI Ratios
> - Conforming loans use 28% front ratio and 36% back ratio (28/36)
> - FHA uses 31% front ratio and 43% back ratio (31/43)
> - VA only uses back ratio of 41% as a guideline
> - Non-conforming loans have very flexible DTI ratios

The **front ratio** is the percentage of the borrower's monthly gross income (before taxes) that is used to pay housing costs, including principal, interest, taxes, and insurance (**PITI**). When applicable, it also includes mortgage insurance and homeowners' association fees.

The **back ratio** is the total monthly PITI and consumer debt divided by the gross monthly income. **Consumer debt** can be car payments, credit card debt, installment loans, and similar expenses. Auto or life insurance is not considered a debt.

When the maximum front-end ratio is 28%, it means that borrowers' housing costs should not be more than 28% of their monthly income. When the maximum back-end ratio is 36%, it means that total debt (housing and consumer) should not be more than 36% of the gross monthly income.

There is a distinct relationship between total-debt-to-income ratios and foreclosure rates.

> Example: Based on the purchases Freddie Mac made in 1994, borrowers with total-debt levels greater than 36% of their income were twice as likely to enter foreclosure as those with ratios below 30%.

While capacity is an important underwriting component, debt-to-income ratios generally are less powerful predictors of loan performance than other factors. The following chart shows the relationship between debt-to-income ratios and foreclosure rates among borrowers.

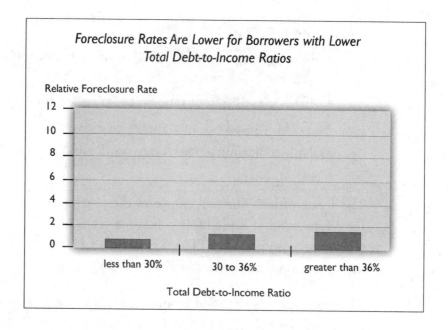

Foreclosure Rates Are Lower for Borrowers with Lower
Total Debt-to-Income Ratios

Relative Foreclosure Rate

Total Debt-to-Income Ratio

FHA guidelines state that a 31/43 qualifying ratio is acceptable. VA guidelines do not have a front ratio at all, but the guideline for the back ratio is 41.

> Example: If Borrower Brenda makes $5,000 a month, to meet 31/43 qualifying ratio guidelines, her maximum monthly housing cost should be around $1,550. Including Brenda's consumer debt, her monthly housing and credit expenditures should not exceed about $2,150.

Lenders who do not provide FHA or VA loans commonly use the guideline that suggests the total of all debt should not be more than 36% of the borrower's gross monthly income. However, the lender may consider other factors and allow a higher debt-to-income ratio. These factors include a larger down payment than normal, a large amount of cash in savings, a large net worth, or an especially solid credit rating.

Creditworthiness of the Borrower

Underwriters look at the borrower's employment history, income, assets, credit history, and credit score. The amount of income indicates the borrower's ability to repay the loan, whereas the credit history reflects the borrower's willingness to repay the loan.

Real estate lenders use credit scores as a significant factor in their decision-making process. A **credit score** is a statistical summary of the information contained in a consumer's credit report. Lenders commonly use the credit score to screen a potential borrower and often it becomes the compelling basis for loan approval. Lenders use credit scores to rank consumer risk and determine loan amounts.

The quality of the credit score also affects the interest rate the lender charges the borrower. Generally, the higher the credit score, the lower the payments. Borrowers with high credit scores are usually offered the lowest rates on loans. The lower the credit score, the less likely the lender is to extend credit. However, if the lender does extend credit, borrowers with low credit scores pay higher interest rates. The higher interest rate reflects the higher risk involved in making such a loan.

The higher the credit score, the lower the interest rate, and the lower the monthly payment. The following chart illustrates this concept for a $225,000, 30-year fixed-rate loan.

Credit Scores Affect the Interest Rates and Monthly Payments		
FICO® Score	**APR**	**Monthly Payment**
760-850	6.146%	$1,370
700-759	6.368%	$1,403
660-699	6.652%	$1,445
620-659	7.462%	$1,567
580-619	9.451%	$1,884
500-579	10.310%	$2,026
*Estimated average over the life of the loan. Payments may vary.		

Although many credit-scoring systems are available, the two most frequently used are FICO® and VantageScore℠.

Collateral for the Loan

Underwriters working for lenders also look at the collateral for the loan. Usually lenders do not wish to make loans that are greater than the value of the collateral. A borrower, who owes more money on a loan than what the home is worth, is more likely to default. One of the risks associated with approving a real estate loan is the type and value of the property used as security for the loan. The property itself is the lender's primary security for repayment of the loan if the borrower defaults. The secondary security is the promissory note, which is the borrower's personal promise to pay. The property must be structurally sound and in good repair. The lender's decision to fund the loan is dependent as much on the value of the property as it is on the borrower's ability to pay off the loan.

The underwriter wants to make sure that the lender is protected from loss because of default and foreclosure by establishing the value of the property to which the loan-to-value ratio is applied. The value of a property is determined by an appraisal. The purpose of the appraisal is to analyze the current market value of the property and determine any adverse factors that might affect value in the near future. Each property is appraised to determine if it has sufficient fair market value to serve as reasonable security for a loan.

Finance Instruments

Real estate finance instruments—promissory notes and security instruments—are legal documents that provide evidence of a debt and secure that debt with a collateral property. The lender or subsequent noteholder holds the promissory note and the security instrument until the loan is repaid.

Promissory Note

When a loan is made, the borrower signs a promissory note. A **promissory note** (note) is a written promise to repay a certain amount of money at a certain time, or in a certain number of installments. The note specifies the amount of the loan (principal), interest rate, terms of repayment, the due  date of the note, and the penalties imposed if the borrower fails to meet the obligations of the note.

Security Instruments

At the same time the promissory note is signed, the borrower is required to execute the security instrument. A security instrument is a separate agreement from the promissory note. A **security instrument** is a legal document given by the borrower to hypothecate (pledge) the property to the lender as collateral for the loan. Mortgages and deeds of trust are the most common types of security instruments used in real estate finance, whereas Georgia uses a security deed.

As you recall, the promissory note is the evidence of the debt. The promissory note can stand alone without the security instrument. It is a personal, unsecured note at that point. However, the security instrument needs the note to validate its existence. If there is a conflict between the terms of a note and the security instrument, the provisions of the note prevail.

Although the lender retains a security interest in the property, the borrower retains right of possession as long as payments are made according to the promissory note. If the borrower does not make payments per the agreement, he or she loses the rights of possession and ownership. If the borrower defaults, the security instrument allows the lender to foreclose on the loan. A security instrument creates a lien against the property.

A mortgage is a lien against a property until the debt is paid

Every security instrument describes the parties to the security instrument. The type of security instrument dictates the parties.

Borrower. Depending on the type of security instrument, the borrower is called the mortgagor, trustor, or grantor.

Lender. Depending on the type of security instrument, the lender is called the mortgagee, beneficiary, or grantee.

Trustee. Only a deed of trust has a trustee.

Type of Security Instrument	Borrower	Lender	Trustee
Mortgage	Mortgagor	Mortgagee	N/A
Deed of Trust	Trustor	Beneficiary	Trustee
Security Deed	Grantor	Grantee	N/A

THE REAL ESTATE MARKET

The appraiser has to understand how real estate markets work to accomplish nearly every step of the valuation process. Recognizing the challenges associated with the real estate market highlights the need for competent and ethical appraisers.

Most commodities are bought and sold in markets that are efficient and organized. An **efficient market** is one in which goods and services are easily produced and readily transferable, there are a large number of buyers and sellers, and market prices adjust rapidly to reflect new information. An **organized market** is one in which participants operate under recognized rules for the purpose of buying and selling a particular commodity. Economists describe this type of market as a **perfect market**.

Characteristics of the Real Estate Market

Due to the nature of real estate, the real estate market is inefficient and disorganized—imperfect. An **imperfect market** is a market that cannot meet the requirements for a perfect market. The real estate market does not meet any of the requirements for a perfect market.

Characteristics of the "Imperfect" Real Estate Market

- There are relatively few buyers and sellers, and one cannot transfer property to the other quickly or easily.
- Information is not readily available, and there is no one source to buy or sell real estate.
- Real estate as a product is unique and immobile.
- Real estate as an investment is illiquid.
- The supply of land is limited, and suppliers cannot produce (i.e., construct) new properties quickly.
- Government influences financing and property-use controls.
- The real estate market is local and segmented.

Limited Number of Buyers and Sellers

Efficient markets have a large number of buyers and sellers creating a free market. Typically, none of the participants in the market has a large enough share to have a direct measurable influence on the prices within the market. In any given real estate market, few people are active in the process of buying and selling of real estate at any particular time. In addition, relatively few sales of real estate in a market can have a significant influence on prices within that market.

Availability of Information

In efficient markets, participants are brought together by an organized market mechanism and sellers enter the market relatively easily in response to demand. Markets such as these provide an abundance of information that buyers and sellers can easily access, and with which they may quickly interact. Buyers and sellers in organized markets are knowledgeable because information on bids, offers, and sales is readily available.

However, buyers and sellers of real estate are often inexperienced. Additionally, information is often difficult to access, since real estate transactions are confidential. Most of the time, buyers and sellers must rely upon those having this specific knowledge to assist them in achieving their goals. This lack of knowledge on the part of buyers and sellers is one of the main reasons participants in the real estate marketplace use services provided by real estate brokers and appraisers.

Unique Product

In efficient markets, products tend to be uniform and virtually identical to one another. One product may be readily substituted for another. For example, an ounce of gold purchased in New York City is identical to an ounce of gold bought in Los Angeles. Likewise, a new car purchased in Texas is virtually identical to the same make and model car that is sold in Minnesota.

On the other hand, each piece of real estate is unique. No two properties are identical. This causes the real estate market to be disorganized. Even if the improvements on two different pieces of land are identical, each property is the only one in its particular location and this makes it unique. Since each property is unique, it is not readily substituted for another property.

Supply of Land is Limited

In organized markets, the price to purchase a particular commodity is relatively uniform, stable, and low. Competition has a limiting effect on the market and keeps supply and demand in balance so prices remain relatively stable.

If there is increased demand, producers of the commodity will see an opportunity to profit and will increase their production relatively quickly to fill the need. More suppliers will enter the market vying for those profits. In turn, the influx of these additional suppliers will act to keep prices down as supply rises to meet the demand. The opposite holds true for decreasing profits. If there are too many producers for a given commodity, suppliers will stop producing that commodity since there is less profit incentive.

This is usually not the case with real estate. Land itself is limited in supply, and once an area has been built up, it can be very difficult to change the supply of a particular type of property. Zoning changes or other modifications may be necessary. Even in an area that has vacant land, production cannot quickly change to match a change in demand for a particular type of property. In the housing market, it can take years to increase the existing housing supply. Because the supply of real estate does not increase quickly or easily, the real estate market is much more susceptible to changes in demand.

Immobility

Real estate markets are relatively inefficient because real estate is immobile. In efficient markets, goods are easily moved, quickly supplied, and readily consumed by buyers. As demands change, commodities move to where they are needed. They move to areas where that commodity is in short supply or they can be stored until needed. This is not true for real estate. Land cannot move elsewhere. It is impossible to relocate land to a location where it would be more desirable.

Land is immobile

Illiquid Investment

In addition to being immobile, real estate is illiquid and cannot be sold quickly for full market value. **Illiquid** means that an asset cannot be readily converted to cash. Although it is true that in some instances real estate is sold very quickly, there are typically unusual circumstances at work. For example, the quick sale may be due to the seller discounting the purchase price, or it may be caused by low supply coupled with high demand in a particular market. However, the reality is that most markets do not allow for the quick sale of real estate at market value.

Other commodities, such as stocks and bonds, tend to be liquid assets. When these types of assets are sold, owners usually receive the cash proceeds within a day or two. In the real estate market, it may take weeks, even months, before a buyer is found and even more time for the transaction to be finalized.

Real estate prices are high in comparison to other commodities. Since very few people have the funds to purchase real estate with cash, financing is necessary. The financing process increases the complexity involved in transferring real estate and substantially increases the time involved.

Government Regulations

The real estate market is also highly regulated. In most markets, there are relatively few government restrictions influencing value; the market is self-regulating. Although government oversight is becoming more widespread all the time, many commodities are still bought and sold with relatively little government regulation. However, in real estate the processes involved in transferring ownership are heavily regulated. In addition, the actual use of a property is restricted by building permits and zoning or subdivision regulations.

Market Segmentation

The real estate market consists of many individual (**specific**) markets. There are specific markets for virtually every kind of real property, including markets for residential property and markets for commercial property. There are markets for industrial and agricultural properties. There are even markets for land that may never be developed.

One of the major tasks appraisers perform is identifying the market in which a property operates. An appraiser starts the analysis by identifying the specific market that describes the market for the subject property.

Markets can be limited to a specific neighborhood within a city. Other times a market for a particular kind of property may range over numerous states. Markets may even be international in scope. Although individual real estate transactions are local in nature, it is important to recognize that forces influencing real estate markets operate at the county, state, regional, national, and in some instances, international level. These market forces include such things as population level, demographics, location characteristics, topography, economic, financial, as well as property specific physical characteristics.

Specific real estate markets have submarkets. A **submarket** is a geographic, economic, or specialized subdivision of a market. **Market segmentation** is the process of identifying and analyzing submarkets within these larger markets.

> For example, there is a specific market for residential property within a city. Within that larger, specific market, there are submarkets for higher priced, luxury homes, moderately priced homes and entry-level homes. Each of those submarkets are further differentiated according to location within the city and physical characteristics such as age, style, bedroom and bath count, gross living area, lot size, etc. Legal considerations such as type of ownership (fee simple, condominium, PUD) also further differentiate the market. When determining which submarket a property operates in, criteria such as these are considered.

Five broad categories of **real estate markets** include residential, commercial, industrial, agricultural, and special purpose. These categories are the starting point to identify the market for the property being appraised. An appraiser will identify which of the broad categories describes the market for the subject property.

Residential Market

Typical submarkets for the residential market include houses, condominiums, apartments, lofts, and co-op buildings. They may be either attached or detached and can be single story, multi-story, mid-rise, or high-rise. They may be further categorized as being low-priced, medium-priced, and high-priced. They can be built using standard construction materials and techniques, or be factory-built. They may be located in a tract of similar homes or situated in a rural location far from any other residences.

Commercial Market

Since commercial properties are designed for a business purpose, the typical submarkets include retail space, office space, and hospitality properties.

Further differentiation includes business size, type of business, and type of space needed. They may be further categorized as single-use, multi-use, and high-rise. The space can be Class A, Class B, or Class C construction quality. They may be located in the downtown, suburban, or rural areas. Differentiation even takes into account the type of investor—small private investor, large private investor, limited partnership, or institutional investor.

Industrial Market

Industrial properties are typically used to assemble, process, or manufacture products. They are also used for industrial services such as storage, warehousing, and recycling facilities. Industrial submarkets include factories, warehouses, industrial plants, and mining facilities.

Agricultural Market

As the name implies, agricultural properties are those devoted to an agricultural purpose, such as farming, pasturing, timberland, orchards, groves, and ranches. Each of these submarkets

is differentiated by the type of crop (fruits, grains, vegetables) produced or animals (cattle, dairy cows, chickens, hogs, or any other livestock) raised. They may be further categorized by acreage, soil type, water rights, and topography.

Special Purpose Market

Special purpose properties include the remaining properties not included in the above lists. Special properties include, but are not limited to, government facilities, parks, open space, houses of worship, cemeteries, landfills, museums, colleges and universities, convention centers, theatres,

recreational and historic properties. Each of these properties would have various submarkets and differentiated users and uses.

Real Estate Market Analysis

A market analysis is a key step in every appraisal assignment. The goal of the **market analysis** is to identify, research, and analyze the particular market in which the appraised property operates. Appraisers rely upon their market analysis to identify the scope of work necessary to produce a reliable opinion of value.

Questions to Address when Identifying the Subject Property's Market

- What is the location of the property being appraised?
- Which kinds of properties are comparable to the subject property?
- What is the location of, and geographic distance from the subject, of possible comparable properties that would compete with the subject?
- Are the comparable sales used in the analysis reasonable substitutes within the market for the subject property?

By categorizing the subject's market, the appraiser can identify where to look for comparable data used in performing the appraisal.

Real estate market analysis reflects the most current market conditions and analyzes development, leasing, sales, and absorption trends that have occurred over the past 10 years. In addition, appraisers interview local development and real estate professionals in order to understand the nuances of the subject market and to identify any structural or regulatory barriers that may be inhibiting local development activity.

The general purpose of a market analysis is to identify future opportunities for growth and development within the region, with a specific emphasis on the subject market. With a few exceptions, it is generally believed that recent development trends will be a reasonable predictor of future development over the next three to five years. Beyond five years, it is very difficult to predict with any certainty how a community might grow. One can only make reasonable assumptions about regional economic trends, land and building absorption rates, and regulatory constraints, and provide a range of possible outcomes.

Demographic Data

Through **demography**, or the study of population statistics, appraisers can reveal a clearer picture of a market's participants. Analyzing median age, income, and family size, among other statistical factors, can tell the appraiser valuable information about who is buying, who is renting, and help to anticipate the future of a market as well. For example, if population trends have been increasing for a certain market for the past eight years, an appraiser might conclude that the need for housing will continue to increase, and consequently the absorption rate will increase in kind.

Absorption Analysis

The purpose of an absorption analysis is to predict the absorption rate of a certain type of property in a given market. An **absorption rate** signifies the rate at which a type of property is bought or leased—that is, absorbed by the market. This is useful because it indicates how fast a property will sell or rent considering the availability of competing properties, the projected supply and space surplus, as well as the needs of that particular market.

> Example: Bob is building a new 16-unit apartment complex. He hired an appraiser to do an absorption analysis, and the appraiser estimated the absorption rate at four units per month. This means that it will take four months to rent the entire building.

An absorption analysis will also reveal the price point for marketing a property to the public so that the units sell or rent at the highest price in the shortest period.

Forecasts

Demographic data and absorption analysis are usually parts of a larger study known as a feasibility analysis. A **feasibility analysis** is a study of the cost-benefit relationship of an economic endeavor. In performing a feasibility study, the appraiser forecasts the likely success of a project and considers the demographics and absorption rates of a market. In addition, the appraiser examines the costs associated with the project and the likely return the investors can expect.

SUMMARY

The availability of funds for financing real estate is tied to monetary and fiscal policies. The **monetary policy** influences the cost and availability of credit to promote economic growth, full employment, and price stability. The **fiscal policy** is the government policy on taxes and government spending and affects demand.

The real estate lending industry is comprised of the primary mortgage market and the secondary mortgage market. The **primary mortgage market** is the market in which mortgage originators provide loans to borrowers. Participants in the primary mortgage market include commercial banks, thrifts, mortgage bankers, and other lenders. The **secondary mortgage market** can be seen as a resale marketplace by purchasing loans from lenders and channeling liquidity into the primary market. There major participants in the secondary mortgage market are Fannie Mae, Freddie Mac, Ginnie Mae, and Farmer Mac.

Loans can be classified as conventional or government-backed. A **conventional loan** is any loan without government insurance or guarantees. **Government-backed loans** are just that—loans with some type of government backing.

The appraiser has to understand how real estate markets work to accomplish nearly every step of the valuation process. The real estate market consists of many individual (**specific**) markets—residential, commercial, industrial, agricultural, and special purpose markets. Specific real estate markets have submarkets. A **submarket** is a geographic, economic, or specialized subdivision of a market. **Market segmentation** is the process of identifying and analyzing submarkets within these larger markets.

Appraisers use many different dynamics in a **market analysis**. The appraiser studies **demographics**, or demography, to obtain statistical data for the market's population. Another important aspect of any real estate market analysis is the **absorption analysis**. By performing an absorption analysis, the appraiser determines how quickly a given property type should sell or rent. By forecasting project costs and profits in a **feasibility study** in conjunction with the above analyses, it can be determined if a certain housing project or commercial center is a worthwhile venture in a specific market.

UNIT 5 REVIEW

Matching Exercise

Instructions: Write the letter of the matching term on the blank line before its definition, and then check your response with the Answer Key that immediately follows the Multiple Choice Questions.

Terms

A. absorption rate

B. amortization

C. conforming loan

D. demography

E. equity

F. feasibility analysis

G. fiscal policy

H. imperfect market

I. market analysis

J. market segmentation

K. monetary policy

L. negative amortization

M. nontraditional mortgage product

N. note

O. primary mortgage market

P. purchase money loan

Q. reserve requirements

R. secondary mortgage market

S. security instrument

T. submarket

Definitions

1. _____ Owner's financial interest in real or personal property at a specific moment in time.

2. _____ Policy that influences the cost and availability of credit to promote economic growth, full employment, and price stability.

3. _____ Government policy on taxes and spending.

4. _____ Percentage certain percentage of each deposit in a bank that must be set aside.

5. _____ Market in which mortgage originators provide loans to borrowers.

6. _____ Market in which existing loans are bought and sold.

7. _____ Loan that is used to purchase property.

8. _____ Liquidation of a financial obligation on an installment basis.

9. _____ Any mortgage product other than a 30-year, fixed-rate mortgage.

10. _____ Increase in the principal balance caused by low monthly payments that do not pay all the interest due on the loan.

11. _____ Loan whose terms and conditions that follow the guidelines set forth by Fannie Mae and Freddie Ma.

12. _____ Written promise to repay a certain amount of money at a certain time, or in a certain number of installments.

13. _____ Legal document given by the borrower to hypothecate the property to the lender as collateral for the loan.

14. _____ Market that cannot meet the requirements for a perfect market.

15. _____ Process of identifying and analyzing submarkets within these larger markets.

16. _____ Geographic, economic, or specialized subdivision of a market.

17. _____ Process of identifying and analyzing submarkets within larger markets.

18. _____ Study of population statistics.

19. _____ Rate at which a type of property is either leased or bought by the market.

20. _____ Analysis of the cost-benefit relationship of an economic endeavor.

Multiple Choice Questions

Instructions: Circle your choice, and then check your response with the Answer Key that immediately follows the Multiple Choice Questions.

1. A synonym for money is capital. Capital consists of:
    a. debt and interest
    b. principal and interest.
    c. equity and debt.
    d. equity and interest.

2. Which statement is INCORRECT regarding fiscal and monetary policies?
    a. The Federal Reserve System is responsible for the monetary policy.
    b. The U.S. Treasury is responsible for the fiscal policy.
    c. Fiscal policy is the government policy on taxes and government spending.
    d. Fiscal policy promotes economic growth, full employment, and price stability.

3. The central bank of the United States is known as the:
    a. Federal Bank of America.
    b. United States Reserve.
    c. Federal Reserve.
    d. National Reserve.

4. Which of the following is true regarding the difference between debt investors and equity investors?
    a. Equity investors are passive and debt investors are active.
    b. Equity investors are active and debt investors are passive.
    c. Debt investors invest in higher risk investments than equity investors.
    d. There is no difference.

5. Which of the following is NOT considered a debt investor?
    a. Mortgage broker
    b. Credit union
    c. Bank
    d. Mortgage banker

6. Which of the following organizations is NOT a participant in secondary mortgage market?

    a. Freda Mae

    b. Fannie Mae

    c. Freddie Mac

    d. Farmer Mac

7. Lenders offer a variety of loans. Which type of loan is used to buy property?

    a. Cash-out refinancing

    b. Hard money loan

    c. Purchase money loan

    d. Refinancing

8. When a repayment schedule has a final payment that is significantly larger than the other payments, this final payment is known as:

    a. amortization.

    b. an interest-only payment.

    c. a balloon payment.

    d. a graduated payment.

9. Of the following, which is not a nontraditional mortgage product?

    a. Adjustable-rate mortgage

    b. 15-year, fixed-rate loan

    c. Graduated payment loan

    d. 30-year, fixed-rate loan

10. Mary has a graduated payment mortgage (GPM). If she had a fully amortized loan, her monthly payment would be $1,500. However, her scheduled payment is only $1,400. The difference of $100 a month:

    a. causes negative amortization.

    b. is added to the loan balance.

    c. increases the principal.

    d. does all of the above.

11. Jane wants to purchase a house for $200,000 using a conventional loan. What would be the minimum down payment if she does NOT want PMI?

    a. $15,000

    b. $20,000

    c. $40,000

    d. $80,000

12. Prime loans are also known as:
    a. "A" paper.
    b. "B" paper.
    c. non-conforming.
    d. hybrid.

13. Which type of loan exceeds the maximum conforming loan limit set by Fannie Mae and Freddie Mac?
    a. Conforming loan
    b. Jumbo loan
    c. Prime loan
    d. Sub Prime loan

14. Which type of government-backed loan has mortgage insurance?
    a. FHA loan
    b. conventional loan.
    c. VA loan
    d. both (a) and (c).

15. Appraisers are reprimanded if they fail to use specialized guidelines when preparing an appraisal for:
    a. friends and family.
    b. Ginnie Mae.
    c. FHA-backed loans.
    d. the Department of Veterans Affairs.

16. The maximum amount that the VA will provide a veteran for a home loan is called the:
    a. eligibility
    b. entitlement.
    c. guaranty.
    d. residual income.

17. Which of the following is responsible for the real estate market's inefficiency?
    a. Each property's uniqueness
    b. Real estate's illiquidity
    c. The limited supply
    d. All of the above

18. Which of the following is NOT one the five broad categories of real estate markets?

    a. Residual
    b. Industrial
    c. Special Purpose
    d. Agricultural

19. An "illiquid" property:

    a. has improper drainage.
    b. cannot be sold quickly for full value.
    c. has poor plumbing.
    d. is in a flood zone.

20. A new subdivision's first phase took a full year to sell and it contained 60 units. The next two phases contain 30 units each, and the appraiser concludes that the absorption rate will decrease by one third per year. How many more years will it take to sell the remaining units?

    a. 1 year
    b. 2 years
    c. 3 years
    d. 3 ½ years

UNIT 5 ANSWER KEY

Answers – Matching

1. E	6. R	11. C	16. T
2. K	7. P	12. N	17. I
3. G	8. B	13. S	18. D
4. Q	9. M	14. H	19. A
5. O	10. L	15. J	20. F

Answers – Multiple Choice

1. **(c)** A synonym for money is capital. Capital consists of equity (one's own money) and debt (borrowed money). **Page 142**

2. **(d)** The monetary policy influences the cost and availability of credit to promote economic growth, full employment, and price stability. It works by affecting demand across the economy. The fiscal policy is the government policy on taxes and government spending and affects demand. The Federal Reserve System is responsible for the monetary policy and the U.S. Treasury is responsible for the fiscal policy. **Page 143**

3. **(c)** The Federal Reserve System is the central bank of the United States. **Page 143**

4. **(b)** Typically, equity investors are active in the management of real estate. They have an ownership interest, and assume a relatively higher risk. Debt investors have a relatively passive role in the operation and management of the real estate. They seek conservative investments, with relatively little risk. **Page 145**

5. **(a)** Mortgage brokers do not fund loans themselves. Instead, they originate loans with the intention of brokering them to lending institutions. **Page 148**

6. **(a)** The major participants in the secondary mortgage market are the Fannie Mae, Freddie Mac, Ginnie Mae, and Farmer Mac. **Page 149**

7. **(c)** A loan that is used to purchase property is called a purchase money loan. It is used strictly for financing the purchase of real property. **Page 151**

8. **(c)** A balloon payment is the single, large payment that pays the remaining balance due. It is much larger than the previous payments because it includes all of the remaining principal and interest. **Page 152**

9. **(d)** Any mortgage product other than a 30-year, fixed-rate mortgage is called a nontraditional mortgage product. **Page 152**

10. **(d)** Negative amortization is an increase in the principal balance caused by low monthly payments that do not pay all the interest due on the loan. **Page 154**

11. **(c)**   When the loan exceeds 80% of the value of the property, lenders usually require private mortgage insurance (PMI) on conventional loans. This means Jane needs a $40,000 down payment (20%) to avoid PMI. **Page 156**

12. **(a)**   Conforming loans have terms and conditions that follow the guidelines set forth by Fannie Mae and Freddie Mac and are called "A" paper loans, or prime loans. **Page 156**

13. **(b)**   A jumbo loan exceeds the maximum conforming loan limit set by Fannie Mae and Freddie Mac. **Page 157**

14. **(a)**   The FHA does not make loans. It insures loans to protect the lenders who make the loans. On loans with less than a 20% down payment, the lender is protected in case of foreclosure by mutual mortgage insurance. **Page 158**

15. **(c)**   Appraisers are reprimanded if they do not use FHA guidelines when preparing appraisals for FHA loans. If an appraiser intentionally misrepresents the subject property's value on an FHA loan appraisal, and the inaccurate appraisal subsequently causes a loss, the appraiser could be fined and face legal action. **Page 159**

16. **(b)**   The entitlement is the maximum guaranty that the VA will provide for the veteran's home loan. It is shown on the Certificate of Eligibility. **Page 160**

17. **(d)**   Some of the causes of these inefficiencies include: the unique nature of real property, its illiquidity, uninformed buyers and sellers, its relatively high cost, the immobile nature of real estate, and the inflexible supply of real estate. **Page 168**

18. **(a)**   The five broad categories of real estate markets are residential, commercial, industrial, agricultural, and special-purpose. **Page 172**

19. **(b)**   Real estate is not liquid, which means that real estate assets cannot be quickly sold for full market value. **Page 170**

20. **(b)**   Between the two phases, there are 60 more units to sell. Year 1 sold 60 units. Year 2 will sell 40 units (two-thirds of 60), and Year 3 will sell the last 20 units (two-thirds of 40 is 26.67). So, it will take approximately two more years to sell the remaining 60 units. **Page 175**

The Appraisal Process

Unit 6

INTRODUCTION

Professional appraisers have developed an orderly, systematic method to arrive at an estimate of value. This method is known as the **appraisal process** or the valuation process.

Although, the appraisal process may be described in different ways, this text discusses five main steps of the appraisal process.

Steps in the Appraisal Process

1. Define the problem.

2. Determine the scope of work.

3. Collect, verify and analyze all relevant information.

4. Reconcile the information analyzed.

5. Report the assignment results.

This unit compares CMAs, BPOs, and appraisal reports and introduces the appraisal process. In the rest of the text, each step of the appraisal process will be explored in detail.

Learning Objectives

After reading this unit, you should be able to:

- identify key differences among CMAs, BPOs, and appraisal reports.
- identify the steps in the appraisal process.
- recognize the key parts of defining the problem.
- recognize the types of data appraisers collect and analyze.
- identify the approaches to value.
- recognize the reconciliation process and its role in appraisal.

CMA, BPO, OR APPRAISAL REPORT

Appraisers are not the only professionals who value property. Valuation services are services that pertain to some aspect of property value whether those services are performed by an appraiser or by someone else.

Although they appear similar on the surface, there are many differences between a comparative market analysis (CMA), broker price opinion (BPO), and an appraisal report. The central difference is that appraisers must follow a more stringent process in preparing an appraisal report than real estate brokers do when preparing a CMA or BPO. Brokers collect and analyze data, apply a version of the sales comparison approach, and report the results to their client. However, they do not follow any of the other steps in the appraisal process.

The goal of a comparative market analysis is to determine an appropriate LISTING PRICE for a property. The goal of a broker price opinion is to determine a PROBABLE SELLING PRICE of a property. An appraiser's goal is to develop an opinion of the VALUE of a property. Although a CMA can also serve as a ballpark estimate of value, an appraisal gives a carefully researched and documented opinion of value.

An even bigger difference can be seen when looking at the parties who create these reports. For a real estate licensee, creating a CMA is only a small part of the job. For an appraiser, creating an appraisal report is the job. Also, since the real estate agent's pay is tied to the price of the house, it could be argued that it is in the agent's best interest to come up with a high number. Appraisers are expected to give an unbiased and impartial analysis. In addition, USPAP's COMPETENCY RULE requires an appraiser, before accepting an assignment, to disclose any lack of knowledge and/or experience that would keep them from competently completing the appraisal assignment.

Comparative Market Analysis

Typically, a homeowner's first experience with any type of valuation service occurs when he or she sees a comparative market analysis (CMA). A **comparative market analysis** is a comparison analysis that real estate licensees use to help potential sellers determine an appropriate listing price for their property or to help buyers determine an appropriate offering price for a property.

To create a CMA when dealing with potential sellers, the real estate licensee finds recently sold houses that are similar to the seller's house in location, style, and amenities. These similar sales are called **comparable sales** or more simply **comps**. If there are any significant differences between the seller's house and the comps, the broker adjusts the selling prices of those properties to derive a market value range and an appropriate list price for the house. The CMA includes a summary of the features of the seller's house, photos of the house, and photos of the comparable houses. A CMA usually includes data on current listings, recently sold houses, and listings that expired recently. This helps the seller to see what other people are asking and what other people have received. They can also see which homes were left unsold because the asking price was too high. Once the seller and the real estate licensee have determined together an appropriate listing price for a property, the property is marketed.

Comps

Real estate licensees use CMAs to help prospective buyers determine an offering price for a specific property. The CMA shows recent closed sales of similar properties and their length of time on the market. This information helps buyers make an informed decision when writing an offer on a property.

Broker Price Opinion

A **broker price opinion** (BPO) is a written opinion of the probable selling price of a property. BPOs are often used by mortgage servicers or loss mitigation companies as an alternative to appraisals because they take less time and are less expensive than appraisals. Frequently, BPOs are requested when houses are in default, for home equity loans or refinancing, and for PMI removal. Usually, BPOs are prepared by licensed real estate agents, brokers, or appraisers for a fee. In some states, BPOs are considered appraisals and must be performed by licensed appraisers.

Broker price opinions are similar in methodology and report appearance to a comparative market analysis and, to a lesser degree, an appraisal. A BPO is usually 2-3 pages and includes specific information regarding the subject property and other properties offered for sale, in escrow, or recently sold within the same area. The two main types of BPOs are drive-by BPO and internal BPO.

Appraisal Report

The **appraisal report** is the appraiser's opinion of value, typically presented in a written format. The appraisal report will state or summarize the information that the appraiser has researched and analyzed. The appraiser's **workfile** for a particular assignment consists of all the documentation necessary to support the analyses, opinions, and conclusions conveyed in the appraisal report.

Lenders use an appraisal to ascertain how much a house is worth. Based on that amount, they then determine how much they are willing to loan. This protects the lender in case of default by the borrower. If a house is priced significantly higher than its appraised value, it can be very difficult to get a loan, since lenders do not want to lend on a house that is priced higher than it is worth. A buyer should think twice before purchasing a home if its price is higher than its appraised value. The buyer may not be able to resell it without losing money.

STEPS IN THE APPRAISAL PROCESS

Each appraiser follows the following steps to create an appraisal report.

1. **Define the problem.** This includes identifying the client and other intended users, the intended use of the appraiser's opinions and conclusions, the type and definition of the value sought, and the effective date of the appraiser's opinions and conclusions. The appraiser must also identify the property, relevant characteristics of the property, and any special or unusual conditions involved in the assignment.

2. **Determine the scope of work.** The scope of work in an assignment is essentially the amount of work that is done. Scope of work applies to the type and extent of research done and the type and extent of analysis applied. While defining the problem, the appraiser gathers the information needed to determine the scope of work.

3. **Collect, verify, and analyze all relevant information.** This includes collecting, verifying, and analyzing both general and specific data. For example, appraisers gather general information about any social, economic, physical, or governmental forces that may impact the value sought. They also collect specific data about the subject property and the comparables. This step also includes applying the relevant approaches to value—sales comparison approach, cost approach, and the income approach.

   The **Sales Comparison Approach** is the most straightforward of the three approaches, and it is typically the most accurate approach when appraising a residential property. Using the sales comparison approach, the appraiser compares the subject property with other, similar homes that have recently sold. By adjusting for any differences in size, amenities, etc., the appraiser is able to develop an opinion of the market value of the subject property.

   The **Cost Approach** values a property by determining what it would cost to replace the improvements, subtracting any deterioration or depreciation from that, and then adding the value of the site. **Improvements** are buildings or other structures that are permanently attached to the land. A **site** is land that has been prepared for use with grading, utilities, and access.

   The **Income Approach** is most accurate for valuing income-producing properties. Using the income approach, an appraiser estimates what an investor would pay for a property based on the income it produces.

Not every approach will apply to every assignment, so the appraiser must determine which approaches apply. Once the appraiser has determined this, he or she must analyze the data using the appropriate approaches.

4. **Reconcile the information analyzed.** Since the three approaches will not give the same exact value, the appraiser must reconcile the quantity of data available, the quality of the data analyzed, and the suitability of the approaches used to develop the most accurate final value estimate.

5. **Report the assignment results.** Once the appraiser has determined the final value estimate, he or she is ready to report to the client.

This structured, detailed, and systematic process is what sets appraisal apart from other valuation services.

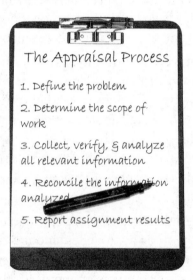

The appraisal process is made up of five basic steps.

Define the Problem

Defining the appraisal problem is the first step in the appraisal process. Appraisers need to identify the essential elements of the problem to be solved.

In order to define the problem, appraisers identify a variety of elements. This step includes identifying what property they are appraising, for whom they are appraising the property, and why they are appraising the property. They also need to identify relevant physical, legal, and economic characteristics of the property being appraised, the effective date of the appraisal, and any conditions or assumptions that need to be considered in the assignment.

Elements That Need Identification When Defining the Problem

- Client and other intended user(s)
- Intended use of the appraisal
- Type of value to be estimated
- Date of the value estimate
- Subject property and its relevant characteristics
- Any unusual assignment conditions

Identify the Client and Intended Users

One of the first things an appraiser needs to do when beginning an appraisal assignment is to identify the client. The **client** is the party, or parties, who hire the appraiser for a specific assignment.

> Example: In a typical appraisal assignment, appraisers are hired by the lender, not the buyer or seller, so the lender is the client.

Identification of a client in an assignment is necessary since the appraiser must know to whom he or she has a responsibility. In the course of completing an assignment, appraisers will often obtain information that is confidential in nature. Appraisers need to protect the legitimate interests of their clients about the use of otherwise confidential information.

Often clients order an appraisal with the intention that other parties will rely upon the report generated by the appraiser. Parties intending to use an appraisal are called **intended users** by USPAP. Appraisers need to identify all intended users of their appraisal reports in order to make sure their reports are meaningful to those parties.

> Example: A mortgage broker may order an appraisal from an appraisal management company with the intention of giving that appraisal, along with other documentation, to a wholesale lender. The wholesale lender will use the appraisal to help determine whether they will make a loan on the property. The mortgage broker is the client, and the wholesale lender is an intended user.

Identify the Intended Use

Along with identifying the client and the intended users, the appraiser must identify the intended use of the appraisal. This lets the appraiser know why he or she is being hired to appraise the property.

Appraisals are requested for many different reasons. They are often performed in order to obtain financing for a real estate purchase. Appraisals are also done in order to settle estates and for use in lawsuits. They may be requested for property tax purposes, condemnation purposes, or for a variety of other reasons.

Appraisers need to identify the intended use of an appraisal in order to know the amount of detail needed in the appraisal report and what types of information should be gathered.

Identify the Type of Value to Be Estimated

Appraisers need to know which type of value they are being asked to analyze in an appraisal assignment. The type of value provides the context upon which a value estimate is based. To simply state that a property is worth $250,000 is relatively meaningless. That could be market value, insurable value, investment value, or possibly even sentimental value. Many types of value may be identified in an appraisal assignment and appraisers need to be aware of the kind of value they are to estimate.

Within each type of value, there are also differing definitions.

> Example: Most of the time, appraisers are requested to develop an opinion of the market value of a property. Market value usually centers on the concept of most probable price. Sometimes however, the definition of market value may be based upon the concept of highest price. This slight change in wording in the definition could have a significant effect upon the final value estimate.

Different kinds of value or different definitions of value produce different value estimates. In order to produce a value estimate meaningful to the client, appraisers need to identify the exact type and definition of value they are using in the appraisal assignment.

Identify the Date of the Value Estimate

Appraisers need to know the effective date of the appraisal. The effective date of an appraisal can be a present, past, or future date. Think of an appraisal as being a snapshot in time, like a photograph. If you were to view a snapshot of yourself at age 10, that picture would appear much different from photos taken at age 20, 30, or 40. Estimating the value of a property as of April 14, 1975 would produce a very different value for that property than if the value were based upon current market expectations.

In most instances, the effective date of an appraisal is the date it is inspected by the appraiser. In this situation, the effective date for the value is the present. In some instances however, the effective date of value is at some point in the past, or may even be at some point in the future.

A **retrospective appraisal** looks at the value of a property at a point of time in the past. A retrospective appraisal could also be used to find the value of a house that has since burned down.

> Example: When appraising properties for estate and probate purposes, appraisers are typically requested to appraise a property as of the date of death of the property owner. It is not unusual for an appraiser to be contacted by an estate attorney 6 months or even a year after the owner died. In instances such as this, the appraiser would not be analyzing the market as it currently is, but as it was at some point in the past.

A **prospective appraisal** looks at the value of a property at a future point of time. Appraisers are sometimes asked to perform a prospective appraisal.

> Example: Properties that are fully rented are usually more valuable than properties that are vacant. New, high-rise office buildings typically have few tenants upon completion of construction. It may take years to fill up that building with tenants. Clients may wish to identify what that high-rise office building may be worth once it has become filled with tenants at some point in the future.

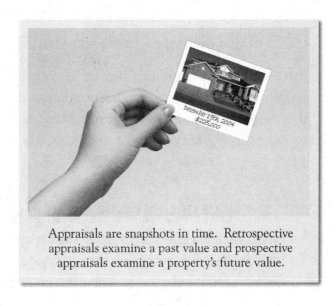

Appraisals are snapshots in time. Retrospective appraisals examine a past value and prospective appraisals examine a property's future value.

Other times, an appraiser might be asked to determine if houses should be built for sale in a particular area. Part of the appraiser's work would be to value the houses as if they were finished. This is a common request from lenders who are providing construction loans.

Identify the Subject Property

The property being appraised is called the **subject property**. Appraisers obviously need to know what property they are appraising, but identifying the property that is the subject of an assignment is not always as easy as one may think. Simply knowing the address of the subject property may not be enough to identify the subject property. Sometimes the property to be appraised is vacant land and has no address. In other instances, the subject of an assignment has only one address but includes multiple distinct parcels of land. Sometimes the owners do not have legal descriptions to their properties but they know that it is the "third property from the corner on the north side of the street."

Some appraisers have mistakenly appraised the wrong subject property because it was incorrectly identified to them. Although the appraiser needs to include enough information in the appraisal report to identify the subject, clients may not always be clear in communicating this information to the appraiser. The appraiser needs to be careful to avoid confusion in this area.

Identify Any Special Assignment Conditions

In some instances, there are certain conditions and assumptions that need to be identified in an assignment. These conditions and assumptions significantly affect how appraisers perform their work. A **hypothetical condition** is defined in USPAP as "that which is contrary to what exists on the effective date of the assignment results, but is supposed for the purpose of analysis." An **extraordinary assumption** is defined as "an assumption, directly related to a specific assignment, as of the effective date of the assignment results, which, if found to be false, could alter the appraiser's opinions or conclusions." These two types of limiting conditions may occur together or separately.

> Example: Appraiser John was asked to appraise a property that is currently under construction. In this assignment, he is appraising the property as if it were complete even though it is not. In fact, the building only exists on blueprints. Essentially, he is appraising an imaginary structure. This is an example of a hypothetical condition. This kind of analysis is usually required to assist a lender in deciding whether to make a construction loan.

In other cases, appraisers need to make assumptions where they do not know all the facts.

> Example: Appraiser Jane was asked to appraise a property that is located near another property that has hazardous waste contamination. There is no information available indicating whether or not the subject property is also contaminated. If there is no evidence to the contrary, she may base her appraisal on the fact that the subject is not adversely affected. This is an example of an extraordinary assumption.

Hypothetical conditions and extraordinary assumptions are covered in more detail in the 15-hour USPAP course that is required for individuals who want to become licensed appraisers.

Determine the Scope of Work

It is necessary to identify these elements in order to determine the scope of work in the assignment. The scope of work in an assignment is essentially the amount of work that is done. Scope of work applies to the type and extent of research done and the type and extent of analysis applied.

> Example: More in-depth research, verification, and analysis are usually required of appraisers appraising homes for litigation purposes than is required of those appraising the same kind of property for loan purposes.

This is because the needs of clients in these instances are different. The scope of work varies from property to property and from assignment to assignment

Reasons Why Scope of Work Varies
- Degree to which property is inspected or identified
- Extent of research into physical or economic factors that could affect the property
- Extent of data research
- Type and extent of analysis applied to arrive at opinions or conclusions

Some appraisals merely require a drive-by visual confirmation that the subject exists. Others require an in-depth, painstaking analysis of the property's operating statement as well as comparable properties' operating statements.

Depending on the scope of work, an appraisal may require only a drive-by property verification or it may require a detailed interior inspection.

Collect, Verify, and Analyze All Relevant Information

Once the appraiser has defined the appraisal problem and determined the scope of work, he or she needs to collect and analyze data applicable to that assignment. In the process of determining the scope of work, the appraiser will be able to identify the amount and kind of data needed in the appraisal assignment.

The amount and kind of data needed to appraise a property varies by assignment and property type. The amount and kind of data an appraiser would gather to appraise a high-rise office building would be drastically different from the data required to estimate the value of a single-family home.

Collect Data

Data is collected and gathered from many sources. When collecting data for an appraisal assignment, appraisers start from a broad, market-wide base and gradually focus more and more on the subject.

They gather general data regarding items affecting the subject's market. This includes general economic, demographic, environmental, and sociological information affecting markets and trends in specific real estate markets. Next, they collect information on local area and neighborhood employment, income levels, trends, access, and convenience of location. Finally, they gather specific data for both the subject and comparable properties.

Appraisers analyze all these levels of data because most factors that influence a property's value occur outside of the subject property itself.

> Example: If Sally's house is identical to Joe's house, Joe's house may still be worth more if it is located in a different neighborhood.

General Data Sources

A substantial amount of data is collected and published by federal, state, and regional government agencies.

National data can be obtained from government publications, newspapers, and magazines. Federal government agencies such as the U.S. Census Bureau and the U.S. Department of Commerce provide a wealth of demographic and employment information.

State offices such as transportation agencies, departments of housing and community development, and departments of commerce and economic development may provide information regarding future development, employment trends, income levels, etc.

Regional data (metropolitan areas such as San Francisco Bay, Southern California, or the Central Coast) can be gathered from monthly bank summaries, regional planning commissions, and government agencies.

Local Data Sources

Community data (town or city) can be obtained from the Chamber of Commerce, City Planning Commission, city government agencies, banks, and real estate boards. Local agencies such as building departments, zoning departments, planning and land use departments, health departments, property tax assessor's offices, county recorder's offices, chambers of commerce, etc., provide a wealth of data regarding local economies and trends, as well as information on both the subject property and comparable sales. Among other things, these local agencies provide information regarding such items as building permits, property zoning information, property tax information, environmental issues, sewage disposal information, and recording information. Information obtained from these sources is often free. However, appraisers may need to travel to the offices to obtain needed information.

Neighborhood data can be obtained from personal inspections, real estate agents, or area builders. The appraiser notices the age and appearance of the neighborhood; any negative influences such as physical or social hazards (run-down buildings, evidence of criminal activity); evidence of future development; and proximity to schools, businesses, recreation, and transportation.

Specific Data Sources

Appraisers must also gather data about the specific property being appraised. In addition, specific data must be collected and analyzed for sales and listing prices of comparable properties in the area.

When determining the value of a particular house, appraisers consider the general condition and age of the house, the size of the building and the surrounding land, the location of the house (including its view or any other remarkable features), the features of the home (e.g. number of bedrooms and bathrooms), any major improvements or additions to the property, and any features that are especially sought after (like a fireplace or a skylight).

Appraisers gather the same kinds of information on the comparable sales or rental comps used in an assignment by either a personal inspection or a drive-by inspection from the street.

Appraisers can verify the legal description of the subject property and comparable properties from county records. They can also double-check the age of the buildings and other information regarding improvements at the tax assessor's office or city building department.

Sales information is usually obtained from data sources such as local multiple listing services (MLS), real estate agents and brokers, property buyers and sellers, county assessor's offices, title companies, on-site sales offices, private data providers offering both online and published sales data, and the appraiser's own database.

Review – Information Gathered for Appraisals

General Data	Local Data	Specific Data
National	Community	Condition of Subject
State	Neighborhood	Comparable Sales
Regional		

Verify Data

Once all the data has been obtained by the appraiser, it is checked for both accuracy and reliability. Some data sources are updated rarely and may be out of date. Sometimes information obtained from one data provider conflicts with data obtained from another source. Appraisers need to make a determination regarding which data sources are the most reliable and which should be given more credence.

An appraiser may also find that, in the course of uncovering one piece of information relevant to an assignment, other items are uncovered that may require additional research.

> Example: Upon verifying building permits for a property, an appraiser may find a permit for environmental remediation. This permit would indicate that property probably had some kind of adverse environmental influence. Additional research by the appraiser would then be needed to identify the problem, the work performed, and its possible effect on value.

The scope of work may need to be increased when additional information is uncovered in the course of an assignment.

Analyze Data

With all of the pertinent facts at hand, the appraiser needs to analyze how the information applies to the value of the subject property. There are three commonly accepted methods used to value real estate. They are the sales comparison approach, the cost approach, and the income approach. Each of these approaches to value has strengths and weaknesses in any given assignment.

Often one or two of these approaches are not performed in an assignment since they may not be applicable to that particular assignment. Even if all three approaches to value are applicable in an assignment, usually one has the greatest significance in the valuation problem.

The "how to" details for each of these approaches will be covered later in this text. Here, we will cover a basic definition of the approach.

Sales Comparison Approach

The **sales comparison approach** is the process of developing an opinion of value by using sales of similar properties to estimate the value of the subject property. These similar sales are called  comparable sales (or more simply comps), and they should be as similar to the subject property in location, style, and amenities as possible. This approach is most useful when a large number of similar properties have recently sold within the subject's market and sales information is readily available.

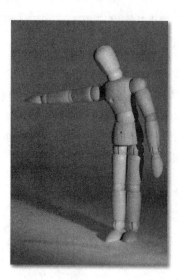

The sales comparison approach uses the comparable property's sales price as an indicator of its market value. For the sales price to be an accurate indicator, the sale must have been an arm's length transaction. An **arm's length transaction** is one in which neither the buyer nor the seller is acting under duress, the property is on the market for a reasonable length of time, and the buyer and the seller both have reasonable knowledge of the property's assets and defects. If there is any indication that the sale was not an arm's length transaction, it should not be used as a comp.

Sometimes it is easiest to understand arm's length transactions by looking at what they are not. A sale is not an arm's length transaction if it has been forced for any reason or if there is some other motivation that would affect the selling price. Foreclosures, tax sales, and estate liquidations are all forced sales. Transactions that are motivated by the need to purchase adjoining property or the need to sell property before the owner is transferred would not be arm's length transactions. In addition, if the buyer and seller are related individuals or corporations, the appraiser must assume that the relationship affected the terms of the sale and prevented it from being an arm's length transaction.

Once the appraiser has found similar properties that sold under normal circumstances, the next step is to collect data on the comparable properties. Typical areas of comparison include property rights being conveyed, financing terms, neighborhood location, square footage, number of bedrooms and bathrooms, age, and architectural style.

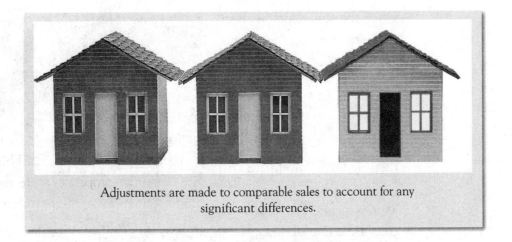

Adjustments are made to comparable sales to account for any significant differences.

The appraiser gathers information on both the subject property and the comps and notes the differences. Then, the appraiser analyzes each comparable property in turn. He or she starts with the sales price of the comparable property and adjusts it for any differences to arrive at the market value for the subject property. The more similar a particular comp is to the subject, the stronger it is as an indicator of value for that subject property.

Cost Approach

As its name implies, the **cost approach** is the process of determining value by adding up the costs involved. This process is based upon the premise that the value of a new building is equal to the cost of the land on which it was built plus the cost of actually building it. When using  this approach on buildings that are not brand new, the appraiser also has to subtract the amount of depreciation that has occurred. **Depreciation** is a loss in value from any cause.

The starting point of this approach is to identify the value of the land component of a property. Typically, recent comparable sales of vacant land are found and are used as indicators for the value of the subject's site. This portion of the cost approach is similar to the sales comparison analysis in that the comparable land sales are adjusted to reflect the differences between those properties and the subject property. Differences such as size, zoning, location, access to utilities, and view are items attributable to a site that appraisers would consider in the adjustment process.

Once the site value has been estimated, the cost to replace or reproduce the existing improvements is estimated. This information can be obtained from a variety of sources. Depreciation is then deducted from the cost estimated for the subject's improvements. The depreciated

cost of the improvements is added to the land value to get the value estimate for the property.

The cost approach is used most often for appraising new buildings and special-purpose or unique structures. This is because depreciation on a new building is relatively easy to determine, so the cost approach is at its most accurate. Also, it is difficult to find comparable sales for buildings that are unique or one-of-a-kind, such as a church, fire station, or hospital, so the cost approach is used with these types of buildings.

Occasionally, the cost approach is the only one an appraiser can use even with residential property. If there have been no recent sales (such as during a recession or when interest rates are very high), there will be no comparables for the sales comparison approach. If the subject is not an income-producing property, the income approach cannot be used. So, the cost approach is a reliable way for an appraiser to arrive at the value of a property when other options are not available.

There are situations where the cost approach is not reliable, however. The cost approach is impractical with older buildings because of the difficulty in estimating depreciation. Also, because the cost approach calculates value by adding the value of the land to the depreciated value of the improvements, this approach may not apply to properties with special ownership interests.

> Example: Condominium owners own their particular unit and have the right to use common areas. The land is not sold with the condo, so condominiums cannot be valued using the cost approach.

Income Approach

The **income approach** is the process of determining value based on the amount of income that the property is expected to produce. The income approach to value is based upon the premise that the more income a property generates for its owner, the more valuable it is. This approach recognizes a direct relationship between the value of a property and the income it is expected to produce.

This method is used to estimate the value of income-producing property, like apartment and office buildings. Single-family residences usually do not generate income (unless the property is being rented), and most single-family residential properties are not purchased for their income-producing potential. Even though an appraiser may use the income approach to value when appraising a single-family residence, it would typically be given little weight in the final estimate of value. It would be necessary, however, for the appraiser to mention this in the appraisal report.

The income approach to value uses mathematical techniques to identify the present value of future benefits from ownership of a property. There are two simple calculations that are the basis of this approach.

Value = Gross Income × Gross Income Multiplier

Value = Net Operating Income ÷ Capitalization Rate

The first calculation is called a gross income multiplier calculation. **Gross income** is total annual income received before any expenses are deducted. Sale prices of comparable properties are divided by the gross income they generate to provide a multiplier. The multiplier indicated by the comparable sales is multiplied by the subject property's gross income to provide a value estimate.

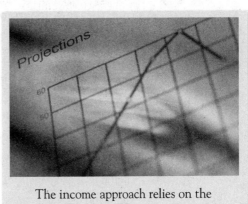

The income approach relies on the anticipation of future income.

Using the second calculation typically involves more detailed and in-depth analysis on the part of the appraiser. Net operating income (NOI) is used instead of gross income. **Net operating income** is gross income minus operating expenses. The net income a property is forecasted to generate over time is divided by a capitalization rate to produce a value estimate. A **capitalization rate** (cap rate) is the appraiser's estimate of the rate of return a property will produce on the owner's investment. The cap rate is used to determine the present value of the property's future earnings. Choosing a capitalization rate is the hardest part for appraisers using the income approach.

To use this approach, an appraiser needs to collect data that will enable him or her to estimate the subject's potential gross income, the loss in potential gross income due to expected vacancy and collection losses, anticipated operating expenses, the pattern of a property's anticipated income, the anticipated resale value of a property at some point in the future, and competitive investments available to potential investors in real estate.

Reconcile the Information Analyzed

The next step in the valuation process is reconciliation of the various approaches to value into a final value estimate. **Reconciliation** is the process of analyzing the values obtained using the different approaches in order to develop an opinion of the final estimate for the property in question. During the reconciliation process, the appraiser reviews his or her work and considers: (1) the scope of work, (2) the quantity and quality of the data collected in each approach, (3) the inherent strengths and weaknesses of each approach, and (4) the relevance of each approach to the subject property and market behavior.

Many times an appraiser will use all three methods to arrive at the market value of a property. In most appraisals, all three approaches will have something to add. Each method is used independently to reach an estimated value.

Among the various approaches to value employed in an assignment, the reconciliation process is used to identify which one provides the strongest and most reliable indication of value. In some instances, one or two of the approaches may not provide strong nor reliable indicators of value.

> Example: Since most single-family residential properties are not purchased for their income producing potential, an appraiser estimating the market value of a single-family residence would typically give little weight to the income approach in the final estimate of value. In this case, the sales comparison approach would be given the most consideration in determining the final estimate of value.

Reconciliation can also be used within a particular approach. When reconciling within the various approaches, the appraiser makes a determination about which data provides the strongest and most reliable indication of value. The data providing the strongest and most reliable indication of value would therefore be given most consideration in a particular approach.

> Example: An appraiser using the sales comparison approach may find that, of the comparables used, Comparable Sale #1 is overall most similar to the subject property. Therefore, that sale would be given the most weight in determining the value of the subject property using this particular approach.

The reconciliation process depends upon the nature of the subject property; the approaches to value that were used in the assignment, and the reliability of the value estimates indicated by the various approaches to value.

Sometimes the appraiser gets to this final step and finds it difficult to state the value. This happens when the appraiser is missing a vital piece of information, and – deep down – knows it. When this happens, it is time to stop the procedure, and go back to the point where the information is missing. This may require the appraiser to make more inquiries or another trip to the field.

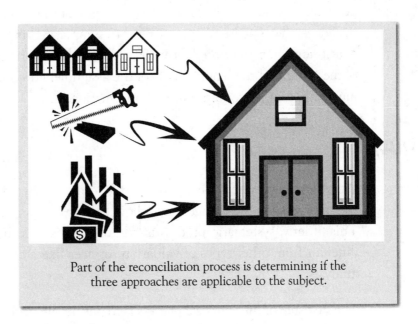

Part of the reconciliation process is determining if the
three approaches are applicable to the subject.

Report the Assignment Results

Once the appraiser has completed formulating his or her opinions and conclusions, the final task is to communicate those assignment results to the client. This is accomplished by presenting either a written or an oral report.

The appraisal report is the expression of the appraiser's service to the client. It usually includes the data considered and analyzed, the methods and approaches used, and the reasoning that to led the final value estimate of the property. Proper reporting allows the reader to understand the appraisal problem and the scope of work performed. This includes the data considered in formulating the opinion of value and the reasoning employed by the appraiser in estimating the final estimate of value for the subject.

The detail and style of report is determined when the appraiser and client first meet to discuss the client's needs and decide on the scope of work. Although most clients require written reports, there are some instances, such as courtroom testimony, where an oral report is requested.

Depending upon the needs of the client, the intended use of the appraisal, and the kind of property being appraised, appraisal reports may go into significant detail and include hundreds of pages of documentation and analysis. In other instances, the appraiser may only need to summarize his or her opinions and conclusions on a preprinted form. There are even situations where the needs of the client and the requirements of the assignment are such that the report must only contain certain minimal information.

SUMMARY

Professional appraisers have developed an orderly systematic method called the **appraisal process** that they follow to arrive at an **estimate of value**. This orderly, systematic process is one of the reasons that an appraisal is different from other types of valuation services like a **comparative market analysis**.

The first step of the appraisal process is to **define the problem**. To do so, the appraiser determines the client, the intended use, and the type of value to be estimated, the date of the value estimate, the subject property, and any special assignment conditions.

The next step in the appraisal process is to **determine the scope of work**. The scope of work varies from property to property and from assignment to assignment.

The third step in the process is to **collect, verify, and analyze the data.** Significant quantities of data must be collected from different sources, whether it is general data, local data, or specific data. The data must be properly analyzed in order for the appraiser to come to an accurate value conclusion. The appraiser analyzes the data using the three approaches to value. The appraiser can use any combination of three different approaches to value the subject, depending on which approaches are applicable to the assignment.

If more than one approach was used, step four is for the appraiser to **reconcile** the different values produced by each approach. When only one approach is used, the appraiser still needs to verify and review the appropriateness, the accuracy, and the quantity of evidence, as well as ascertain that the problem originally defined has been solved and that the predetermined scope of work has been met.

Finally, after a supportable conclusion has been reached, step five is to convey the appraiser's findings to the client, usually by way of a **written appraisal report.**

UNIT 6 REVIEW

◻ Matching Exercise

Instructions: Write the letter of the matching term on the blank line before its definition, and then check your response with the Answer Key that immediately follows the Multiple Choice Questions.

Terms

A. appraisal process	I. intended users
B. arm's length transaction	J. prospective appraisal
C. broker price opinion	K. reconciliation
D. client	L. retrospective appraisal
E. comparative market analysis	M. sales comparison approach
F. comps	N. scope of work
G. extraordinary assumption	O. workfile
H. hypothetical condition	

Definitions

1. _____ Orderly, systematic method to arrive at an estimate of value.

2. _____ Analysis that real estate licensees use to help potential sellers determine an appropriate listing price for their property or to help buyers determine an appropriate offering price for a property.

3. _____ Similar properties used in the sales comparison approach to estimate the value of the subject property.

4. _____ Written opinion of the probable selling price of a property.

5. _____ Consists of all the documentation necessary to support the analyses, opinions, and conclusions conveyed in the appraisal report.

6. _____ Party who hires the appraiser for a specific assignment.

7. _____ Parties intending to use an appraisal.

8. _____ Appraisals that look at the value of a property at a point of time in the past.

9. _____ Appraisals that look at the value of a property at a future point of time.

10. _____ That which is contrary to what exists but is supposed for the purpose of analysis.

11. _____ Assumption, directly related to a specific assignment, which, if found to be false, could alter the appraiser's opinions or conclusions.

12. _____ Type and extent of research done and the type and extent of analysis applied in an appraisal assignment.

13. _____ Process of determining value by using sales of similar properties to estimate the value of the subject property.

14. _____ Transaction in which neither the buyer nor the seller is acting under duress, the property is on the market for a reasonable length of time, and the buyer and the seller both have reasonable knowledge of the property's assets and defects.

15. _____ Process of analyzing the values obtained using the different approaches in order to determine the final estimate for the property in question.

Multiple Choice Questions

Instructions: Circle your choice, and then check your response with the Answer Key that immediately follows the Multiple Choice Questions.

1. Regarding valuations services, CMAs, and BPOs, which of the following statements are true?
   a. Valuation services are performed by appraisers and brokers perform CMAs.
   b. CMAs are different from BPOs in that only brokers can perform BPOs.
   c. CMAs, BPOs, and appraisals are all types of valuation services.
   d. CMAs, BPOs, appraisals, and valuation services are all one in the same.

2. When using CMAs, if there are significant differences between the seller's house and the comps, a broker will:

    a. adjust the selling prices of the comparable properties.

    b. adjust the selling price of the subject property.

    c. tell the seller there are no comparable properties.

    d. not take the listing.

3. Broker price opinions are similar in methodology and report appearance to a:

    a. workfile.

    b. summary appraisal report.

    c. oral report.

    d. comparative market analysis.

4. If a house is priced _____ than the appraised value, lenders may _____.

    a. lower, not fund the loan

    b. higher, not fund the loan

    c. same as, not fund the loan

    d. lower, require mortgage insurance

5. Identifying the client, the definition of value, and the effective date are all included in which step of the appraisal process?

    a. Identify the assignment

    b. Determine the scope of work

    c. Define the problem

    d. Reconciliation

6. Parties intending to use an appraisal report are known as:

    a. clients.

    b. intentional users.

    c. customers.

    d. intended users.

7. Social forces are an example of:

    a. general data.

    b. economic influence.

    c. specific data.

    d. physical influence.

8. Sam was hired to appraise a house in a tax dispute on July 11, 2011. The dispute was over how much property tax the owner should have paid in November, 2005. The completed report was submitted to the tax authority on August 1, 2011 and used in a court proceeding on August 16, 2011. Which of the following is the effective date of the appraisal?

   a. July 11, 2011
   b. November, 2005
   c. August 1, 2011
   d. August 16, 2011

9. If Bill hires Frank to appraise the value of vacant land as if it were fully developed with an apartment building, this would be considered a(n):

   a. effective appraisal.
   b. retrospective appraisal.
   c. prospective appraisal.
   d. objective appraisal.

10. Donna, an insurance appraiser, is hired to appraise a residence that recently burned down. When Donna appraises the home as if it were still in existence, she is using:

    a. a hypothetical condition.
    b. a retrospective appraisal.
    c. a limiting condition.
    d. all of the above.

11. When verifying data, should an appraiser encounter conflicting information, he or she must:

    a. determine which source is more reliable and give it more credence.
    b. ignore both pieces of data.
    c. count both pieces of information without explanation.
    d. count both pieces of information with brief explanation.

12. Which of the following is important when choosing comps for sales comparison analysis?

    a. All comparable sales should be arm's length transactions.
    b. All comparable sales should be similar in location to the subject.
    c. All comparable sales should be similar in style to the subject.
    d. All of the above are true statements.

13. Which of the following is NOT a typical application for the cost approach?

  a. Post office, library, hospital
  b. 40-year old tract home
  c. Brand new office complex
  d. Frank Lloyd Wright inspired mansion

14. Which of the following is the formula used when calculating the income approach?

  a. Gross income multiplied by net income multiplier equals value.
  b. Net operating income multiplied by cap rate equals value.
  c. Net operating income divided by cap rate equals value.
  d. Net income multiplied by net income multiplier equals value.

15. When should an appraiser use reconciliation in the appraisal process?

  a. In every instance
  b. Only when two or more approaches to value are used
  c. Only when there is conflicting information
  d. When he or she is having difficulty expressing a property value

UNIT 6 ANSWER KEY

Answers – Matching

1.	A	5.	O	9.	J	13.	M
2.	E	6.	D	10.	H	14.	B
3.	F	7.	I	11.	G	15.	K
4.	C	8.	L	12.	N		

Answers – Multiple Choice

1. **(c)**   Although they appear similar on the surface, there are many differences between a comparative market analysis (CMA), broker price opinion (BPO), and an appraisal report. The central difference is that appraisers must follow a more stringent process in preparing an appraisal report than real estate brokers do when preparing a CMA or BPO. **Page 186**

2. **(a)**   If there are any significant differences between the seller's house and the comps, the broker adjusts the selling prices of those properties to derive a market value range and an appropriate list price for the house. **Page 187**

3. **(d)**   Broker price opinions are similar in methodology and report appearance to a comparative market analysis and, to a lesser degree, an appraisal. **Page 88**

4. **(b)**   If a house is priced significantly higher than its appraised value, it can be very difficult to get a loan, since lenders do not want to lend on a house that is priced higher than it is worth. A buyer should think twice before purchasing a home if its price is higher than its appraised value. **Page 188**

5. **(c)**   The step called "define the problem" includes identifying the client and other intended users, the type and definition of the value sought, and the effective date of the appraiser's opinions and conclusions, among others. **Page 189**

6. **(d)**   Often clients order an appraisal with the intention that other parties will rely upon the report generated by the appraiser. Parties intending to use an appraisal are called intended users by USPAP. **Page 191**

7. **(a)**   When collecting and analyzing information, appraisers gather general data including social, economic, physical, or governmental forces that may impact the value sought. **Page 189**

8. **(b)**   In most instances, the effective date of an appraisal is the date of inspection. In some instances however, the date of value is at some point in the past, which makes it a retrospective appraisal. **Page 193**

9. **(c)**   A prospective appraisal looks at the value of a property at a future point of time. **Page 193**

10. **(d)**   A hypothetical condition is that which is contrary to what exists but is supposed for the purpose of analysis, which is what Jaime is doing for the purpose of this insurance appraisal. Also, a hypothetical condition is a type of limiting condition. Since she is appraising the property as it was before it burnt down, this also becomes a retrospective appraisal. **Page 194**

11. **(a)**   Sometimes, information obtained from one data provider conflicts with data obtained from another source. Appraisers need to determine which data sources are the most reliable and deserve more credence. **Page 199**

12. **(d)**   When choosing comparable properties for analysis, select comps that are arm's-length transactions because non-arm's-length transactions do not truly reflect the market. Also, select properties that are as similar to the subject as possible to minimize the need for adjustments. **Page 200**

13. **(b)**   The cost approach is used most often to appraise new buildings and special-purpose or unique structures. A post office, library, and hospital are all classified as special-purpose and famous architectural buildings are considered unique. **Page 202**

14. **(c)**   Two simple calculations are the basis of the income approach: (1) Value = Gross Income $\times$ Gross Income Multiplier and (2) Value = Net Operating Income $\div$ Capitalization Rate. **Page 203**

15. **(a)**   Though the definition of reconciliation refers to the analyzing of the three value approaches, it also includes revisiting the scope of work, the quantity and quality of the data collected in each approach, the inherent strengths and weaknesses of each approach, and the relevance of each approach to the subject property and market behavior. These steps should be taken in every assignment even if only one approach is used. **Page 204**

Highest and Best Use & Site Valuation

Unit 7

INTRODUCTION

In the appraisal process, the first step of data collection and analysis is to determine the highest and best use of the subject property. Closely related to this step is developing an opinion of the value of the land or site separately from the value of any improvements. This unit discusses both of these different, but interrelated ideas.

Appraisers often need to develop an opinion of the value of a site. There are many different reasons for this. Sometimes the subject property is a vacant lot. At other times, the subject property has improvements, but the appraiser needs to ascertain the land value separately in order to apply the cost approach or the income approach's building residual technique. Site value may be needed in appraisals done for taxation purposes or condemnation proceedings.

This unit focuses on site value, and the most important factor that influences site value. The highest and best use of a particular site has a direct effect on its value and on the property's overall value.

This unit does not cover every aspect of site value. However, this unit covers in detail the different contributing factors that influence land value. These factors include the afore mentioned highest and best use, physical aspects such as size, shape, soil and topography, as well as off-site factors like utilities and access.

The information presented applies to assignments in which vacant land is being appraised, as well as in situations where the land has been developed and built upon, but the value of the land needs to be identified separately.

Learning Objectives

After reading this unit, you should be able to:

- recall the tests of highest and best use and how they influence site value.
- designate the correct order of applying the four tests.
- differentiate between a site and a tract.
- recognize physical aspects that influence site value.
- designate lot descriptions based on their shape and placement.
- recall offsite factors that may influence site value.

INFLUENCE OF HIGHEST AND BEST USE ON SITE VALUE

The concept of highest and best use is one of the most important and least understood principles in real estate appraisal. The highest and best use of a property, more than anything else, is what determines its value. **Highest and best use** is the use, from among reasonably probable and adequately supported alternative uses, that meets four tests.

Four Tests of Highest and Best Use
1. Physically possible
2. Legally permitted
3. Economically feasible
4. Maximally productive

When appraising a property, an appraiser first has to determine highest and best use. He or she does this with a site analysis and by applying the four tests. Appraisers cannot value land if they do not understand how the land is best used. They apply the four tests to vacant land (or improved property as if it were vacant) and to improved property.

The same process of analysis applies to each of these situations. The following examples demonstrate how important it is for the appraiser to analyze highest and best use in order to develop an opinion of the property's market value, whether the property is vacant or improved.

Example 1:

Highest and best use strongly influences land value. To illustrate this point, assume a site is currently improved with only a single-family dwelling; however, the zoning allows ten apartment units. The value of this land would, in most instances, be less if it were valued as a single-family lot than if it were valued as an apartment site. Typical buyers or sellers would consider its potential as an apartment site when making their buying or selling decisions.

Example 2:

In one Southern California community, many vacant lots flanked a major east-west thoroughfare. These were large parcels—5, 10, even 20 acre lots. Gradually, as the local and regional economies picked up, the lots sold and major corporations began building corporate headquarters and large office complexes on these lots. The last vacant lot in this area produced strawberries up until last year. Currently, it is being developed into a similar office complex.

Due to the growing economy and changing demands, these lots have the capacity to produce income. It is no longer prudent to leave them vacant. Moreover, it is not in the highest and best use of the land to grow strawberries. Growing strawberries produced some income, but a more profitable use is now possible. Building corporate headquarters and office complexes represents that highest and best use. When the economy is growing and demand is present, the use of land will transition to produce a greater net income.

Example 3:

A similar situation occurred in another community located in Southern California. A mobile-home park had a 50-year lease on beachfront land. When the lease expired, the owners of the land thought there might be a higher and better use. They did their research and went through all of the legal processes with the city council and public participation. They are now developing plans for a hotel resort community that will include major hotels, condominiums and a park. Although leasing to a mobile-home park produced decent income, the new use of the land will produce more income.

Example 4:

Improvements are valued according to how they contribute to (or detract from) the value of the land. If a property is not already at its highest and best use, a building may need renovation. In other situations, a building may demolished to make way for a replacement that would make the property more valuable.

Consider an older, run-down, single-family house in an area zoned for commercial use. If there is a greater demand for residential property than that of commercial, it most likely will benefit the owner to remodel the house and make it a rental. In fact, if residential demand is great enough, the highest and best use might be to expand the rental into a duplex to create more income. Then, as commercial demand increases, converting the house into office space may produce the best revenue opportunity. However eventually, if demand for conventional retail buildings becomes high enough, demolition and reconstruction becomes the most prudent alternative.

Sometimes highest and best use is easy to determine. Other times, it is not so clear. Through the four tests, a property's highest and best use is determined. Much of the highest and best use analysis is a study of cost/benefit relationships. Each of the tests will yield or eliminate alternative uses that may be possible but not plausible because of the costs associated with transforming the property.

A property's value may benefit from renovation, remodeling, or even demolition of the improvements.

Physically Possible

Every site has physical characteristics that determine its highest and best use. Some properties have value-enhancing views and frontages like beach or lake properties. Other properties are limited by poor access, steep topography, or unstable soil. The site may have poor drainage and require an expensive type of septic system. It may be in the path of urban growth or in the middle of nowhere.

Sometimes you have to balance the positive and negative attributes. For example, an ocean front property may have geologic problems that require special foundation work, but the value of the ocean frontage may be worth the expense.

The first test for highest and best use is to verify if the use is physically possible.

Legally Permitted

Current zoning and other land use regulations normally define **legally permitted** uses. As previously discussed, zoning is the legal way a municipality or local government regulates the use of privately owned real property. These restrictions govern property use (commercial or residential applications), height restrictions for buildings, signage height and size restrictions, and parcel and lot sizes. They also regulate setbacks for fences and buildings from property lines, as well as the number of units that are allowed to be built within an area.

There are many different types of zoning laws and classifications. **Zoning laws** execute general plans and control the mix of properties in a particular area. Most local governments include organizations that are responsible for planning and zoning. Generally, the Planning Commission develops a general plan and the City Council / Board of Supervisors adopts and implements the general plan.

Zoning is not the only legal barrier an appraiser needs to consider. There are also easements and restrictions that may limit the property's legal uses. For example, the developer may have included a condition that prohibits the sale of alcohol on the land. This would certainly preclude a liquor store or bar as the highest and best use of the subject property.

Often, if zoning prevents a certain use, the owner can petition for a zoning change. However, this is costly, so the appraiser must analyze and determine the cost versus the benefit of implementing these changes.

Local zoning laws will determine if a current or proposed use is legally permissible.

Non-Conforming Uses and Use Permits

Legally non-conforming uses are those uses that are **grandfathered** when new zoning regulations are adopted. Legally non-conforming uses can change the highest and best use and often produce a higher value than what the current zoning ordinance will allow.

> Example: James opens a convenience store in an area zoned for mixed residential and commercial use. A few years later, the city council rezones the neighborhood to allow only single-family homes. Although the store is now a non-conforming use, James may operate his business as a legally non-conforming use.

Most zoning ordinances allow non-conforming uses to continue until they fall out of use for a period (usually one year) or they are destroyed by fire, disaster, or neglect.

Typically, the local zoning authority issues **conditional use permits** or **variances**. These permit certain uses that are not otherwise allowed in a certain zoning district, but which are beneficial to the community. A city may grant conditional use permits to daycare centers, parking lots, and churches in residential zones.

> Example: Amy wants to have a pool installed in her backyard. However, her city has a zoning ordinance that requires swimming pools in R1 residential zones to be set back at least 25 feet from the property lines. The dimensions of Amy's

property do not provide adequate space to place a pool 25 feet from the rear property line. Amy can apply for a variance permitting her to install the pool only 20 feet from the property line.

Interim Use

Interim use is a short-term and temporary use of a property until it is ready for its expected highest and best use.

Example: If a ten-acre lettuce field gets rezoned R-1, the highest and best use would be single-family homes. However, there may already be hundreds of lots on the market and little or no demand for them. Until the market can support more single-family homes, its interim use will remain a lettuce field.

Economically Feasible

The principle of supply and demand is the basis for **economic feasibility**. This often requires extensive market research and the accurate prediction of trends. This entails finding out who the competition and the potential buyers, tenants, and customers are.

Franchise operations such as McDonald's and Starbucks have made a science out of location studies. They analyze traffic patterns and study community age and income profiles. In this way, they have been able to successfully predict financial feasibility and effectively operate many different locations within a concentrated area.

The test of economic feasibility is highly dependent
on current supply and demand trends.

Maximally Productive

A **maximally productive use** produces the greatest return on investment. For income property, determining the highest rate of return might involve studying several alternatives and design configurations.

> Example: It has been determined that the highest and best use for a site is an apartment complex. Determining its maximum production would include distinguishing the appropriate mix of one, two, and three bedroom apartments the property can sustain; whether or not to have laundry facilities or hookups built into each apartment; garages or centralized parking, etc.

Even when building or remodeling a house, there are ways to determine what will produce the highest value. If the owner decides to build a four-car garage in a neighborhood typically consisting of two-car garages, it may be considered an over-improvement, even if it serves his personal interests. If he under-improves, like eliminating a garage in favor of a large garden, he may not be creating the highest value either.

A residence located in a commercial district most likely will not be maximally profitable.

> **Review – Four Tests of Highest and Best Use**
> Physically possible
> Legally permitted
> Economically feasible
> Maximally productive

Application of the Tests

The convention is that these criteria usually be considered sequentially, as a process of elimination. A use may be economically feasible but this is irrelevant if it is physically impossible or legally prohibited. Only when there is a possibility that one of the prior, unacceptable conditions can be changed is it appropriate to proceed with the analysis. For example, if current zoning does not permit a potential highest and best use, but there is a possibility that the zoning can be changed, the proposed use can be considered in that case.

Order of the Application of the Four Tests
1. Physically possible
2. Legally permitted
3. Economically feasible
4. Maximally productive

Physically possible and legally permitted aspects are considered together, but for the sake of semantics, physically possible considerations edge out legally permitted ones as the primary consideration in the sequence. This is because if a potential use were contrary to the laws of nature, considering the other three criteria would be futile. Legally permitted uses are checked next. Many zoning laws will limit the property's uses to a few or even one use, thus eliminating multiple options. Remaining possibilities are then analyzed for economic feasibility and finally maximum production.

> Example: Joe is appraising a vacant lot located in a commercial district. He immediately supposes that some variety of commercial use would most likely meet the highest and best use for this property. However, upon investigation, he discovers that it is zoned non-commercial, which leaves only agricultural, residential, and industrial possibilities. Because of the nature of the soil on the lot, an agricultural use is not physically viable, not without expensive soil cleaning or importation, the cost for which far exceeds the benefit. Appraiser Joe also determines that any type of residential use would not be economically feasible because there would be significant loss in demand due to its commercial surroundings. After analyzing the surrounding area, he deduces that local businesses have a need for a storage and distribution facility and concludes that a warehouse would yield the best production of the remaining industrial options for the site, as there is virtually no competition for this type of use.

Non-Economic Highest and Best Use

Analyzing the property on as many levels as possible will lead to the most thorough and sound result possible. An appraiser may need to consider one other highest and best use consideration. There is a controversy within the appraisal profession and conservation movement regarding something termed **non-economic highest and best use**. According to this belief, sometimes the highest and best use does not necessarily produce the most income, but instead takes into account the contribution of a specific use to the community and community developmental goals. These uses include parks, greenbelts, open spaces, wetlands, wildlife habitats, and other types of natural lands.

Land that is at a non-economic highest and best use is for community enjoyment.

Although the support for this type of highest and best use is on the rise, there exist no widely accepted methods of estimating non-economic value. Current appraisal practice requires that properties are appraised based on their conventional economic use (residential, commercial, industrial, etc.) regardless of their conservation potential.

PHYSICAL ASPECTS INFLUENCING SITE VALUE

When the appraiser shows up at the subject property, it must first be determined if it is a tract or a site. A **tract** is a piece of land in an unimproved state, i.e. it does not have utilities, sewer lines, etc. It is not ready to build on. Once a tract has been prepared for construction, it becomes a **site**.

Once a tract has been prepared to be built upon, it becomes a site.

The appraiser must be able to describe the site in the report based on its physical characteristics and any neighborhood characteristics that affect the site. It is also important for the appraiser to be able to distinguish between favorable and unfavorable characteristics and to determine their affect on the value of the property.

Size

The size of a site is a key factor in determining its value because the size influences how the site may be used. For example, zoning laws may require that a property meet certain size requirements before development of the land can commence.

Appraisers can often find the size of the appraisal site in official legal documents. Acres or square feet make up the measurements for size in appraisal.

However, legal documents do not report the usable area of the site, which is more important than gross area. **Usable area** is the portion of the site that is suitable for building. Some areas of the site may not be usable because the soil or topography cannot support buildings. Usable areas can be limited also by zoning regulations such as setback requirements.

If the size of a particular piece of land limits its utility, the limitation can be overcome in various ways.

Assemblage and Plottage

Land is often worth more as one entirely incorporated and unified unit than it is as a number of divided individual parcels. **Assemblage** is the process of combining two or more small sites to form a larger one. This usually happens with income or commercial properties in order to create a larger building, with higher income, on the larger site.

> Example: Imagine a major farming enterprise. To become more efficient, it would try to control as many adjacent acres as possible. As it acquires more lots to add to its farmland, the total of the entire body as a single site exceeds the value of the individual lots that comprise it.

Plottage is the added value that results from the assemblage process.

> Example: Each of the separately owned businesses in one block of a major metropolitan area is viable and generates good income. When the lots are appraised as if vacant and divided, they are valued at approximately $400,000 total. A developer wanting to build a large luxury hotel with conference rooms and other business related facilities hires an appraiser to perform a feasibility study for such a venture. The appraiser finds that lots similar to the size of the combined individual parcels are valued from at least $500,000. This indicates that the plottage of the assembled lots would be $100,000 minimum.

Assemblage does not always result in higher land values. Sometimes, the assembled lot will result in a lower value than the combined values of the separate lots.

Excess and Surplus Land

Excess land (for an improved site) is the land not needed to serve or support the existing improvement. For a vacant site (or site considered vacant), excess land is land beyond that which is needed to support the property's highest and best use. FHA Guideline 4150.2 (4-4) states that excess land is larger than is typical in the neighborhood and is capable of a separate use. Excess land may be separated from the larger site and have its own highest and best use, or it may allow for future expansion of the existing or anticipated improvement.

Conversely, **surplus land** is land that is not necessary to support the highest and best use of the existing improvement. Additionally, it cannot be sold off separately due to physical limitations, building placement, or neighborhood norms. Surplus land might contribute positively to value and might allow for future expansion of an existing or anticipated improvement.

> Example: A house is situated on a 100' residential double lot which is larger than the typical 50' lot in the neighborhood. If the 100' lot can be subdivided legally into two 50' front sites, it is excess land. However, if the house is located on a 75' lot in an area that only allows 50' front lots (or larger), it surplus land because it cannot be separated.

Shape

After estimating the size of the parcel of land, the **shape** of it comes into play. The appraiser should note its shape in a geometric form if possible. The shape of a site can affect both its usable area and its overall utility. Lot descriptions are based on their shape and placement.

A **cul-de-sac lot** is located on a dead-end street. A cul-de-sac (dead-end street) has no other outlet except by the entrance. Cul-de-sac lots may be oddly pie-shaped if they are on the turn-around section of the street. They are desirable for residential use because of the privacy and quiet. The lack of access makes them less desirable for industrial or commercial purposes.

A **corner lot** is at the intersection of two streets. It may be desirable for a gas station or convenience store because of its accessibility and visibility, but may also be noisy and expensive to maintain because of the increased frontage. Usually, a corner lot is less desirable for residential use due to lack of privacy, noise, and potential pollution from multiple sides.

A **key lot**, so named because it resembles a key fitting into a lock, is surrounded by the back yards of other lots. It is the least desirable because of the lack of privacy and visibility.

A **T-intersection lot** is fronted head-on by a street. The noise and glare from headlights detract from this type of lot for residences, but these same influences may make it desirable for commercial use.

An **interior lot** is surrounded by other lots, with frontage on the street. It is the most common type of lot and may be desirable or not, depending on other factors.

A **flag lot** looks like a flag on a pole, with the pole representing the access to the site. The lot is usually behind another lot fronting a main street and has access and visibility problems.

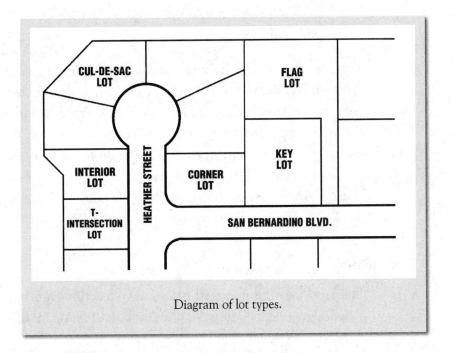

Diagram of lot types.

Soil and Topography

The composition of the soil determines the ability of the soil to support the weight of the building. There is a great deal of variation in soil composition in different parts of the country, and the appraiser must be familiar with the local conditions. Soil formation is a product of time, climate, and the characteristics of the native plants and animals.

The **topography** of a parcel of land refers to its contours and features. Terms like flat, hilly, rolling, and sloping (moderately or severely) all describe the site's topography. Topography also includes items like creek beds or swamps that may be on the parcel of land.

The site's topography can affect its value. A site may decrease in value if the irregular topography decreases the usable area or makes it difficult for construction. However, sometimes irregularities can actually increase property value. For example, a home built on hilly land may have a good view of the surrounding area that can significantly increase the value of the home.

Drainage and Flood Hazards

The site's soil and its topography affect the site's drainage. **Drainage** refers to natural processes or artificial pipes and drains that remove water and moisture from land. Drainage helps to keep water from building up on a parcel of land and flooding a home.

The appraiser should be aware of hazardous drainage conditions not only for the inspected parcel but also for other neighboring land that may drain onto the inspected parcel. The **Federal Emergency Management Agency (FEMA)** is a government agency that is involved with all the different aspects of emergency management from preparation to recovery and prevention. As a part of its work, FEMA identifies flood-prone areas called **Special Flood Hazard Areas**. Appraisers note in the appraisal report whether the subject property is within a flood hazard zone.

Grading

The land must be prepared before any structures are built on a lot. This includes grading, building retaining walls and foundations, and landscaping.

Grade is the slope of the surface of the ground expressed as a percentage. An example would be a 2% grade, where the slope climbs 2 feet for every 100 feet of horizontal distance. Sometimes the level or elevation of the ground has to be changed or altered using bladed machines that literally scrape the earth in a process known as **grading**.

Grading is important so that water runs away from the foundation and the structure itself. If the pitch or slope of the soil is toward the house, basements or crawlspaces may flood during storms, and damage to the foundation may occur over time.

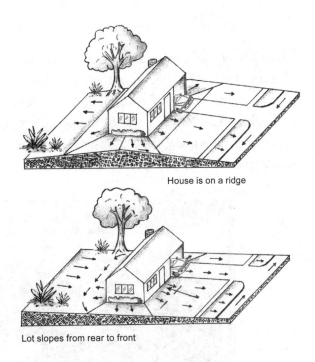

House is on a ridge

Lot slopes from rear to front

Diagram of typical grading methods.

Retaining Walls

Retaining walls hold back earth. They are built where elevation changes on a property and soil must be held back from falling down. Retaining walls come in many material types and have some type of reinforcement. There are numerous guidelines for their construction. They also should have drainage by means of spaces or holes in the face of the wall or drain tiles at its base.

Landscaping

Landscaping is the use of vegetation around a house to prevent erosion and improve its aesthetic appearance (curb appeal). **Curb appeal** is the visual appeal of a property when viewed from the street. Appropriate landscaping usually increases the value of a property. Sometimes, poor landscaping causes structural damage. For example, improperly planted trees could allow roots to penetrate the foundation or branches to hang over the roof.

Different types of landscaping are appropriate for different climate zones. For example, desert climates use a form of landscaping known as **zeroscaping**, because it needs little or no water. Another type, **xeriscaping**, achieves water efficiency by using plants appropriate for the natural environment.

View

The **view** of the surrounding area can be one of the most favorable physical characteristics for a property. Views that usually increase value include those of mountains, water (ocean, lake, river, etc.), golf courses, greenbelts, and city lights. Obviously, views of industrial property or refuse dumps are not appealing. Either way, the appraiser should note in the report if there is a view that could affect the property value.

A property's view can have a positive influence on value.

Off-Site Factors Influencing Site Value

Real estate is immobile. "Therefore, the value of a given parcel of land is affected by factors outside its boundaries. These **off-site factors** include the uses that are made of neighboring parcels, the quality of public services (e.g., schools, parks, and police and fire protection), and the availability and quality of off-site infrastructure (e.g., water, sewer, utility, and transportation systems). All of these off-site factors originate outside of a particular parcel of real estate.

Utilities

Public utilities originate off-site, so they are off-site factors. However, appraisers should note whether utilities are available to the property when inspecting the site. The utilities in question include municipal water service or wells, electrical service, and/or solar panels. Utilities also refer to storm sewer or septic systems, solid waste disposal systems like trash removal, and natural gas or bottled propane. Amenities such as telephone and cable television service are included in this category as well.

Utilities are an important value component.

Utilities can be above ground or below ground. If the visual inspection does not reveal which ones are present, the appraiser should interview the property owner to find out which ones may be present. The appraiser can also contact the city or municipality in which the property exists to confirm which utility services are used.

Access

Another key off-site factor is **access**. Accessible land is more valuable than inaccessible land. The appraiser must note the **ingress** (entrance to the site or property) and **egress** (exit from the site or property) and how they contribute to the property's use. This is important because accessibility directly relates to a site's use potential or value if developed.

Traffic volume of the surrounding area can also affect the access to a parcel. The **traffic volume** is the number of cars and pedestrians that travel by a location in a given span of time. Generally, high traffic volume benefits a retail location and negatively affects a residential location.

Traffic flow can also be a factor in an appraisal. Not only does it produce noise and air pollution, in some areas traffic tends to bog down, causing a hazard for residents of surrounding areas. Poor flow or movement of traffic can adversely affect the value of a home.

SUMMARY

Highest and best use is a foundational concept that appraisers apply every time they value a property. Regardless of its current use, a site is always valued at its highest and best use—the use that is **physically possible**, **legally permitted**, **economically feasible**, and **maximally productive**.

When analyzing a property's highest and best use, appraisers consider **vacant land or improved property as if it were vacant**, and **property as improved**. Valuing a site separately from its improvements is also necessary when finding the land value component for the cost approach, and is an important factor in other uses as well.

There are many different physical characteristics and features of a site that appraisers need to consider in order to determine the highest and best use and value of a site. Similarly, appraisers gather legal and financial information to analyze as well. Determining highest and best use is a process of weighing alternative uses.

UNIT 7 REVIEW

Matching Exercise

Instructions: Write the letter of the matching term on the blank line before its definition, and then check your response with the Answer Key that immediately follows the Multiple Choice Questions.

Terms

A. assemblage

B. cul-de-sac

C. curb appeal

D. drainage

E. excess land

F. grading

G. highest and best use

H. ingress

I. maximally productive use

J. plottage value

K. site

L. surplus land

M. topography

N. tract

O. usable area

Definitions

1. _____ The use, from among reasonably probable and adequately supported alternative uses, that is physically possible, legally permitted, economically feasible, and maximally productive.

2. _____ Use that produces the greatest return on investment.

3. _____ Piece of land in an unimproved state, i.e. it does not have utilities, sewer lines, etc. and is not ready to build on.

4. _____ Parcel of land ready for construction.

5. _____ Portion of the site that is suitable for building.

6. _____ Process of combining two or more small sites into a larger one.

7. _____ Increment of change between a parcel's value as divided, compared to its value as one unified unit.

8. _____ Land not needed to serve or support the existing improvement.

9. _____ Land that is not necessary to support the highest and best use of the existing improvement.

10. _____ Dead-end street.

11. _____ Contours and features of a parcel of land.

12. _____ Natural processes or artificial pipes and drains that remove water and moisture from land.

13. _____ Changing the elevation of the ground using bladed machines.

14. _____ Visual appeal of a property when viewed from the street.

15. _____ Entrance to the site or property.

Multiple Choice Questions

Instructions: Circle your choice, and then check your response with the Answer Key that immediately follows the Multiple Choice Questions.

1. What is the primary factor that determines a property's value?
    a. Its highest and best use
    b. The cost of its improvements
    c. Its proximity to the beach
    d. Its zoning

2. A property is at its highest and best use when it is:
    a. at its most legally permitted state.
    b. most profitable while being possible both physically and legally.
    c. physically feasible.
    d. vacant.

3. Which of the following tests of highest and best use would a business operating in a residential neighborhood most likely violate?
    a. Economically feasible
    b. Physically possible
    c. Legally permitted
    d. Maximally productive

4. A church in the middle of an area zoned for single-family residences is an example of:
    a. a legally nonconforming use.
    b. a variance.
    c. an interim use.
    d. non-economic highest and best use.

5. Converting a gas station into an orange grove would NOT be:
    a. economically feasible.
    b. physically possible.
    c. legally permitted.
    d. maximally productive.

6. Tom drives to the subject property and discovers that it is vacant except that there are major utility hook-ups installed. On his report, Tom would identify the subject as a:
    a. parcel.
    b. tract.
    c. site.
    d. lot.

7. Mary purchases two adjoining lots. Her appraisal estimates that the value of the lots combined into a single lot will almost double the total value of lots if kept separate. This added value is known as:
    a. yield.
    b. assemblage.
    c. plottage value.
    d. acreage.

8. The most common type of lot is a:
    a. cul-de-sac lot.
    b. corner lot.
    c. interior lot.
    d. flag lot.

9. Each of the following is an off-site improvement, except:
    a. a retaining wall.
    b. access.
    c. zoning.
    d. utilities.

10. Heavy traffic in front of a property may adversely affect:
    a. noise and air pollution.
    b. ingress.
    c. egress.
    d. all of the above.

UNIT 7 ANSWER KEY

Answers – Matching

1. G	5. O	9. L	13. F
2. I	6. A	10. B	14. C
3. N	7. J	11. M	15. H
4. K	8. E	12. D	

Answers – Multiple Choice

1. **(a)** The highest and best use of a property, more than anything else, is what determines its value. **Page 216**

2. **(b)** Highest and best use is the use, from among reasonably probable and adequately supported alternative uses, that meets these four factors: physically possible, legally permitted, financially feasible, and maximally productive. "Most profitable" implies both financial feasibility and maximal productivity. **Page 216**

3. **(c)** Legally-permitted uses are normally defined by current zoning and other land use regulations. An area zoned for residential use would not typically permit a business use. **Page 219**

4. **(b)** Most zoning ordinances allow the local zoning authority to issue conditional use permits or variances, which permit certain uses that are not otherwise allowed in a certain zoning district, but which are beneficial to the community. **Page 220**

5. **(b)** Gas stations contaminate the soil. Therefore, cultivating any type of crop on contaminated soil is physically impossible in the context of highest and best use (HBU). Because the first step in determining HBU is to test if a site is physically possible, all other tests are inconsequential if it cannot pass the first step. **Page 219**

6. **(c)** A site is a piece of land that either has been built on already or is ready to build on. **Page 224**

7. **(c)** Assemblage is the process of combining two or more small sites into a larger one. The added value that results from this process is called plottage value. **Page 224**

8. **(c)** An interior lot is surrounded by other lots, with frontage on the street. It is the most common type of lot and may or may not be desirable, depending on other factors. **Page 227**

9. **(a)** A retaining wall is an on-site improvement. While aspects of the other choices may exist on-site, their origins are off-site, and therefore they are classified as off-site improvements. **Page 229**

10. **(d)** Ingress (access to the property) or egress (exit from the property) as well as noise and air pollution most likely will be negatively affected by heavy traffic volume. **Page 231**

Inspecting the Subject Property

Unit 8

INTRODUCTION

One of the most important parts of the data collection process is the inspection of the subject property by the real estate appraiser. Depending on the intended use of the appraisal, the on-site inspection may involve driving by the property or actually entering the house, measuring it, and photographing it.

Previously, we covered key features and characteristics of the site itself. This unit covers the key features and characteristics of the improvements, i.e., buildings, located on the site. Most appraisers start their career appraising single-family residences, so inspecting and describing a home is the focus of this unit. Although the process is similar, an appraiser inspects and describes different characteristics when appraising other types of buildings.

Learning Objectives

After reading this unit, you should be able to:

- recognize architectural styles of houses.
- choose the appropriate definitions for substructure and superstructure.
- recall the elements of a visual inspection of the exterior of a dwelling.
- indicate the interior features of a dwelling that are included in a visual inspection.
- determine the mechanical systems used in a home.
- recall contributory value of onsite improvements.

INSPECTING THE PROPERTY

To illustrate what an appraiser's property inspection is, first we will explain what it is not. An appraiser's inspection of a house is significantly different from one done by a home inspector. Appraisers perform unbiased valuation services for their clients; whereas home inspectors work in the interest of the homebuyer. A home inspector never assigns value; he or she merely examines the home for defects or signs of possible defects. Home inspectors perform a much more thorough inspection to different standards.

When an appraiser is appraising a property for an FHA-backed loan, the FHA (Federal Housing Administration) requires that appraisers must disclose any defects uncovered through customary inspection to the client. General ethics also dictate this practice. However, appraisers are not responsible for issues or adverse conditions undetectable by the standard visual walk-through.

An appraiser's inspection includes a general description of the structure and a visual inspection of the exterior and interior of the dwelling. In a typical appraisal, the appraiser measures, sketches, and photographs both the exterior and interior of the home. Appraisers also look at the mechanical systems and equipment within the home, as well as the car storage available, and any other site improvements that may affect the home's value.

When appraising a new home or appraising a home from the plans, an elevation sheet for the home can aid the appraiser. The **elevation sheet** is a labeled diagram or cutaway of the home detailing its features and building components, both interior and exterior.

Throughout the inspection, the appraiser judges the condition and quality of the building. Terms such as "good" or "average" are used to describe features that are adequate and equal in quality and utility to that same feature in similar homes. "Fair" or "poor" are used to describe features that are less than adequate and below average for that neighborhood. In order to judge effectively the condition and quality of the building and its features, an appraiser must have at least a general knowledge about the different aspects of house construction and the advantages and disadvantages of each.

General Description

When an appraiser arrives at a site, one of the first things he or she notices is the type of home and its architectural influence or design. The **type of home** refers to the number of stories—one, one-and-one-half, two, split-level, or multi-level. **Architectural design** is the cohesive element that blends the structural, functional, and decorative elements of a property into a whole.

Appraisers should have a basic understanding of the different architectural designs of the homes in their area. This gives appraisers a perspective on which homes are appropriate comparables for the subject of the appraisal. In some neighborhoods, only a few styles may be present, whereas others may exhibit a wide variety of architectural styles.

It is important that the subject property's architectural design is harmonious with other homes in the immediate neighborhood. There may be considerable variety in the architectural design of the homes in a neighborhood and yet each may present a pleasing appearance when viewed in relation to its surroundings. On the other hand, a home may be without any architectural faults and yet clash so violently with the design of neighboring properties that marketability may be seriously limited.

Housing styles continuously change. The architectural design of the home affects its value in some cases because trends occur in architecture and interior design as in anything else. As a result, the cute Cape Cod in perfect condition may be "in" and sell very quickly, or be "out" and begging for a buyer.

Most houses built since the late 1970s do not fall into a single category. Instead, designers and builders incorporate decorative details and features from many of the previous historic styles. Sometimes only one style is used to influence the house. Other times, the ideas are taken from more than one architectural source and create an eclectic mixture that is difficult to categorize. Whether one or more features are chosen, the result alludes to, but does not mimic, the historic styles. These styles are called **Postmodern** or **Neo-Eclectic**.

Ranch Styles

Since its debut in San Diego in 1932, the **Ranch** style house has become the most popular style in the country. Ranch style houses are one-story, rambling, rectangular, L-shaped or U-shaped, with a low-pitch gable or hipped roof, attached garage, stucco, wood, or brick  exterior walls, picture windows, and sliding doors leading to patios. Due to the horizontal nature of the style, these houses need wide lots. These homes are built on raised foundations with a very shallow crawlspace or directly onto a concrete slab-on-grade foundation.

A **Raised-Ranch** style house has two stories. The lower story is at ground level or partially submerged below grade. From the main entrance, a full flight of stairs leads to the main living areas on the upper level. It allows for more livable square footage because the basement is partially above ground and usually finished with extra bedrooms and/or a bonus room.

 The **Split-Level Ranch style** is a variation of the Ranch style. Instead of just one level floor plan, split-levels usually have three levels at varying heights. The mid-level entry has stairs leading to the other two levels. The upper level is used for sleeping areas; the mid-level has the living room, dining room, and kitchen, while the lower level has the family room, hobby or game rooms, laundry area, and the garage. These houses are asymmetrical, with a rectangular, L-shaped, or U-shaped design. The low-pitched roof may be hipped or gabled. Any siding may be used, but the most common is stucco or wood siding with brick or rock trim.

Mediterranean Style

The **Mediterranean** style is the blend of the Italian, Moorish, Byzantine, and the early California mission styles. This style utilizes white or light-colored stucco on the exterior and a red tiled gable roof with very little or no overhanging eaves. Additional features include arched doorways and windows, courtyard entrances, patios, ornamental tile, and wrought iron ornamentation.

This is a single story Ranch with Mediterranean influences (low pitch, red tile roof, arched, recessed entry to resemble a courtyard).

This house has a red tile roof and stucco as seen in the Mediterranean style.

This house exemplifies the mixed look of the Mediterranean style.

Cape Cod Style

The **Cape Cod** home is usually rectangular-shaped, one to one-and-one-half stories, and has a steeply pitched gable roof with a small overhang. The multi-paned windows with ornamental wood shutters are placed symmetrically on both sides of the front door. Masonry chimneys are usually located at the side. Aside from shutters, this style has very little ornamentation and no front porch. The garage is detached and placed at the back of the lot.

Colonial Styles

Colonial style homes are rectangular, symmetrical, two to two-and-one-half story houses with windows arranged in an orderly fashion around a central front door. Living areas are on the first floor, with bedrooms on the second floor. The windows usually have many small, equally sized square panes and decorative shutters. Typically, roofs are hip or gable.

Variations of the Colonial style home include Colonial Revival, Georgian, Regency, Federal, Dutch Colonial Revival, Spanish Colonial Revival, and the Florida Caribbean.

Colonial Revival homes feature wood exteriors with tall wood columns that typically are painted white. On occasion, this type of home may have a brick exterior. In the 1920s and 1930s, the Colonial Revival was the most popular revival house style in the United States. The **Georgian Colonial Revival** style has paired chimneys (one on each side) and five windows across the front of the second story. The **Regency** style is very similar to the Georgian except it has an octagonal window over the front door, double-hung windows, and a chimney on the far left or right side of the house. The **Federal** style is similar to the Georgian except it has more ornamentation, dentil moldings, decorative garlands, Palladian-style windows, and fanlights.

Like all of the colonial styles, the **Dutch Colonial Revival** houses are one to two-and-one-half stories with shed-like dormers. They are identified easily by a distinctive **gambrel roof**. The front door may be a **Dutch door**, which is a horizontally divided double door.

Typical to the colonial style, the **Spanish Colonial Revival** houses are rectangular, symmetrical, and two stories high. They have low-pitched gable roofs with ceramic tiles, eaves with little or no overhang, stucco walls, wrought iron, and windows and doorways with round arches.

Although predominantly a Classic Revival style, the **Florida Caribbean** homes reflect the influence of Bahamian, African, Creole, and Victorian design. Typical to the Florida Keys area, these homes incorporate a bit of everything from New England down the southeastern seaboard, including Cuba and the Bahamas. These one to two-and-a-half story, wooden homes are handcrafted. They include such elements as shell infused walls to keep the interiors cool, wooden gables and posts, and spacious verandas with simple balustrades. Many details such as ship's walks, crow's nests, and roof hatches for ventilation were adopted from the shipping and fishing industries.

Victorian Styles

The term **Victorian** describes many styles built between the 1830s and early 1900s. This style is known for its elaborate bric-a-brac, excessive gingerbread, trim work, and other ornamentation. Three popular Victorian styles are the Queen Anne, Folk Victorian, and Second Empire.

Queen Anne homes have multiple stories with projecting wings, a complicated roofline with very steep cross-gabled roofs, towers, turrets, vertical windows and balconies, multiple chimneys with decorative chimney pots, scrollwork, bric-a-brac, gingerbread, and gingerbread with frosting. Queen Anne style houses usually have several wide porches with turned posts and decorative railings. The wood siding is painted white or pastel with contrasting trim and it probably has a round tower or enormous round bay windows.

The **Folk Victorian** style is the affordable version of the Queen Anne house. They are asymmetrical, rectangular, or L-shaped, with white wood siding, steep gabled roofs, and a front porch with turned spindles. They are adorned with flat jigsaw cut trim in a variety of shapes and patterns. These practical houses are found in small towns and farms across the United States.

Second Empire style houses are symmetrical, boxy, and two-to-three stories. Typical ornamentation includes paired columns and elaborate wrought iron along the rooftop. The most striking feature is the high, boxy **Mansard roof**, which allows more usable living space in the upper story. The windows are tall and narrow with no shutters. The exterior walls are usually stucco, brick, or wood siding.

Bungalow Styles

Bungalows are one of the most common houses found in older neighborhoods and are characterized by simplicity and emphasis on horizontal rather than vertical lines. The bungalow style remains one of the most popular styles even today and can be seen influencing new residential developments.

California Bungalow

The **California Bungalow** has a low profile, with one to one-and-one-half

stories, a square shape, with a low-slung gable or hip roof, an offset entry with a wide front porch, and exterior walls finished with stucco and natural stone. These smaller, affordable bungalows were very popular between 1900 and the mid-1920s. Currently, this look is incorporated into modern houses.

Craftsman Bungalow

The **Craftsman Bungalow** is larger than the traditional California Bungalow. Other differences include rows of high, small "ribbon" windows, full-width porches framed by tapered columns, and overhanging eaves with exposed rafters. Craftsman Bungalows frequently include built-

ins, such as window seats, and dining room buffets, and partial walls with bookshelves used as room dividers.

Period Styles

Period styles get their inspiration from the architectural styles of the past. In the early half of the 20th century, the trend was toward historical interpretations of European styles. Many styles existed, but some period styles were very popular throughout the country.

Monterey

The first two-story **Monterey** style was built in 1853 when Thomas Larkin designed a house that blended the English Colonial with the single-story Spanish Colonial style, which was then prevalent in Monterey. The most distinguishing feature of the Monterey style is the second-story balcony on

the front of the house. The over-hanging balcony creates a shaded, protected entry. These houses often have a courtyard and wrought iron trim and fencing. The roof is a shallow pitched gable or hipped roof with red tiles or wood shakes. Windows are often tall and in pairs with false shutters.

Mission

Since the **Mission** style house originated in California, the style is often called the California Mission style. These houses are easily recognized by the round parapets on the roof. A **parapet** is a low wall projecting from the edge of a platform, terrace, or roof. They are one to two stories, rectan-

gular shaped, and have flat roofs with red tile accents. The exterior walls are adobe or smooth stucco. Most Mission style houses have arched windows and a small courtyard entry with an arched front door.

Santa Fe

The thick, earth-colored adobe walls and flat roofs with rounded parapets of the **Santa Fe** style make these houses look chunky, but they are suitable for hot, dry climates. Because of the thickness of the walls, the windows and heavy wooden doors are set into deep open-

ings. Sometimes red clay tile accents on the roof and enclosed patios add a Spanish influence.

The **Pueblo Revival** style is another version of the Santa Fe, which is characterized by roof beams (**vigas**) that protrude through the walls and help support the roof.

Typical of the **Territorial** style is a more angular look, with square corners replacing the round corners of the Santa Fe style. In addition, the windows of the Territorial style are framed with straight, unpainted, wooden moldings and brick detailing is present in the parapets.

Tudor Revival

The traditional **English Tudor** is a large, two-story masonry or stucco, steep-gabled house with a definite medieval feel. The **Elizabethan (Tudor Revival)** variation of this style is asymmetrical, has a very steep cross-gabled roof, a prominent chimney, and half-timbered exteriors. Both styles are

characterized by patterned brick or stone walls, rounded doorways, and multi-paned casement windows. Inside, Tudor houses have intricate wood paneling or moldings. They feature arched entries, projecting oriel windows on the second floor, and large leaded-glass windows with stone mullions. Another characteristic is the massive chimney placed in a prominent location and often topped with a decorative chimney pot. They are expensive to build because of the various features such as the complex roof system with various gables of alternating heights, dormers, and large sculpted brick chimneys.

English Cottage

The **English Cottage** style is patterned after the rustic cottages constructed in the Cotswold region of southwestern England since medieval times. Like their Tudor cousins, they are asymmetrical with an uneven sloping roof of slate or cedar that mimics the look of thatch. The exterior may have  brick, stone, or stucco with half-timbering. The multi-pane casement windows and low entry door help create a cozy feeling. Many homes have a prominently placed chimney made of brick or stone.

French Provincial

French Provincial style houses are large, square, symmetrical two-story houses with a distinctive steep, high, hip roof. The exterior is usually white brick or stucco. Windows and chimneys are symmetrical and perfectly balanced. Frequently, tall second floor windows break through the cornice. They have  balcony and porch balustrades; rectangular doors set in arched openings; and double French windows with shutters. Unlike French Normandy houses, French Provincial houses do not have towers.

French Normandy

The main characteristic of **French Normandy** style is the round stone tower topped with a cone-shaped roof. Sometimes the tower is the entrance to the house. In addition, vertical half-timbering (reminiscent of Tudor style) adds height to the house. Unlike a Tudor, French Normandy houses have

hip roofs, not cross-gabled roofs. The houses use stone, stucco, or brick as siding.

Modern Styles

Modern style homes have clean lines, smooth surfaces, and little or no ornamentation. This resulted in the Art Deco, Art Moderne, International, and Contemporary styles.

Art Deco

The **Art Deco** style, which became popular in the 1920's and 30's, is two or more stories, and emphasizes the vertical lines of the house. It is angular and boxy with a flat roof and simple, clean, crisp lines. Glass blocks, metals, plastics, and

other machine-made materials are used extensively. The walls are smooth texture stucco or stone. Geometric designs such as zigzags, chevrons, diamonds, and sunbursts are arranged in horizontal bands and painted or cut out near the roofline.

Art Moderne

The **Art Moderne** style is the precursor of future house design, displaying extreme simplicity. It has a horizontal, cube-like shape with a flat roof and rounded corners. The exterior walls are smooth stucco with rounded corners. Casement windows are evenly spaced. Other than the use of glass brick, there is little or no

ornamentation. Window and door trim and balustrades are made from polished aluminum and stainless steel.

International

The **International** style is modern, asymmetrical, and very practical in its use of concrete, glass, and steel to create sleek lines. With a flat roof and floor-to-ceiling "window walls", the design is avant-garde.

Contemporary

Contemporary style houses are characterized by attractive, simple, clean lines and the combination of stone, glass, masonry, and wood in the exterior.

These asymmetrical houses can be one or more stories with a roof that is flat or very low-pitched. Windows are often an odd shape because they follow the roofline. Sometimes the roof extends from a higher level down over a lower level. Ornamentation is simple with a vertical orientation.

Factory-Built Houses

The types of factory-built houses include manufactured, modular, panelized, and precut homes. **Manufactured houses** are built entirely in the factory. Then they are transported to the site where they are hooked up to utilities and anchored to the foundation. **Modular** homes are comprised of units (or modules) built at a factory that are transported to the home site and assembled on-site. **Panelized homes** arrive to the site in smaller units, usually as completed walls with all the wiring and plumbing intact. Once the foundation is poured, the walls are enclosed and the two-piece roof is attached. Finally, the **precut home** is like a house in a box. All the materials are delivered unassembled, but precut to fit exactly in place. It saves the time and cost of measuring and cutting on-site.

Exterior Inspection

In addition to the housing type and architectural design, appraisers should have basic knowledge of the substructure and the superstructure of a house. The **substructure** refers to all the **below grade** improvements. The main underground component is the foundation; however, if there is a basement, it is also part of the substructure. The **superstructure** refers to all the above grade improvements. **Above grade** refers to anything above ground level. These include the wood framing, the materials used to finish both the interior and exterior walls, as well as the various coatings, doors, and windows.

The appraiser will take note of the exterior characteristics of the home, and use a tape measure to get the accurate dimensions of the home. Then, the appraiser sketches the dimensions on graph paper, a laptop computer, or a handheld computer.

Foundations

The **foundation** or substructure of a home supports the entire building, and transfers the weight of the building to the ground. Types of house foundations include slab-on-grade and pier and beam (raised) foundations. Local climate and soil conditions affect the type of foundation chosen, as do the size and weight of the structure and the location of the water table.

Slab-on-Grade Foundation

Depending on the climate, soil conditions, and architectural requirements, the builder may use a **slab-on-grade** foundation, where the structure sits directly on the ground. In this case, the foundation and footings are one integral unit. A properly designed slab supports the weight of the entire structure and is unaffected by soil movement.

Raised Foundation

A **raised foundation** is a foundation that is the main floor of a home that is raised above the plane of the surrounding earth. A raised foundation is a grid system of beams (girders), piers, and footings. Typically, raised foundations are made of poured concrete, cinder or concrete blocks, or wood. Raised foundations have a space underneath them. Depending on the size, it is a crawlspace or a basement.

A **crawlspace** is a low space beneath a floor of a building to give workers access to wiring and plumbing. The crawlspace is not large enough to be a finished or livable space. It serves the same purpose as the basement in that it connects the foundation of the home to footings and piles that are pounded into the earth below the frost line.

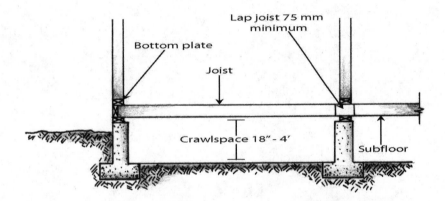

Crawlspaces range from 18 inches to 4 feet in height.

A **basement** is partially or entirely below ground. Basements can be finished spaces or unfinished spaces. Since basements may add value to a home, their presence should be noted by the appraiser. In some cases, the basement is a finished space with livable area. **Finished areas** are the enclosed areas in a home that are suitable for year-round use. These areas have flooring, insulation, etc. that is similar to the rest of the house. **Unfinished areas** are the areas of a home that do not meet these criteria. Sometimes, a finished basement can be what is known as a walkout, finished basement. In this case, the basement is not completely underground. At least one side is exposed and a door connects the livable space to the grade level outside.

Crawlspaces and basements are subject to flooding and will have a sump pump. A **sump pump** is essential in keeping crawlspaces or basements dry and preventing moisture and mildew problems.

Roofing

The style and condition of a roof can affect the value of a home, and a roof in poor condition can significantly detract from the value of the home. There are many types of roof styles.

Roof Styles

Gable

Hip

Cone

Gable with Dormers

Mansard

Dome

Dust Pan

Pyramid

Flat

Salt-Box

Pagoda

Shed

A-Frame

Gambrel

False Thatched

Roof Coverings

There are a number of different materials used for roof coverings, but they all must share some common characteristics. They must be able to shed water and protect the interior of the home from the weather. Materials used for roofing must be durable, aesthetically pleasing, easy to apply, reasonably priced, and not too heavy. The appraiser should be familiar with all the different types of roofing materials used in his or her market area.

Common Roofing Materials
- Built-up roofing
- Slate
- Tile
- Asphalt composition shingles
- Metal roofing and shingles
- Wood shingles and shakes

Roof Framing

Normally the roof system uses joists and rafters spaced from 12 inches to 24 inches apart on centers. The **rafters** and **joists** support the weight of the sheathing, roofing material, and roof mounted equipment. They also bear weight from weather such as wind, rain, or snow. Rafters may carry the ceiling loads below when cathedral ceilings are present. Rafters and joists also create attic and ventilation space.

Roof Flashing

Flashing defines the material used to prevent the intrusion of water at the place where dissimilar materials or surface planes intersect. Typically, flashing is installed at any roof penetration where leaks may occur such as chimneys or vents, and any exterior wall openings such as windows or doors. Flashings seal the edges of membranes or seal where the membranes overlap. They direct water away from the structure and its components. Flashing is by nature corrosion resistant and can be made from copper, stainless steel, galvanized steel, and various plastics.

Ventilation

Adequate ventilation is essential to prolong the life of the roof covering as well as the building materials used in the roof structure. In addition to obtaining maximum life for the roof, proper ventilation can dramatically reduce the heating and cooling costs for the house. Soffit vents and attic fans aid ventilation of the roof.

Doors

Doors usually come as packaged units that need to fit squarely in their frames, open, and close smoothly without binding. They come in solid, hollow, or paneled varieties. Typically, exterior doors are solid and interior doors are hollow.

Doors can be hung in different ways. Traditional doors are hung with hinges on one side. French doors are double doors hinged at either side. Others run in tracks and are sliding doors. Others yet are suspended overhead on tracks, like pocket doors. Doors have different surfaces as well. They may be flush or level, glazed, paneled, or even louvered.

Door Styles

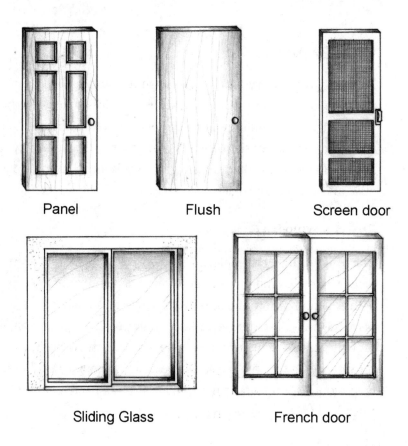

Panel   Flush   Screen door

Sliding Glass   French door

Windows

Windows allow light and air into a home and improve airflow and circulation. A description of windows usually starts with the types of the frames and sashes that hold the panes in place. **Window frames** and **sashes** are usually made of wood, metal, vinyl, or fiberglass.

Most **windowpanes** are conventional glass but some may be laminated glass, tempered glass, or even wired-glass. Acrylic coatings are used in many skylights, and polycarbonates are used to strengthen windows for security purposes. **Energy-efficient windows** (low E, dual-glazed, and triple-glazed) decrease the amount of heat loss in cold months and the cool air escaping during warm months.

Most decorative and picture windows are fixed windows. **Fixed windows** do not open or move at all. Skylights are a type of fixed window. Skylights are estimated to let five times more light into a house than another window of the same size. Skylights also help a space look much larger than it is and add value to the house.

Windows that open have either a traverse sliding mechanism or hinges. **Traverse windows** slide from side to side. Sliding glass doors are simply large, traverse windows. In single-hung windows, the bottom portion slides up. In double-hung windows, both top and bottom parts move up and down.

Types of **hinged windows** include casement, awning, transom, and hopper. Casement windows have hinges on the sides and are opened with cranks. A French window is actually two casement windows placed side by side. An awning window is hinged at the top and opens out. A transom window is hinged at the top and opens into the room. A hopper window (or eyebrow) is hinged at the bottom and opens into the room.

Jalousie windows do not slide or use a hinge, instead, they have narrow glass slats like Venetian blinds that are opened and closed with a crank.

Window Styles

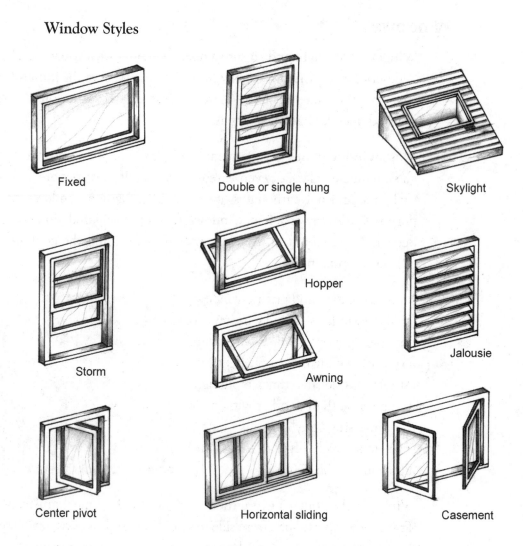

Fixed

Double or single hung

Skylight

Storm

Hopper

Awning

Jalousie

Center pivot

Horizontal sliding

Casement

Cladding

Cladding in general can refer to any external, weatherproof protective skin or device for the exterior surfaces of the home and includes surface coatings and exterior cladding systems.

Surface Coatings

The outermost layer of house is a layer of paint or similar coating and is only a few thousandths of an inch thick. If properly applied and replenished, paint will protect tens of thousands of dollars worth of siding. Although there are several different chemical systems used in common home coatings, they are all applied as a liquid and, when dry, form tough plastic-like layers of protection on the surfaces to which they are applied. Common surface coating types include enamel, latex, epoxy, lacquer, shellac, and stain.

Exterior Cladding Systems

Exterior cladding systems, such as wood siding, shingles, or brick have both an aesthetic and a functional role. Aesthetically, what is on the exterior of the house creates the first and often lasting impression of the home. Functionally, the cladding material protects the house's structure from the elements, mainly rain and wind driven moisture. Commonly used cladding includes siding, shingles, stucco, and brick.

Siding. **Siding** refers to overlapping horizontal boards made from wood, vinyl, or aluminum. Vinyl siding is widely used today due to its low cost, low maintenance, and relative durability. Sometimes a house has "**board and batten**" which is an application of vertical boards with joints that are finished by thin vertical strips.

Shingles. Wood **shingles** are commonly used in combination with wood siding. Shingles can be plain or patterned and vary in shape from rectangular to diamond.

Stucco. **Stucco** is a mixture of cement, sand, and lime which is applied over a frame construction. **Half-timbering** is a method of construction in which the wooden frame and principal beams of a structure are exposed, and the spaces between are filled with stucco, brick, or stone.

Brick. Bricks are made in a variety of colors, and can be laid in many patterns to create a distinctive and pleasing appearance. **Bricks** are rectangular blocks of clay or shale baked dry by the sun or in a kiln. Due to earthquake considerations, many houses in California have a brick veneer. **Adobe bricks** are made with a mixture of clay and straw, formed into brick shapes, and dried in the sun rather than in a kiln. Adobe bricks are larger than standard bricks. Although very energy efficient, they do not withstand earthquakes, which is why you will find this material in Arizona and New Mexico rather than in California.

Trim

Trim refers to the finishing materials in a building, such as moldings applied around openings (window and door trim) or at the floor and ceiling of rooms (baseboard, cornice, and other moldings). Trim around windows is also known as casing. Trim is usually a different color or material than the adjacent wall. It is located either on the outside or inside of the building and covers the space between the window frame or doorjamb and the wall. Although largely cosmetic in nature, trim serves the purpose of protecting other more vital structural parts.

Interior Inspection

Once the basic examination of the outside is complete, the appraiser can then move to the inside of the home. At this point, the appraiser has already drawn a sketch of the exterior of the house. The appraiser now uses that perimeter sketch and fills in the room layout and other interior details.

Size for the interior of the home is reported in terms of **gross living area** (GLA), which is the total amount of finished, above ground habitable space. In most cases, attics, crawlspaces, and basements are unfinished and do not count in the GLA measurement. The **gross building area** (GBA) is the total amount of all enclosed floor areas and does include basements and attics. The American National Standards Institute (ANSI) has a standard method for calculating floor areas in single-family dwellings, "Square Footage - Method for Calculating", ANSI Z765-2003. Some state appraisal regulatory agencies adopted this standard method as an assignment condition that appraisers must follow. Copies may be purchased from the NAHB Research Center, a subsidiary of the National Association of Home Builders (NAHB).

The appraiser also takes note of the features present in the interior of the home. Most appraisal reports contain a checklist that reminds the appraiser to check all the important features and provides a space for noting the condition of features present.

In many cases, the current owner can provide additional information about the condition or quality of improvements. If the homeowner is present during the appraiser's on-site inspection, he or she is usually happy to talk about the remodeling of the kitchen, when the interior of the home was last painted, and any recent major repairs.

Floors

Floors need to be level, well supported, smooth, and easy to navigate so they do not trip occupants. Floors should also be very durable as they are the most used components of the home interior. Floors get support from floor joists, which span the floors perpendicularly to the floor sills.

Finish flooring can be made of concrete, wood strips or planks, carpet, resilient tile, ceramic tile, or quarry tile (stone and marble). Some types of flooring, such as travertine, may add to the value of the home.

Walls and Ceilings

Interior walls and ceilings conceal the electrical, mechanical, and plumbing systems and serve to strengthen the vapor barrier. They also improve overall rigidity and help to prevent racking and twisting of the structure.

Interior Walls

Interior walls are a decorative finish made from different materials like plaster or drywall, wood planks or panels, fiber cement panels, masonry or concrete. **Plaster** and **drywall** are the two most common types of interior walls. They are durable materials, considered inexpensive, and easy to paint, cover, or wallpaper. Additionally, they are easy to fix when damaged, resistant to rodents and insects, good for blocking sound, and resistant to fire.

Ceilings

Ceilings are made from the same basic types of material as walls. Materials used in ceilings include plaster, drywall, wood, paneling, or even acoustic tiling. Metal ceilings appear in some homes as well.

There are also different styles of ceilings. Textured ceilings are quick to apply to a drywall backing and are relatively inexpensive. However, because they tend to collect dirt and grease, they should not be used in kitchens or bathrooms. Dropped or suspended ceilings consist of **t-bars**, a framework of steel or metal channels suspended by wires, into which pre-cut acoustic tiles are placed.

Counters and Cabinets

The appraiser should also note the quality, condition, and type of material used for the counters and cabinets located throughout the home.

Counters come in a number of materials like particleboard or plywood and have a variety of materials like wood, slate, granite, marble, stainless steel, and tile covering them. The choice of materials and colors is often dramatically affected by the prevailing styles. This is a reason why remodeling a kitchen can be an important way to modernize a home and increase its value. Whichever covering is used for the countertop, it should be waterproof, abrasion-resistant, durable, scorch-proof, and non-porous.

Cabinets provide storage in rooms like the kitchen and bathrooms. They are usually made from solid wood, particleboard, or even different types of metal. Plastic laminate covers the particleboard type of cabinet for protection. Quality cabinet materials and an abundance of cabinet space is another factor that can add to the value of the home.

Attics

The **attic** is the area of the home bounded by the underside of the roof and the upper side of the ceiling of the top floor. It may be large enough to stand up in or just barely large enough to be considered an attic. If large enough, some attics are finished and heated and could be considered part of the living area. A hatchway built into the ceiling at an upstairs hallway or closet usually accesses the attic. Some have a ladder or a folding drop stair to provide access.

Mechanical Systems and Equipment

The main mechanical systems are heating, cooling, plumbing, and electrical. Homes vary in their type and quality of systems. Similarly, although almost every home has plumbing and electricity, there can be wide variations in the quality of plumbing fixtures and electrical capacity.

Heating and Cooling Systems

Appraisers need to be familiar with the variety of home heating systems, e.g., forced air, radiant, hydronic, steam, and geothermal.

Forced Air Heating and Cooling System

The **forced air system** is the most common type of home heating (and cooling) system. The air is heated in a furnace and then forced throughout the ductwork of house using blowers until the warm air goes into the rooms via registers. To heat the air, furnaces use various fuel sources, such as natural gas, propane, oil, or electricity. The ductwork and registers are also used for cooling the home.

Radiant Heating System

The **radiant heating system** works through the process of radiation or direct transfer of heat from a hot to a cold surface. The radiant heat can be distributed by radiant panels may be used in ceilings or floors, by hot water tubing embedded in the floor or directly below the floor surface, or by heating stoves or fireplaces.

Radiant systems use hot water heated by a boiler, which may be fueled by natural gas, propane, oil, coal, or electricity. Typically, heating stoves and fireplaces use pellets or wood. A heating stove is normally associated with pelletized wood. However, many will also burn fuels such as grain, corn, seeds, or woodchips.

Fireplaces are an inefficient heat source. Now, fireplaces are a focal point for winter comfort and provide a cozy atmosphere rather than being the sole source of heat for a home.

Hydronic Heating System

The **hydronic system** (hot water) is similar to a radiant heat system. This system uses a combination of radiation and convection. Hot water is heated by boiler, which may be fueled by natural gas, propane, oil, coal, or electricity. The hot water is piped to baseboard units mounted along walls. Warm air is distributed by convection as air rises and is heated by the baseboard unit.

The **steam radiant heating system** is a variation of the hydronic system. Boilers heat water to steam, which is distributed via steam piping and radiator units.

Geothermal Heat Pump

Some homes may be heated (and cooled) by using Geothermal Heat Pump (GHP). Heat pumps work like a refrigerator that can run in reverse. Heat is taken from one source and deposited in another location. For example, with a ground loop geothermal system, heat is taken from or deposited to the earth by use of a ground loop pipe.

Plumbing System

Residential plumbing consists of the pipes that deliver clean water (aseptic system), the drains that remove used water (septic system), and the various fixtures needed to use the water.

The **aseptic system** is the clean water system and is also known as potable water. **Potable water** is water that does not have enough impurities to cause health problems. Most homes are connected to a public water supply system. However, some homes may have a private source, such as a well, cistern, or access to a river, lake, or pond.

The **septic system** is the wastewater system. Homes either are connected to a public sewage system or have a private sewage system (e.g., septic tank and field lines). The type of system depends on the location of the property.

Plumbing fixtures generally refers to parts of a plumbing system that have a distinct use and application. Most plumbing fixtures for home use can be broken down into three categories: kitchen fixtures, bathroom fixtures, and plumbing system fixtures. Kitchen fixtures include sinks, faucets, and taps and bathroom fixtures include bathtubs, showers, toilets, faucets, and sinks. Porcelain, stainless steel, fiberglass, brass, copper, and cast iron are some of the materials used for fixtures. Additionally, the plumbing connections are installed to hook up the various appliances that use water, such as water heaters, dish and clothes washers, and water softeners.

Electrical System

Most homes get their electrical power from a utility company that is delivered to the main electrical panel of the house by overhead or subterranean transmission lines. However, increasingly more homeowners are installing renewable energy systems (solar and wind) to provide all or part of their electricity needs.

Solar panels gather the sun's heat for use in a solar water heater, solar heating system and even as a source of electricity in the residence. Most solar panels are installed on the roof, but if the site is large enough the solar panels can be installed on the ground.

Solar panels are becoming more prevalent.

Although it is common for people in sunny areas to install solar panels, small wind turbines for residential use are a relatively new technology. **Small wind turbines** are wind turbines that have lower energy output than large commercial wind turbines, such as those found in wind farms. Small wind turbines should not be used in heavily populated areas, because tall buildings break up the wind pattern, which makes the wind energy erratic.

Car Storage

Once the appraiser has examined the exterior and interior of the home, he or she should also make note of any space designed for car storage. Usually, there are four places to park a car at the home site. Homes may have an attached garage, detached garage or a carport. Other homes have only an uncovered driveway or on-street parking.

Garages

The appraiser should note whether the **garage** is attached to or detached from the home, its size, and the number of cars it accommodates. The appraiser usually includes the garage in his or her sketch of the home.

Carports

Like garages, carports cover the car. Unlike garages, carports do not enclose it. **Carport**s have no walls or doors with which to control access.

Driveways

Most homes with a garage have a **driveway**; but sometimes, older homes have no garage and no carport. Instead, they possess only a driveway, and that is the private parking for the home.

The appraiser should also note the driveway surface and its condition. Driveways are made of solid materials like concrete or asphalt or pieced materials like stones, pavers, bricks, or gravel. They should be free of cracks and trip hazards where subsurface upward heaving has caused the concrete to crack or become uneven. Driveways should be sloped to drain water away from the home and garage.

On-Street Parking

In some cases, a home has no garage, carport, or even a driveway to park a car. The owner of the home must resort to parking the car on a public street in front of the home. Obviously, the appraiser should note this on a report if encountered.

INSPECTING SITE IMPROVEMENTS

In addition to the dwelling, the appraiser should note other improvements made to the site. These improvements include things around the perimeter of a building like fences, patios, pools, lighting, ponds, out buildings, and even sports courts.

The appraiser also has to give contributory value to site improvements after identifying them. **Contributory value** is the contribution a particular component has to the value of the whole property. Sometimes the contributory value of site improvements does not equal the cost of building them. For example, swimming pools contribute to the overall value of a home, but their contributory value is less than the expense of building the pool itself. As with all other property features, the appraiser determines the value of site improvements by considering market data.

Fences. Fences add to the security of a property and can add to its value. They are usually made of masonry (brick or block) or various types of wood.

Patios. Patios are surfaced exterior areas used for outdoor enjoyment of the home. Barbeques and patio furniture are often located out on these areas. Their construction type varies, as some are concrete, brick, stone, asphalt, or wood. No matter the type, they are usually at ground level. If the patio is more than two feet off the ground, it should have a guardrail.

Swimming Pools and Spas. Swimming pools are becoming more prevalent in residential areas. They may be above ground or level with the backyard. The most common materials used in pool construction are concrete, fiberglass, and vinyl.

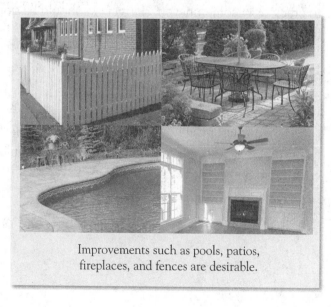

Improvements such as pools, patios,
fireplaces, and fences are desirable.

A **spa** or hot tub is a small pool filled with circulating hot water for therapeutic soaking. It can be freestanding, attached to a pool, above ground or set into the ground. Although similar in construction to a swimming pool, a spa or hot tub is much smaller. The distinction between spa and hot tub is largely semantic, but the term "hot tub" usually refers to a round structure made from woods like cedar, redwood, cypress, oak, or teakwood.

Sauna. A **sauna** is a Scandinavian invention consisting of a small, wood-lined room or house with the provision to be heated to 150°F or more. Like spas, saunas are considered therapeutic. The dry heat in a sauna increases perspiration, which causes "toxins" to be removed from the body, cleansing the skin pores. The heat also increases circulation and relaxes muscles.

SUMMARY

Depending on the scope of work involved with the assignment, the appraiser's inspection sometimes is a simple **drive-by visual verification**. Usually an appraiser will actually make an **on-site inspection** of the subject property, as well as the comps.

Appraisers inspect properties to develop an opinion of the market value, NOT to discover defects. However, if a defect or adverse condition is known, the appraiser must factor this information into the **value conclusion**. Appraisers are not responsible for any **defects** or **adverse conditions** that could not be identified in the course of his or her customary inspection.

Appraisers inspect the **exterior and interior of the home**. They identify features that are or are not included, and they note the quality of the features that are present. In addition, they note **car storage** options and any other **site improvement**s that may affect the value of the subject property. For this reason, a basic knowledge of the **substructure** and the **superstructure** of a house and its **architectural style** is of benefit to the appraiser.

UNIT 8 REVIEW

Matching Exercise

Instructions: Write the letter of the matching term on the blank line before its definition, and then check your response with the Answer Key that immediately follows the Multiple Choice Questions.

Terms

A. architectural design

B. Bungalow

C. cladding

D. contributory value

E. Dutch Colonial

F. flashing

G. forced air system

H. foundation

I. French Normandy

J. gross building area

K. gross living area

L. hydronic system

M. potable water

N. Ranch

O. septic system

P. siding

Q. substructure

R. superstructure

S. traverse

T. Victorian

Definitions

1. _____ Elements that blend the structural, functional, and decorative elements of a property into a whole.

2. _____ House style that is one-story, low-pitch gable or hipped roof, attached garage, stucco, wood, or brick exterior walls, picture windows, and sliding doors leading to patios.

3. _____ House style easily identified by a distinctive gambrel roof.

4. _____ House style known for its elaborate bric-a-brac, excessive gingerbread, trim work, and other ornamentation.

5. _____ House style found in older neighborhoods that is characterized by simplicity and emphasis on horizontal rather than vertical lines.

6. _____ House style characterized by the round stone tower topped with a cone-shaped roof.

7. _____ All the below grade improvements.

8. _____ All the above grade improvements.

9. _____ Substructure of a home that supports the entire building.

10. _____ Material used to prevent the intrusion of water at the place where dissimilar materials or surface planes intersect.

11. _____ Windows that slide from side to side.

12. _____ Any external, weatherproof protective skin or device for the exterior surfaces of the home.

13. _____ Overlapping horizontal boards made from wood, vinyl, or aluminum.

14. _____ Total amount of finished, above ground habitable space.

15. _____ Total amount of all enclosed floor areas and does include basements and attics.

16. _____ Most common type of home heating (and cooling) system.

17. _____ Heating system that uses a combination of radiation and convection.

18. _____ Water that does not have enough impurities to cause health problems.

19. _____ Wastewater system.

20. _____ Contribution a particular component has to the value of the whole property.

Multiple Choice Questions

Instructions: Circle your choice, and then check your response with the Answer Key that immediately follows the Multiple Choice Questions.

1. An appraiser's inspection of the improvements is:
    a. more thorough than the home inspector's inspection.
    b. an unbiased valuation service for the homebuyer.
    c. significantly different from one done by a home inspector.
    d. an unimportant step in the appraisal process.

2. The cohesive elements that blend the structural, functional, and decorative elements of a property into a whole is known as the:
    a. architectural design of a home.
    b. superstructure of a home.
    c. dissimilarity of a home.
    d. type of a home.

3. Homes built after the 1970s do not have a single design. Instead, ideas are taken from more than one architectural style. What is the name of this style?
    a. Art Modern
    b. Colonial Revival
    c. International
    d. Postmodern

4. The most popular architectural style in the country.
    a. Cape Cod
    b. Mission
    c. Ranch
    d. Tudor

5. Popular style that is a blend of the Italian, Moorish, Byzantine, and the early California mission styles.
    a. Bungalow
    b. Contemporary
    c. Mediterranean
    d. Victorian

6. The high, boxy Mansard roof is the most striking feature of which architectural style?
    a. Territorial
    b. Second Empire
    c. Queen Anne
    d. Florida Caribbean

7. Monterey, Mission, Santa Fe, English Cottage, and French Normandy are all considered:
    a. Bungalow styles
    b. Colonial styles
    c. Period styles
    d. Victorian styles

8. Which type of factory-built house is comprised of units (or modules) built at a factory that are transported to the home site and assembled on-site?
    a. Manufactured home
    b. Modular home
    c. Panelized home
    d. Precut home

9. Which part of a structure is the support for the entire building?
    a. Crawlspace
    b. Flooring
    c. Foundation
    d. Superstructure

10. What is the commonality of siding, shingles, stucco, and brick?
    a. Cladding
    b. Energy efficiency
    c. Flooring
    d. Ventilation

11. Kelly has just completed her inspection of the subject property. Her measurements identified the total area of 1,524 square feet (SF). The attic measured 298 SF and the combined area of the 2 ½ baths measures 132 SF. The kitchen and dining area measured 102 SF and the basement measured 121 SF. What is the gross living area for this property?

    a. 1,524 SF

    b. 871 SF

    c. 1,105 SF

    d. 1,094 SF

12. Which is the most common type of home heating and cooling system?

    a. Forced-air heating system

    b. Geothermal heating system

    c. Hydronic heating system

    d. Radiant heating system

13. A pellet stove is used to create:

    a. forced-air heat.

    b. geothermal heat.

    c. hydronic heat.

    d. radiant heat.

14. What is the commonality of septic, aseptic, and fixtures?

    a. Air conditioning system

    b. Electrical system

    c. Heating system

    d. Plumbing system

15. Of the following types of car storage, which encloses the car?

    a. Carport

    b. Driveway

    c. Garage

    d. On-street parking

UNIT 8 ANSWER KEY

Answers – Matching

1. A	6. I	11. S	16. G
2. N	7. Q	12. C	17. L
3. E	8. R	13. P	18. M
4. T	9. H	14. K	19. O
5. B	10. F	15. J	20. D

Answers – Multiple Choice

1. **(c)**   An appraiser's inspection of a house is significantly different from one done by a home inspector. Home inspectors perform a much more thorough inspection to different standards. **Page 238**

2. **(a)**   Architectural design is the cohesive element that blends the structural, functional, and decorative elements of a property into a whole. **Page 239**

3. **(d)**   Most houses built since the late 1970s do not fall into a single category. Instead, designers and builders incorporate decorative details and features from many of the previous historic styles. Whether one or more features are chosen, the result alludes to, but does not mimic, the historic styles. These styles are called Postmodern or Neo-Eclectic. **Page 239**

4. **(c)**   Since its debut in San Diego in 1932, the Ranch style house has become the most popular style in the country. **Page 240**

5. **(c)**   The Mediterranean style is the blend of the Italian, Moorish, Byzantine, and the early California mission styles. **Page 241**

6. **(b)**   The most striking feature of the Second Empire style house is the high, boxy Mansard roof, which allows more usable living space in the upper story. **Page 244**

7. **(c)**   Period styles get their inspiration from the architectural styles of the past. In the early half of the 20th century, the trend was toward historical interpretations of European styles. **Page 245**

8. **(b)**   Modular homes are comprised of units (or modules) built at a factory that are transported to the home site and assembled on-site. **Pages 249-250**

9. **(c)**   The foundation is the support for the entire structure and its purpose is to transfer the weight of the building to the ground. **Page 250**

10. **(a)**   Commonly used cladding includes siding, shingles, stucco, and brick. **Page 257**

11. **(c)**   Gross living area (GLA) is the total finished above ground habitable space. Usually attics, crawlspaces, and basements are unfinished and not counted in this measurement. Therefore, subtract the attic and backyard areas from the total area to determine the GLA. **Page 258**

12. **(a)**   The forced air system is the most common type of home heating (and cooling) system. **Page 260**

13. **(d)**   The radiant heating system works through the process of radiation or direct transfer of heat from a hot to a cold surface. Heating stoves use pelletized wood and many burn fuels such as grain, corn, seeds, or woodchips. **Page 260**

14. **(d)**   Residential plumbing consists of the pipes that deliver clean water (aseptic system), the drains that remove used water (septic system), and the various fixtures needed to use the water. **Page 261**

15. **(c)**   Whether attached or detached, garages have walls and doors to create a complete enclosure. **Page 263**

Sales Comparison Approach

Unit 9

INTRODUCTION

The **sales comparison approach** is an appraisal method in which the property being appraised (subject) is compared to sales of similar properties in order to arrive at a value for the subject property. It is regarded as the simplest and the most commonly used approach among residential appraisers. The sales comparison approach even appears in a limited form when using the cost and income approaches to value.

In the real estate market, no two properties are ever exactly alike (if only because no two properties may be in the same location), so exact comparability is impossible to obtain. However, by using market analysis, it is possible for appraisers to identify any aspect of a real estate transaction or any characteristic of the property that may affect the property's sales price. From this, appraisers are able to identify economic comparability, which is essential to proper estimation of market value.

This unit introduces the comparison grid (matrix) and explains how adjustments are determined and applied. Additionally, it covers the topic of reconciling the adjusted prices of the comparable properties to develop an opinion of the market value of the subject property.

Learning Objectives

After reading this unit, you should be able to:

- specify the applications and the limitations of the sales comparison approach.
- identify sources of the data used in the sales comparison approach.
- recognize the elements of comparison considered when selecting comparables.
- recall the importance of and ways used to verify market data.
- identify the methods and sequence of applying adjustments to the comparables.
- determine the reliability of the indicated values derived from the comparables.

OVERVIEW OF THE SALES COMPARISON APPROACH

The sales comparison approach relies heavily upon the principle of substitution. The **principle of substitution** states that the maximum value of a property is set by the cost of acquiring an equally desirable and valuable substitute property. Based on the principle of substitution, appraisers can assume that similar properties have similar market value. In the sales comparison approach, the market value of the subject property is estimated by comparing it to other similar properties that have recently been sold, been listed for sale, or for which offers to purchase have been made.

Appraisers obtain an indication of the subject property's value by adjusting the prices of the comparable properties to account for their differences from the subject property. Real estate appraisers compare the legal, economic, locational, and physical characteristics of the property they are appraising to those corresponding characteristics of similar sales, listings, or pending sales. Then, they adjust up or down the sales price of each of the comparable properties to account for differences between the subject property and the comparable properties. These **adjustments** are values expressed in percentage or dollar amounts that appraisers add to or subtract from the sales prices of the comparable properties, as shown by the following formula.

Adjusted Value = Comparable Property Sales Price ± Adjustments

The adjusted prices are then reconciled into an estimate of value for the subject property.

Comparable House A sold for $355,000 with a garage.

Subject House B has no sales price and is virtually identical to *House A* except it has no garage.

Your job as an appraiser is to determine a value for *Subject House B*. If a garage is valued at $5,000 in this neighborhood, and the two houses are identical in every way except *Comparable House A* has a garage,

then, subtract the value of the garage from *Comparable House A* to determine an appropriate value for Subject *House B*.

$355,000 - $5,000 = $350,000
Comparable Property Sales Price ± Adjustments = Adjusted Value

Applications of the Sales Comparison Approach

The sales comparison approach is applicable when appraising all kinds of real property interests. It is most reliable in situations with a sufficient number of arm's-length sales transactions to indicate patterns within that market.

Uses for the Sales Comparison Approach
- Property types that are bought and sold on a regular basis
- Single-family residences
- Condominiums
- Small multi-residential properties
- Vacant land

Although it is not usually the primary method employed, sales comparison analysis is often useful when appraising many kinds of commercial property. If sufficient sales data is available, appraisers use this approach as a check on the reasonableness of the value estimates obtained from the income and cost approaches to value.

Limitations of the Sales Comparison Approach

Lack of market data can limit the usefulness and reliability of the sales comparison approach. Some types of properties are sold infrequently, so there is not enough market data to apply this approach. In situations with only a few comparable sales that are close substitutes for the subject property, the reliability of this approach is limited. In fact, the sales comparison approach usually is not applicable when appraising special-use properties or unique properties, such as churches or historic landmarks.

Limited Usefulness of the Sales Comparison Approach

- Property types that are bought and sold infrequently
- Properties in a market with few arm's length transactions
- Property in a rapidly changing market
- Special-use properties
- Unique properties

Another limitation is that the sales comparison approach to value is based on the assumption that a property's sales price is equal to its value. Although this assumption is valid in most cases, in some instances a sales price is not indicative of what a property is actually worth. The appraiser's job is to find sales that are truly reflective of the market. This means that appraisers must research the conditions of each sale before using it as a comparable. Sales that do not meet the conditions of an arm's length transaction are not good indicators of market value.

The reliability of the sales comparison approach is also limited by its heavy reliance on historical data. When a property sells, the purchase price is agreed upon sometimes months prior to the actual close of escrow. Consequently, that sales price is indicative of market perceptions as of the date an offer to purchase was accepted; not necessarily of market conditions as of the date it closes escrow. It also follows that a comparable sale's purchase price is indicative of market reactions at some point in the past and may not be reflective of the present market. If appraisers are attempting to estimate the current value of a property, they need to consider current market data, such as active listings and pending sales, in the analysis.

Uniform Residential Appraisal Report

File #

| There are | comparable properties currently offered for sale in the subject neighborhood ranging in price from $ | | to $ | |
| There are | comparable sales in the subject neighborhood within the past twelve months ranging in sale price from $ | | to $ | |

FEATURE	SUBJECT	COMPARABLE SALE # 1		COMPARABLE SALE # 2		COMPARABLE SALE # 3	
Address							
Proximity to Subject							
Sale Price	$		$		$		$
Sale Price/Gross Liv. Area	$ sq. ft.	$ sq. ft.		$ sq. ft.		$ sq. ft.	
Data Source(s)							
Verification Source(s)							
VALUE ADJUSTMENTS	DESCRIPTION	DESCRIPTION	+(-) $ Adjustment	DESCRIPTION	+(-) $ Adjustment	DESCRIPTION	+(-) $ Adjustment
Sale or Financing Concessions							
Date of Sale/Time							
Location							
Leasehold/Fee Simple							
Site							
View							
Design (Style)							
Quality of Construction							
Actual Age							
Condition							
Above Grade	Total Bdrms. Baths	Total Bdrms. Baths		Total Bdrms. Baths		Total Bdrms. Baths	
Room Count							
Gross Living Area	sq. ft.	sq. ft.		sq. ft.		sq. ft.	
Basement & Finished Rooms Below Grade							
Functional Utility							
Heating/Cooling							
Energy Efficient Items							
Garage/Carport							
Porch/Patio/Deck							
Net Adjustment (Total)		☐ + ☐ -	$	☐ + ☐ -	$	☐ + ☐ -	$
Adjusted Sale Price of Comparables		Net Adj. % Gross Adj. %	$	Net Adj. % Gross Adj. %	$	Net Adj. % Gross Adj. %	$

I ☐ did ☐ did not research the sale or transfer history of the subject property and comparable sales. If not, explain

My research ☐ did ☐ did not reveal any prior sales or transfers of the subject property for the three years prior to the effective date of this appraisal.

Data source(s)

My research ☐ did ☐ did not reveal any prior sales or transfers of the comparable sales for the year prior to the date of sale of the comparable sale.

Data source(s)

Report the results of the research and analysis of the prior sale or transfer history of the subject property and comparable sales (report additional prior sales on page 3).

ITEM	SUBJECT	COMPARABLE SALE # 1	COMPARABLE SALE # 2	COMPARABLE SALE # 3
Date of Prior Sale/Transfer				
Price of Prior Sale/Transfer				
Data Source(s)				
Effective Date of Data Source(s)				

Analysis of prior sale or transfer history of the subject property and comparable sales

Summary of Sales Comparison Approach

Indicated Value by Sales Comparison Approach $

SALES COMPARISON ANALYSIS PROCEDURE

The sales comparison analysis procedure is a part of the appraisal process, and if applicable, it is only one of many steps. When using the sales comparison approach, USPAP requires appraisers to "collect, verify, and analyze all information applicable to the appraisal problem." There is a systematic process an appraiser should follow when performing the sales comparison analysis.

Steps for the Sales Comparison Analysis

- **Collecting Market Data.** Researching and collecting data regarding comparable sales, listings, and offers to purchase properties that are considered substitutes in the market for the subject property.

- **Selecting Comparables.** Selecting the most appropriate comparable properties.

- **Verifying Market Data.** Verifying the comparable sales information to ensure that it is accurate and reflective of open market activities.

- **Applying Adjustments.** Applying appropriate adjustments to the comparable properties chosen for the analysis.

- **Reconciling.** Reconciling the various adjusted indicators of value into a value estimate.

Collecting Market Data

After an appraiser has identified the appraisal problem, determined the scope of work, and decided that the sales comparison analysis needs to be performed, he or she then collects data applicable to the assignment. The quality of the analysis performed in an appraisal assignment is directly related to the quality of the data relied upon in an assignment.

The **data sources** appraisers use may vary from area to area and from property type to property type. For example, the data sources an appraiser would rely upon when appraising a large commercial facility typically would not be the same as those relied upon by an appraiser performing single-family residential appraisals. Likewise, the various real estate data services in existence do not provide information for all geographic areas or for all property types. Often, a data source heavily relied upon in one area is not even available in another area.

The Internet is a useful resource because sales and listing data, market area trends, and in some cases, local zoning and assessors' information is available.

Since no single data source is absolutely complete or accurate, appraisers need to rely upon multiple data sources. Local practices often dictate which data sources an appraiser uses for a particular assignment. Consulting multiple data sources helps appraisers minimize any discrepancies, inaccurate details, and incomplete records. If discrepancies are found between differing data sources or if data is incomplete, an appraiser needs to do additional research to determine why the discrepancy exists or where to find the missing information. An appraiser can provide a good analysis of the assignment only if the data used is complete and accurate.

Data Service Companies

Data service companies sell data to real estate appraisers. Almost all of these data services obtain their data from the local county recorder's and assessor's records. Some on-line data service companies provide unlimited access to their database for a flat monthly fee. Others may charge per record, and, in some instances, the data is free. The companies may provide residential data, commercial data, or both.

Although many of these services have good search capabilities, appraisers need to remember they often provide only raw data such as addresses, sales prices, sale dates, bedroom and bath counts, and improvement size. In most cases, they do not provide information concerning quality, condition, income and expense information, buyer and seller motivation, or special amenities associated with a property. Appraisers who rely solely upon information obtained from these sources may misstate some critical aspect of the property.

Multiple Listing Service

Commonly referred to by the acronym "MLS", the **multiple listing service** is an invaluable source of data provided by local real estate boards to its members. Real estate brokers input individual records, called **listings**, into the MLS system to notify other brokers of properties available for sale. Real estate brokers and sales associates use information in the MLS for purposes of buying and selling real estate.

Although not specifically designed as a data source for appraisers, MLS systems provide a wealth of information. Information such as the seller's asking price and the property's total days on the market is usually included in MLS listings. This information is often difficult, if not impossible, to obtain elsewhere. Usually, MLS systems also provide comments specific to a property describing items of interest to buyers (and appraisers) of real estate. MLS systems often provide neighborhood specific statistical data such as average sales prices and median days on market before a property sells. One of the most important pieces of information found in an MLS listing is the phone number(s) of the real estate brokers directly involved in the transaction.

MLS systems are Internet-based and provide extensive search capabilities. Most listings have multiple interior and exterior photos that show items not visible to an appraiser performing a drive-by inspection from the street. Virtual tours of a property showing 360° views from various locations both inside and outside of a property are commonplace. These items enable appraisers to compare comparable sales and listings with the subject property more accurately.

Although MLS systems are a good source of data, appraisers need to remember that the purpose of the listings on MLS systems is to sell properties and not specifically to assist appraisers. Since listing records are generated by individuals desiring to sell properties, there is a tendency toward overstating positive attributes and understating negative factors of a property.

Example: In some listings, houses suffering from deferred maintenance are labeled as "handyman's delights" and properties with small rooms are labeled as being "cozy". Separating hype from facts in MLS listings is another task appraisers perform.

Public Records

In most states, the county recorder's records and the tax assessor's information are considered public. Some counties provide this information on-line through the Internet, whereas others require a trip to county offices.

Public records are documents like those in the County Recorder's Office that show evidence of the conveyance of title or transfer of an interest in real property. Data obtained from these sources varies in accuracy, quality, and completeness from county to county and state to state. In some instances, this information is not computerized, so an appraiser is required to manually search through cumbersome card catalogues and property lists. Sometimes, sales information does not appear in public record systems until months after the actual sale occurred.

Title Companies

For years, title companies have maintained title plants or abstract plants. A **title plant** consists of fully indexed records showing all instruments of record affecting lands. The records are used as the basis for issuance of title insurance policies. In the last few years, many of the larger title companies have started to provide free on-line access to their databases to real estate brokers as a tool to assist them in their marketing efforts. Sometimes appraisers can obtain free access to these databases by contacting a title representative from one of the major title insurance companies.

Other Sources of Market Data

There are numerous other sources available to appraisers. Though these sources rarely provide all the information appraisers require to perform their services, they may provide a starting point for further investigation by an appraiser.

Appraiser Office Files

Appraisers also rely on information obtained when performing previous appraisals. Although this may be a very good source of information, appraisers have to be careful to maintain confidentiality. Sometimes, an appraiser is precluded from using information obtained in an earlier assignment since using it would violate confidentiality laws. Appraisers need to be aware of the Confidentiality section of the Ethics Rule of USPAP in order to comply with this requirement.

Parties to the Transaction

Parties to the transaction are the people directly involved—the buyer, the seller, the buyer's broker, and the seller's broker. In many cases, owners are more than willing to talk to appraisers regarding the property they just purchased.

> Example: Assume that Bob, a licensed appraiser, becomes aware of a sale that was not recorded. He talks to the owner of the property who shows Bob an unrecorded deed, a purchase agreement, and the price that was paid. This information could not have been obtained from any of the paid data services.

Although the information an appraiser learns from people in the field can be invaluable, it must be verified. This is because buyers and sellers may not convey that information accurately to the appraiser.

On-Site Sales Offices

There is often no on-line or public record information available for a property in a new development. In many instances, newly constructed properties do not appear on these data sources until months after they are completed and sold. In such instances, often the only reliable source of sales and information within that development is the on-site sales office. **On-site sales offices** are often very good sources of data, since the person providing the information is involved in all the transactions within that tract. Additionally, the sales agreements for both the subject and comparable sales are often available for inspection.

Selecting Comparables

After appraisers gather information, they must select the comparables that are the most appropriate. They need to identify which data is appropriate and applicable to the assignment at hand. For instance, sales from high-rise

condominiums are not usually good indicators of value for single-family detached homes. However, in some instances, sales of single-family detached condominiums are very strong indicators of value for detached, single-family homes in nearby planned unit developments.

The geographic area an appraiser would typically search for comparable sales data depends upon the nature of the real estate being appraised. If similar properties are bought and sold within a neighborhood, an appraiser typically would limit the search for sales data to similar properties located within that area. On the other hand, the market for some kinds of properties may be national or even worldwide in scope. Appraisers valuing regional malls, golf courses, high-rise office buildings, and industrial properties would consider properties located large distances from the subject property.

Most clients require a minimum of three comparable sales to be included in the appraisal report. Often, active listings and pending sales are included in the sales comparison analysis. Even though these additional comparable properties may not be closed sales as of the date of the appraisal, they provide a glimpse of current market expectations and can lend support to the final estimate of value. The more comps an appraiser can analyze, the more sound and supportable his or her conclusions will be. Therefore, an appraiser should utilize as many comps as necessary to arrive at his or her conclusion.

Elements of Comparison

When appraising single-family residential properties, appraisers consider numerous elements of comparison. An element of comparison is any aspect of a real estate transaction or any characteristic of the property that may affect the property's sales price. Appraisers need to consider different elements of comparison for different assignments. Selecting truly comparable sales minimizes the amount and size of adjustments.

Requirements for Comparable Properties

- Sale date as close to the effective date of the appraisal as possible
- Similar in age as possible to the subject property
- Similar in location as possible to the subject property
- Similar, if not identical, in physical, legal, and economic characteristics to the subject property

Although it is not possible in every instance to find sales or listings that are identical to the subject in all these areas, appraisers should strive to find sales, offers to purchase, and listings that are as similar to the subject property in all aspects as possible. Using comps that are as similar as possible to the subject property enables appraisers to produce the most credible, and the most reliable, estimate of value.

Appraisal report forms in general use, such as the Fannie Mae Forms 1004 and 2055, identify most of these elements in a grid format. However, the adjustment grids in these forms do not include all items that may need to be adjusted. Items such as zoning, landscaping, auxiliary units, etc., are not specifically listed in the grids on these commonly used forms. If items such as these are applicable within a particular assignment, appraisers are obligated to consider them in the adjustment process as well.

FEATURE	SUBJECT			COMPARABLE SALE # 1		COMPARABLE SALE # 2		COMPARABLE SALE # 3	
Address									
Proximity to Subject									
Sale Price	$			$		$		$	
Sale Price/Gross Liv. Area	$	sq. ft.	$	sq. ft.		$	sq. ft.	$	sq. ft.
Data Source(s)									
Verification Source(s)									
VALUE ADJUSTMENTS	DESCRIPTION		DESCRIPTION	+(-) $ Adjustment		DESCRIPTION	+(-) $ Adjustment	DESCRIPTION	+(-) $ Adjustment
Sale or Financing Concessions									
Date of Sale/Time									
Location									
Leasehold/Fee Simple									
Site									
View									
Design (Style)									
Quality of Construction									
Actual Age									
Condition									
Above Grade Room Count	Total	Bdrms.	Baths	Total	Bdrms. Baths	Total	Bdrms. Baths	Total	Bdrms. Baths
Gross Living Area	sq. ft.		sq. ft.			sq. ft.		sq. ft.	
Basement & Finished Rooms Below Grade									
Functional Utility									
Heating/Cooling									
Energy Efficient Items									
Garage/Carport									
Porch/Patio/Deck									
Net Adjustment (Total)			☐ + ☐ -	$		☐ + ☐ -	$	☐ + ☐ -	$
Adjusted Sale Price of Comparables			Net Adj. % Gross Adj. %	$		Net Adj. % Gross Adj. %	$	Net Adj. % Gross Adj. %	$

Items needing consideration include the property rights conveyed, financing terms, any conditions of sale, expenditures immediately after purchase, and market conditions. Additionally, the appraiser must examine locational, physical, and legal differences between the subject and the comparable property.

Property Rights Conveyed

In a majority of appraisal assignments, the assignment is to appraise the fee simple interest in a property. In other instances, the assignment is for a leasehold or leased fee interest in a property. The owner of a leasehold interest in a property does not own the complete bundle of rights in that property. That owner only has a portion of the rights associated with that property, and therefore, the leasehold interest in a property is usually not equal to the fee simple interest in a property.

Though it is not always possible, appraisers should try to use comparable properties that include the same property rights as the subject property in their analyses since property rights tend to have a large influence on value. Once the property rights for the subject and the comparable sales are established, appraisers can relate and, if necessary, adjust the market data for the comparable properties to the subject property.

Financing Terms and Cash Equivalency

The **financing terms** used to purchase a property can affect the price a seller will accept. In fact, differences in financing can cause the sales price of one property to be significantly higher than that of an almost identical property that sold in the same period.

Financing can vary in many ways. Sometimes, to facilitate a sales transaction, a seller pays fees that a buyer would traditionally pay, such as discount points, loan origination fees, and closing costs. In those situations, the seller usually adds those additional fees to the sales price. Seller financing, installment sales contracts, or a buyer assuming an existing loan with a favorable interest rate can all have significant effects upon sales prices.

Adjustments for financing are different from other adjustments in one very significant way. Other adjustments are based upon differences between the comparable sale and the subject. However, adjustments for financing are based upon the difference in financing for the comparable sale and financing typically found in the market. When typical financing is used, the sale is referred to as a **cash equivalent sale**.

When adjusting for financing, appraisers typically adjust for cash equivalency. The **cash equivalency technique** is a procedure whereby the sales prices of comparable properties selling with atypical financing are adjusted to reflect financing that is typical in a market. The calculations used to derive cash equivalency adjustments vary depending upon the kind of financing used to purchase the comparable property and the terms associated with that financing.

> Example: The seller paid discount points to the lender so that the buyer could obtain financing at a below-market rate. (Points refers to prepaid interest lenders accept in order to finance a loan at below-market interest rates.) The seller added the additional points to the accepted sales price. If using this sale as a comp, an appraiser would deduct a dollar amount equal to the amount paid by the seller from the sales price.

In some cases when atypical financing is used, appraisers may not be able to adjust for its effect on the sales price, so they use a different comp.

Conditions of Sale

Appraisers look for arm's length transactions in which all parties involved are knowledgeable, acting in their own self-interest, and under no undue influence or pressure from other parties. However, **conditions of sale** may affect the final purchase price of a comparable sale and cause the sales price to reflect the market improperly. For example, if the buyer's motivation is atypical for the market, the sales price may be atypical as well. If buyers or sellers are acting under duress, properties may be bought and sold at prices that are not indicative of market value.

> Example: An extremely wealthy property owner desired to purchase his next-door neighbor's property. The adjacent property owner did not wish to sell; however, the wealthy neighbor wanted the adjacent property so much that he eventually offered an extremely high price—much higher than the actual worth of the property. The offering price was so high the adjacent property owner could not refuse. This selling price would not be a good indicator of market value.

Sometimes the conditions of a sale lead to a lower price. A seller who wants to sell quickly may discount the property's price, or family members may sell properties at a discount to other family members.

Obviously, it is best to use comparable sales that have no unusual conditions of sale. However, if an appraiser finds it necessary and unavoidable to use a sale of this type, he or she must make appropriate, market-based adjustments to compensate for these conditions and their effect on the sales price of the comparable property.

Expenditures Immediately after Purchase

A knowledgeable buyer often analyzes a potential purchase in terms of improvements needed to make it suitable to his or her needs. For example, if a property were sold, but needed a new roof at the time of sale, the sale price for the property would be the price paid plus the cost of the new roof covering.

Reasons for Expenditures Immediately After Purchase
- Curing deferred maintenance
- Removing and remodeling parts of the structures
- Change in use with special use permits and sometimes zoning changes
- Costs for remediation of any contamination

This is often seen in very expensive properties because buyers in a high-end market consider what needs to be done to the property immediately after the purchase.

> Example: A residential property is under contract for $5,000,000. The appraiser's search for comparable sales indicates that nearly every sale involved an extensive remodel immediately after purchase. In many of these comparables, it appears that the majority of the sales price was attributable to the location of the property and its land value.

Often, the buyer does not know exactly what the costs will be—though the buyer and seller are likely to negotiate some kind of price adjustment to reflect the potential expenditures.

Market Conditions and Time Considerations

An appraisal is a snapshot in time. Just as a photograph documents an instant in time, an appraisal documents a property and its value at a specific point in time. In most instances, the date of value of an appraisal is the date an appraiser inspects the subject property. However, appraisers perform appraisals with a date at some point in the past (**retrospective appraisal**). On other occasions, appraisers develop an opinion of the value of a property as of some point in the future (**prospective appraisal**). Appraisers consider market data that reflects the market conditions effective as of the date of value.

> Example: Market data effective in the summer of 2011 is a poor indicator of value for a property valued as of June 1, 2005. Sales, offers to purchase, and listings in early 2005 would be the data an appraiser would need to rely upon in that assignment.

Market conditions and property values change over time. Some markets have relatively stable values, whereas property values in other markets may increase or decrease at an astonishingly fast pace. In changing markets, adjustments need to be applied in order to reflect the change in the market from the time a property sold to the time it was used as a value indicator.

Although the term, **time adjustment**, is usually applied to adjustments made because of changing market conditions, these adjustments are not based merely on the passage of time. In a stable market, a relatively long length of time may have elapsed, but no adjustment would be needed. Likewise, in a quickly changing market, relatively significant adjustments may be necessary even though only a short length of time has elapsed between the sale of the comparable property and the date of the appraisal. The passage of time by itself is not sufficient reason to apply a time adjustment. Changes in market conditions that are spread over time are what really constitute time adjustments.

Many things bring about changes in market conditions. Any changes in interest rates, inflation, deflation, employment trends, building trends, and inward and outward population shifts produce changes in supply and demand. As supply and demand change, property values change.

Time adjustments are based upon the change in market conditions between the date the comparable property sold and the date of the appraisal. Time adjustments usually are expressed as a percentage increase or decrease over time. Then the percentage change is converted to a dollar adjustment and is applied to the sales price of the comparable property.

Often the percentage of change is expressed as a yearly amount. Appraisers convert this yearly percentage change to a monthly amount and multiply the monthly amount by the number of months that have elapsed between the sale of the comparable property and the date of the appraisal.

Example: Appraiser Abe identifies a comparable within the same planned development (PUD) as the subject. The comparable sold ten months ago for $250,000. Because each property has the same floor plan and is in the same PUD, only the time of sale must be adjusted. From his research, Abe concludes that the property values in the local market have increased an average of 3% per year. To convert this to a monthly percentage, he divides the yearly percentage by 12 and then multiplies this by the number of months for which he must account.

$$0.03 \div 12 = 0.0025$$

$$0.0025 \times 10 = 0.025 \ (2.5\%)$$

The final step is to adjust the comparable's sales price up by the percentage.

$$\$250,000 \times 2.5\% = \$6.250$$

$$\$250,000 + \$6,250 = \$256,250$$

Location

The comparable properties should be influenced, if possible, by the same market forces as the subject. Since real estate is immobile, the market forces that influence a property usually are determined by the property's **location**. In any neighborhood, many forces combine to influence the market perception, and therefore the values, within that neighborhood. Appraisers identify the boundaries of the neighborhood in which the subject property is located.

A **neighborhood** may be defined by physical boundaries such as a freeway, a body of water, or the base of a mountain. In other cases, the neighborhood boundary is established by a change in land uses, such as a transition from residential to commercial uses. Items that may not be evident when passing through an area may establish other neighborhood boundaries include ZIP code boundaries, school district boundaries, city limits, or improvement district boundaries.

If possible, appraisers should rely upon comparable properties located in the same neighborhood as the subject. Using comparable properties outside the subject's neighborhood requires additional analysis to account for locational differences between the subject and the comparable properties.

A **location adjustment** is usually required when the subject property has locational influences that are significantly different from those influencing a comparable sale. Even though the subject and the comparable sales are located in the same neighborhood, sometimes variations within that neighborhood would affect value.

> Example: In a desirable neighborhood, a residential property may back to a major interstate freeway, whereas another home in that same neighborhood may back to a private lake.

Commercial properties can be extremely susceptible to differences in location. For example, most gasoline service stations are located in corner locations because these are more advantageous. Studies have shown that customers patronize retail businesses with good vehicular access over those with inferior access. In some instances, the side of the street a property is located on has a significant effect on value.

A location that is detrimental for one land use is often beneficial for another land use. Single-family residential properties located on very busy thoroughfares tend to be less desirable than similar properties located on quiet streets. Busy street locations, on the other hand, are much more desirable for retail establishments than quiet street locations.

Physical Characteristics

The **physical characteristics** of a subject property and a comparable may vary greatly. Differences in site area, view, amenities, quality, condition, design and appeal, age, and size of improvements are all items that have an influence on a property's value. For example, all other things being equal, a three-bedroom home is usually the best indicator of value for a three-bedroom home. Likewise, a property with a panoramic ocean view is usually the best indicator of value for another property with a panoramic ocean view. Other items, such as functional utility (usability), amenities, room count, and architectural style, are all things that appraisers need to consider when making adjustments for physical differences between the subject and a comparable property.

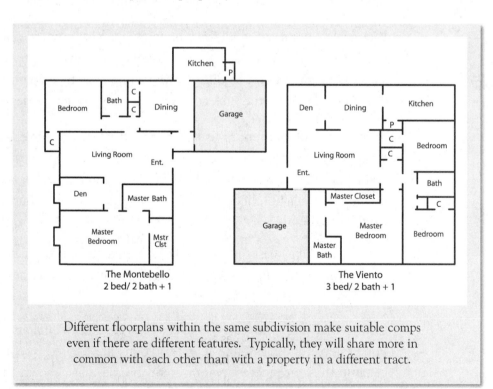

Different floorplans within the same subdivision make suitable comps even if there are different features. Typically, they will share more in common with each other than with a property in a different tract.

Other Characteristics

Other physical, legal, and economic characteristics of the subject and comparable properties should be considered. For example, properties with similar zoning (legal) or similar income producing capacity (economic) are usually better indicators of value than properties that differ in these characteristics.

Non-real Property

Occasionally, personal property is sold along with real property. For example, a seller may include all appliances in the sale of the house. If the sales price of the comp includes such items, an adjustment may be needed.

Highest and Best Use

As we discussed previously, the highest and best use of a property is the main factor that determines its value. For this reason, most appraisers will not use a comp if its highest and best use is different from that of the subject property. One of the simplest ways to check highest and best use is to see if there is a difference in zoning.

Differences in zoning may have a large influence on a property's value. An appraiser should attempt to use comparable sales that have the same zoning designation as the subject. An adjustment may be necessary if the subject and comparable properties have different zoning. Typically, properties with zoning that allows a more intensive use are more valuable than properties with zoning that allows a less intensive use. This is because the owner of the more intensively zoned property has more options for how he can use his property.

Economic Characteristics

Most beginning appraisers start with residential property appraisals. However, the sales comparison approach is used with income-producing properties as well. Ideally, if the subject property is producing income, the comps should produce similar amounts. If not, an adjustment may be necessary.

> Example: Appraiser Jane is using the sales comparison approach to value a convenience store that has annual revenue of $900,000. Two similar convenience stores sold recently: one has annual revenue of $820,000 and sold for $700,000; and the other has annual revenue of $600,000 and sold for $490,000. In this situation, the first comp is more similar to the subject in its capacity to produce income.

Verifying Market Data

After identifying the best comparable properties, the next step is to verify the data. The verification process is extremely important since it is used to identify which possible comparable properties are, or are not, reflective of activity in the open market. **Verification** is an inquiry into the circumstances surrounding and affecting a sale. This includes the reason for the sale of the property and any items affecting its price. Appraisers must be careful that data used to formulate their opinions and conclusions reflect arm's length transactions within the market.

It is important to verify the information of the comparable properties to confirm that the physical, legal, and economic information about each comparable property found in other data sources is accurate and correct. Verification also identifies whether or not the comparable property is an open market and arm's length transaction. In this part of the process, appraisers identify buyer and seller motivations and resolve any apparent conflicts and/or discrepancies found in the data sources. Additionally, they resolve any questions they may have regarding any gaps in the data or any other items that may need further explanation.

The verification process may take a number of forms and may vary as to its depth depending upon the scope of work of an assignment. Whenever possible, appraisers should verify sales by contacting the parties directly involved in the transaction. Appraiser may also verify some of the market data with parties, such as tenants, property managers, developers, etc. Some appraisal assignments require appraisers to verify the sale with the buyer (or buyer's agent) and the seller (or seller's agent).

Sometimes the verification process performed by appraisers is minimal and entails simply confirming the transaction through more than one data source. Appraisers performing only this level of verification are at much greater risk of improperly analyzing the comparable data. Although this level of verification is a relatively common practice, it does not relieve appraisers of liability associated with negligent appraisal practice.

In some instances, verification of the data may cause appraisers to eliminate a sale as a value indicator in an assignment. This happens when information uncovered during the verification process shows that the reported transaction is not indicative of the market. It also may happen when information about a comparable property cannot be verified to an appraiser's satisfaction.

Applying Adjustments

After analyzing and verifying the comps, appraisers narrow down the number of sales, listings, and pending sales to those most similar to the subject. The next step is to **apply adjustments** to the comps. Appraisers apply adjustments to the sales prices of comparable properties in an effort to "equalize" the comparable sale to the subject property. As a result, the adjusted sales price of the comparable property is indicative of the value of the subject property.

The accuracy and the reliability of the sales comparison approach hinges upon the accuracy of the adjustments applied to the comparable properties. The importance of making proper adjustments to the comparable properties cannot be overemphasized. The adjustments applied to the comparable properties must be derived from the market and reflective of the actions of typical buyers and sellers in the real estate market within which the subject property operates. One of the pitfalls in performing the sales comparison analysis is the tendency for some appraisers to apply improper, unsupported, and even arbitrary adjustments to comparable properties. In more than a few instances, appraisers have significantly over-valued properties based on improper adjustments. USPAP is very clear when it states, "…an appraiser must be aware of, understand, and correctly employ those recognized methods and techniques that are necessary to produce a credible appraisal…"

Applying Adjustments

1. Identify differences between the comp and the subject property.
2. Decide if the difference makes the comp more or less valuable.
3. Determine the value of the difference.
4. Make value adjustments in order.

Identify Differences

When looking at the various elements of comparison, appraisers first identify if there is a difference for which adjustment is necessary. Appraisers look at the elements of comparison and check for any special sales and financing considerations and for any differences between the comps and the subject property in time-related, locational, and physical characteristics.

The subject and the comparable sales usually are entered onto an adjustment grid, or matrix. The **adjustment grid** lists important items affecting value such as site area, location, design and appeal, quality, condition, gross building area, basement area, room count, view, age, amenities, etc. Using this grid helps to ensure that the comparable sales are adjusted consistently. It also shows, how the subject compares to the comparable properties.

Decide if the Comp is More or Less Valuable

Once differences are identified, an appraiser's next step is to analyze each of the differences and determine if a particular difference makes the comparable sale superior or inferior.

Example: The comparable property shown in the grid is not in as good condition as the subject property and does not have as many bathrooms. However, it does have a larger garage and a pool, whereas the subject property does not.

	Subject Property	Comparable Sale	
Sales Price	???	$205,000	
Condition	Good	Fair	Inferior
Bedrooms	4	4	Same
Bathrooms	3	2	Inferior
Garage	2-car	3-car	Superior
Pool	No	Yes	Superior

The appraiser knows the sales price of the comparable property, and is trying to develop the probable sales price of the subject property. Since the comp's condition and number of bathrooms are inferior to the subject, the subject property would be worth more than the comp in these areas. However, the comp has a larger garage and a pool, so the subject would be worth less than the comp in those areas.

By comparing the two properties in this way, an appraiser knows if he or she has to make a positive or a negative adjustment to the comparable sales price, even before he or she determines the actual dollar value of the adjustment.

Direction of Adjustments

Adjustments are always made to the comparables. An appraiser cannot adjust the value of the subject property because the value of the subject is not known.

1. If the comparable property has a feature that is superior to the subject property or if the comparable property has a feature that is missing from the subject property, the comparable property is considered to be worth more than the subject in regard to that item. In that case, the sales price of the comparable would need to be adjusted down to account for the contributory value of that superior feature and its effect upon the sales price of that property.

2. If the comparable property has a feature that is inferior to the subject property or if the comparable property is lacking a feature that the subject property has, the comp is worth less than the subject in regard to that item. In that case, the sales price of the comparable property would be adjusted up to account for that difference.

Example: Through careful analysis, it is determined that a pool in this marketplace is worth $10,000. The comparable property has a pool and the subject property does not, so the adjustment process requires that $10,000 is subtracted from the sales price of the comparable. In essence the question is, "What would the comparable have sold for if it were like the subject property and did not have a pool?"

Additionally, the subject property has three bathrooms and the comparable sale has only two bathrooms. An extra bathroom in this marketplace is worth $5,000. In this case, add $5,000 to the sales price of the comparable, to answer the question, "What would the comparable have sold for if it had a third bathroom, just like the subject property?"

Determine the Adjustment Value

After identifying a particular characteristic in which the subject property and the comparable property are different, appraisers identify the amount the market would pay for that difference. By tabulating the pluses and minuses of all of the adjustments made to the comparable sale, we arrive at the adjusted selling price.

Example: Features that are superior to those of the subject property require a negative adjustment. Features that are inferior require a positive adjustment. Totaling the positive and negative adjustments enables an appraiser to zero in on an indicated value for the subject property.

	Subject Property	Comparable Sale	
Sales Price	???	$205,000	
Condition	Good	Fair	+$5,000
Bedrooms	4	4	
Bathrooms	3	2	+$5,000
Garage	2-car	3-car	-$5,000
Pool	No	Yes	-$10,000
Adjusted Sales Price		$200,000	

Adjustments made to the prices of the comparable sales may be applied either in dollars or as a percentage. For example, an enclosed patio may add $15,000 in value (dollar adjustment) or a home located adjacent to a noisy freeway may be found to be worth 15% less (percentage adjustment) than other homes not similarly affected.

The manner in which the adjustment is extracted from the market determines which way the adjustment is applied. Some adjustments are applied to reflect specific property features or physical characteristics. Views, swimming pools, and additional garage parking spaces fit this category. Dollar values are used for these types of adjustments. Other adjustments are made to the sales prices of comparable properties to reflect items affecting the overall value of that property. Sales and financing concessions as well as property rights conveyed would be items fitting this description. Since these items affect the overall value, the sales price of the comp is adjusted by a percentage.

In some appraisal assignments, appraisers make adjustments to a particular unit of comparison rather than to the property as a whole. For example, when appraising an apartment complex, or a large hotel, the appraiser may analyze comparable sales based on price per unit. Theaters, sports facilities, and auditoriums may be analyzed in terms of price per seat. RV and mobile home parks and parking lots may be analyzed in terms of price per space. Some properties are analyzed based on price per square foot, price per acre, or even price per cubic foot.

Example: Karl is appraising a warehouse. He found a comparable that recently sold for $21 per cubic foot. Karl's market investigation reveals that a negative 4% adjustment for age should be made and a positive 7% adjustment for physical differences. Karl would first subtract 4% from the price per unit ($21 − 4% = $20.16), and then add 7% ($20.16 + 7% = $21.57) to find the adjusted value per unit, $21.57 per cubic foot.

Identifying how much to adjust for a particular item is the most difficult aspect of the sales comparison approach. Adjustments must be market derived, and in some situations, readily available market data is inconclusive. There are numerous methods for identifying how large an adjustment should be, and some methods work better than other methods. Common methods include paired sales analysis, sale-resale analysis, multiple regression analysis, and contingent valuation methodology.

Paired Sales Analysis

The **paired sales analysis** (also called model match) is used to identify the amount of an adjustment when at least two sales are found that are virtually identical in all aspects except one. The one differing item between the sales logically accounts for the difference in price between the two properties.

Example: Assume two homes sold in a tract of homes all developed by the same developer. Both of the homes in this example have the exact same floor plan and both are in similar locations. The two homes are virtually identical in all regards except one has a remodeled kitchen and the other does not. The home with the upgraded kitchen sold for $225,000 and the one without sold at about the same time for $210,000. Both homes sold with similar financing in a market where values are stable. In the above scenario, the difference in price is $15,000. The only significant difference between the two properties is the fact one has a remodeled kitchen and the other does not. In this example, it would be reasonable to assume that the kitchen has a contributory value of $15,000.

In that particular neighborhood, an appraiser would be able to state, with a high degree of certainty, that a similar kitchen in that same neighborhood would warrant a $15,000 adjustment upwards or downwards. The direction of the adjustment would be dependent upon whether the subject or the comparable sale was the property with the upgrade.

Example: Suppose an appraiser needs to know the value of a pool in a particular marketplace. He or she searches for two sales that are similar in all characteristics, except for the pool. The two properties have the same number of bedrooms and bathrooms. They are close enough in size that no adjustment needs to be made (a 25 square-foot difference is not perceptible in the marketplace).

| Sale 1 | 3 bedroom | 2 bath | 1600 sq. ft. | pool | $200,000 |
| Sale 2 | 3 bedroom | 2 bath | 1625 sq. ft. | no pool | $192,000 |

Assuming that all other characteristics are similar, the only recognized difference is the pool. This paired sales analysis reveals that a pool in this marketplace is worth about $8,000.

Sale 1
$200,000

Sale 2
$192,000

This marketplace appears to support the value for a pool at $8,000. The diligent appraiser continues to search and finds another pair to analyze. This time the two properties match with the exact same square footage, room count, and floor plan. The only recognized difference is Sale 1 has a pool, whereas Sale 2 does not.

| Sale 1 | 4 bedroom | 2.5 bath | 2000 sq. ft. | pool | $232,000 |
| Sale 2 | 4 bedroom | 2.5 bath | 2000 sq. ft. | no pool | $223,500 |

The difference in the selling prices is $8,500. Since the properties are a bit more expensive, the slightly higher pool value can be justified. However, the difference is not significant and still supports the opinion that a pool in this marketplace is worth approximately $8,000.

The more evidence appraisers can extract from the marketplace, the stronger their opinions will be. Although, this method is accurate, it is often impractical. In most cases, there are not enough sufficiently similar sales available to identify the contributory value of a particular variable. Typically, very few sales are available that have only one significant difference between them, and most of the time, when sales like this do exist, the difference between the two is not the item an appraiser is trying to identify. When this method is used, frequently a series of adjustments is required in order to isolate the effect of a single characteristic. The problem arises in this scenario in knowing how much to adjust for the other items when attempting to isolate the effect of that single characteristic.

Even though the data available to perform the paired sales analysis may be limited, appraisers should not discard this method of extracting adjustments. In many cases, this method provides meaningful results, in spite of the limited available data. In these cases, an appraiser would check the reasonableness of the data by using some of the other available analytical methods.

Case Study

Appraiser Jane was hired to appraise a new house in an upscale development situated in the hills overlooking a valley and a freeway. She began her investigation by pulling comparable sales and setting up a workfile. She then went to the site to examine the circumstances.

Upon doing the physical inspection, she discovered that the subject property was situated at the end of a short cul-de-sac. Looking from the rear of the property, the subject property definitely had an outstanding view of the valley and the freeway. Comparable 1 was situated on the same cul-de-sac, but was on the opposite side of the street. Because of a hillside and the homes opposing it, its view was obstructed. Comparables 2 and 3 were situated in the same subdivision so as not to have any view at all. From her physical inspection thus far, she knew that the subject property did indeed have a superior view to the comparables but still did not know how much the view was worth or what the adjustment should be.

These homes were about a year old and the subdivision was still under construction, so she went to the sales office to see if any recent sales could be paired up, isolating the view in order to determine what the view was worth. No such comparison could be made, but she was able to verify in the sales office that the owner of the subject property had paid a $50,000 view premium for that particular lot. By then, though, the subdivision was a year older and there was still no concrete proof of what a view was worth in this subdivision.

Case Study *(Continued)*

Jane revisited the data pulled at the beginning of the assignment and noticed five sales of new homes in a less expensive neighboring community on the other side of the freeway, about five miles away, all on the same street. She observed that the five sales were described almost identically: approximately 2,200 square feet with all the same amenities, but there was a disparity in the prices. They ranged from $275,000 to $329,000, three of the sales clustered between $275,000 and $279,000, and the other sales were $325,000 and $329,000. They evidenced no descriptive difference in amenities, yet the price range was $50,000.

She decided to drive over and investigate. The top level of the street was about 15 to 20 feet higher than the lower level of the street, and the street was shaped like a horseshoe. House A sold for $325,000 and had an outstanding view from the rear yard, a view of the same valley and freeway but from the other side. Houses B, C and D on the opposite side of the street sold for $275,000, $277,000, and $279,000 respectively. They were very similar homes to House A, but they had no views because of the obstruction of the homes on the opposite side of the street. House E, situated on the corner of the upper level of the street, sold for $329,000, and had an outstanding view from the rear yard over the housetops of the homes on the lower level of the street.

These five properties matched up perfectly as being practically identical, except for their views. The sales prices were approximately $50,000 apart, indicating that the view in this neighborhood was worth about $50,000. Because this is a lower priced neighborhood than that of the subject property, it is logical to say that since the view was worth approximately $50,000 in this marketplace, it would be worth at least $50,000 in the more expensive marketplace.

Sale-Resale Analysis

Sometimes a property sells and is resold in a relatively short time. Assuming both sales are arm's-length, open market transactions, and assuming that there have been no significant changes to the property during the time between the two sales, the difference in price could be a basis for a time adjustment. This is called the **Sale-Resale Analysis**.

> Example: Assume a property was purchased for $275,000 on June 1 and resold 6 months later for $280,500. This $5,500 increase was spaced over a 6-month period and was a 2.0% increase over the original sales price. The 2.0% increase equals a .33% increase in value per month or approximately 4% per year.

In some instances, a property may be in a stable market where values are not changing to any significant degree. If the improvements have been remodeled during the time between the two sales, the sale-resale analysis method could identify the contributory value of the remodeling.

However, like the paired sales analysis, this method is not always practical. Rarely do properties sell and resell with no other changes taking place. In many instances, properties are purchased, remodeled, and resold in markets that are also increasing in value. To identify how much of the increase in value between the two sales was attributable to the remodeling and how much was attributable to the increasing market may be difficult to determine. The Sale-Resale analysis can prove to be a powerful analytical tool in an appraiser's set of analytical techniques.

Multiple Regression Analysis

Multiple regression analysis is an analytical technique using statistical methods to analyze comparable sales and estimate individual adjustments. Appraisers use multiple regression analysis not just to identify the amount of an adjustment, but also to help estimate property values. The problem with using multiple regression analysis is that most of the time all sales in an area are factored into the analysis, not just the sales that are comparable to the subject. Less than arm's length transactions and even fraudulent sales often get included in these analytical models. Obviously, these non-market based transactions can distort the results obtained from a multiple regression analysis.

Like the other methods, multiple regression analysis has benefits and limitations. Since it is a statistical method, multiple regression analysis works best when distinct, quantifiable data can be identified. Items such **as age, building size, sales price, room count, site area, etc., are easily** quantifiable. Other items having an effect on value such as quality, condition, view, design and appeal, and location are not easily quantifiable and therefore not readily applicable in a program that is based upon mathematical calculations.

In areas where properties have a high degree of homogeneity—same age, size, quality, condition, design and appeal, etc.—a multiple regression analysis may produce credible results. In areas where all the properties are custom built and are dissimilar, multiple-regression analysis does not usually produce meaningful results.

Contingent Valuation Methodology

Also called the survey method, the **contingent valuation methodology,** if performed properly, can yield very good results. There are participants in any given market that are active in, and extremely knowledgeable about, that market. Sometimes, all the appraiser has to do to identify how much a particular feature affects the value of a property is to ask those who are knowledgeable about that market. If an appraiser surveys enough knowledgeable participants within a market in a systematic manner, the appraiser can generate data that is found nowhere else.

The major benefit to this method is that it can be used even when there is no sales data available, since this method does not rely on sales data to determine the adjustment value.

However, this method has limitations as well. Like any type of survey, appraisers need to perform a significant number of interviews in order to obtain accurate and quantifiable results. Additionally, in order to get meaningful results, the appraiser should ask all interviewees the same questions.

Make Adjustments in Order

Appraisers use both dollar and percentage adjustments. If the adjustments are made strictly on a dollar basis, the sequence in which adjustments are made is unimportant.

However, the adjustments must be made in a specific sequence if the adjustments are entirely percentage adjustments or if they are made in combination with dollar adjustments. Adjustments that affect the overall property value are made first, followed by those that only affect individual property features.

Typical Order of Adjustments

1. Rights conveyed
2. Financing and sales concessions
3. Conditions of sale
4. Expenditures immediately after purchase
5. Market conditions (time)
6. Location adjustments
7. Physical characteristics

Making Dollar Adjustments

Comparables with dollar adjustments only are relatively uncomplicated. This is because the sequence in which adjustments are made is unimportant.

Example: A comp sold for $335,000 but required several adjustments:

Comparable	
Sales Price	$335,000
Condition	- $5,000
1/2 bath	+ $8,000
Garage	-$12,000
Adjusted Price	$326,000

Since this example only involves dollar adjustments, the appraiser can add up the adjustments in any order, and the adjusted price will always be $326,000.

The appraiser can even total the adjustments, and then combine the net adjustment amount with the sales price to get the adjusted price: − $5,000 + $8,000 − $12,000 = − $9,000 net adjustment; $335,000 − $9,000 = $326,000.

Making Percentage Adjustments

Since a percentage adjustment affects the overall property value, applying several percentage adjustments can cause the outcome to vary considerably.

Unlike dollar adjustments, one cannot simply add the percentages together and then apply the ultimate percentage to the comparable's price. When applying percentage adjustments, intermediate adjusted prices are calculated. Subsequent adjustments are applied to the previous intermediate price thereby calculating a new intermediate price. This results in a cumulative value estimate that could be significantly affected by the sequence in which adjustments are applied. An example should help to illustrate this.

Example: A suitable comparable has been found and it sold for $310,000. However, three percentage adjustments are required to account for its differences to the subject.

The location of the comparable is superior to the subject, which requires a 10% negative adjustment to make up for its superiority. The appraiser also discovered that the financing used to purchase the property was not typical of that market, so the sales price of the comp needs to be adjusted up by 2%. Finally, it sold 14 months ago, and due to changing market conditions, it will need to be adjusted up 5%.

Correct Sequence: By making the adjustments in the correct sequence, the adjusted price is $298,999 (rounded).

Sequence	
Sales Price	$310,000
Financing Terms	× 1.02
	$316,200
Market Conditions	× 1.05
	$332,010
Location	× .90
Adjusted Price	$298,800 (rounded)

Incorrect Combined Percentages: Adding the three percentages together to get a net percentage of -3% (2%+5%-10%) and applying the combined percentage to the sales price of the comparable results in an adjusted price of $300,700.

Combined	
Sales Price	$310,000
Net %	× .97
Adjusted Price	$300,700

There is a difference of almost $2,000 when using the correct sequence of percentage adjustments, and with larger numbers, the discrepancy becomes more glaring.

Making both Percentage and Dollar Adjustments

When this scenario arises, it is crucial to follow the sequence of adjustments, for any improperly applied adjustment will affect the following adjustment(s).

Example: Appraiser Kate is appraising a large, million dollar home. She found a comparable property that recently sold for $5,500,000. However, she needs to make several adjustments—a $20,000 adjustment for the presence of a pool, a 7% adjustment for market conditions, and a -10% adjustment for external obsolescence associated with proximity to a freeway. In addition, Kate discovered during her research that the seller bought down the buyer's loan, which accounted for $111,000 of the sales price.

When applied properly, the sequence of adjustment reveals that the proper adjusted value of this particular comparable is $5,209,600 (rounded).

Sequence 1	
Sales Price	$5,500,000
Financing	− $111,000
	$5,389,000
Market Conditions	× 1.07
	$5,766,230
Location	× .90
	$5,189,607
Physical Characteristics	+ $20,000
	$5,209,607

If the adjustments are applied in any other order, the final result will be off from as little as $4,000 to as much as $12,500.

Sequence 2	
Sales Price	5,500,000
Physical Characteristics	+ $20,000
	$5,520,000
Location	× .90
	$4,968,000
Financing Terms	– $111,000
	$4,857,000
Market Conditions	× 1.07
	$5,196,990

Reconciling the Sales Comparison Analysis

When reconciling the sales comparison analysis, it is important for appraisers to weigh the reliability of all indicated values derived from the sales, pending sales, and listings that were considered.

When the adjustment process is completed, each comparable sale produces an adjusted sales price that is an indicator of value for the subject property. Sometimes these adjusted sales prices may match one another; most often, they do not. Appraisers do not simply average the adjusted sales prices. At this point, appraisers identify which of the comparable sales is given the most weight in this analysis and the reasoning why it is the one most heavily weighted. They must use sound reasoning and judgment, not mere mechanical calculation, to reconcile the individual value indicators into a value estimate.

Often, the comparable sale having the smallest amount of gross adjustments is the sale given most weight in the sales comparison analysis. This stands to reason since the property requiring the least amount of adjusting on a gross basis is likely the one that is overall most similar to the subject. Additionally, sales that require the largest amount of adjusting on a gross basis would tend to be the least similar sale to the subject and consequently the weakest indicator of value.

Although the property having the least amount of adjusting on a gross basis is often the one given the most weight, this is not always the case. Sometimes the sale having the fewest number of adjustments, or the sale that is most recent in time to the date of the appraisal is weighted most heavily.

Fannie Mae's Adjustment Guidelines

Sometimes a comp ceases to be an appropriate comparable. This occurs when an appraiser makes too many adjustments to the comparable, but what is too many? Fannie Mae has established **adjustment guidelines**.

Single Line-Item Adjustments

Fannie Mae states that a single line item adjustment should not exceed 10% of the sales price of the comparable. For example, if a property sold for $200,000, no single adjustment should exceed $20,000. Keep in mind that this is not a steadfast rule; it is a guideline. Appraisers can make the adjustment, even if it exceeds the 10% guideline for a single line item, as long as market data supports it.

Total Adjustments

Fannie Mae has also established guidelines for the total adjustment amounts. There are two types of totals—net and gross.

Net Adjustment Guidelines. The net adjustment amount is determined by combining all the adjustments and adding or subtracting them as indicated. Appraisers divide this amount by the sales price to determine the percentage of net adjustments. Fannie Mae's guideline is that the percentage of net adjustments should not exceed 15%.

However, the net adjustment guideline is not enough, since the net adjustment amount allows for offsetting adjustments. In theory, an appraiser could apply 100 different adjustments that balance each other out and result in a net adjustment amount of $0.

Gross Adjustment Guidelines. Fannie Mae has also established a guideline for the acceptable percentage of gross adjustments in a single comparable sale. The amount of the gross adjustment is determined by adding all individual adjustments, without regard to whether they are positive or negative adjustments. Then, appraisers divide that sum by the comparable property's sales price to determine the percentage of gross adjustment. Fannie Mae states that this percentage should not exceed 25% of the sales price of the comparable.

Example: Net and Gross Adjustments

In this example, the percentage of net adjustments is well within the guideline at only 2.5%. However, the gross percentage adjustment is 27.5%, which is too high.

Sales Price	$100,000
Condition Adjustment	+$5,000
Bedroom Adjustment	– $3,000
Bathroom Adjustment	– $2,000
Pool Adjustment	– $7,500
Location Adjustment	+$5,000
Age Adjustment	+$3,000
Gross Living Area Adjustment	+$2,000
Net Adjustment	$2,500
Percentage of Net Adjustments	2.5%
Gross Adjustment	$27,50
Percentage of Gross Adjustments	27.5%

This is a clearly a red flag, because there seem to be too many significant quality differences between the two properties for them to be comparable. Again, this is only a guideline that can be exceeded within reason, but in those occasional cases, appraisers need to include discussion about why such large adjustments were necessary.

Bracketing

At this point, appraisers should check the appropriateness of the subject property's value by bracketing. **Bracketing** is the idea that the sales prices of the comparables chosen for the appraisal will not all be higher than the value of the subject property, nor will they all be lower.

The comparable sales will bracket the value of the subject—that is, one or two of the sales will be higher, and one or two will be lower. When considering the marketplace, bracketing produces a solid conclusion.

> Example: A property appraised for $200,000, but all of the comparable sales sold for a price in the low $190,000s. How can an appraiser justify this opinion of value when all of the comparable properties were lower? If the appraiser cannot find an appropriate comp that sold for $200,000 or more, then the value may be questionable.

Similarly, if all of the comparables are higher in price than the value of the subject property, a question should arise as to whether or not appropriate comparables were used.

> Example: If the subject property appraises for $200,000, but all of the comparable sales are between $210,000 and $215,000, there must be several significant differences that account for the difference in values. If they are truly similar, then the subject should be worth between $210,000 and $215,000. If the comps chosen are not that similar, the appraiser should look for comparables that are more appropriate.

SUMMARY

Deeply rooted in the **principle of substitution**, the **sales comparison approach** is a powerful tool in the marketplace for appraising land and residential properties (1 to 4 units). This approach is the least complicated and most widely used method. It is an accurate tool when appraisers follow proper procedures to extract the relevant data from the marketplace and appropriately apply the information to the appraisal problem at hand. Appraisers must always objectively read the marketplace, not try to make the marketplace fit a predetermined notion. With practice and varied experience, appraisers become proficient at applying these techniques and using this methodology.

However, the sales comparison approach does have its limitations. The fact that it relies so heavily on historical data is the primary drawback. Additionally, the requisite of multiple arms' length transactions of similar property types can limit it for unique properties, but makes it a powerful tool when working in an active market.

This approach to value relies heavily on bona fide market data and proper verification. Therefore, appraisers must be careful when collecting, analyzing, and verifying their information and when applying and reconciling the data.

UNIT 9 REVIEW

Matching Exercise

Instructions: Write the letter of the matching term on the blank line before its definition, and then check your response with the Answer Key that immediately follows the Multiple Choice Questions.

Terms

A. adjustment

B. bracketing

C. cash equivalency technique

D. element of comparison

E. matrix

F. Multiple Listing Service

G. multiple regression analysis

H. paired sales analysis

I. public records

J. title plant

Definitions

1. _____ Value expressed in dollar or percentage amounts that is added or subtracted from the sales price of a comparable property.

2. _____ Service provided by local real estate boards for its member agents and brokers and is designed as a tool for marketing real estate.

3. _____ Documents that show evidence of the conveyance of title or transfer of an interest in real property.

4. _____ Fully indexed records used by the title companies for research related to the issuance of title insurance policies.

5. _____ Any aspect of a real estate transaction or any characteristic of the property that may affect the property's sales price.

6. _____ Procedure whereby the sales prices of comparable properties selling with atypical financing are adjusted to reflect financing that is typical in a market.

7. _____ Grid that identifies important items affecting value such as site area and location.

8. _____ Method to determine adjustment value that uses at least two sales that are virtually identical in all aspects, except one.

9. _____ Analytical technique that uses statistical methods to analyze comparable sales and estimate individual adjustments.

10. _____ Concept that the sales prices of the comparables chosen for the appraisal will not all be higher than the value of the subject property, nor will they all be lower.

Multiple Choice Questions

Instructions: Circle your choice, and then check your response with the Answer Key that immediately follows the Multiple Choice Questions.

1. The overruling principle behind the sales comparison approach is:
    a. anticipation.
    b. substitution.
    c. multiplication.
    d. supplication.

2. Adjustments are applied to:
    a. the comparable properties.
    b. the subject property.
    c. the property being appraised.
    d. both the subject and comparable properties.

3. The comparison approach is LEAST applicable when:
    a. there is a sufficient number of comps.
    b. appraising property types that are bought and sold regularly.
    c. appraising vacant land.
    d. appraising a large shopping center.

4. In which situation can the sales comparison approach be used?
    a. When appraising single-family residences, multi-residential properties, and vacant land only
    b. When appraising residential and income property
    c. Any property when sufficient comparable data is available
    d. When appraising special purpose buildings, residential property, and qualified income properties

5. Which of the following lists the steps for the sales comparison approach in order?
    a. Collect data, verify data, apply adjustments, reconcile values
    b. Collect data, analyze data, reconcile values, apply adjustments
    c. Analyze data, verify data, reconcile values, apply adjustments
    d. Analyze data, apply adjustments, verify data, reconcile values

6. The service that appraisers and real estate agents use to research information on properties currently for sale is called the:
    a. County Recorder's Office.
    b. Multiple Regression Service.
    c. Title Plant Distributor.
    d. Multiple Listing Service.

7. As a market data resource, a party to a transaction is:
    a. a principal like the buyer or the seller.
    b. a local real estate agent.
    c. other appraisers in the area.
    d. owners of properties used as comparable sales.

8. Sales information for a 30,000 square foot warehouse is a good indicator of value for:
    a. high-rise office space.
    b. single-family residences.
    c. warehouses of similar volume.
    d. strip center.

9. Which of the following statements regarding comps and geographic area is INCORRECT?
    a. It may be necessary to consider comparables in other neighborhoods.
    b. Appraisers must limit the comparables to the neighborhood of the subject.
    c. Depending on the property type, an appraiser may need to look in different states for a comparable.
    d. The distance an appraiser will have to go for comparable information varies from assignment to assignment.

10. How many comparables should an appraiser use on each assignment?
    a. Three closed sales
    b. Three closed sales and three pending sales
    c. Three sales of any kind
    d. As many as it takes to arrive at a credible analysis

11. While researching comparable properties, Frank finds an identical comp in the same tract of homes. He notes that as part of the sales agreement, the seller partially financed the sale. Frank should:

    a. use the comparable with no further action.

    b. not use the comparable because it has atypical financing.

    c. apply a cash equivalency formula to the comparable to adjust for the non-market financing.

    d. apply a cash equivalency formula to the subject to adjust for the non-market financing.

12. A comparable sold nine months ago for $268,000. The appraiser concludes that property values have increased by 5% per year. What should the adjustment be?

    a. $278,000

    b. $10,000

    c. $27,800

    d. $13,400

13. Locational adjustments may be based on:

    a. changes in zoning.

    b. proximity to negative influences like an airport.

    c. market perception.

    d. all of the above.

14. If the subject property has a feature that the _____ property does not have, _____ the value of the feature _____ the comparable price.

    a. comparable, add, to

    b. subject, add, to

    c. subject, subtract, from

    d. comparable, subtract, from

15. Adjustments are made on:

    a. a dollar basis only.

    b. a percentage basis only.

    c. a fractional basis.

    d. both dollar and percentage basis.

16. Which of the following lists the proper sequence of adjustments?

    a. Conditions of sale, rights conveyed, financing, and time

    b. Financing, time, conditions of sale, and location

    c. Location, financing, time, and expenditures after purchase

    d. Rights conveyed, financing, time, and physical characteristics

17. The transaction price of a comparable property is $200,000. The appraiser determines that the comparable is 5% more desirable because of special financing, the conditions of the sale affected the subject negatively by 8%, the location of the comparable is 15% better but it is physically 5% worse than the subject, and since the comparable sold, the market has improved by 20%. What is the indicated value of the subject?

    a. $187,000

    b. $253,000

    c. $220,000

    d. $169,000

Use the following grid to answer 18-20:

Characteristic	Subject	Sale 1	Sale 2	Sale 3
Price		$200,000	$235,000	$190,000
Square Feet	1,500	1,500	1,500	1,5000
Fireplace	One	One	One	One
Pool	Yes	No	Yes	No
Garage	1-car	2-car	2-car	1-car

18. What is the adjustment value for a pool in this neighborhood?

    a. $35,000

    b. $45,000

    c. $17,500

    d. $10,000

19. What is the adjustment value for an extra garage space in this neighborhood?

    a. $35,000

    b. $45,000

    c. $17,500

    d. $10,000

20. According to the adjustments above, what is the indicated value of the subject property?

    a. $245,000

    b. $210,000

    c. $225,000

    d. $190,000

21. A flower shop was purchased in the summer of 2009 for $500,000. It sold in the summer of 2011 for $450,000. Using the sale-resale analysis, determine the annual rate at which this market is decreasing.

    a. 10%

    b. 1%

    c. 5%

    d. 9%

22. A comparable sold recently for $100,000 and requires a positive adjustment for locational differences of $12,000 and a negative adjustment for physical differences of $7,500. Under normal practice, should an appraiser use this comp?

    a. Yes.

    b. No, because it exceeds the federal guideline for single line item adjustments.

    c. No, because it exceeds the Ginnie Mae guideline for gross adjustments

    d. No, because it exceeds the Fannie Mae guideline for single line item adjustments.

23. Based on the following information, is this comp acceptable?

Selling Price	$160,000
Bedroom Adjustment	$8,000
Fireplace Adjustment	−$3,000
Garage Adjustment	$7,000
Locational Adjustment	−$10,000
Age Adjustment	$8,000

    a. Yes

    b. No, because it exceeds the federal guideline for single line item.

    c. No, because it exceeds the Ginnie Mae guideline for gross adjustments.

    d. No, because it exceeds the Fannie Mae guideline for single line item.

24. Using the information from question 23, what is the adjusted value of the comparable?

    a. $196,000

    b. $170,000

    c. $124,000

    d. $150,000

25. After careful analysis, Brandi determines the adjusted value for her three best comparable properties are $400,000, $420,000, and $425,000. What is the indicated value of the subject?

    a. $415,000

    b. $412,500

    c. $422,500

    d. It depends on which property or properties Brandi gives most weight to in her analysis.

UNIT 9 ANSWER KEY

Answers – Matching

1. A	4. J	7. E	10. B
2. F	5. D	8. H	
3. I	6. C	9. G	

Answers – Multiple Choice

1. **(b)** This valuation approach relies heavily upon the principal of substitution, which states that a typical buyer in a market will pay no more for a property than what he or she could pay for a reasonable substitute. **Page 274**

2. **(a)** Comparable Property Sales Price ± Adjustments = Adjusted Value. **Page 274**

3. **(d)** The sales comparison approach is most applicable in situations where there are a sufficient number of reliable, arm's-length sales, and when appraising property types that are bought and sold on a regular basis. It is the predominant approach used when appraising single-family residences, multi-residential properties, and vacant land. **Page 275**

4. **(c)** The sales comparison approach is best suited for appraising single-family residences (including condominiums, small multi-residential properties, and vacant land). It is also applicable anytime sufficient sales data is available. **Page 275**

5. **(a)** Although the "Analyze market data" step is missing, the remaining four steps are in correct order. The other choices are missing steps and out of order. **Page 278**

6. **(d)** The Multiple Listing Service (MLS) is a service is provided by local real estate boards for its members and is designed as a tool for marketing real estate. Listings are input into the MLS system to notify real estate licensees of properties available for sale. Listings include information such as the asking price and the total days the property has been on the market. **Page 279**

7. **(a)** Parties to the transaction are buyers, sellers, and their brokers. **Page 281**

8. **(c)** Sales information for like properties to the subject will provide the most credible, reliable, and appropriate market data for an appraisal. **Page 283**

9. **(b)** The geographic area an appraiser would typically search for comparable sales data depends upon the nature of the real estate being appraised. If similar properties are commonly bought and sold within a neighborhood, such as single-family residences, an appraiser would typically limit the search for sales data to similar properties located within that area. On the other hand, the market for some kinds of properties may be national or even worldwide in scope. **Page 282**

10. **(d)** Most clients require a minimum of three comparable closed sales to be included in their reports. However, the more comps an appraiser can analyze, the more sound and supportable his or her conclusions will be. Therefore, an appraiser should utilize as many comps as necessary to arrive at his or her conclusion. **Page 283**

11. **(c)** The cash equivalency technique is a procedure whereby the sale prices of comparable properties selling with atypical financing are adjusted to reflect financing that is typical in a market. **Page 285**

12. **(b)** $5\% \div 12 = .4167\%$ per month. $0.4167\% \times 9$ months $= 3.75\%$ (rounded). $268,000 $\times 3.75\% = \$10,050$ (10,000 rounded) adjustment value. **Page 288**

13. **(d)** Locational adjustments may be based on changes in neighborhood (zoning, zip code, school district, et al), proximity to negative or positive influences, street orientation, and market perceptions. **Page 289**

14. **(a)** If the subject property has a feature that the comparable sale lacks, add the value of that feature to the comparable. **Page 295**

15. **(d)** Adjustments may be made solely on the basis of percentage or dollars, or adjustments may be made by using a combination of both. The manner in which the adjustment is extracted from the market determines which way the adjustment is applied. **Page 303**

16. **(d)** The proper sequence of adjustments is rights conveyed, financing, conditions of sale, expenditures immediately after purchase, time, location, and physical characteristics. **Page 305**

17. **(a)** Comparables are always adjusted to mimic the amenities of the subject. **Page 305** Following the sequence of adjustments, the math is as follows:

Financing:	$200,000 – 5%	= $190,000
Conditions of sale:	$190,000 – 8%	= $174,800
Market conditions:	$174,800 + 20%	= $209,760
Location adjustments:	$209,760 – 15%	= $178,296
Physical characteristics:	$178,296 + 5%	= $187,210
Round the number	$187,000	

18. **(a)** The paired sales analysis identifies the amount of an adjustment when at least two sales are found that are virtually identical in all aspects except one. The one differing item between the sales equals the difference in value between the two properties. For the pool, the difference between Sale 1 and Sale 2 equals the value of a pool. $235,000 − $200,000 = $35,000. **Page 305**

19. **(d)** The difference between Sale 1 and Sale 3 equals the value for an extra garage space. $200,000 − $190,000 = $10,000. **Page 305**

20. **(c)**   To determine the value of the subject, select any one of the comparables and apply the proper adjustments to it. Select the comparable that is as similar as possible to the subject, in this case, either Sale 2 or Sale 3 would work. If we use Sale 3, the only difference is that the subject has a pool and the comparable does not. To account for the difference, add $35,000 (the value of a pool) to the comparable, answering the question, "What would this comparable sell for if it had a pool like the subject?" If you select any of the other two comparables and apply the adjustments correctly, you will arrive at the same conclusion. **Page 305**

21. **(c)**   The difference between the sales prices is $50,000. Divide that figure by the original price ($500,000) to calculate the total percentage the market has declined, 10%. It has been two years, however, and the question is asking for a yearly rate. Divide the total rate by 2 to calculate the annual rate of 5%. **Page 301**

22. **(d)**   Fannie Mae has a guideline that states a single line item adjustment should not exceed 10% of the sales price of the comparable. In this problem, the $12,000 adjustment for physical differences equals 12%. **Page 307**

23. **(a)**   This comparable does not have a single adjustment that exceeds Fannie Mae's 10% single line adjustment guideline, nor does the gross adjustment value of $36,000 exceed the 25% guideline for gross adjustments. **Page 307**

24. **(b)**   When determining the gross adjustments, ignore the positive or negative aspects of the adjustment. When applying the adjustments, pay close attention to if they are positive or negative adjustments. After the listed adjustments are applied, the adjusted value of this comparable property is $170,000. **Page 307**

25. **(d)**   It is the appraiser's job at this point to identify which of the comparable sales is given most weight in this analysis and the reasoning why it is the one most heavily weighted. It is not proper appraisal practice simply to average the adjusted sale prices together. Sound reasoning and judgment, not mere mechanical calculation, must be used on the part of the appraiser in order to reconcile the individual value indicators into a value estimate. **Page 306**

Income Approach

Unit 10

INTRODUCTION

Properties are purchased for a variety of reasons, one of which is the anticipation of future benefits associated with owning a particular property. People acquire real estate based not only upon the property's expected use, but also on the anticipation of the benefits they will receive because of owning that property. However, investors also consider secondary benefits such as income tax and investment benefits, location, prestige, and privacy.

Real estate investors purchase or develop properties with the expectation of receiving revenue. From that perspective, the income earning potential of a property is a major consideration for prospective buyers. Therefore, the more net income (after expenses) a property generates for an owner, the more valuable that property should be.

Learning Objectives

After reading this unit, you should be able to:

- recall the basis of the income approach.
- specify the applications and the limitations of the income approach.
- estimate potential gross income, effective gross income, and net operating income.
- recognize the direct capitalization technique using income multipliers.
- recognize the direct capitalization technique using capitalization rates.
- recall the purpose of and the steps to perform for yield capitalization.

OVERVIEW OF THE INCOME APPROACH

The **income approach** is a method of appraising property based on the property's anticipated future income. In its simplest form, the income approach is based on the principle of anticipation—that there is an identifiable relationship between the income a property can generate and its value. All of the income approach techniques rely upon the expectation that a property will produce income. The amount an investor will pay for a property is directly proportional to the future income benefits the investor expects to derive from that property

When using the income approach, appraisers estimate the value of the present worth of future benefits. Identifying this relationship between the income a property generates and value of that property is at the core of the income approach.

Application of the Income Approach

The application of the income approach is straightforward. The income approach is most useful when appraising properties whose ability to produce income is considered by potential investors.

The income approach depends on a property's income—real or potential. If a property's ability to produce income is an important factor to potential buyers, then this approach is the best indicator of value. Even if the property is not currently producing income, this approach can convert its potential income into a current value.

Limitations of the Income Approach

The income approach has limited usefulness when current rental data and operating statements are not available.

The income approach requires current market data for rentals of like properties as well as careful analysis of the operating statements. Sometimes this information is difficult to obtain and analyze. In addition, determining the appropriate capitalization rate is very difficult, and at times, can become very complex.

This approach is not pertinent if the income-producing capability of the subject and comparable properties is not a factor to potential buyers.

Converting Income to Value

There are numerous methods used to analyze the income a property produces to develop an opinion of the market value of that property. The basic methods are direct capitalization, and discounted cash flow analysis (or yield capitalization). These methods are discussed later in the Unit. An appraiser decides which method to use based on the type of property being appraised and the data available.

ESTIMATING INCOME

Income is estimated both as **gross income** (total income before deducting expenses) and as **net operating income** (income received after expenses have been deducted). An appraiser examines an income property's income statement and analyzes the information to calculate the income properly. This section covers potential gross income, effective gross income, and net operating income (NOI).

Potential Gross Income

Potential gross income (PGI) is the maximum income a property could generate. The most obvious income a property produces is the rent paid by tenants of a property. However, rent may not be the only source of income a property produces.

Sources of additional income include laundry and vending machines, parking fees, interest earned on security deposits, and possibly, income resulting from government programs. Potential gross income encompasses all of these possible sources. This is important because, in some instances, such as retail stores in shopping centers, rents are based upon a percentage of gross sales generated by the business leasing that store.

When determining the subject property's potential gross income, the first step is to identify its current gross income. Once the current gross income is established, that income level needs to be analyzed to determine if it will continue into the near future.

Questions an Appraiser Must Consider
- What is the likelihood this property will continue to generate that same amount of income into the near future?
- Can the income be increased?
- If so, by how much?
- If not, why not?

Appraisers should investigate any lease arrangements that limit the amount of rent a landlord can charge, or if there are government restrictions such as rent control or low-income occupant limitations.

During this process, appraisers need to be aware of market trends. There are both positive and negative influences, which are either actual or merely perceived, that appraisers must identify and analyze when projecting potential income for a property. For example, a large company that closes could have a serious negative effect on the local market for rental housing. Similarly, a large retailer that is opening a superstore in an area may obliterate the demand for commercial properties in the downtown business districts of some smaller towns. Conversely, a new university campus under construction or a newly built sports facility can draw large numbers of people to an area, causing greater demand for rental properties.

Additionally, appraisers should compare the subject's income to properties that are similar to the subject property and perform a rental survey of those properties. A **rental survey** is an analysis of competitive rents. The purpose of this task is to identify the amount of income the subject property might generate. By identifying the current gross income and analyzing the current terms of the rental/lease agreements of the comparable properties, appraisers can forecast a reasonable estimate of the subject's potential income.

The rental comps chosen should be as indicative of the subject's current market as possible. Just because a nearby rental property is similar to the subject in physical characteristics does not necessarily mean it is indicative of the subject's rental market. Small, multi-residential income properties with long-term tenants often rent below market levels and may be unsuitable for use as rental comps. Items such as physical characteristics, location, and amenities, and rental/lease terms all deserve consideration. Similarly, rent concessions offered to tenants or premiums being demanded by landlords also need analysis. A **rent concession** is a discount given to induce a tenant to rent.

Differences between the subject property and the rental comps in terms of physical characteristics, amenities, and lease arrangements need to be analyzed when forecasting the subject property's income. In a process similar to that used in the sales comparison approach, appraisers develop an estimate of the subject's projected income by adjusting the rents obtained from the rental comps to compensate for differences between the subject and the rental comps.

Effective Gross Income

Effective gross income (EGI) is the property's income after deducting vacancy and collection losses from the estimate of projected potential gross income (PGI). **Vacancy loss** is the amount of income lost due to vacant units in a property. **Collection loss** represents an amount due to bad debts or losses attributed to slow pay.

Though good management may minimize vacancy and collection losses, no property is immune to suffering losses in income. Usually, vacancy and collection losses are combined and are expressed as a percentage of the potential gross income.

EGI = PGI – Vacancy and Collection Loss

Net Operating Income

Net operating income (NOI) is the income remaining after the operating expenses are deducted from the effective gross income. NOI is probably the best value indicator for any income property since it most accurately reflects the income for a given property.

To calculate net operating income, an appraiser deducts operating expenses from effective gross income.

NOI = EGI – Operating Expenses

Operating Expenses

Operating expenses are those expenses necessary to maintain the property and to help ensure the continued production of income. They include, but are not limited to, items such as property management, insurance, property taxes, utilities, and maintenance. Operating expenses vary from property to property. Operating expenses are divided into three broad categories: fixed expenses, variable expenses, and replacement reserves.

Fixed expenses are ongoing expenses not affected by vacancy, such as property taxes, insurance premiums, and licenses.

Variable expenses are operating expenses that vary based upon numerous criteria such as the level of occupancy, the income a property generates, and the amount of services provided by the owner to the tenants. Variable charges vary from property type to property type but usually include:

Variable Expenses

- Administrative
- Advertising
- Decorating
- Landscaping
- Maintenance/repairs
- Management

- Pest control
- Pool, spa, tennis court
- Security
- Snow removal
- Trash removal
- Utilities

Replacement reserves are funds set aside to replace short-lived components of the property, such as carpeting, painting, roofing, or mechanical equipment. These items routinely wear out and need replacement. The amount is set aside on an annual basis and usually is calculated by dividing the replacement cost of the item by its remaining useful life.

Since property owners know they eventually will need to replace these items, setting aside replacement reserves ensures they will have the funds necessary to perform these replacements when needed.

> Example: Replacing all the roofs and repainting all the buildings in a 500-unit apartment complex may cost hundreds of thousands of dollars. Unless replacement reserves are set aside, the owners may not be able to afford the replacements when needed.

Excluded Expenses

Operating statements prepared by accountants for accounting or tax purposes typically include all the expenditures an owner makes for a property, even those that are not operating expenses. However, some items listed as expenses for accounting or tax purposes are not included as operating expenses when calculating net operating income. The most notable are mortgage payments (debt service), depreciation for tax purposes, and income taxes. Appraisers reconstruct the operating statements by omitting these expenses.

> **Review —Types of Income and Expenses**
>
> **Potential Gross Income** (PGI) – total estimate of all possible income sources for a property without any deductions
>
> **Effective Gross Income** (EGI) – income remaining after vacancy and collection losses are deducted from the potential gross income
>
> **Operating Expenses** – expenses that are necessary to maintain a property and that help it to continue the production of its effective gross income
>
> **Net Operating Income** (NOI) – income left after deducting operating expenses from effective gross income

DIRECT CAPITALIZATION

Any interest in real property may be estimated by the technique known as direct capitalization. Direct capitalization relies upon the premise that there is a relationship between the income a property produces and the value of that property. Direct capitalization involves the use of income multipliers or capitalization rates.

Direct Capitalization - Income Multipliers

Direct capitalization using an income multiplier (or factor) is a method of estimating the value of income-producing real estate based on the gross— rather than the net income. An **income multiplier** is a number that, when multiplied by the income, gives an indicator of value.

The key benefit of using a multiplier is its relative ease of use. The advantage of this approach is that it is widely used and understood by both the investing public and the appraisal community.

Although the income multiplier technique is a simple tool to use, it has some significant drawbacks that cause it to be inapplicable. The main drawback is that this technique is based on gross income, and it ignores the net income that a property generates. Two properties may generate very similar levels of gross income; however, one may have significantly higher net income since it has lower operating expenses. All other things being equal, the property with the higher net income would tend to be in greater demand and therefore more valuable. When using the income multiplier technique, this difference is ignored.

Typical income multipliers used are the gross rent multiplier and the effective gross income multiplier. The difference between the two is that GRMs are based on monthly rents and GIMs are based on annual income.

Gross Rent Multipliers

One of the simplest ways to estimate a property's value (V_o) based on its gross monthly income is to use a gross rent multiplier. The **gross rent multiplier** (GRM) is the relationship (ratio) between the sales price (value) and gross monthly rent for residential properties. The GRM is the most commonly used income approach method when valuing 1-4 unit residential properties. The GRM does not account for a vacancy or collection factor. Usually, properties in prime locations have higher GRMs than properties in less desirable locations. Then when comparing similar properties in the same area or location, the lower the GRM, the more profitable the property.

$$GRM = V_0 / \text{Gross Monthly Rent}$$

Example: A duplex property that recently sold for $270,000 has monthly rental income of $3,000. The GRM is 90. ($270,000 / $3,000).

Multiplying the subject property's gross rent by the GRM gives an indication of the value of the subject property.

$$V_0 = \text{Gross Rent x GRM}$$

Example: Appraiser Dan wants to get a quick estimate for a duplex that rents for $2,500. If the GRM for comparable duplexes is 90, the value of the subject duplex will be $225,000. ($2,500 x 90).

Because it is based on monthly rent, a GRM is easy to calculate, but consequently, it is not as accurate as the EGIM.

Effective Gross Income Multipliers

The **effective gross income multiplier** (EGIM) is the relationship (ratio) between sales price (value) and the annual effective gross income from income producing properties. The annualized income stream includes rents and other sources of income derived from the property. Non-residential properties—apartments with 5+ units as well as other office, retail, commercial, and industrial uses—are valued using EGIMs.

The EGIM is obtained from recent comparable sales and calculated by dividing the sale price of the comparable sale by its effective gross income (EGI) at the time of sale.

$$\text{EGIM} = V_0 \text{ / EGI}$$

Multiplying the subject property's effective gross income by this multiplier gives an indication of the value of the subject property.

$$V_0 = \text{EGI} \times \text{EGIM}$$

Illustration - EGIM

The subject property is a 10-unit apartment complex that has five 1-bedroom apartments and five 2-bedroom apartments. By looking at the property's actual gross income and performing a rental survey of similar properties, appraiser Joe determined that the 1-bedroom apartments can rent for $725 per month and the 2-bedroom apartments can rent for $850 per month. The following chart illustrates the subject's potential gross income forecast.

Subject Property

Five Units × $725 rent/month	=	$3,625
Five Units × $850 rent/month	=	$4,250
Total Forecasted Monthly Gross Income	=	$7,875

Comparable Sales

Three recent apartment sales comparable to the subject were found. Unfortunately, no sales were found that have the same number of units as the subject. The comparable sales are described as follows:

Comparable Sale #1

A twelve-unit apartment complex, it has nine 1-bedroom units that are rented for $725 per month and three 2-bedroom units that are rented for $850 per month. It recently sold for $1,115,000.

Nine Units × $725 rent/month	=	$6,525
Three Units × $850 rent/month	=	$2,550
Total Gross Monthly Income	=	$9,075

Divide the sale price of this property ($1,115,000) by its monthly income ($9,075) to get a GRM of 122.86 (rounded to 123).

Comparable Sale #2

A nine-unit apartment complex, it has nine 1-bedroom units that are renting for $725 per month. It sold for $830,000.

Nine Units × $725 rent/month = $6,525
Total Gross Monthly Income   = $6,525

Divide the sale price of this property ($830,000) by its monthly income ($6,525) to get a GRM of 127.20 (rounded to 127).

Comparable Sale #3

A thirteen-unit apartment complex, it has ten 1-bedroom units that are rented for $725 per month and three 2-bedroom units that are rented for $850 per month. It sold recently for $1,220,000.

Ten Units × $725 rent/month   = $7,250
Three Units × $850 rent/month = $2,550
Total Gross Monthly Income   = $9,800

Divide the sale price of this property ($1,220,000) by its monthly income ($9,800) to get a GRM of 124.5 (rounded to 125).

The three comparable sales produced gross income multipliers ranging from 123 to 127 (summarized on grid). Based upon this information, one could reasonably indicate the gross income multiplier for the subject at 125.

Comparable	Income	Sales Price	GRM
Comp 1	$9,075	$1,115,000	123
Comp 2	$6,525	$830,000	127
Comp 3	$9,800	$1,220,000	125

As stated earlier, the subject's estimated income is $7,875. The indicated GRM is 125. Multiplying the forecasted income by the GRM produces an indication of the subject's value.

$7,875 × 125 = $984,375

Rounded down, the subject's value is $984,000.

Direct Capitalization – Cap Rates

Direct capitalization using a capitalization rate is a method of estimating the value of income-producing real estate based on the net operating income—rather than the gross income. The **capitalization rate** (R_0) is a ratio reflecting the relationship between the net operating income a property generates and its value. Sometimes called the overall capitalization rate, or simply the cap rate, this method converts annual expected net operating income (NOI) generated by a property into a value estimate (V_0) for that property.

The following capitalization formulas are used by real estate investors, lenders, and appraisers to estimate the value of income producing properties.

Capitalization Formulas	
Calculate a property's value:	$V_0 = NOI \div R_0$
Calculate the cap rate:	$R_0 = NOI \div V_0$
Calculate a property's NOI:	$NOI = V_0 \times R_0$

In general, riskier investments typically have higher capitalization rates and low-risk investment have low capitalization rates. Because the risk is lower, the value will be higher.

Example: If an income producing property has a yearly NOI of $45,000 and an 10% cap rate, its value is $450,000. ($45,000 / 0.10). However, if the cap rate were 5% (more safe), the value of the property would be $900,000. ($45,000 / 0.05).

Illustration - Capitalization Rate

The subject property consists of 25 apartments. The units in this development are leased for $700 per month. There is a laundry room in the development generating approximately $5.00 per month per unit in the development. The vacancy and collection losses in this development are estimated to be 4% of potential gross income. Operating expenses are forecasted to be 35% of effective gross income. Relying upon similar sales in the subject market, an overall capitalization rate of 9.25% is used.

Solution:

Rental Income *(25 Units @ $700 per month)*	$17,500
Laundry Income *(25 Units @ $5.00 per month)*	+ $125
Monthly Potential Gross Income (PGI)	$17,625
Potential Gross Income *(Monthly PGI x 12)*	$211,500
less Vacancy & Collection Loss *(4% of Yearly PGI)*	− $8,460
Effective Gross Income (EGI)	$203,040
less Operating Expenses *(35% of EGI)*	− $71,064
Net Operating Income (NOI)	$131,976
NOI ÷ Cap Rate = Value *($131,976 ÷ 0.0925)* =	$1,426,768
Indicated Value (Rounded)	$1,427,000

Deriving Capitalization Rates

Appraisers use several methods to derive capitalization rates. The quality and quantity of data available to an appraiser determines which technique is most appropriate. Typically, capitalization rates are market extracted using comparable sales or constructed, such as the band of investment method.

Market Extracted Cap Rates

When determine a capitalization rate using comparable sales, an appraiser analyzes the relationship between the sales prices of competing properties in the subject's market and the yearly net operating incomes generated by those properties.

The comparable sales method to estimate capitalization rates is preferred when there is sufficient comparable data available. In order to use this method, appraisers research the comparable properties' sales price, income, expenses, financing arrangements, and market conditions at the time of sale. Appraisers must be sure that the net operating income for each of the comparable sales used is calculated in the same manner as it is for the subject. Failure to perform this task results in incorrect estimates.

Once the comparable sales are identified and the appropriate data about each sale is researched, appraisers divide each comparable sale's net operating income by its sale price resulting in an overall cap rate estimate for each property.

Appraisers choose the cap rate for the comparable sale that is overall most similar to the subject property.

Example: The operating statement for the subject property shows that its NOI is $575,000. After researching the market area, appraiser Mary came up with the following comparable information.

Comparables	NOI	Sales Price	Cap Rate
Comp 1	$450,000	$5,000,000	9.%
Comp 2	$357,750	$3,578,000	10.%
Comp 3	$1,506,800	$25,113,000	6.%
Comp 4	$600,000	$6,316,000	9.5%

After further analysis, Mary concludes that Comp 3 is not especially indicative of the market, even though on the surface it appeared to be wholly comparable to the subject. Looking at the remaining comps, Mary concludes that the cap rate most likely should be in between 9-9.5%. Mary ultimately selects 9.5% because Comp 4 was the most comparable to the subject. $575,000 ÷ 9.5% = $6,052,631. The subject has a value of $6,053,000 (rounded).

Band of Investment Method to Develop Cap Rates

The **band of investment method** determines the capitalization rate based on the two primary sources of funds used to purchase a property—equity funds and debt funds. In a typical purchase transaction, a portion of the purchase price is paid directly from funds a borrower already has and the remainder of the purchase price is paid for by funds the buyer borrows from a lender. The amount a buyer invests into a property is called **equity capital** and the amount borrowed by the buyer to purchase a property is called **debt capital**. Almost all real estate investments have an equity component and a debt component. In the band of investment technique, capitalization rates for both the equity and debt positions in a property are determined and then combined into an overall rate for the property.

Example: Assume a property is being purchased for $800,000. The buyer makes a 20% down payment ($160,000) and the balance of the purchase price ($640,000) is financed with a mortgage. The following diagram shows both the equity and the debt (mortgage) components of that investment.

Equity Value   (20%)   = $160,000

Mortgage Value (80%)   = $640,000

Total Property Value (100%)   = $800,000

Mortgage Constant

The capitalization rate for the debt component in a property is called the mortgage constant. The **mortgage constant** is the ratio of the loan amount (principal) to the annual sum of the individual loan payments. It is a function of the interest rate, the time length of the loan, and the frequency of loan amortization. Mortgage constants may be calculated on a financial calculator or by referring to financial tables that are discussed later in this unit.

Equity Cap Rate

The capitalization rate for the equity position in a property is called the equity capitalization rate. The **equity cap rate** reflects the anticipated return on a percentage basis to the investor who owns the property and is typically reflective of the first year of the investment. Equity capitalization rates may be identified a couple of ways. One way is to divide the pre-tax cash flow of a sale by the amount of equity investment in that sale. Often this information is very difficult to confirm; however, if it is available, it is a very strong indicator. Another way is to identify the interest rates being paid on competing investments. Often the interest rates being paid on 6-month or 1-year treasury bills are the basis for estimating an equity capitalization rate.

Once the mortgage constant (debt cap rate) and the equity cap rate are identified, the overall rate indication can be calculated. The overall cap rate is a composite of both the equity and debt positions in a property and is proportionally weighted by each of the property investment positions.

To calculate the weighted debt rate, multiply the debt percentage of the property value by the mortgage constant.

Weighted Debt Rate = Debt Percentage × Mortgage Constant

To calculate the weighted equity rate, multiply the equity percentage of the property value by the equity cap rate.

Weighted Equity Rate = Equity Percentage × Equity Cap Rate

Add the debt and equity rates together to derive the overall cap rate.

Overall Cap Rate = Debt Rate + Equity Rate

Example: The subject property is a 50-unit apartment complex. The buyer is putting a 30% down payment on the property and can obtain financing for the remaining 70% of the property's value at 7% for 20 years fully amortized with monthly payments. Competing non-real estate investments are currently paying 12% annual interest.

Using the bank of investment method, the overall capitalization rate is computed as follows:

Percent of Property Value	×	Cap Rate	=	Weighted Rate
Mortgage (70%)	×	0.093	=	0.0651
Equity (30%)	×	0.120	=	0.0360 +
Overall Cap Rate			=	0.1011

Based upon the above calculation, the overall capitalization rate is 0.1011 (10.11%).

(Note: The mortgage capitalization rate of 0.0930 is the mortgage constant for a 7% loan amortized over 20 years with monthly payments.)

Residual Techniques

A **residual technique** is a method of estimating the value of a building or land, given the value of one and the rate of return. Real estate is divided into two components—the land and its improvements. In income producing properties, a portion of its total net income is attributable to its land and the remaining portion is attributable to its improvements (buildings). Similarly, there are capitalization rates that are attributable to the land and other capitalization rates that are attributable to the improvements (rarely are they the same).

Example: Imagine a stand-alone gas station with an annual NOI of $200,000 and a cap rate of 10%. This technique says that the property improvements (building, pumps, gas reserves, etc.) contribute to the NOI ($80,000) and that the land component of the property contributes a portion (the remaining $120,000).

This technique subsequently states that the property's cap rate can be split to represent the rate the improvements and the rate the land contribute to the overall rate. In this case, the land-contributed cap rate is 2.2% and the improvements account for the remaining 7.8%.

If the value and the capitalization rate of one of the components are known, the net operating income attributable to that component may be deducted from the total net operating income for the property to arrive at a net operating income attributable to the other component. Capitalizing that income results in a value indication for the unknown component. Adding the value of the two components together results in a value indication for the overall property.

Keep in mind that, for these methods to be reliable, the property must be at its highest and best use. If the highest and best use of the land is different from the highest and best use of the improvements, the residual techniques cannot accurately determine value.

When using a residual technique, an appraiser divides the subject property into a land component and an improvement component.

Building Residual Technique

The value of the total property may be estimated, by using the **building residual technique** if the land value is known (or easily estimated). In the following illustration, the capitalization rates for the subject's land and building are 9% and 6% respectively.

Known Land Value	$800,000
Total Net Operating Income	$225,000
Less Net Operating Income Attributable to the Land	
(Land Value × Land Cap Rate) ($800,000 × 0.09)	−72,000
Residual Income Attributable to the Building	$153,000
Building Value	
(Building NOI ÷ Building Cap Rate) ($153,000 ÷ 0.06)	$2,550,000
Indicated Total Property Value	$3,350,000

In order for the building residual technique to be meaningful, appraisers need to have information about the current land value, net operating income information for the property, and capitalization rates for both the land and the improvements. The drawback to this method is the fact this information may be difficult to extract from the market.

This method is used in situations when the improvements have suffered significant accrued depreciation. In some instances, accrued depreciation may be estimated by this technique when the indicated building value by this method is subtracted from the estimated building cost new.

Land Residual Technique

The value of the total property may be estimated by using the **land residual technique** if both the total net operating income for a property and the value of the building are known. This method also assumes an appraiser has obtained information regarding cap rates for both the land and for the building. The following example illustrates this method for estimating property values.

Known Building Value	$2,550,000
Total Net Operating Income	$225,000
Less Net Operating Income Attributable to the Land	
(Building Value × Building Cap Rate of 6%)	−153,000
Residual Income Attributable to the Land	$72,000
Land Value ($72,000 ÷ 9%)	$800,000
Indicated Total Property Value	$3,350,000

This method is often used when comparable land sales data is not available. It typically relies upon the cost approach to value in order to estimate the value of the improvements. As such, it relies upon the assumption that the cost to build a building is equal to its market value, which is not necessarily reflective of market realities. Like the building residual technique, appraisers need the appropriate capitalization rates for both the building and for the improvements as well as information regarding the subject's total net operating income.

Yield Capitalization

Yield capitalization, also known as discounted cash flow analysis, is a method in which the value of future benefits is discounted to a present value. Future benefits include the periodic flow of income generated by a property for its owner (return on investment) as well as a reversion. **Reversion** is the lump sum amount the investor expects to receive upon sale of a property at some future point in time (return of investment).

The process when the periodic future income flows and the reversion are converted into a present value estimate is called **discounting**. Discounting is a form of capitalization that is specifically concerned with calculating present worth based upon future income. The **discount rate** is the yield rate to the investor and assumes a satisfactory return on and return of investment to the investor.

Conceptually, it is helpful to look at the property being appraised as an investment over time and note the direction of cash flow. When the initial purchase of a property is made, funds flow from the buyer to the seller.

Although not always the case, there is usually an expectation at this point that the property will generate funds that will flow to the investor who just bought the property. There is also an expectation that at some point in the future, the property will be sold with the investor receiving a lump sum amount of capital at that time. Yield capitalization converts these various cash flows into a value estimate.

Steps to Perform for Yield Capitalization

1. Project the holding period of the investment. The **holding period** is the length of time the property will be used as an investment.

2. Estimate and forecast all the future cash flows associated with the investment. At times, monies will flow from the investor toward the investment. This is called **negative cash flow**. At other times, income generated by the property flows toward the owner which results in **positive cash flow**.

3. Identify an appropriate discount rate. The rate chosen needs to be reflective of investor's expectations and provide for an acceptable return on investment and return of investment.

4. Convert the future benefits into a present value estimate for the property.

Six Functions of One Dollar

To understand yield capitalization, it is necessary to have an understanding on the time element of money. People place their funds in investments with the expectation those funds will earn interest. The investor is a "lender" and the investment is the "borrower". The individual invests (loans) capital in an investment and that investment is expected to compensate the investor with some kind of return. If an individual puts $100 into a savings account at a bank and it pays 7% per year, at the end of one year, the initial $100 investment has grown to $107. In a different light, to accumulate $107 in one year, it would be necessary to deposit $100 into an account bearing 7% interest.

Three Overall Ways to Look at Money

1. The future worth (amount) can be calculated based upon compounding.
2. The present worth (amount) of money may be calculated through discounting.
3. The amount of equal payments to retire a debt or to accumulate a specific amount of money may also be analyzed.

Overall, the six functions of a dollar are tied to the time element of money. These six functions are included in the following chart. With computer technology and modern financial calculators, charts like the one following this discussion have pretty much fallen into disuse. Charts like these however, are helpful to illustrate the various functions of a dollar and that is why one is included here.

The following chart includes the six functions of a dollar calculated at a 7% interest rate and projected out for 40 years. In order to use this chart, simply multiply the appropriate factor by the appropriate amount of money. The result includes the original investment plus any interest or discount.

> Example: To find out how much $250 would be worth if it were placed in a savings account untouched for 15 years, look at column 1 (Future Value of $1) for 15 years. Multiply that factor (2.759032) by $250. At the end of 15 years, the original investment of $250 will have grown to $689.76

Column 1, Future Value of $1

This column is used to calculate the future worth of a present amount assuming the amount invested draws interest at the rate stated at the top of the chart.

> Example: The future value factor of $1.00 invested for 17 years is 3.158815. If $100 were invested for 17 years with a rate of 7% per year, the interest plus the initial investment of $100 would total $315.88.

Column 2, Future Value of $1 per Period

This column is used to calculate the future value if regular additions of $1.00 are made every year and the interest stays constant during the investment period. In this instance, not only is interest added to the original investment amount, but additional capital is added to the investment at regular intervals as well.

> Example: If $100 is invested at the end of every year for five years and that amount earns 7% per year, the investment will build up to $575.07 at the end of the fifth year.

Column 3, Sinking Fund Factor

This column will tell the investor how much must be invested each year to accumulate to a specific amount at the end of the stated period.

> Example: If a person wants to accumulate $1,500,000 in savings over a 20-year period, an annual deposit of $36,589.50 ($1,500,000 × 0.024393) must be placed into an account bearing 7% interest every year for those 20 years.

Column 4, Present Value of $1

This column is used to calculate the present value of a future amount.

> Example: A person who will inherit $750,000 in 5 years could sell his or her rights to that inheritance. If the investor buying the rights to that inheritance required a 7% return on his investment, he or she would pay $534,739.50 ($750,000 × 0.712986).

Column 5, Present Value of an Annuity of $1 per Period

This column is much like Column 4, but instead of one future lump payment, it is used to discount future cash flows into a present worth.

> Example: Assume a woman won a $20,000,000 state lottery payable at $1,000,000 per year for 20 years. If the state required a 7% discount, the woman would receive $10,594,014 ($1,000,000 × 10.594014) as a lump sum (prior to taxes).

Column 6, Installment to Amortize $1

This column is often used to identify the size of regular payments (annually in this case) required to pay off a debt over a specified period.

> Example: If a couple obtained a 30-year, $300,000 loan at 7% to buy their house, they would have to make annual payments to the lender of $24,175.50 ($300,000 × 0.080586).

The 7.00% Annual Interest Rate Chart identifies six individual functions. Columns 1 and 2 are for compounding, columns 3 and 6 are for asset accumulation or debt retirement, and columns 4 and 5 are for discounting.

7.00% Annual Interest Rate					
1	2	3	4	5	6
Years	Future Value of $1	Future Value of $1 Per Period	Sinking Fund Factor	Present Value of $1 (Reversion)	Present Value of $1 Per Period	Installment to Amortize $1
1	1.070000	1.000000	1.000000	0.934579	0.934579	1.070000
2	1.144900	2.070000	0.483092	0.873439	1.808018	0.553092
3	1.225043	3.214900	0.311052	0.816298	2.624316	0.381052
4	1.310796	4.439943	0.225228	0.762895	3.387211	0.295228
5	1.402552	5.750739	0.173891	0.712986	4.100197	0.243891
6	1.500730	7.153291	0.139796	0.666342	4.766540	0.209796
7	1.605781	8.654021	0.115553	0.622750	5.389289	0.185553
8	1.718186	10.259803	0.097468	0.582009	5.971299	0.167468
9	1.838459	11.977989	0.083486	0.543934	6.515232	0.153486
10	1.967151	13.816448	0.072378	0.508349	7.023582	0.142378
11	2.104852	15.783599	0.063357	0.475093	7.498674	0.133357
12	2.252192	17.888451	0.055902	0.444012	7.942686	0.125902
13	2.409845	20.140643	0.049651	0.414964	8.357651	0.119651
14	2.578534	22.550488	0.044345	0.387817	8.745468	0.114345
15	2.759032	25.129022	0.039795	0.362446	9.107914	0.109795
16	2.952164	27.888054	0.035858	0.338735	9.446649	0.105858
17	3.158815	30.840217	0.032425	0.316574	9.763223	0.102425
18	3.379932	33.999033	0.029413	0.295864	10.059087	0.099413
19	3.616528	37.378965	0.026753	0.276508	10.335595	0.096753
20	3.869684	40.995492	0.024393	0.258419	10.594014	0.094393
21	4.140562	44.865177	0.022289	0.241513	10.835527	0.092289
22	4.430402	49.005739	0.020406	0.225713	11.061240	0.090406
23	4.740530	53.436141	0.018714	0.210947	11.272187	0.088714
24	5.072367	58.176671	.017189	0.197147	11.469334	0.087189
25	5.427433	63.249038	0.015811	0.184249	11.653583	0.085811
26	5.807353	68.676470	0.014561	0.172195	11.825779	0.084561
27	6.213868	74.483823	0.013426	0.160930	11.986709	0.083426
28	6.648838	80.697691	0.012392	0.150402	12.137111	0.082392
29	7.114257	87.346529	0.011449	0.140563	12.277674	0.081449
30	7.612255	94.460786	0.010586	0.131367	12.409041	0.080586
31	8.145113	102.073041	0.009797	0.122773	12.531814	0.079797
32	8.715271	110.218154	0.009073	0.114741	12.646555	0.079073
33	9.325340	118.933425	0.008408	0.107235	12.753790	0.078408
34	9.978114	128.258765	0.007797	0.100219	12.854009	0.077797
35	10.676581	138.236878	0.007234	0.093663	12.947672	0.077234
36	11.423942	148.913460	0.006715	0.087535	13.035208	0.076715
37	12.223618	160.337402	0.006237	0.081809	13.117017	0.076237
38	13.079271	172.561020	0.005795	0.076457	13.193473	0.075795
39	13.994820	185.640292	0.005387	0.071455	13.264928	0.075387
40	14.974458	199.635112	0.005009	0.066780	13.331709	0.075009

Annuities

Column 5 is the one real estate appraisers use the most frequently, and it is used to estimate the present value of an annuity. An **annuity** is regular payment of a predetermined amount. Though the term annuity technically refers to an annual amount, it applies to any kind of regular payment of a specific amount. For any income producing property, there is the expectation that tenants will pay rent at regular intervals, usually monthly, to the property owner. Because of this, proprietors come to expect a regular amount of income generated at a predictable schedule.

Since real estate income flows in a similar pattern, it is reasonable to analyze real estate income from the point of view of an annuity. Estimating the present value of an annuity is the same process that one may use to value real estate that produces a predictable steady stream of income at regular intervals.

When discounting, the present value of an annuity is always assumed to be less than the sum total of all the cash flows during the period of the annuity. This procedure is tied to the premise that benefits received today are worth more than benefits received in the future.

The formula for calculating the present value of an annuity is rather complex and beyond the scope of this discussion. However, the factors found in the above table can be used to calculate the value of an income producing property.

Illustration – Yield Capitalization

An income producing property has been leased to a very reliable tenant for 18 years. The property produces a net annual operating income of $250,000 to the owners. The yield on the property has been estimated to be 7%. Though it would not work out this way in the real world, for purposes of simplicity, the net operating income is forecast to be level for the next 18 years. (This would be making the assumption that taxes, maintenance costs, management costs, etc. would not go up for the next 18 years.) At the end of the 18-year lease period, the subject property's building is estimated to be at the end of its remaining economic life and have no value at that time. Consequently, at the end of the lease period, all the value of the subject property will be solely in its land.

Current comparable land sales indicate the current value of the land at $450,000. On average, land value has historically appreciated 1% per year for the last 20 years and is forecast to increase at this rate. (The future value of a property is obviously very difficult to predict; however, this assumption is made for illustration purposes.) The assignment is to estimate the current value of this property.

Solution:

To solve this valuation problem, the value of the income stream needs to be estimated as well as the value of the reversion.

1. The value of the income stream may be estimated by multiplying the Net Operating Income (NOI) by the Present Value of an Annuity Factor at 7% for 18 years.

Current annual NOI	$250,000
Annuity factor/18 years @ 7%	× 10.059087
Present value of the NOI	= $2,514,772

2. To estimate the value of the land, the subject's land is currently estimated to be worth $450,000. Assuming it increases in value by 1% per year, 18 years in the future it is estimated to be worth $538,300 (rounded).

Current Land Value	$450,000
Future Value of $1 factor/18 years @ 1%	× 1.196147
Future value of the land	= $538,266
Rounded	$538,300

3. The future value of the land needs to be discounted to its present value by multiplying it by the reversion factor (Column 4) for 7% at 18 years.

Future Land Value	$538,300
Present value of the reversion factor	× 0.295864
Present value of the land	= $159,264
Rounded	$159,300

4. The final step is to add the present values of the income and of the reversion.

Present value of the NOI	= $2,514,772
Present value of the land (rounded)	$ 159,300
Present value of the reversion	$2,674,072
Rounded	$2,675,000

SUMMARY

The **income approach** to value is for properties that produce income and is based on the premise that a property is worth the amount of money it produces, or is expected to produce. There are numerous methods used to analyze the income a property produces to develop an opinion of the market value of that property. The basic methods are direct capitalization, and discounted cash flow analysis (or yield capitalization).

The first step in each of the methods is to determine the subject's income. Income is estimated both as **gross income** (total income before deducting expenses) and as **net operating income** (income received after expenses have been deducted). An appraiser examines an income property's income statement and analyzes the information to calculate the income properly. **Potential gross income** (PGI) is the maximum income a property could generate. **Effective gross income** (EGI) is the property's income after deducting vacancy and collection losses from the estimate of projected potential gross income. **Net operating income (NOI)** is the income remaining after the operating expenses are deducted from the effective gross income. **Operating expenses** (fixed expenses, variable expenses, and replacement reserves) are those expenses necessary to maintain the property and to help ensure the continued production of income.

Any interest in real property may be estimated by the technique known as direct capitalization. Direct capitalization involves the use of income multipliers or capitalization rates. Direct capitalization using an income multiplier (or factor) is a method of estimating the value of income-producing real estate based on the gross—rather than the net income. An **income multiplier** is a number that, when multiplied by the income, gives an indicator of value. Typical income multipliers used are the **gross rent multiplier** (GRM) and the **effective gross income multiplier** (EGIM). The difference between the two is that GRMs are based on monthly rents and GIMs are based on annual income.

Direct capitalization using a capitalization rate is a method of estimating the value of income-producing real estate based on the net operating income—rather than the gross income. The **capitalization rate** (R_0) is a ratio reflecting the relationship between the net operating income a property generates and its value.

Yield capitalization, the most complex and accurate technique, accounts for the present worth of future benefits. Yield capitalization condenses forecasted future income streams into a singular, present day value. In order to do this, appraisers must be familiar with the six functions of a dollar. The six functions of a dollar are tied to the time element of money.

UNIT 10 REVIEW

Matching Exercise

Instructions: Write the letter of the matching term on the blank line before its definition, and then check your response with the Answer Key that immediately follows the Multiple Choice Questions.

Terms

A. annuity

B. capitalization rate

C. EGI

D. EGIM

E. debt capital

F. equity cap rate

G. fixed expenses

H. GRM

I. income approach

J. mortgage constant

K. NOI

L. PGI

M. residual technique

N. variable expenses

O. yield capitalization

Definitions

1. _____ Method of appraising property based on the property's anticipated future income.

2. _____ Maximum income a property could generate.

3. _____ PGI minus vacancy and collection loss.

4. _____ EGI minus operating expenses.

5. _____ Ongoing expenses that not affected by the vacancy, such as property taxes, insurance premiums, and licenses.

6. _____ Operating expenses that vary based on level of occupancy, the income a property generates, and the amount of services provided by the owner to the tenants.

7. _____ Relationship between the sales price (value) and gross monthly rent for residential properties.

8. _____ V_0 / EGI

9. _____ Ratio reflecting the relationship between the NOI a property generates and its value.

10. _____ Amount borrowed by the buyer to purchase a property.

11. _____ Ratio of the loan amount (principal) to the annual sum of the individual loan payments.

12. _____ Capitalization rate for the equity position in a property.

13. _____ Method of estimating the value of a building or land, given the value of one and the rate of return.

14. _____ Method in which the value of future benefits is discounted to a present value.

15. _____ Regular payment of a predetermined amount

⬛ Multiple Choice Questions

Instructions: Circle your choice, and then check your response with the Answer Key that immediately follows the Multiple Choice Questions.

1. The main principle behind the income approach is:
    a. anticipation.
    b. production.
    c. multiplication.
    d. supplication.

2. Potential gross income includes income from:
    a. rent.
    b. parking fees.
    c. laundry and vending machines.
    d. all of the sources mentioned.

3. Over the last year, a 10-unit apartment complex had 2 units that were vacant for 1 ½ months. What was the vacancy loss?
    a. 2.5%
    b. 5%
    c. 15%
    d. 20%

4. Which of the following is an example of a fixed expense?
   a. Marketing fees
   b. Cleaning expenses
   c. Property taxes
   d. None of the above

5. Advertising, maintenance, repairs, management, and utilities are:
   a. capital expenditures.
   b. fixed expenses.
   c. replacement reserves.
   d. variable expenses.

6. An accountant provided an appraiser with the subject property's operating statement. It included the following expenses: utilities - $2,150, repairs - $1,075, management - $3,000, property taxes - $4,000, and debt service - $12,000. From the appraiser's perspective, the operating expenses total:
   a. $ 3,225.00.
   b. $ 7,225.00.
   c. $10,225.00.
   d. $22,225.00.

7. If a townhouse rents for $1,025 per month and the gross rent multiplier is 240, what is the value of the property?
   a. $246,000
   b. $258,300
   c. $634,050
   d. $2,952,000

8. A property's net operating income is $92,250 and the estimated cap rate is 9%. What is the value of the property?
   a. $100,553
   b. $1,025,000
   c. $1,206,630
   d. None of the above

9. Low-risk investments would have a:
   a. low capitalization rate and low value.
   b. low capitalization rate and high value.
   c. high capitalization rate and high value.
   d. high capitalization rate and low value.

10. A property has $100,000 annual income and $35,000 operating expenses. In the area where the property is located, an appropriate cap rate for this type of property is 8%. Which of the following statements is true?

    a. The value of the building is $437,500.

    b. The NOI is $65,000.

    c. The EGI is $35,000.

    d. The value of the property cannot be calculated from the information provided.

11. In the band of investment method, the mortgage constant is:

    a. a market derived percentage of the debt capital.

    b. the pre-tax cash flow divided by the amount of debt investment.

    c. an amount that is deducted from a property's income to account for the mortgage payments that a typical owner would make.

    d. the ratio of the loan amount to the annual sum of the individual loan payments.

12. The building residual technique is used when:

    a. the building value is known.

    b. the land value is known.

    c. comparable land sales data is not available.

    d. a building has burned down and an appraiser must determine the value of the remaining structural elements.

13. What is the commonality of present value, future benefits, and discounting?

    a. Direct Capitalization

    b. Yield Capitalization

    c. Land Residual Technique

    d. Gross Rent Multiplier

14. All of the following are steps in the yield capitalization process, except:

    a. projecting the holding period of the investment.

    b. estimating and forecast all the future cash flows associated with the investment.

    c. identifying an appropriate discount rate.

    d. determining the gross income multiplier.

15. Which function of one dollar is most commonly used by appraisers?

    a. Column 1, Future Value of $1

    b. Column 2, Future Value of $1 per Period

    c. Column 3, Sinking Fund Factor

    d. Column 5, Present Value of an Annuity of $1 per Period

UNIT 10 ANSWER KEY

Answers – Matching

1. I	5. G	9. B	13. M
2. L	6. N	10. E	14. O
3. C	7. H	11. J	15. A
4. K	8. D	12. F	

Answers – Multiple Choice

1. **(a)** The income approach is based on the principle of anticipation—that there is an identifiable relationship between the income a property can generate and its value. **Page 320**

2. **(d)** Potential gross income (PGI) is the maximum income a property could generate. Sources include rent and additional income from laundry and vending machines, parking fees, interest earned on security deposits, and possibly, income resulting from government programs. **Page 321**

3. **(a)** 10 units multiplied by 12 months = 120 months of rent due. 2 units times 1 ½ months vacant = 3 months of rent lost due to vacancy. 3 months divided by 120 months = .025 or 2.5%. **Page 323**

4. **(c)** Fixed expenses are ongoing expenses not affected by vacancy, such as property taxes, insurance premiums, and licenses. **Page 323**

5. **(d)** The expenses shown are all types of variable expenses. **Page 324**

6. **(c)** Although some items (debt service, depreciation for tax purposes, and income taxes) are listed as expenses for accounting or tax purposes, appraisers do not include them as operating expenses. Appraisers reconstruct the operating statements by omitting these expenses. Of the expenses listed, appraisers would omit the debt service. $2,150 + $1,075 + $3,000 + $4,000 = $10,225. **Page 323**

7. **(a)** $1,025 multiplied by 240 = $246,000. **Page 326**

8. **(b)** $92,250 divided by .09 (9%) = $1,025,000. **Page 329**

9. **(b)** In general, riskier investments typically have higher capitalization rates and low-risk investment have low capitalization rates. Because the risk is lower, the value will be higher. **Page 329**

10. **(b)** The EGI is $100,000. The NOI is $65,000 ($100,000 − $35,000) and the value of the property using an 8% cap rate is $812,500. **Page 329**

11. **(d)** The mortgage constant is the ratio of the loan amount (principal) to the annual sum of the individual loan payments. **Page 332**

12. **(b)** The building residual technique is used when the land value is known (or easily estimated). **Page 334**

13. **(b)** Yield capitalization, also known as discounted cash flow analysis, is a method in which the value of future benefits is discounted to a present value. **Page 335**

14. **(d)** When performing yield capitalization, the appraiser completes certain steps: 1. Project the holding period of the investment. 2. Estimate and forecast all the future cash flows associated with the investment. 3. Identify an appropriate discount rate. 4. Convert the future benefits into a present value estimate for the property. **Page 336**

15. **(d)** Column 5 is the one real estate appraisers use most frequently, and it is used to estimate the present value of an annuity. **Page 340**

Cost Approach: Estimating Cost of Improvements

Unit 11

INTRODUCTION

The **cost approach** is based upon the proposition that an informed buyer will pay no more than the cost of producing a substitute property with equal utility as the subject property. It is a method of appraising property based on the depreciated reproduction or replacement cost (new) of improvements, plus the market value of the site.

The cost approach recognizes there are two major components in real estate: land and improvements. Land includes the ground itself, and the rights inherent in the use of that ground. Improvements are buildings or other structures that are attached permanently to the land. Houses, detached garages, barns, office buildings, and shopping centers are all examples of improvements. Other improvements, such as sidewalks, curbs, drainage structures, retaining walls, grading, streets and utility hook-ups, are called site improvements and need to be analyzed in this approach as well.

Estimating land value is straightforward. Previously, we discussed site characteristics that may influence land value. In this unit, we cover six different methods to develop an opinion of the value of a site.

Estimating the value of the improvements is a little more complex. Using the cost approach, appraisers first estimate the cost to build the improvements, as if new. However, buildings do not stay new; they **depreciate**, or lose value over time. Depreciation of improvement is discussed in the next unit.

Learning Objectives

After reading this unit, you should be able to:

- recall the basis of the cost approach.
- specify the applications and the limitations of the cost approach.
- identify the methods commonly used to estimate the value of land.
- differentiate between reproduction cost and replacement cost.
- recognize the difference between entrepreneurial incentive and entrepreneurial profit.
- identify on-site improvements.

OVERVIEW OF THE COST APPROACH

Like the sales comparison approach, the cost approach is based on the principle of substitution. However, in this case, the substitution is not purchasing another similar improvement—it is building it. When using the cost approach, appraisers compare the value of the subject improvement with the cost of building a similar improvement.

Applications of the Cost Approach

In some instances, the cost approach is the only reliable indicator of value in an assignment. When appraising single-family residences using the sales comparison approach, appraisers also use this approach to support the value conclusion reached. This valuation method can have much use in appraising unique homes, church buildings, schools, museums, public buildings, and special use properties.

Applications of the Cost Approach
- Appraising new properties
- Appraising properties with unique improvements
- Appraising special use properties
- Appraising properties that cannot be analyzed using the other approaches to value, i.e. not enough comparables and no income produced

Variations on this approach are often useful in identifying market reactions when appraising oddball properties that have unique designs and characteristics.

The cost approach to value is applicable for unique properties
and special-use properties like a stadium.

Limitations of the Cost Approach

Like the other two approaches to value, the cost approach to value is not
applicable to every appraisal assignment.

Limitations of the Cost Approach

- Appraising properties with older improvements
- Appraising properties in a market with minimal land value
  indicators
- Appraising properties that are not at their highest and best use

This approach is also limited in other
ways. The cost approach assumes
that the cost to build an item is
equal to its value in the market,
but that is not always the case. In
addition, depreciation can be difficult
to determine accurately. At times,
estimating accrued depreciation
is based on subjective reasoning,
which lessens the applicability of this
approach. **Accrued depreciation** is
the difference between the cost to
replace the property and the property's current appraised value.

The cost approach is inapplicable
when appraising older buildings
because it is difficult to measure
accurately the depreciation.

In certain assignments, like appraising vacant land or a condominium, the
cost approach to value is completely inappropriate. This is because the cost
approach requires both an estimate for land and an estimate for improvements.

Vacant land, of course, is missing improvements and the condominium form of ownership does not include the land, but rather airspace and its contents.

Because of these limitations, the cost approach to value is often omitted in an assignment. When it is developed, the primary role of the cost approach to value is to lend support to the value estimates derived by the sales comparison approach or the income approach.

COST APPROACH TO VALUE (not required by Fannie Mae)					
Provide adequate information for the lender/client to replicate the below cost figures and calculations.					
Support for the opinion of site value (summary of comparable land sales or other methods for estimating site value)					
ESTIMATED ☐ REPRODUCTION OR ☐ REPLACEMENT COST NEW		OPINION OF SITE VALUE			= $
Source of cost data		Dwelling	Sq. Ft. @ $		=$
Quality rating from cost service	Effective date of cost data		Sq. Ft. @ $		=$
Comments on Cost Approach (gross living area calculations, depreciation, etc.)					
		Garage/Carport	Sq. Ft. @ $		=$
		Total Estimate of Cost-New			= $
		Less Physical	Functional	External	
		Depreciation			=$( )
		Depreciated Cost of Improvements			=$
		"As-is" Value of Site Improvements			=$
Estimated Remaining Economic Life (HUD and VA only)	Years	Indicated Value By Cost Approach			=$

STEPS IN THE COST APPROACH

The steps in the cost approach follow a logical sequence. This unit discusses the first three steps in the cost approach.

Steps Appraisers Use When Applying the Cost Approach

1. Estimate the value of the land of the subject property as if vacant and available to be put to its highest and best use.

2. Estimate the replacement (or reproduction) cost new of the building, as of the effective date of the appraisal.

3. Estimate and deduct the amount of accrued depreciation from the replacement (or reproduction) cost new of the building(s).

4. Add entrepreneurial incentive, when appropriate.

5. Estimate "as-is" value of additional site improvements, if necessary.

6. Add the land value estimate, the depreciated value of the improvements, the entrepreneurial incentive, and the value of the site improvements together to arrive at the total property value.

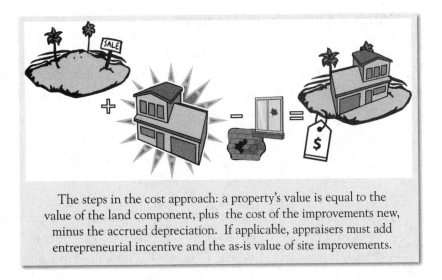

The steps in the cost approach: a property's value is equal to the value of the land component, plus the cost of the improvements new, minus the accrued depreciation. If applicable, appraisers must add entrepreneurial incentive and the as-is value of site improvements.

Estimate Value of the Land

The principles of supply and demand, change, anticipation, substitution, and balance all influence land value. All of these principles are used when estimating the value of land.

> Example: The principle of anticipation causes value to be created in anticipation of benefits that may be derived at some point in the future. Buyers acquire properties in anticipation of what may be done with that property in the future; not necessarily what is economically feasible immediately upon acquisition. The competition among buyers creates a price level for land that may have little, or nothing, to do with its current use.

Appraisers may use numerous techniques in order to identify the land value for the subject. It is important to recognize that the following techniques produce estimates of the fee simple interest in land. If there is another interest in land required in an assignment, such as a leasehold, leased fee, or reversionary interest, the land value estimate will need to be adjusted.

The methods used to estimate land value are all derived from and are variations on the three basic approaches to value.

Six Methods Commonly Used To Estimate the Value of Land

- Sales comparison method
- Allocation method
- Extraction method
- Land residual method
- Ground rent capitalization method
- Subdivision development method

Sales Comparison Method

The **sales comparison method** is the most commonly used method for valuing land and is preferred over the other methods. This technique is best used when there are recent comparables of vacant land sales. When using this technique, appraisers compare the subject site with other vacant land sites that have sold recently. Appraisers must be sure to use the same units of comparison. The units of comparison for land may be per acre, per square foot, per front foot, etc.

This method follows the same steps as the sales comparison approach. An appraiser collects data of vacant land sales, selects the comparables, and verifies the information gathered. Comparable sales used in valuing land should be as similar as possible to the subject. Zoning is often the most important criterion when selecting comparable sales for the subject because it may create limitations on how a lot may be used, making it inappropriate for comparison with another lot. One lot may have available utilities, whereas another does not. Then, he or she analyzes the comparables and applies adjustments to the sales prices of the comparable sales to reflect the differences between the comparables and the subject site. After adjusting a representative number of comparable sales, the adjusted prices are reconciled into an estimate of value. When performing the reconciliation process, the sales requiring the least amount of adjusting tend to be the strongest indicators of value.

Although this approach is the most commonly used, there are situations when it does not apply. For example, the subject property may be in a heavily developed area with very few vacant sites, and even fewer vacant land sales. Similarly, in some rural areas, vacant land sales may occur so seldom that the available data is inadequate to develop a credible estimate of value land using the sales comparison method.

Allocation Method

The **allocation method** is based upon the principle of balance as well as on the concept of contributory value. The allocation method assumes that there is a typical ratio between the land value of a property and the value of its improvements. Since the ratio varies by area, appraisers must extract the ratio from the local market. Then, they can apply it to other improved sales in the subject's neighborhood in order to establish the land value.

Example: Assume that there have been no recent sales of vacant land in the subject's neighborhood. Appraiser John has found that houses in a nearby neighborhood sell for prices ranging from $200,000 to $300,000. He found a property in that same area where the developer purchased lots for $100,000 and built houses that sold for $300,000 upon completion. In this case, the value of the land ($100,000) represents 33.3% ($100,000 ÷ $300,000) of the overall value of that property.

John then finds a sale of an improved property with a site virtually identical to the subject. This property sold for $360,000. Applying the ratio to this sale, he estimates that the land is worth $120,000 (33.3% × $360,000).

The allocation method holds that the property value is composed of a typical ratio of land to improvements.

Although this method does not produce conclusive value estimates, it can be used to establish land values in situations when recent comparable land sales are scarce or non-existent. The weakness of this method is that it does not take into account individual property differences.

Extraction Method

The **extraction method** (or abstraction method) is a variation on the allocation method and is based on the same principles.

Using this method, appraisers derive the land value of a comparable property by deducting the depreciated costs of the improvements on that property from the property's known sale price. The remaining value represents value attributable to the land.

This method may be best applied in situations when the improvements contribute a relatively small amount of value to the overall property.

Land Residual Technique

The **land residual technique** is based upon the premise that the income of a property is generated by both the land and the improvements, and that there is a relationship between the income a property produces and the value of that property.

This technique is useful when building value is known or can be accurately estimated. If appraisers know or can reliably estimate the income for the whole property, they can subtract the portion of that income attributable to the improvements to determine the income attributable to the land. The income attributable to the land is converted into a land value by applying a capitalization rate.

However, when using this analytical technique, the forecasted income must be at the property's highest and best use. Estimating this income upon some other use will a provide less than accurate indication of value.

Ground Rent Capitalization Method

In the **ground rent capitalization method**, the annual ground rent is divided by a market derived capitalization rate. **Ground rent** is the rent that is payable under a ground lease, which is a long-term lease (sometimes up to 99 years).

The calculation under this method is similar to that used in the land residual method. However, when using this method, the income is determined by the land lease amount rather than calculating the residual of the whole property's income. Variations in the terms of the lease such as renewal options and escalator clauses as well as the reversion need to be considered in this analysis.

This technique is useful in situations when comparable sales of leased land are available and the terms of those leases are known.

Subdivision Development Method

The **subdivision development method** (or land development method) is used to value land when subdivision and development of the subject site represent the highest and best use of the property and sales information for finished lots is available. This method is applicable to all kinds of land including residential, commercial, recreational, or industrial. It requires accurate forecasting of market demand and risk factors.

In performing this analysis, appraisers estimate the number, size, and price of lots that may be created by subdividing the subject property. Although it may be impossible to determine this information precisely without performing surveys or engineering studies, analyzing zoning and subdivision requirements may enable appraisers to formulate a reasonable estimate. Appraisers may also estimate the subdivision potential of the subject property by analyzing the number of lots created in other nearby subdivisions.

Example: Appraiser Baker estimates that a parcel can be subdivided into 50 lots of the same size. From market data, she determines that this size lot is worth approximately $30,000. The total projected gross income from lot sales once developed is $1,500,000 total.

After the development potential of the subject property is estimated, the time required to develop the subject into individual sites needs to be estimated. Additionally, the period required to sell all these newly developed lots created from the subject property, called the absorption rate, needs to be calculated.

Example: If the subject is developed into 50 single-family residential lots, the absorption forecast may project that the first 20 homes will sell in the first year for $300,000 each, the second 20 for $330,000 in the next year, and the final 10 for $375,000 in the third year.

The owner will incur many different costs in the process of subdividing the land into individual lots, developing the lots, and marketing them. All these costs need to be deducted from the sum of the projected sales prices for the sites. Then, the projected net proceeds from these sales are discounted to their present value in order to arrive at an indication of the land's present value in its raw state.

The subdivision method is useful in situations when comparable sales are scarce or non-existent. It is also useful in developing feasibility studies. However, it is often necessary to make speculative assumptions when performing this approach, which lessens the reliability of this technique. Although the complexity of this technique may cause appraisers to use it less than other methods, it is useful when others are not available.

Estimate Replacement (Reproduction) Cost

After estimating the land value, the next step is to determine the cost to reproduce or replace the improvements. Reproduction cost and replacement cost are calculated differently, and it is important to understand the difference.

Reproduction vs. Replacement

The decision to use replacement cost or reproduction cost is usually related to the intended use of the appraisal. Fannie Mae and Freddie Mac require reproduction cost estimates in appraisals for loans they purchase. For insurance purposes, replacement cost may be desired.

Reproduction Cost

Reproduction cost is the dollar amount required to construct an exact replica of the property being appraised. This cost estimate assumes the cost of using like kind and quality of materials, identical construction and workmanship standards, as well as identical design and layout. It reflects construction prices current as of the date of the appraisal.

When performing a reproduction cost estimate, appraisers estimate the costs using the exact same building materials, construction standards, floor plan, layout, and quality of workmanship existing in the property being appraised. This option is more suited to estimating unique or historical structures when an exact replica is requisite.

In some instances, reproduction cost is difficult, if not almost impossible, to estimate accurately because identical building materials may no longer be available and construction standards may have changed.

> Example: Asbestos was used widely for siding and insulation in years past. Today it is virtually impossible to buy building materials containing asbestos.

> Similarly, in years past, 60-amp electrical service using "knob and tube" wiring was the standard for most homes. This kind of electrical system is no longer compliant with building codes.

In such instances, appraisers estimate costs using building materials and construction methods that are nearly equal.

Replacement Cost

Since estimating the reproduction cost of an existing structure is not always feasible, it may be more reliable and more prudent to estimate the cost to replace the existing improvements. **Replacement cost** is the dollar amount required to construct improvements having the same utility and quality as the subject property using current construction materials, methods, and techniques. Like reproduction cost, replacement cost reflects construction prices current as of the date of the appraisal.

To estimate the replacement costs for an older subject property, appraisers may find the costs of newer homes with similar bedroom and bath counts, similar-sized gross living areas, and similar room sizes. Generally, similar sized structures of similar quality construction and similar utility will have very similar values. An exact replica is not necessary to achieve the same value in the marketplace, and it may not even achieve maximum value if depreciation due to excess construction offsets perceived worth in the marketplace. Because of this, residential appraisers are mostly concerned with replacement cost, and this text focuses on replacement cost.

Sources of Data

When using the cost approach, the most important data that appraisers collect is information on the building area and construction costs.

Building Area

Appraisers can determine the square footage of the building(s) by personally inspecting and measuring the improvements. Additionally, the size of the improvements may be obtained from local county tax assessor's records, blueprints, sales brochures, or from previous appraisals, if provided by the client.

However, if appraisers rely on third party sources, they increase their risk of producing a misinformed appraisal. By personally measuring the improvements, appraisers avoid the need to make an extraordinary assumption regarding the size of the improvements, which lessens the risk of poorly appraising the property.

Construction Costs

Appraisers rely on reliable cost data in order to formulate the cost approach. As such, gathering and identifying this information is essential.

Some of the best indicators of cost are construction contracts for buildings that are similar to the one being appraised. Although these are not often available, they provide a very strong basis upon which to base a cost estimate.

Data sources such as Marshall & Swift®/Boeckh, R.S. Means Company, and Craftsman Book Company all are sources of construction cost data. Computer assisted cost estimator programs as well as internet based cost estimator resources are also available.

Discussions with builders and cost estimators are also a very good way to determine local building costs to incorporate into appraisal assignments.

Some appraisers maintain extensive records including costs of various kinds of buildings they have appraised. Although this method is very reliable, an appraiser needs to maintain confidentiality according to USPAP.

Appraisers should compare data obtained from different sources, such as contractors and cost estimators, in order to verify the accuracy of the information provided. If there are significant discrepancies when comparing one data source to another, additional investigation is needed to identify the reason for the discrepancy.

Direct Costs and Indirect Costs

Cost estimating services all provide direct cost estimates; however, they vary in their level of accurately identifying indirect costs. **Direct costs** or hard costs refer to costs directly related to labor and materials. **Indirect costs** (soft costs) are costs for items not directly linked to construction that are still incurred in the overall process. Appraisers need to be certain if the cost information obtained from other sources include the indirect costs. If not, indirect costs need to be added into that cost estimate.

Examples of Direct Costs

- Building materials, products, and equipment used in construction

- Labor used to construct the building(s)

- Contractor's profit and overhead, including both project and worker supervision, worker's compensation, fire, liability, and unemployment insurance, as well as performance bonds

- Equipment rental, including an on-site temporary office, material storage facilities, security fencing, barricades, and portable toilets

- Temporary power, water, phone service, and utility costs

- Security, including guards and video monitoring

- Temporary construction easements

Examples of Indirect Costs

- Professional fees, such as architect's fees, surveyor's fees, civil, geotechnical, mechanical, electrical, and structural engineering fees
- Environmental and building permit fees including plan check fees
- Building construction inspector fees
- Zoning change, conditional use permit, and environmental consultant's fees
- Accounting, legal, and appraisal fees
- Financing fees, including costs and interest paid on construction loans, permanent financing costs, processing fees, and service charges
- Lease-up, marketing, and sales costs, including commissions, sales incentives, and administrative costs
- Escrow, title insurance, and recording fees
- Insurance and property taxes during construction

Some indirect costs are calculated as a percentage of the direct costs. Others are calculated as a lump-sum amount to the overall cost since they are not related to the size or direct costs of the building(s) being constructed. Appraisers must be sure that the cost estimate in an appraisal reflects the costs likely to be incurred by an owner/developer. For example, constructing a high-rise office tower incurs different costs than those incurred when building a detached, single-family home.

Methods Used to Estimate Cost

Once the size of the improvements is determined, that information is incorporated into the cost approach using any of the four commonly used methods— index method, comparative unit method, unit-in-place method, and quantity survey method.

The **index method** and the **comparative unit method** are the quickest and easiest to calculate. However, they also tend to be the least accurate of the methods used for cost estimation. The **unit-in-place method** is a more in-depth cost estimate that provides more detail than the square-foot or index method. The **quantity survey method** is the most in-depth and detailed of the commonly used processes for estimating costs, but it also is the most time-consuming and arduous of the four. It is the method least used by appraisers.

Index Method

Many cost services have information regarding cost trends. **Cost-index trending** involves converting known historical costs into current cost estimates. Usually, the cost reporting service keeps track of building cost trends over time. The reporting service assigns a numerical index to a cost relative to a base year. By comparing the current cost index with the cost index when a property was constructed, an estimate for current costs may be obtained.

To update the known historical cost to the current date of valuation, it is necessary to divide the present index by the historical index at the time of construction and multiply that result by the original cost of construction. The following equation illustrates this concept:

$$\frac{\text{Current Cost Index}}{\text{Historical Cost Index}} \ \times \ \text{Historical Cost} \ = \ \text{Present Cost Estimate}$$

Example: Appraiser Joe is appraising a single-family detached home that was constructed in 1973. From his research, he identified the historical cost index figure at 177. He also identified the cost to construct the subject property at $64,000 from examining the contractor's records. The current cost index is 587. To estimate the current replacement cost of the subject property, Joe uses the above formula to calculate the cost:

$$587 \div 177 = 3.32 \text{ (rounded)}$$
$$\$64,000 \times 3.32 = \$212,480$$

Limitations of this Method

There can be problems with estimating costs using this method.

- Historical costs do not always indicate typical costs for that period.

- Historical data does not always correspond in its individual components with current costs.

- Construction methods at the time of the historical cost may differ from the methods at the time of the appraisal.

Cost-index trending is rarely accurate when used as the only method of estimating current costs. Used alone, this method is not a reliable replacement for more traditional cost estimating methods. It may be used to help verify one of the other ways costs are estimated, however, and give further support to the final cost estimate.

Comparative Unit Method

The **comparative unit** or **square-foot method** is based on costs of similar structures computed on a unit of measurement. The comparative unit method is a relatively uncomplicated way of estimating costs and is widely used. The cost to construct a building is multiplied by the area of the building being appraised.

Units of Measurement

The two **units of measurement** that are most commonly used are square foot and cubic foot. A **square foot** is an area equal to one foot by one foot square. A **cubic foot** is a measurement for volume. It is an area one foot long, by one foot wide, by one foot high.

When appraising residential property, the cost approach is typically calculated on a per-square foot basis. Since the cubic-foot method measures the volume of a building, it is used when appraising commercial, industrial, or special use buildings, when the heights of floors within a structure are varied and a simple square foot measurement would not accurately account for all the materials used in the structure. Cubic foot measurements are also used for structures like warehouses or silos that are very tall with no floors other than the ground floor. Obviously, a square-foot measurement would not account for all the materials used in the height of the walls.

Even though both units of measurement are used, the remainder of this section concentrates on using the cost-per-square foot as the comparative unit. In either case, the process is overall the same.

Using the Cost-per-Square Foot Unit

Data on the cost to construct a property on a per square-foot basis may be obtained from cost estimate services such as Marshall & Swift®/Boeckh or may be obtained from developers or contractors who have built other similar properties. When appraising single-family properties, the cost to build a structure on a per-square-foot basis is multiplied by the gross living area of the building being appraised. The cost of additional components, such as garages, basements, driveways, pools, patios, etc., is added to this calculation to arrive at the total cost estimate. This method applies whether calculating replacement cost or reproduction cost.

> Example: An appraiser contacts a contractor who just built a brand new tract about four blocks away from the subject. The new complex averaged about $105 per square foot of construction and contained both two and three bedroom homes. The subject is a three-bedroom house and has 2,124 square feet of living area. Using the comparative unit method, the appraiser estimates that it will cost approximately $223,000 to rebuild the subject property (2,124 sq. ft. × $105).

The example is over-simplified. In reality, appraisers must account for a multitude of variables and make adjustments to those variables.

Cost estimating services typically generate the cost-per-square-foot estimate starting with a base price, which is usually reflective of the subject's quality and size. This base cost estimate is adjusted up or down depending upon features found in, or lacking from, the subject property.

Adjustments for Quality of Construction. In a middle-income area where homes are built in subdivisions and floors are linoleum, the quality of construction might be called average. In a high-end area of luxury and custom homes, where the floors are marble and the kitchens have polished granite counter tops, a higher quality of construction a higher price per square foot is used. When using costs obtained from similar buildings, appraisers need to apply adjustments to reflect the differences between the costs to build those similar properties and the subject.

> Example: Assume homes that are similar to the subject are being built at a cost of $110 per square foot and have average-quality kitchen cabinetry and equipment. The subject may be estimated to cost $115 per square foot if it has superior kitchen cabinetry and equipment.

Regional Adjustments. Additionally, appraisers apply regional and local cost multipliers to the subject's base cost, because the same house built in Los Angeles and Des Moines will have different costs associated with the project. Regional and local cost multipliers account for the differences in regional median wages, materials that have regional cost differences due to supply or transportation costs, as well as regional building requirements. These adjustment figures and locational multipliers are also supplied by the cost estimating service. Be careful when identifying building costs in this manner. For instance, some developers build so many homes that they are able to take advantage of economies of scale and spend much less money building properties than it costs others. Building costs should be reflective of the cost to build one unit, not one of many units.

Size Adjustments. Similarly, costs on a per-square-foot basis vary with size. All other things being equal, it typically costs less to build a larger building on a per-square-foot basis than to build a smaller building. First, this is due to **economies of scale**; larger quantities of building materials typically cost less, on a per unit basis, than smaller quantities of the same materials. Second, certain items, such as heating, plumbing, doors, windows, elevators, and insulation, do not cost proportionately more to install in a larger building than in a smaller one.

Adjustments for Type of Structure. Costs on a per-square-foot basis also vary depending on the type of structure. For example, costs vary depending on whether the structure is finished or unfinished. **Finished structures**, like the house, require a higher cost per square foot. Construction within a home includes insulation, fine carpentry, finishing of all surfaces, expensive carpeting, and so forth. **Unfinished structures**, like the garage or carport, require a lower cost per square foot because they lack the details and added costs of the dwelling. Often a garage is a shell with no flooring, insulation, or drywall. Therefore, it is calculated separately from the calculation for the gross living area of the single-family residential property.

Combine Adjusted Base Costs of GLA, Garage, and Other Improvements. Once an appraiser has determined all the costs, he or she adds the adjusted base cost of the subject's gross living area to the costs of the garage and any other improvements.

> Example: Assume the property being appraised is a single-family residence that has 1,565 square feet of gross living area. The reproduction cost of the gross living area is estimated to be $81.00 per square foot. The subject has a tile roof that, according to the cost estimating service, adds $6.25 per square foot to the base cost. The subject property is two stories tall which lowers the overall cost $7.50 per square foot. The subject has no basement; however, it does have a 420 square foot garage that is estimated to cost $19.50 per square foot to build. The regional multiplier supplied from the cost service is 1.05.

House	Base Cost Tile Roof Premium Two-Story Design	$81.00 + $ 6.25 − $ 7.50
	Cost per Square Foot Gross Living Area	$79.75 1,565 ft.²
	Reproduction Cost	$124,808.75
Other	Garage Cost per Sq Foot Garage Area	$19.50 × 420 ft.²
	Garage Reproduction Cost	$8,190.00
Reproduction Costs Subtotal Regional/Local Multiplier		$132,998.75 × 1.05
Total Reproduction Cost		$139,648.69
Rounded Estimate		$139,600.00

With experience, appraisers become accustomed to what price per square foot is appropriate for which type of construction in the area, and do not have to perform such laborious research for each appraisal. However, they should be aware of any economic changes in the area that could cause building costs to increase or decrease. Appraisers must be in touch with the market for all relevant data, including cost data. Consulting available cost handbooks, as well as builders, contractors, and other appraisers in the area is necessary.

Unit-in-Place Method

The **unit-in-place method** is an accurate way to calculate building costs since every building component must be identified. However, it is also much more time-consuming than the comparative unit method.

In this method, the costs of the various building components are calculated separately, as installed. Building components include items such as the foundation, exterior walls, interior walls, roof structure, ceiling, electrical system, plumbing system, kitchen cabinetry, kitchen equipment, windows, doors, mechanical systems, stairways, etc.

The costs to build each of these component parts in place is calculated then added together with the cost of the other component parts in order to estimate the value of a property. The individual costs estimated for each of the building components required in this method are in terms of the standardized units typically used for the individual building component.

> Example: Concrete for a foundation is measured in dollars per cubic yard. Roofing may be calculated in terms of a square, which equals 100 square feet. The cost of a raised foundation made of concrete block may be expressed as dollars per linear foot. Carpeting may be calculated in terms of square yardage.

Cost estimates for the individual components need to include a proportionate share of all direct costs including labor, contractor's profit, etc. Indirect costs are usually calculated separately when using this method.

As in the comparative unit method, costs to perform the unit-in-place method may be obtained from local developers and contractors. Additionally, unit-in-place estimates may be calculated with cost estimating services. Even though cost information obtained from developers and contractors may be more accurate, it is more time consuming.

Limitations of this Method

This method breaks down the cost of a building into the cost of its component parts. Unfortunately, the market is not always reflective of valuing a property on this basis. The knowledge about costs concerning materials, equipment, labor, and contractor's profit associated with every component of a building, or buildings, on a site may be very difficult to estimate. Additional specialized knowledge may be required to perform this procedure accurately.

Quantity Survey Method

The **quantity survey method** is the most thorough and accurate method of estimating building costs. It is also the most time-consuming and intricate method. As the most comprehensive way to estimate costs, the quantity survey method duplicates a contractor's method of developing a bid for construction. When employing this method, the quality and quantity of all the materials used and all labor associated with building the structure is identified and estimated.

For example, the number of bricks used in construction are identified, the number of yards of concrete needed are determined, the amount and type of electrical wire calculated, the number and type of plumbing fixtures counted, and the number of hours associated with each category of labor necessary to construct the building are estimated. The cost of each of these items is then calculated and the labor associated with assembling and building all these items is calculated.

The quantity survey method is the most comprehensive way to estimate cost new and it accounts for all materials used.

The quantity survey method breaks down the indirect costs in an in-depth manner as well. Permit fees, taxes, insurance costs, surveys, financing fees and interest, and developer's profit are all calculated in as precise a manner as possible.

Limitations of this Method

This method for estimating costs is very precise when properly executed. However, it is also very time consuming and costly to perform. Many appraisers may lack the expertise needed to perform this kind of cost estimate. Usually, this method requires the services of a professional construction cost estimator. Due to the level of expertise required and the costs and time required to develop this method properly, the quantity-survey method is not often used.

Estimate Entrepreneurial Incentive

No matter which method an appraiser uses to reproduce the cost estimate of the improvements, the entrepreneurial incentive must also be estimated. **Entrepreneurial incentive** represents the amount an entrepreneur expects to receive for his or her contribution to a project and risk. **Entrepreneurial profit** is the compensation the owner or developer actually receives from the undertaking. It is typically reflected as the property value once construction is completed minus the developer's costs (including direct and indirect costs) and the land value.

Entrepreneurial incentive is a necessary element of the cost approach estimate. Based upon the principle of anticipation, entrepreneurial incentive reflects the usual motivation within the market. If the value of a property were only equal to its cost plus its land value, there would be no motivation for an owner to build.

When applying the cost approach, appraisers must estimate the appropriate amount to allow for entrepreneurial incentive, since cost estimator services like Marshall & Swift®/Boeckh do not include entrepreneurial incentive in their listed costs. Usually appraisers survey builders in their area to estimate entrepreneurial incentive. Depending on the market, estimating entrepreneurial incentive may be calculated as a percentage of cost, a percentage of cost plus land value, or a percentage of the final estimate of value.

Estimate Value of Site Improvements

Although adding the value of on-site improvements is one of the final steps in the cost approach, it will be addressed here before we cover depreciation since on-site improvements are typically valued "as-is", and the value of the site improvements is not depreciated. Items like landscaping, sprinkler systems, driveways, brickwork, fences, etc. fall into the category of site improvements. For some properties, the contribution of site improvements to value is negligible. In other situations, it is significant. Appraisers use market data to determine the "as-is" value.

This method is used because the cost to install site improvements does not necessarily equal the value they contribute to the site. For example, a swimming pool may cost $35,000 to install, but only add $10,000 to the value of the property. Appraisers determine this with a paired sales analysis or by other appropriate market abstraction. Other items of site improvements may add more value to the property than their cost to install. Landscaping, for example, may cost $3,000, but add $5,000 to the value. This, too, must be referenced to data from the marketplace.

After appraisers have determined the land value, and developed a depreciated value of improvements, those two factors are combined with the "as-is" value of site improvements to create an entire property value based on the cost approach to value.

SUMMARY

The **cost approach** to value is not used as frequently as the sales comparison or income approaches. However, there are situations when the cost approach is the only way to estimate a property's value.

The first step in the cost approach is to develop an opinion of the value of the **site**. The methods used to estimate land value include the sales comparison method, allocation method, extraction method, land residual technique, ground rent capitalization method, and subdivision development method.

The next step is to estimate the **reproduction cost** or **replacement cost** of the subject property. This includes researching costs through cost estimating services or by contacting developers or contractors, and choosing an appropriate method to use. The methods used to estimate cost are the **index method**, the **comparative unit method**, the **unit-in-place method**, and the **quantity survey method**. They vary in complexity and reliability. In this unit, they are presented in order from the least complex and least reliable (index method) to the most complex and most reliable (quantity survey method). The comparative unit method is the one most widely used when appraising residential properties.

As a part of calculating the cost new for the subject, appraisers account for the **entrepreneurial incentive** when necessary.

Estimating the "as-is" value of other site improvements is another separate step.

After appraisers have determined the land value, and developed a depreciated value of improvements, those two factors are combined with the "as-is" value of site improvements to create an entire property value based on the cost approach to value. Because the subject property is almost never brand new, appraisers must decide how much the improvements have depreciated, which is the subject of the next unit.

UNIT 11 REVIEW

Matching Exercise

Instructions: Write the letter of the matching term on the blank line before its definition, and then check your response with the Answer Key that immediately follows the Multiple Choice Questions.

Terms

A. allocation method

B   cost approach

C. direct costs

D. entrepreneurial incentive

E. ground rent

F. indirect costs

G. replacement cost

H. reproduction cost

I. sales comparison method

J. unit-in-place method

Definitions

1. _____ Valuation method based upon the proposition that an informed buyer will pay no more than the cost of producing a substitute property with equal utility as the subject property.

2. _____ Most commonly used method for valuing land in the cost approach.

3. _____ Method that assumes that there is a typical ratio between the land value of a property and the value of its improvements.

4. _____ Rent that is payable under a ground lease.

5. _____ Dollar amount required to construct an exact replica of the property being appraised.

6. _____ Dollar amount required to construct improvements having the same utility and quality as the subject property using current construction materials, methods, and techniques.

7. _____ Construction costs directly related to labor and materials.

8. _____ Construction costs for items not directly linked to construction.

9. _____ Method in which the costs of the various building components, as installed, are calculated separately and then added together into a single value estimate.

10. _____ Compensation the owner/developer expects to gain by supplying the necessary funds to begin and maintain the project as well bearing the risks associated with the development.

Multiple Choice Questions

Instructions: Circle your choice, and then check your response with the Answer Key that immediately follows the Multiple Choice Questions.

1. The cost approach recognizes that there are two major components in real estate. They are:

    a. cost and value.
    b. land and improvements.
    c. supply and demand.
    d. income and expenses.

2. Regarding the cost approach to value, which of the following statements is true?

    a. It is the best approach to appraising new condominiums.
    b. The cost to build an item usually equals its value.
    c. It is best suited for older buildings because of its reliance on depreciation.
    d. Like the other two approaches to value, the cost approach to value is not applicable to every appraisal assignment.

3. Which method of valuing land is most useful when building value is known or can be accurately estimated?

    a. Allocation method
    b. Extraction method
    c. Land residual method
    d. Sales comparison method

4. In Anytown, the ratio of land value to improvement value is historically 2 to 1. If a typical improved comp value is $300,000, what is the typical lot value?

    a. $100,000
    b. $150,000
    c. $200,000
    d. Cannot be determined

5. Linda must identify the value of the land component for a developed property. The property sold recently for $500,000 and she has determined the improvement value, through the cost approach, to be $289,000. Thus, the land value must be $211,000. Linda used which method of land valuation?

    a. Allocation

    b. Abstraction

    c. Sales comparison

    d. Land residual

6. The dollar amount to replicate an improvement using like kind and quality of materials, identical construction and workmanship standards is known as the:

    a. replacement cost.

    b. reproduction cost.

    c. index cost.

    d. entrepreneurial cost.

7. Which of the following is the most in-depth method for estimating cost?

    a. Index

    b. Square-foot

    c. Unit-in-place

    d. Like-quality

8. In 1984, a three bedroom, two bath single-family detached home cost $65,000 to construct in Anytown, Arizona. The historical cost index for that area is 220 and currently is 378. Using the index method, what is the current replacement cost for this structure?

    a. $112,000

    b. $378,000

    c. $ 37,800

    d. $ 78,000

9. According to a cost estimating service, a 2,000 square foot office building cost $300,000 to build. What is the cost per square foot?

    a. $140

    b. $150

    c. $160

    d. $660

10. A starter home that Earl is appraising contains 978 square feet of above grade improvements and a garage that contains 168 square feet. Earl estimates the land value at $75,000 from recent comparables. If the cost estimating service Earl uses has a base cost of $81 per unit of above grade improvements and $23 per unit for the garage and a regional multiplier of 1.19, what is the reproduction estimate for the subject home?

    a. $ 98,868
    b. $173,867
    c. $ 83,082
    d. $141,829

11. Which method of cost estimation would use the following list?
Foundation - $30 per linear foot, Floor Construction - $3.60 per sq. ft., Framing - $4.50 per sq. ft. of support area, Roof Construction - $3.70, Exterior Walls - $10.20 per sq. ft., Windows - $14.20 per sq. ft.

    a. Index method
    b. Comparative unit method
    c. Unit-in-place method
    d. Quantity survey method

12. Which of the following is not considered a direct cost?

    a. Site utility costs
    b. Labor
    c. Financing costs
    d. Portable toilets

13. In the context of the cost approach to value, an appraisal fee would be considered:

    a. entrepreneurial incentive.
    b. a direct cost.
    c. an indirect cost.
    d. necessary cost.

14. Entrepreneurial incentive is based on the principle of:

    a. depreciation.
    b. anticipation.
    c. reproduction.
    d. substitution.

15. Items that are not attached to the main structure of the property, but still add value are:

    a. added to the depreciated value of improvements and land value.
    b. not depreciated.
    c. site improvements.
    d. all of the above.

UNIT 11 ANSWER KEY

Answers – Matching

1.	B	4.	E	7.	C	10.	D
2.	I	5.	H	8.	F		
3.	A	6.	G	9.	J		

Answers – Multiple Choice

1. **(b)** The cost approach recognizes there are two major components in real estate; land and improvements. **Page 349**

2. **(d)** The cost approach to value is not applicable to every appraisal assignment. Cost approach is inapplicable for condominiums. The cost to build an item rarely equals its value. It is difficult to apply this approach to older buildings, specifically because of its reliance on depreciation. **Page 351**

3. **(c)** The land residual technique is based on the premise that the income of a property is generated by both the land and the improvements, and that there is a relationship between the income a property produces and the value of that property. This method is useful when building value is known or can be accurately estimated. . **Page 355**

4. **(c)** If an improved property is $300,000 and the land to improvement ratio is 2:1, then the land is worth $200,000 and the improvements are worth $100,000. Remember to account for both parts of the ratio: 2 to 1 means 3 parts total. **Page 355**

5. **(b)** The extraction (or abstraction) method derives the land value of a comparable property by deducting the depreciated costs of the improvements on that property from its known sale price. **Page 355**

6. **(b)** Reproduction cost is the dollar amount required to construct an exact replica of the property being appraised. This cost estimate assumes the cost of using like kind and quality of materials, identical construction and workmanship standards, as well as identical design and layout. **Page 358**

7. **(c)** The unit-in-place method is a more in-depth cost estimate that provides more detail than the square-foot or index method. The quantity survey method is the most in-depth of the commonly used methods for estimating costs; however, it was not given as a choice. The like-quality method does not exist. **Page 361**

8. **(a)** Divide the current index by the historical index (378 ÷ 220 = 1.718) and then multiply the result by the historical (or original) cost (1.718 × $65,000 = $111,682). Rounded, the best answer is $112,000. **Page 362**

9. **(b)** A 2,000 square foot building that cost $300,000 to build has a cost per square foot of $150 ($300,000 ÷ 2,000 = 150). **Page 364**

10. **(a)** The math is as follows:

Base above grade x above grade area ($81 × 978 sf) = $79,218
Base garage x garage area ($23 × 168 sf) = $3,864
Total before regional multiplier $83,082
Total after regional multiplier ($83,082 × 1.19) = $98,868
The land value is not part of the reproduction cost. **Page 365**

11. **(c)** The unit-in-place method breaks down the cost of a building into the cost of its component parts. The individual costs estimated for each of the building components required in this method are in terms of the standardized units typically used for the individual building component. **Pages 366-367**

12. **(c)** Direct costs include all the costs directly involved with construction including any costs associated with maintaining a construction site. **Page 360**

13. **(c)** Indirect costs are costs that are part of the overall process of building a project, but are not directly linked to construction. **Page 360**

14. **(b)** Entrepreneurial incentive reflects the amount developers expect to receive for their efforts and it is based upon the principle of anticipation. **Page 368**

15. **(d)** Items like pools, fences and landscaping that are not part of the main primary structure but still add value are called site improvements. Typically, these items are not depreciated. As the final step in the cost approach section on the URAR form, they are added to the depreciated value of improvements and land value to create the overall property value. **Page 369**

Cost Approach: Depreciation of Improvements

Unit 12

INTRODUCTION

After estimating the reproduction or replacement cost of a structure, an appraiser's next step is to determine the depreciation amount. This step is required to determine the present value of the structure. An estimation of value by the cost approach is not complete until the depreciation of the improvements has been deducted.

Learning Objectives

After reading this unit, you should be able to:

- recall the purpose of depreciating the improvements in the cost approach.
- differentiate between effective and economic age.
- distinguish between incurable and curable depreciation.
- classify the types of depreciation and identify the causes.
- identify the different methods used to calculate accrued depreciation of improvements.
- recognize the steps in the cost approach process.

DEPRECIATION

Depreciation is a loss in value to a property due to any cause. **Accrued depreciation** is depreciation that has already occurred. This loss in value is equal to the difference between the replacement cost new of the improvements and their market value. Depreciation may be due to the physical wearing out of a building, functional problems of the building, or locational problems that affect the property. After estimating the accrued depreciation, appraisers deduct it from the replacement (or reproduction) cost of the building(s) on a property. The resulting figure is the depreciated cost of the improvements.

Effective Age and Economic Life

Before exploring the different types of depreciation, appraisers must know the difference between effective age and economic life.

Effective Age

The chronological age of the structure is its **actual age**. However, properties often appear younger or older than the structure's actual age and have an effective age that varies from its actual age. **Effective age** describes the age of a structure based on its condition and usefulness.

Appraisers use effective age instead of chronological age because properties physically depreciate at different rates based on the quality of materials, maintenance levels, and workmanship. Effective age is a more accurate representation of the desirability of the property in the marketplace.

Although not an exact science, an experienced appraiser can produce a very meaningful figure with effective age. Appraisers usually express effective age in five-year increments (e.g., 5, 10, 15, 20, etc.), reflecting that it is just an estimate.

Economic Life

Buildings have a certain useful life in which a property's improvements contribute to property value. For residential properties, the structure's utility and physical appeal contribute to its useful life. For income-producing properties, the estimated period during which the structure will profitably produce income is its **economic life**.
The difference between the structure's estimated economic life and its effective age is the **remaining economic life**.

There are many structures in urban areas that have just about used up their economic life.

Example: Old gas stations once were called service stations because you could actually have your car serviced at these facilities. Today, the majority of these structures have been transformed into mini-marts. The customer can buy gas on

a self-serve basis, but a huge profit center is the little store inside that has practically all the products of a downsized supermarket. The old service station buildings have worn out their usefulness and been torn down.

Example: Most movie theaters today are located in large complexes rather than in stand-alone buildings. These theaters tend to show older movies at reduced prices. Sometimes they show a particular genre of film and have an eclectic following. Often, their use is entirely different from the original intent. Perhaps churches or live theater groups have taken over their use. However, at some point the owners of such buildings may conclude that they cannot make enough money operating these buildings to justify their use. At this point, the building is no longer an asset to the land and may be demolished.

Typically, an appraiser uses the comparison method to identify what length of economic life to use. This means talking to other appraisers and comparing data. Economic life usually is shorter than physical life, as a structure generally will still physically exist but not be viable in the marketplace. Commercial property, due to dependence on the ability to produce income, generally has a shorter economic life than that of a residential property.

Types of Depreciation

Adverse physical, functional, and locational influences cause property improvements to depreciate. There are three types of depreciation: physical deterioration, functional obsolescence, and external obsolescence. **Physical deterioration** of a building and its equipment includes physical wear and tear, disintegration, decay or rot, or physical damage of any kind caused by the elements. **Functional obsolescence** refers to deficiencies, superadequacies, or simply undesirable features found in a building. **External obsolescence** is attributable to external adverse conditions that affect a property.

A property may suffer from any combination of the three types of depreciation, or it may not suffer from any depreciation at all. However, unless brand new, a building will probably have incurred some degree of depreciation. Like a brand new car driven off the showroom floor, a structure begins to lose value the moment it is built.

Physical deterioration and functional obsolescence are further divided into two-sub categories: curable and incurable depreciation.

Curable depreciation refers to a loss in value that is economically feasible to correct. In other words, the cost to fix the problem is less than the loss in value, so fixing the problem makes economic sense.

> Example: If a house is estimated to have $2,000 worth of depreciation due to poor exterior paint and the cost to repaint is $1,500, then it is economically feasible to do so. This is an example of curable physical deterioration.

Incurable depreciation refers to items of depreciation that either are physically impossible to cure or are too expensive to be worth curing. If the cost to fix the problem exceeds the loss in value caused by the problem, then it does not make economic sense to repair it.

> Example: A house with a seriously cracked foundation can be repaired, but it typically costs far too much to take the necessary steps to fix a damaged foundation. In fact, depending on the cost of the repairs, it makes more sense from an economic standpoint to raze the structure than to try to repair it. This is an example of incurable physical deterioration.

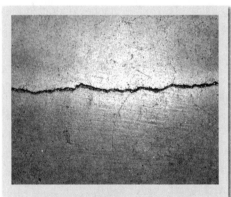

A cracked foundation is repairable, but the cost to cure may outweigh the benefit.

Physical Deterioration

Physical deterioration is the loss in value from all causes of age and action of the elements. It is caused by a number of sources—wear and tear, disintegration, decay or rot, or physical damage by the elements.

The wear and tear from these various elements on a building accounts for the physical deterioration affecting that building. For example, walking on carpeting eventually wears it out. Heating and cooling systems eventually wear out too. Sometimes naturally occurring elements, such as ultraviolet sunlight, wind, and water wear on a property. Storms, extreme temperatures, earthquakes, termites, carpenter ants, and floods all work in varying degrees to affect properties physically. Fire, explosion, vandalism, and neglect also have a detrimental physical effect upon properties.

Property components that exhibit **curable physical deterioration** can be repaired or replaced economically. This includes deferred maintenance and easily repairable items. **Deferred maintenance** refers to items that are in need of repair due to lack of upkeep. Items such as roof repair or replacement, painting, building maintenance, floor covering replacement, and forced air heater replacement are items that are typical examples of curable physical deterioration.

Repairing items of deferred maintenance like broken windows and flaking paint is relatively easy and is economically feasible.

Physical items that are incurable cannot be replaced or repaired economically. **Incurable physical deterioration** typically occurs with structural components that are expected to last for the life of the entire building. Structural components such as foundations, framework, walls, masonry, and ductwork usually are considered incurable. When incurable physical deterioration is evident, it may make more sense from an economic standpoint to tear down the building rather than to try to repair it.

Appraisers classify physical deterioration of components based on economic considerations. Since structural components rarely depreciate at similar rates, appraisers classify them on the length of time they are expected to last—either as short-lived or long-lived. **Short-lived** items are components that are expected to be replaced during the improvement's economic life. **Long-lived** items are components of the improvement that are expected to last as long as the building itself. Paint, floor coverings, and fixtures are examples of short-lived items, whereas the building foundation is an example of a long-lived component.

Functional Obsolescence

Functional obsolescence is depreciation that is attributable to an item or feature within the subject property that is no longer useful or functional. This impaired feature results in loss of value (depreciation) for the entire property. Functional obsolescence is caused in part by changing market requirements and can appear in several different forms, including outdated architectural design, layout problems, lack of modern facilities, and superadequacy.

Outdated Architectural Design. Historically, some interesting construction style changes have taken place. A house built 50 years ago may have been appealing to people at that time, but today, the style may be considered outdated and tiresome. Ornate molding and sculpting, once considered desirable, may be outdated today.

Layout Problems. Appraisers must recognize that the tastes and preferences of society change over time. At one time, the living areas were completely separate from the kitchen and the concept of the Great Room or the open flow was an unusual concept. Not too long ago, a one-car garage was perfectly adequate because families typically owned one car. Today, older homes with one-car garages can still be found, but often sell for less than similar homes with two-car garages.

Lack of Modern Facilities. Outmoded features and equipment also are examples of functional obsolescence. Today, computers dominate every aspect of our lives, and the Internet is here to stay. Any house built without computer and Internet capabilities would be considered functionally obsolete.

Lack of modern facilities most often is curable, but the cost to cure must be measured against the benefit to property value. When adding modern facilities that are valued in the marketplace, usually the enhancement to value offsets the cost of installation.

Today's marketplace demands certain modern kitchens and bathrooms to maximize value. For example, older homes often do not have a dishwasher. A house without a dishwasher will sell, but will sell for less. If installation costs are less than what the dishwasher will contribute, then the obsolescence is curable. If more, it is incurable.

Air conditioning, as a modern convenience, must be measured within the context of its marketplace. In the desert, a house lacking air conditioning is definitely at a disadvantage. However, at the beach, air conditioning is not as essential.

Superadequacy. A **superadequacy** (or over-improvement) is a feature that is too large or of a higher quality than needed for a property. The cost to add the feature is more than the value contributed by the feature. Examples of superadequacies include a 10,000 square foot home in the middle of a tract of homes ranging in size from 1,200 to 1,800 square feet, an excessive number of bedrooms, or 1-foot thick, wood-framed exterior walls.

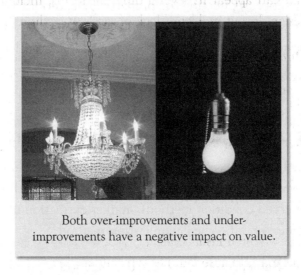

Both over-improvements and under-improvements have a negative impact on value.

External Obsolescence

External obsolescence takes place when influences that are external to a property adversely affect that property. These external influences can be locational or economic.

Locational obsolescence is caused by the physical location of the subject property and its proximity to a negative influence. Heavy traffic noise, such as that generated by freeways and airports, may cause locational obsolescence. Recurring smoke, dust, and noxious odors from sources external to a property, like a dairy farm or sewage plant, also tend to have an adverse influence on the value of a property.

Economic obsolescence occurs when changes in the local economy affect the subject property's value. Some cities rely on one major industry or employer. If the industry shuts down or the employer ever moves, a devastating impact on real estate values could result.

Unfavorable zoning ordinances, environmental restrictions, or other legislative decisions that restrict use can also cause external obsolescence. Since these factors originate externally to the property itself, they are considered external obsolescence.

External obsolescence is incurable in virtually all cases since the adverse condition(s) affecting the property are exterior to the subject and few owners are willing or able to spend money to change adverse conditions that are not located on their own property. Changes such as relocating a freeway or a nearby airport simply make no economic sense and are well beyond the financial means of most property owners.

Methods of Calculating Accrued Depreciation

Methods of calculating accrued depreciation include the cost to cure method, economic age/life method, modified age/life method, breakdown method (or observed condition method), market extraction using sales comparison techniques, and income capitalization method.

> Remember that accrued depreciation is calculated for improvements only, because land does not depreciate. Land is factored into the cost approach at its market value. Since the value of the land is already at market value, making additional deductions to the land value would cause it to be doubly penalized for any condition adversely affecting value.

Cost to Cure Method

The **cost to cure method** is the most basic and straightforward method to calculate accrued depreciation. It is based on observed deferred maintenance and the application of current building costs at the time of the appraisal. Its basic premise states that the cost required to replace an item is the amount lost due to accrued depreciation.

It is relatively easy to estimate physical deterioration using this method. If certain items such as the floor coverings wear out, estimating the cost to repair or replace these items often gives a credible estimate of the physical deterioration. If a stairway needs to be replaced, the amount of accrued depreciation is the cost to accomplish that. If a roof needs to be replaced, the amount of accrued depreciation is the cost to do it, including labor and materials.

This method is used to calculate curable functional obsolescence. Generally, if the functional problem involves a new or newer property, the cost to cure the functional problem is used as the estimate. In an older property, the cost to cure minus the remaining value of the item being replaced is a way to determine the loss.

Limitations of this Method

This simplistic method only allows for a 100% depreciation of any item. The cost to cure method is not very useful when dealing with items that have partial depreciation, like a roof that is not brand new but still has years left before it needs replacement.

Economic Age/Life Method

The **economic age/life method** of calculating accrued depreciation is conceptually one of the easiest to use and to understand. This method compares a structure's effective age to its economic life. Also known as the **straight-line method** or **age/life method**, this method is used most frequently by residential appraisers. With this method, an equal amount of accrued depreciation is attributed to each year of the economic life of the structure. An effective age is estimated and assigned to the structure, and the remaining economic life is determined.

In the age/life method, the ratio of the improvements' effective age to its total economic life is multiplied by the current reproduction or replacement cost of those improvements. The resulting number is the accrued depreciation of the subject property.

The equation to calculate accrued depreciation using this method is Accrued Deprecation = Effective Age divided by Economic Life times Replacement/ Reproduction Cost.

> Example: The subject property is a 50-year-old house with an economic life of 70 years. After close inspection, the effective age of the structure is determined to be only 15 years. The cost to reproduce the structure is $200,000. In this example, the structure is only 21% depreciated, despite its chronological age of 50 years (15 ÷ 70). Multiplying the reproduction cost of the improvements by the depreciation percentage, $200,000 × 21%, the accrued depreciation is calculated at $42,000, and the depreciated value of the improvements at $158,000 ($200,000 − $42,000).
>
> With an effective age of 15 years, and an economic life of 70 years, despite the chronological age of 50 years, the structure can be said to have a remaining economic life of 55 years. This structure still has a long, useful life remaining.

Sometimes, not all the variables are expressly provided. A skilled appraiser, with a complete understanding of effective age and economic life, is able to extract the needed variable from the provided information, as in this following example.

Example: Suppose a commercial office building is 20 years old, has a remaining economic life of 25 years, and an effective age of 15 years. The cost to reproduce the improvements is $350,000.

In this example, the total economic life is not expressed, but can be determined easily by adding the effective age of 15 years to the remaining economic life of 25 years for a total economic life of 40 years. Since the effective age is 15 years, the percentage of accrued depreciation to the building is 38% (15 ÷ 40). If the cost to reproduce the building is $350,000, the accrued depreciation is $133,000 ($350,000 × 38%) and the depreciated value of the improvements is $217,000 ($350,000 - $133,000).

Limitations of this Method

Although the economic age/life method is relatively simple to calculate, it tends to obscure the overall accrued depreciation estimate since it lumps all items of accrued depreciation together. A significant weakness in this method is that curable items of accrued depreciation are not treated separately from incurable items of accrued depreciation. It also does not recognize that certain items in a building have a shorter remaining economic life than the total economic life of the structure. This method accounts for physical, functional, and locational obsolescence, but it does not differentiate among the different kinds of accrued depreciation.

Modified Age/Life Method

In the **modified age/life method**, curable physical and functional items of accrued depreciation are identified. The cost to cure all these items is deducted from the reproduction or replacement cost of the improvements. The ratio derived from the age/life method is then multiplied by the remaining cost to arrive at an estimate of accrued depreciation from all other causes.

Example: The subject property's replacement cost is estimated at $550,000. Items that can be cured economically include the roof, the carpet, and several bathroom fixtures, and total $20,000 in expenses. The remainder of the structure has an effective age of 35 years and an 85-year economic life. An appraiser first subtracts the curable items from the cost estimate, and then applies the age/life ratio to the remaining cost.

Mathematically, it looks like this:

Replacement cost new	$550,000
Less curable items	− $20,000
Remaining cost	$530,000
Age/life ratio (35 ÷ 85)	× 41%
Less amount of accrued depreciation	$217,300
Current building value	**$312,700**

Limitations of this Method

Although curable items are recognized by this method, it still does not account for differences in the remaining economic life of the other building components. This method is a little more accurate, but it is based upon the same assumption as the economic age/life method. Both methods assume that a single age/life ratio can be applied to every component of the improvements.

Breakdown Method

In the **breakdown** or **observed condition method**, an appraiser analyzes each type of accrued depreciation separately, measures the amount of each, and totals the individual estimates to determine the total accrued depreciation. Then, the total accrued depreciation is deducted from the reproduction or replacement cost.

If the accrued depreciation is deducted from the replacement cost, some kinds of functional obsolescence, such as that attributable to outdated equipment or materials, are not to be deducted since, upon replacement, current equipment and materials would be used.

As the name implies, an appraiser observes the condition of various component parts of the structure and observes the percent of deterioration (or loss in value as-is) in comparison to a new properly planned structure not suffering from any loss in value.

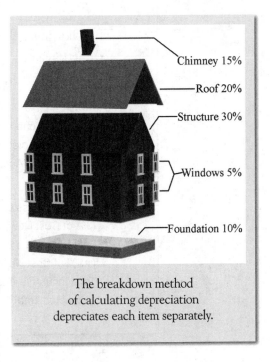

The breakdown method of calculating depreciation depreciates each item separately.

Physical deterioration and functional obsolescence can be measured in this way, although success with this method requires experience and an up-to-date knowledge of current building costs.

Illustration of the Breakdown Method

The following table shows the observed condition method applicable to physical deterioration estimates of accrued depreciation for a property that would cost $400,000 to replace at current market conditions.

Item	Item Reproduction Cost	Observed Deterioration	Dollar Amount of Deterioration
Foundation	$17,500	5%	$875
Basic Structure	$125,000	25%	$31,250
Finished Floors	$18,500	20%	$3,700
Electrical	$10,000	20%	$2,000
Heating/AC	$16,000	25%	$4,000
Kitchen Cabinets	$10,000	20%	$2,000
Plumbing	$18,000	30%	$5,400
Fireplaces/Chimneys	$14,000	20%	$2,800
Insulation	$5,000	5%	$250
Total	$234,000		$52,275

The following table shows the observed condition method applicable to functional obsolescence estimates of accrued depreciation, both curable and incurable for the same property.

Curable

Remodel Kitchen	$12,750
Replace Obsolete Lighting Fixtures	$1,600
Total Curable Accrued Depreciation	$14,350

Incurable

Estimated Loss Due to Obsolete Floor Plan (3% of Cost New)	$12,000
Estimated Loss Due to Excessive Ceiling Heights (1.5% of Cost New)	$6,000
Total Incurable Accrued Depreciation	$18,000
Estimated Total Functional Obsolescence	**$32,350**

> If there is no accrued depreciation due to economic obsolescence, an appraiser's next step is to subtract $84,625, a figure that represents all losses attributable to accrued depreciation ($32,350 + $52,275) from the reproduction cost of the improvements to obtain the current market value of the improvements, $315,400 rounded ($400,000 - $84,625).

Market Extraction using Sales Comparison Techniques

Appraisers use market extraction using sales comparison techniques, such as the sale-resale analysis, paired-sales analysis, and the extraction method to estimate accrued depreciation. They must be sure that the sales prices of all the sales are truly indicative of the market. Seller incentives such as loan discount points, prepaid homeowner's association fees, rebates, seller-paid closing costs, personal property included in the sale, etc., usually have an effect upon sales prices and can affect the results.

Sale-Resale Analysis

In a **sale-resale analysis**, a property that sells and resells in a relatively short period of time is analyzed. By finding properties in a stable market that had two open market, arm's-length sales in a relatively short period of time, any difference in price could be attributable to changes to that property.

> Example: A property in a stable market had deferred maintenance when originally purchased. The purchaser remodeled the building, so the subsequent sale would be reflective of the market's reaction to that remodeling. In this scenario, if the cost of the remodeling is known, the difference between cost and value can be used to identify any functional obsolescence attributable to the remodel. If the market has been increasing or decreasing, a time adjustment would be warranted. After any time adjustments have been applied, any difference would still be attributable to changes affecting that property. If the changes to the property are known, market reaction may be identified.

Similarly, a sale-resale analysis may be employed to determine external obsolescence if the adverse influence was present during the time of one transaction and not the other.

Paired Sales Analysis

In a **paired sales analysis**, two similar properties that sell during the same time period in the same market are analyzed. If the sales are open market, arm's-length transactions, any difference in price could be attributable to physical differences between the two properties. If that physical difference can be identified, the market reaction to that difference may be identified.

> Example: Imagine there are two homes with the same floor plan within the same development. One house is near the complex's main entrance, and thus closer to a busy thoroughfare. The other house is nestled deep inside the development and is shielded from external obsolescence. Both homes sold within one week of each other, but the one near the entrance sold for $3,000 less. From this paired sales analysis, an appraiser could conclude that within this particular neighborhood, the external obsolescence caused by traffic is approximately $3,000. Then, he or she could convert this dollar amount to a percentage so that it could be applied to properties of different size and quality in the area.

Extraction

Similar to the method of the same name used for calculating land value, **extraction** enables appraisers to determine the depreciated value of the improvements of the subject property by estimating the cost new of recently sold comparables, minus the sales price of those comparables, and minus the value of the land in the transaction.

Extraction is an accurate way of reading the marketplace, because arm's-length transactions reveal the amount of accrued depreciation recognized by purchasers. The more samples that can be extracted from the marketplace, the more reliable the assembled data. Among the comparable sales that are analyzed, correlations should be made to arrive at appropriate percentages. With similar comparable sales, the percentage of accrued depreciation can be directly applied to the subject property.

Because an appraiser is simply reading the marketplace with this method, all sources of accrued depreciation are included—physical deterioration, functional obsolescence, and economic obsolescence. If it were necessary to separate out one source of accrued depreciation, a further application of the abstraction method could be used. An appraiser could estimate accrued depreciation attributed to two of the sources by other appropriate methods, and then subtract the amount of accrued depreciation attributed to those sources from the total amount of accrued depreciation. The difference will be the accrued depreciation belonging to one isolated source.

Income Capitalization Method

Depreciation is calculated differently for income-producing properties. Instead of totaling dollar amounts of depreciation and then subtracting that amount from the estimated cost new, appraisers formulate an estimate based upon a loss of income attributable to the item(s) causing the depreciation. In order for this technique to work, the subject needs to be an income-producing property.

The **income capitalization method** is like the market extraction method because it is necessary to find similar income-producing properties both with and without the same influencing defects. Once these properties are isolated, the influence of the defects can be analyzed to determine how it causes the accrued depreciation. This method takes it a step further, though, by applying a market-derived capitalization rate to that income to estimate the overall loss in value.

Accrued Depreciation Based on Functional Obsolescence

Example: A four-bedroom, two-bath house in Marketplace Z rents for $1,200 per month. A four-bedroom, one-bath house in the same marketplace rents for only $1,100 per month. This factor of functional obsolescence (less one bath) costs $100 per month in income for the second house. If an appraiser has determined that the appropriate monthly gross multiplier for the area is 150, the loss in value caused by functional obsolescence is $15,000 (150 × $100). If this condition is incurable, that is, there is no room to add a second bathroom or it is not economically feasible, the amount of accrued depreciation for this item is $15,000.

However, if the item is curable and the cost to cure is only $12,000, an appraiser would use the $12,000 figure to represent accrued depreciation.

Accrued Depreciation Based on Economic Obsolescence

Example: A three-bedroom, two-bath house rents in a particular marketplace for $925 per month. Another three-bedroom, two-bath house in the same marketplace rents for only $850 per month because of a less favorable location, backing up to a main street and suffering excessive traffic noise. The difference in rental income is $75 per month. If the appropriate monthly gross multiplier is 130, the loss in value is $9,750 ($75 X 130). Since the external obsolescence is incurable, $9,750 is the amount of the accrued depreciation charged against the subject property.

PUTTING IT ALL TOGETHER

When all of the causes of depreciation are calculated and deducted, the depreciated value of the improvements will be known. Now we are ready for the last step in the cost approach process:

1. Estimate the value of the land component of the subject property as though vacant and available to be put to its highest and best use.

2. Estimate the reproduction or replacement cost new of the building improvements on the subject site as of the effective date of the appraisal.

3. Estimate accrued depreciation from all sources (physical, functional, or external), and deduct from estimated reproduction or replacement cost.

4. Add entrepreneurial incentive, when appropriate.

5. Estimate "as-is" value of additional site improvements, if necessary.

6. Add the land value estimate, the depreciated value of the improvements, the entrepreneurial incentive, and the value of the site improvements together to calculate the value estimate by the cost approach.

The following example ties all the steps of the cost approach to value together and demonstrates how each step is vital to the final value conclusion.

The subject is a single-family residence in an average subdivision in Anytown, America. The house is 1,800 square feet with a 360-square-foot garage. The cost of construction for homes in this area has been determined to be $70 per square foot and $25 per square foot for garages. The improvements sit on a 5,000-square foot lot, valued at $45,000, which is typical for the area and the subdivision. The lot is surrounded on three sides by a block-wall fence, worth approximately $5,000. The house backs to a main street and suffers from traffic noise. The market shows that similar houses with similar external obsolescence lose roughly $3,000 in value. The house is 12 years old with an effective age of 7 years, and its estimated economic life is 70 years.

1. Estimated Site Value		$45,000
2. Estimated Reproduction Cost New of Improvements		
Dwelling: 1,800 sq. ft. × $70 per square foot	$126,000	
Garage: 360 sq. ft. × $25 per square foot	9,000	
Total Estimated Cost New	135,000	
3. Less Depreciation:		
Physical 10% of Total Cost New	13,500	
Functional 0%	0	
External (from market)	3,000	
Total Depreciation	16,500	
Depreciated Value of Improvements		$118,500
4. Entrepreneurial Incentive		2,000
5. Value of Site Improvements		3,000
6. Indicated Value by Cost Approach		**$168,500**

In this cost approach analysis, the indicated value is $168,500.

If the property appraised at $165,000 using the sales comparison approach, the indicated value by the cost approach would support that value, since the consensus among appraisers is that the cost approach represents the upper limits of value. The rationale behind this is that, if a buyer could purchase the land for $45,000 and build the structures for $124,000, then he would have no reason to pay more than that for a similar property. There is an exception, however. The exception is time and convenience. It could take a year or more for a buyer to acquire the land, get plans approved and build the structure. If a buyer could find a similar property that met his or her needs and be using that property in 45 days, the buyer might, in fact, be willing to pay more for that property. So the old adage does not always hold true.

SUMMARY

After determining the **cost new of the improvements**, an appraiser must calculate the **accrued depreciation**. Depreciation can be **curable** or **incurable** and is categorized as **physical deterioration, functional obsolescence,** or **external obsolescence**. Appraisers can use several different methods to calculate accrued depreciation. These methods vary in their complexity and in the amount and type of data that they require. Appraisers choose which method to use based on the particular assignment they are completing.

Once the accrued depreciation has been determined, an appraiser can calculate the depreciated value of the improvements by adding the cost new of the improvements to the entrepreneurial incentive and then subtracting the accrued depreciation. When the land value is added to the depreciated value of the improvements and the **"as-is" value** of the additional on-site improvements, the resulting number is a value estimate for the subject property.

UNIT 12 REVIEW

▢ Matching Exercise

Instructions: Write the letter of the matching term on the blank line before its definition, and then check your response with the Answer Key that immediately follows the Multiple Choice Questions.

Terms

A. accrued depreciation

B. age/life method

C. curable depreciation

D. economic life

E. effective age

F. external obsolescence

G. functional obsolescence

H. physical deterioration

I. short-lived items

J. superadequacies

Definitions

1. _____ Loss in value to a property due to any cause as of the effective date of the appraisal.

2. _____ Effective age describes the age of a structure based on its condition and usefulness.

3. _____ Time in which the property's improvements contribute to property value.

4. _____ Loss in value that is economically feasible to correct; it adds value equal to or greater than the cost of curing the item.

5. _____ Physical wear and tear, disintegration, decay or rot, or physical damage of any kind caused by the elements.

6. _____ Items that are expected to be replaced or repaired on a consistent basis throughout the life of the structure.

7. _____ Deficiencies, superadequacies, or undesirable features found in a building.

8. _____ Features that are too large or of a higher quality than needed for a property and have a negative effect on property values.

9. _____   Almost always considered to be incurable, conditions affecting a property that are external to that property.

10. _____   Method that uses a ratio of the building's age to its expected life.

Multiple Choice Questions

Instructions: Circle your choice, and then check your response with the Answer Key that immediately follows the Multiple Choice Questions.

1. The difference between the improvements' market value and the cost to build them new is called:

    a. deferred maintenance.

    b. future depreciation.

    c. accrued depreciation.

    d. internal obsolescence.

2. A house in a middle-income neighborhood is under-valued by $20,000 due to extreme deferred maintenance. The cost to paint, re-floor, replace the broken windows, repair the fixtures, and patch the roof is approximately $15,000. This scenario describes:

    a. curable physical deterioration.

    b. incurable functional obsolescence.

    c. curable external obsolescence.

    d. short-lived economic obsolescence.

3. A house's value suffers because of its proximity to an airport. An appraiser would identify this as:

    a. curable.

    b. incurable.

    c. deferred.

    d. long-lived.

4. A furnace would qualify as a(n):

    a. incurable item.

    b. short-lived item.

    c. long-lived item

    d. superadequacy.

5. When constructed, an office building was projected to last 80 years. It is currently 24 years old. Using the square foot method, an appraiser concludes that the building new would cost $500,000. Using the age/life method, estimate the office building's current value.

    a. $150,000
    b. $166,666
    c. $333,333
    d. $350,000

6. A house located in an area where the recommended insulation is R-19 has insulation rated at R-42. This home suffers from:

    a. superadequacy.
    b. external obsolescence.
    c. internal obsolescence.
    d. none of the above.

7. A property valued at $300,000 contains a single-car garage in a neighborhood that predominately contains two-car garages. The typical house value in the neighborhood is $310,000. A contractor estimates the cost of converting the single car garage into a two-car at $15,000. This is an example of:

    a. incurable subadequacy.
    b. curable economic obsolescence.
    c. incurable functional obsolescence.
    d. single-car deficiency.

8. Which of the following is almost always incurable?

    a. Functional obsolescence due to lack of modern facilities
    b. External obsolescence
    c. Deferred maintenance
    d. Physical deterioration of a tile roof

9. What is the best way to depreciate the value of land?

    a. Cost to cure
    b. Age/life method
    c. Breakdown method
    d. None of the above

10. What is the biggest weakness of the cost to cure method of estimating depreciation?

    a. Cost does not equal value.

    b. It does not allow for partially depreciated items.

    c. It does not account for fully depreciated items.

    d. Curing is not always economically viable.

11. A barn was built 40 years ago; however, it has been abandoned and looks 20 years older than it actually is. What is its effective age?

    a. 20

    b. 40

    c. 50

    d. 60

12. A strip mall was built with the expectation that it would be economically viable for 99 years. Currently, it is 40 years old. The property management company and tenants have exceptionally managed and maintained it, and local architectural tastes have not changed. An appraiser concludes that the property has an effective age of 25 years. What is the strip mall's remaining economic life?

    a. 15 years

    b. 59 years

    c. 74 years

    d. 25%

13. A duplex is 30 years old, has a remaining economic life of 75 years and an effective age of 20 years. The current cost to reproduce the improvements is $450,000. How much depreciation should be charged against this structure?

    a. $120,000

    b. $330,000

    c. $95,000

    d. $180,000

14. Which of the following is not a market extraction technique for estimating depreciation?

    a. Abstraction

    b. Sale-resale

    c. Paired sale

    d. Extraction

15. An office building was renting space for $25 per square foot per month but the recent installation of a nearby dump has forced the price down by $4. If the building has 28,000 square feet of rentable space, how much income is being lost each year due to external obsolescence?

    a. $1,344,000

    b. $7,056,000

    c. $112,000

    d. $588,000

UNIT 12 ANSWER KEY

Answers – Matching

1.	A	4.	C	7.	G	10.	B
2.	E	5.	H	8.	J		
3.	D	6.	I	9.	F		

Answers – Multiple Choice

1. **(c)** Accrued depreciation is a loss in value to a property due to any cause as of the effective date of the appraisal. It is the difference between the market value of the improvements and the cost-new of the improvements. **Page 377**

2. **(a)** Curable depreciation is a loss in value that is economically feasible to correct. Roof repair or replacement, painting, building maintenance, floor covering replacement, and forced air heater replacement are examples of curable physical deterioration. If spending $15,000 to improve the home returns a value of $20,000 then it is economically feasible, and thus curable. **Page 380**

3. **(b)** Incurable depreciation refers to items of depreciation that either are physically impossible to cure or are too expensive to be of any worth. Moving a property away from an airport is impossible. **Page 380**

4. **(c)** A furnace typically lasts 20-30 years and may never need to be replaced. If it does need replacement, it is usually a curable item. **Page 381**

5. **(d)** The age/life method uses the ratio of the building's age (or component) to its expected life. 24 divided by 80 = 30%. If 30% of the life has been used, 70% remains. To convert this to value, multiply the cost-new by 70% to get $350,000. **Page 385**

6. **(a)** Superadequacies are features that are too large or of a higher quality than needed for a property and have a negative effect on property values. Having a home over-insulated for an area qualifies as consisting of higher quality than needed. **Page 383**

7. **(c)** Lack of modern facilities most often is curable, but the cost to cure must be measured against the benefit to property value. When adding modern facilities that are valued in the marketplace, they must add equal or greater value than the cost to add in order to be considered curable. From the information given, converting the garage would cost $15,000, but would only add $10,000 to the property's value. **Page 382**

8. **(b)** External obsolescence takes place when influences that are external to the property adversely affect that property. External obsolescence is almost always incurable. **Page 383**

9. **(d)**   While certain physical, functional, and external forces can cause land to lose value, losses attributed to these factors will already have been reflected in the market value estimate of the land. **Page 384**

10. **(b)**   The cost-to-cure method, while simplistic, only allows for a 100% depreciation of any item. When an item like a roof is not brand new, but still has years left before it needs to be replaced, the cost to cure method is not very useful. **Page 385**

11. **(d)**   The effective age accounts for improvements that appear younger or older than the structure's actual age due to quality maintenance, or lack thereof. 40 years actual age plus 20 years equals 60 years. **Page 378**

12. **(c)**   The difference between the structure's estimated economic life and its effective age is its remaining economic life. (99 – 25 = 74 years.) **Page 378**

13. **(c)**   Using the economic age/life method, divide the effective age by the economic life (20 ÷ 95 = 21%). Then multiply the result by the replacement cost of $450,000 to calculate the amount of accrued depreciation. 450,000 × 21% = $95,000 (rounded). **Page 385**

14. **(a)**   Depreciation may be extracted from the market by performing sale-resale analysis, by paired-sales analysis, and by extraction. **Page 389**

15. **(a)**   If the property is losing $4 per square foot per month then: $4 × 28,000 × 12 (months) equals the total loss per year of $1,344,000. **Page 383**

Reconciliation & Reporting

Unit 13

INTRODUCTION

The final steps in the appraisal process are reconciliation and reporting. After analyzing the subject and other data critical to the appraisal, an appraiser will have a range of value or several values that have been calculated from the three approaches. **Reconciliation** is the process of refining the range or set of values into a single supportable value opinion, called the **final value estimate**.

Once an appraiser has reconciled all of the work into a value, he or she must then report it to the client. The detail and format depends on the client's needs.

Learning Objectives

After reading this unit, you should be able to:

- differentiate between what reconciliation is and what it is not.
- determine the validity and reliability of each approach used for the assignment.
- designate items that require verification when using each approach.
- identify types of appraisal reports recognized by USPAP.
- specify the main components of each of the appraisal reports.
- identify the styles of appraisal reports.

RECONCILIATION AND FINAL VALUE ESTIMATE

In a perfect world, each approach would be flawless, and each would result in the exact same value for the subject property. However, in practice, each approach has so many variables that there is a very small chance that the value derived using one approach will ever exactly match the value derived using another approach. In fact, the chance of arriving at the same value conclusion from two or three different approaches is so remote that, if it did occur, it should be considered a major red flag.

Since appraisers arrive at different values from each approach, they have to examine the choices carefully, weigh each one against the other, and then arrive at a single supportable value conclusion. This process is reconciliation.

Ideally, all three approaches should be used on every assignment, but sometimes an approach is inapplicable, unwanted by the client, or lacks enough supportable data to apply.

For example, when appraising vacant land, there is no physical way the cost approach can be used. Because the land is vacant and the cost approach requires the valuing of improvements, the method is inapplicable.

The client's wishes may also determine which approaches are or are not used. The most common example of this occurs when the client, i.e., the lender, asks an appraiser to use Fannie Mae Form 2055. This form only allows room for the sales comparison approach. An appraiser could include the other approaches in an addendum, but the lender's request to use Form 2055 typically means that the lender only wants the one approach used. An appraiser has to make this decision based upon the type of property and his or her experience. If an appraiser thinks that market value can be estimated accurately, using only the sales comparison approach, then that is all he or she will use. However, if an appraiser determines that other approaches are needed, he or she must notify the client.

In other situations, there simply may not be enough data to apply a particular approach. For instance, when appraising a single-family home, the income approach may be unnecessary, especially when there is no rental data in the area for that type of property. Similarly, an instance may occur when the sales comparison approach does not have enough supportable data to be applicable to a single-family residence, even though it is commonly thought of as the strongest indicator of value for that type of property.

How an appraiser decides which approaches are appropriate for an assignment depends on the client's needs coupled with an appraiser's understanding of the nature of the property and the purpose of that particular assignment. Appraising is an assignment-by-assignment decision.

Reconciliation includes not just analyzing the different values derived from the appraisal approaches. It also includes revisiting the steps in the appraisal process and re-verifying that the value defined and the data collected was both valid and relevant. In addition, an appraiser must weigh the strengths and weaknesses of each approach used and consider how those approaches are pertinent to the process as a whole, and to the subject property.

Reviewing the Approaches

When reviewing the approaches chosen for an assignment, appraisers consider the validity and reliability of each approach. They also review the quantity, quality, appropriateness, and accuracy of data for each approach that is used. In order to do this properly, they should know that each approach has certain limitations and advantages.

The strengths and weaknesses of each approach were discussed in previous units. The following section summarizes the strengths and weaknesses for the three major approaches, and lists the items an appraiser should reexamine in the reconciliation process.

Sales Comparison Approach

The sales comparison approach has both advantages and limitations. Its simplicity is an advantage. It is easy to understand how adjusted  comparables can represent a current value for the subject. When available, sales information is usually easy to obtain. In addition, the sales comparison approach is the best determinate for frequently sold property types, namely residential properties.

Things to Verify When Using the Sales Comparison Approach

- Comparables are significantly comparable to the subject property
- An adequate amount of sales data
- Sales data is both accurate and reliable
- Adjustments made to the comps are logical and in good order
- Adjustments are mathematically correct
- Value conclusion drawn from the adjusted comparables is legitimate

This approach is a poor indicator of value for infrequently sold properties and properties that are unique. It is not as useful with insufficient or inaccurate data. Finally, its reliance on historical data can be a limitation, even though information might be easy to gather, it may be outdated or completely erroneous.

Cost Approach

The cost approach is very precise for newer buildings. Also, it is the best indicator of value when the building is specialized or there is a lack of comparable properties.

Things to Verify When Using the Cost Approach

- Sites used to develop an opinion of the subject's site value are comparable to the subject
- Any adjustments made to comparable sites are logical and accurate
- Reproduction or replacement cost is identified correctly
- Unit chosen for the comparative-unit method is appropriate
- Data obtained for the unit-in-place or quantity survey method is current and accurate
- Accrued depreciation is deducted properly, without under-depreciating or double-depreciating certain items
- External influences researched include all possible ones

However, the older the building becomes, the more difficult it is to calculate its accrued depreciation accurately. This approach is a more complicated approach. The cost approach lends itself to multiple errors because of the sheer number of calculations. Lastly, the cost approach tends to identify the upper levels of the value range for a property. If all three approaches are applied to a property, the value derived by the cost approach analysis will most likely be the highest, and therefore is not entirely representative of what that property may sell on the open market.

The cost approach to value probably has more limitations than benefits. As a result, the cost approach is best suited as a very valuable support approach to the other two major approaches, unless special circumstances dictate otherwise.

Income Approach

As the name implies, the income approach to value depends on a property's income, real or potential. Therefore, this approach is the best indicator of value for income producing properties. Even if the property is not currently producing income, this approach can convert its potential income into a current value.

Things to Verify When Using the Income Approach
- Market rents are mathematically accurate
- Reconstructed operating statement is accurate
- Gross income estimate is mathematically accurate
- Net income estimate is mathematically accurate
- Capitalization rate (GRM or direct Cap rate) is mathematically accurate
- Comparable sales are sufficiently comparable to the subject property
- An adequate amount of rental data available from the subject market

The income approach requires current market data for rentals of like properties as well as careful analysis of the operating statements. Sometimes these pieces of information are difficult to obtain and analyze. In addition, determining the appropriate capitalization rate is very difficult and, at times can become very complex.

Weighing the Choices

After revisiting all of the information used during the appraisal process, an appraiser weighs the approaches to determine which one best indicates value.

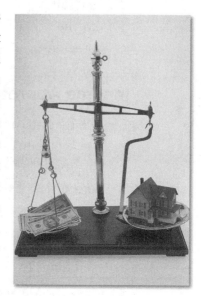

Typically, one of the approaches to value is determined to be the best value for the subject property. At times, the final reconciled value may be a combination of two or three approaches. In addition, an appraiser must be aware of factors that may weaken an approach's validity. For example, even though the sales comparison approach is usually the best indicator for residential property, if the market is unstable, this approach may become less reliable than if it were located in a stable market. In this instance, an appraiser should not simply discard the sales comparison approach analysis, but should depend more heavily on the cost and/or income approaches.

Case Study

Karen is appraising a single-family residence in a neighborhood near a college. Because of the need for student housing, many similar properties in the area are rented. Additionally, because of the nature of this type of tenancy, the neighborhood is in decline. The neighborhood as a whole suffers from excessive deferred maintenance as well as negative external influences like noise pollution and roving bands of drunken students.

From the sales comparison approach, Karen estimates the subject's value at $251,000. From the cost approach, she arrives at an estimate of $260,500, and from the income approach $255,800.

Based on the information provided above, Karen sees a range of value from $251,000 to $260,500. This range of $9,500 is relatively narrow considering all of the factors that affect the subject and its neighborhood. Karen's next step is to analyze and weigh these three value determinates and arrive at a single value conclusion that is supported by them. She should be comfortable with any

Case Study (*continued*)

conclusion reached that falls in the range of the three estimates, from $251,000 to $260,500. In addition, the final value may reflect one approach's estimate exactly, or may be a hybrid of two or three of them.

Karen knows that because of the age of the subject property and its excessive deferred maintenance, her calculation of accrued depreciation may not be the most accurate. She also knows that the cost approach tends to flank the higher end of the value range. Therefore, she decides to give the cost approach the least amount of weight.

When analyzing the result based on the sales comparison approach, Karen recognizes that although this approach is typically the best indication of value for this type of property, in this instance, the neighborhood is in serious decline. Therefore, the sales comparison approach may lose some of its credibility. That said she is still convinced that the value derived from her sales comparison analysis reflects current market value of the subject property. She double-checks her comps and determines that all of the comps used in her sales comparison analysis are legitimately comparable to the subject and none needs extensive adjustments.

Finally, Karen reviews the income approach to value and carefully reexamines all of the information and data used in arriving at her conclusion. She determines that this approach seems to be a strong indicator of value and gives it the most weight. This is because her analysis of the neighborhood revealed several similar rental houses. The rentals are all on a month-to-month basis and are all very competitive. Therefore, they are representative of current market rent.

Karen's final analysis comes down to a value somewhere in between the sales comparison value of $251,000 and the income value of $255,800. She could pick one of the values and use it as the final value estimate for the property, but this does not satisfy her. She determines that the income estimate receives the strongest consideration, but cannot completely discount the sales

Case Study (*continued*)

comparison estimate because it is typically the best indicator of value for single-family detached residences. Karen finally reconciles that the market value for this type of property in this neighborhood is $255,000. She chose to round the income estimate figure down instead of rounding up, which she would typically do in most other circumstances, to account for the influences and disparity from the comparison analysis.

An appraiser should round the final value estimate to the nearest thousand to emphasize the fact that it is indeed an estimate. If Karen were to become too finite in her estimation, say by stating the final value at $254,654, it would be too exact for the marketplace.

What Reconciliation is Not

Reconciliation is often not clearly understood. Although the reconciliation process is strongly rooted in factual data and mathematics, it is subjective. Therefore, no one standardized system applies to all appraisal assignments.

Reconciliation is not a mathematical process. If appraisers have three different values derived from the major approaches to value to consider, they should never simply add the values together and divide by three. Instead, they should carefully analyze the different values and use their judgment. If Karen would have averaged the three approaches in her analysis, she would have ignored the cost approach's inadequacy due to excessive deferred maintenance, and she would not have considered the market conditions that weakened the sales comparison approach. Averaging, as well as applying other statistical functions to the approaches, may be used as a check and balance and is an excellent way to analyze the figures used throughout the appraisal. However, averaging should never determine the result. Mathematical formulas cannot account for an appraiser's opinions or any other intangibles. Averaging implies that each approach receives equal weight. This just is not the case because certain approaches typically are better indicators for certain types of properties.

Reconciling is not a way to fit the conclusion into a preconceived value. Appraisers should always be independent, open minded, and objective. If, at some point in the analysis, an appraiser gets the feeling that the subject property will probably be worth about so much, he or she must be open to other alternatives that may develop during the final value reconciliation. Of course, an experienced appraiser may have a feeling during the appraisal that comes to fruition in the reconciliation. However, an appraiser must not use the process of reconciliation to bend the three values into a single matching value.

Reconciliation is not the narrowing of the range of value estimates. This means that when reconciling, appraisers do not make changes to the three separate value estimates so that they all match. As mentioned earlier, all value estimates will probably be different, and appraisers must report them that way. The only reason to make changes to a value previously derived is if an error was discovered in the data or process used to arrive at that value. Remember, reconciling is weighing the choices and using expertise and analysis to develop an opinion of a final value based on each approach. The thought process used in reconciling the value will require explanation so that the client can see exactly how an appraiser arrived at the value. Therefore, the three separate values need to be included in the report.

APPRAISAL REPORTS

An appraiser must carefully decide which type of report to use. Appraisal standards set minimum requirements for the content and level of information in each type of report. The type of report chosen does not determine the amount of work put into the actual appraisal process. Whether the client requests a detailed report or just a summary, the steps, methods, and amount of work should be identical. The report type chosen only affects how much detail an appraiser uses when communicating his or her findings to the client.

Types of Reports

Uniform Standards of Professional Appraisal Practice (USPAP) lists the type of reports an appraiser can use.

Types of Real Property Appraisal Reports Recognized by USPAP
- Self-Contained Appraisal Report
- Summary Appraisal Report
- Restricted Use Appraisal Report

It is an appraiser's responsibility to understand the designated types of reports, to apply the correct type of report to the appropriate appraisal assignment, and to compose the report correctly.

Self-Contained Report

The **Self-Contained Report** is the most elaborate report and contains the most detailed information. Self-contained means that everything the user of the report needs to fully understand it is contained within the report. The user does not have to rely on an appraiser's workfile like in the other report options.

A Self-Contained Report could be as many as 300 pages long, or more. Appraisers typically do not use this type of report for single-family residences. Rather, it is more common for income producing properties, like apartment complexes, office buildings, hotel resorts, and so forth. Since these kinds of properties are valued based on the income they produce, the report must show all pertinent information about the subject property that influences the value, as well as all pertinent information about the economy of the area that drives the income.

The main thing that distinguishes the Self-Contained Report from the others is what USPAP terms as "describe". When an appraiser describes information, it is presented in a more elaborate level of detail than "summarizing", or "stating."

Items Described in a Self-Contained Report

- Real estate to be appraised
- Value to be estimated
- Information considered
- Appraisal procedures followed
- Reasoning that supports the analyses, opinions, and conclusions
- Appraiser's opinion of the highest and best use of the real estate when appropriate
- Any additional information that may be suitable to show compliance with, or clearly identify and explain permitted departures from the specific guidelines of STANDARD 1 of USPAP

The Self-Contained Report must include sufficient information to indicate that an appraiser complied with the requirements of STANDARD 1, including the requirements governing any permitted departures from the appraisal guidelines. USPAP states that the amount of detail required will vary with the significance of the information to the appraisal.

The Self-Contained Appraisal Report includes the identity of the client and any intended users (by name or type), the intended use of the appraisal, the real estate involved, the real property interest appraised, the purpose of the appraisal, and dates of the appraisal and of the report. It also describes work used to develop the appraisal, the assumptions, and limiting conditions, the information that was analyzed, the procedures followed, and the reasoning that supports the conclusions. The report states the current use of the real estate and the use reflected in the appraisal, the support for an appraiser's opinion of the highest and best use, and any departures from the Standards. It also includes a signed certification.

Appraisals can be delivered in a traditional written format or orally.

Note that the length of the report does not dictate which type it is. An appraiser can create a one-hundred-page report, but if it does not contain the proper detail, it will not be a Self-Contained Report.

Summary Report

The **Summary Report** contains less detail than a Self-Contained Report, but more than the Restricted-Use Report. It is also the most commonly used report option. An appraiser summarizes the information instead of describing it in detail.

Items Summarized in a Summary Report

- Extent of the process of collecting, confirming, and reporting data

- Information considered

- Appraisal procedures followed

- Reasoning that supports the analyses, opinions, and conclusions; and an appraiser's opinion of highest and best use of the real estate when appropriate

- Any additional information that may be relevant to show compliance with, or clearly identify and explain permitted departures from, the specific guidelines of STANDARD 1 of USPAP

To summarize is to elaborate but not provide every detail required to reach that conclusion. For example, the Uniform Residential Appraisal Report (URAR) is a Summary Report. It contains many fields of information in organized categories, and allows for proper summarizing statements and even an addendum to support and clarify concepts when necessary. Most residential appraisals would be done on this standardized form and would be considered Summary Reports.

The Summary Appraisal Report covers the same categories as the Self-Contained Appraisal Report, but where the Self-Contained Appraisal Report includes descriptions, the Summary Appraisal Report contains summaries.

Restricted-Use Report

The **Restricted-Use Appraisal Report** is the briefest presentation of an appraisal and contains the least detail. This type of report is called restricted-use because there can only be one intended user of the report.

Normally, the term **intended user** includes the client and any other party identified by an appraiser as users of the appraisal report. However, for the Restricted-Use Appraisal Report, the client is the only intended user. Since an appraiser always has the responsibility to include enough information that the intended user(s) can understand the report, an appraiser should only complete this type of report when the client is very familiar with the property, and, therefore be able to understand such a brief report. Anyone else who tries to use a Restricted-Use Report is an unintended user.

Restricted-Use Appraisal Reports are used only when they convincingly meet the client's needs, and the client clearly understands their restricted use. The Restricted-Use Appraisal Report covers the same categories as the other two reports with a few differences

Differences Shown in a Restricted-Use Report
- Only the client is named because there are no other users.
- The use of the report is limited to the client.
- The report refers to an appraiser's workfile as the source of necessary additional information about the appraisal.

Much of the information in a restricted report is just stated, which is the briefest method of presenting information. There is no elaboration when information is stated. For example, to state the zoning, simply indicate R-1 (residential-one unit).

Because of the restricted report's brief nature, an appraiser should describe the extent of the process of collecting, confirming, and reporting data. An appraiser must also include a prominent use-restriction that limits reliance on the report to the client, and warns that the report cannot be understood properly without additional information in the workfile of an appraiser.

Information Stated in a Restricted Report

- Real property interest being appraised
- Purpose and intended use of the appraisal
- Effective date of the appraisal and date of the report
- Assumptions and limiting conditions that affect the analyses, opinions, and conclusions
- Appraiser's opinion of highest and best use
- Definition of the value to be estimated
- Exclusion of any of the usual valuation approaches
- Appraiser's opinion of value

Report Styles

A distinction needs to be made between the different report types (discussed above) and the styles in which the reports are presented. All three types of reports can be presented as a form report, in a narrative style, or even verbally.

Form style report means that an appraiser is presenting the report using preprinted forms. Fannie Mae Form 1004, called the **Uniform Residential Appraisal Report (URAR)**, exemplifies the form report. A **narrative style report** does not use a form. Instead, it is an account of the particulars of the appraisal, usually written in a free-form style. Regardless of whether the report is labeled a form or a narrative, an appraiser is responsible for complying with USPAP STANDARD 2 report options when writing the assignment results. **Oral reports** are usually reserved for litigation purposes, but may be used at any time if requested by the client. According to USPAP, an oral report must have a workfile that is as complete as the file for a written report. Additionally, a written summary of the oral appraisal report must be added to the workfile within a reasonable time.

Routinely, the client that requires the Summary Report wants it to be in form style. Because of its length, a Self-Contained Appraisal Report is best suited for the narrative style. However, this certainly does not disqualify an appraiser from using a narrative report for either of the other two report types, nor creating a form that can contain all of the detail required to qualify it as a Self-Contained Report.

SUMMARY

Appraisers spend countless hours collecting and verifying data, analyzing that data, and then using it to implement one, two, or three approaches to value. Once these separate approaches to value have been successfully applied, appraisers reconcile these separate values into a singular supportable value.

A great deal of effort is put into the reconciliation process. Besides weighing and scrutinizing the different values, appraisers review the data, methods, and computations used while arriving at those value opinions. They also analyze the different value conclusions in comparison with each other, as well as in the context of the subject property and its neighborhood.

Once this process is completed, appraisers have a **final value estimate** to present to the client. Depending on the client's needs, an appraiser may have to include every possible detail of the appraisal process or just merely summarize or state the pertinent information. This can be done in a written **form report**, in a written **narrative report**, or an **oral report**. Whichever report type and style is chosen, an appraiser has a responsibility to communicate clearly and accurately his or her analyses, opinions, and conclusions to the client in a credible, comprehensible report.

UNIT 13 REVIEW

Matching Exercise

Instructions: Write the letter of the matching term on the blank line before its definition, and then check your response with the Answer Key that immediately follows the Multiple Choice Questions.

Terms

A. final value estimate

B. form style report

C. intended user

D. narrative style report

E. oral report

F. reconciliation

G. Restricted-Use Appraisal Report

H. Self-Contained Report

I. Summary Report

J. Uniform Residential Appraisal Report

Definitions

1. _____ Process of refining the range or set of values into a single supportable value opinion.

2. _____ Single supportable value opinion.

3. _____ Most elaborate report that contains the most detailed information.

4. _____ Most commonly used report option.

5. _____ Briefest of the appraisal reports.

6. _____ Client and any other party identified by an appraiser as a user of the appraisal report.

7. _____ Report that is presented using preprinted forms.

8. _____ Example of a form style report.

9. _____ Report that is an account of the particulars of the appraisal, usually written in free form.

10. _____ Type of report usually reserved for litigation purposes.

Multiple Choice Questions

Instructions: Circle your choice, and then check your response with the Answer Key that immediately follows the Multiple Choice Questions.

1. Which of the following statements is TRUE regarding the process of reconciliation?
    a. Every approach is applicable in all assignments.
    b. Applying the three appraisal approaches to value to the same property will typically produce the same figure.
    c. The most credible reconciliation uses the average of the different three values derived from the three approaches.
    d. Identical values produced from different approaches are a red flag.

2. In which instance would an approach definitely be inapplicable?
    a. Cost approach not listed on the appraisal form
    b. Income approach on a residential subject
    c. Cost approach for vacant land
    d. Sales comparison approach on a strip mall

3. When using the sales comparison approach, an appraiser should:
    a. ensure there is an adequate number of comparable sales.
    b. double-check all mathematics used.
    c. re-verify that comparables used are in fact comparable to the subject.
    d. do all of the above.

4. Out of the different approaches to value, which would most likely yield the highest value?
    a. Sales comparison approach
    b. Cost approach
    c. Income approach
    d. They all yield the same value.

5. The income approach applies to:
    a. income producing properties only.
    b. any property type.
    c. any property that has income potential.
    d. special-purpose properties that produce income.

6. An appraiser should round the final value estimate:
    a. because numbers confuse clients.
    b. because exact figures cease to be an estimate.
    c. to make the estimate easier to read.
    d. to allow more room for error.

7. While reconciling a final value conclusion, an appraiser should:
    a. reduce the process to a mathematical calculation.
    b. bend the values to fit a preconceived notion.
    c. never make changes to values, calculations, or data unless a genuine mistake was discovered.
    d. decide which approaches are appropriate for an assignment.

8. Regarding appraisal and appraisal reporting, which of the following is TRUE?
    a. An appraisal with a summary report requires more work than an appraisal with a restricted-use report.
    b. Self-contained appraisals require the most work out of all appraisals.
    c. Appraisal reports dictate the amount of detail conveyed to the client, but have no bearing on the amount of work put into an appraisal.
    d. All of the statements are true.

9. Which is the most elaborate of the appraisal report options?
    a. Narrative-form
    b. Summary
    c. Self-contained
    d. Restricted-use

10. A work file is required:
    a. when using a restricted-use report.
    b. when using an oral report.
    c. when using the narrative style.
    d. any time an appraisal is performed.

UNIT 13 ANSWER KEY

Answers – Matching

1. F	4. I	7. B	10. E
2. A	5. G	8. J	
3. H	6. C	9. D	

Answers – Multiple Choice

1. **(d)** Each approach has so many variables that there is a miniscule chance that one value approach will ever match another if performed on the same property. In fact, if it does occur, it should be considered a major red flag. **Page 402**

2. **(c)** One example of when an approach is inapplicable to the assignment is appraising vacant land. There is no physical way of using the cost approach since this method requires the valuing of improvements. **Page 402**

3. **(d)** If the sales comparison approach was used in the assignment, the appraiser should re-verify that the comparables are comparable to the subject property; there is an adequate amount of sales data; the sales data is both accurate and reliable; the logic of adjustments made between subject and comps is in good order; the adjustments are mathematically correct; and the value conclusion drawn from the adjusted comparables is legitimate. **Page 404**

4. **(b)** If all three approaches were applied to a property, the value derived by the cost approach analysis would probably be the highest, and not entirely represent what that property may sell for on the open market. **Page 404**

5. **(c)** The income approach is the best indicator of value for income-producing properties; however, if a property is not currently producing income, this approach can convert its potential income into a current value. **Page 405**

6. **(b)** The final value estimate should be rounded to the nearest thousand to emphasize the fact that it is indeed an estimate. If an estimate were too distinct, it would cease to be an estimate of market value and become too exact for the marketplace. **Page 408**

7. **(d)** While reconciling, appraisers should never limit themselves to a mathematical equation, should never bend values to fit preconceived notions, and never make changes to data or values unless truly warranted. **Page 408**

8. **(c)** Reports will vary on amount and detail of information disclosed, but the type of report used should never affect how much effort is put into the actual appraisal. **Page 409**

9. **(c)** The Self-Contained Report is the most elaborate report and contains the most detailed information. **Page 410**

10. **(d)** An appraiser should always keep his or her workfiles in case he or she must revisit the appraisal or defend his or her appraisal. **Page 410**

Ethical Appraisal Practice

Unit **14**

INTRODUCTION

Since real estate is a major purchase, most people need financing to make that purchase possible. The appraisal profession exists primarily to protect lenders and to bring an impartial eye to the valuation of real estate.

In order to ensure that appraisers meet this responsibility, each state has a program in place to license and regulate appraisers. Nationwide, the *Uniform Standards of Professional Appraisal Practice* (USPAP) are the recognized standards that appraisers must follow. This unit introduces USPAP and discusses some of the ethical challenges that appraisers face.

Learning Objectives

After reading this unit, you should be able to:

- name the different sections of USPAP.
- recall the Rules and describe the conduct each one covers.
- name the subsections of the ETHICS RULE.
- identify the ten USPAP Standards and the appraisal discipline to which each Standard applies.
- differentiate fraud schemes from lender pressure.
- identify ways to avoid deceptive appraisal practices.

OVERVIEW OF USPAP

The *Uniform Standards of Professional Appraisal Practice* (USPAP) are the generally recognized and accepted standards of appraisal practice in the United States. They are the standards for ethics and competency in professional appraisal practice. USPAP permeates what real estate appraisers do, and the professional appraiser must have a thorough knowledge of USPAP. USPAP requirements are referred to throughout this textbook. Since professional appraisers must take a USPAP course, only a short overview is given here.

USPAP has legal authority as it is adopted, cited, or implemented by government agencies through regulation or administrative action. USPAP also may become enforceable through private enterprise when following USPAP is a part of the client's contract with the appraiser. At this point, all licensed and certified appraisers in each state are expected to follow USPAP.

The USPAP document, as it is currently structured, contains five sections—DEFINITIONS, PREAMBLE, Rules, Standards and Standards Rules, and Statements on Appraisal Standards. For convenience, the USPAP document also includes the Advisory Opinions (AOs), but these are not technically part of USPAP.

DEFINITIONS

The **DEFINITIONS** section is the first section of USPAP. The definitions that appear in the USPAP document are specific to USPAP. You will see words with which you are familiar, but the definitions found in this section may or may not correspond to definitions of the same word in other sources. Keeping the definitions straight will aid in understanding USPAP. In fact, confusion as to what USPAP requires often centers around a misunderstanding of the definitions.

> Example: The terms "appraisal" and "appraisal report" are often used synonymously. According to USPAP, an appraisal is an "act or process" of developing an opinion of value. An appraisal report is "any communication, written or oral, of an appraisal, appraisal review, or appraisal consulting service that is transmitted to the client upon completion of the assignment." Therefore, an appraisal is considered a mental process according to USPAP. One cannot mail an appraisal to a client. One would mail an APPRAISAL REPORT to a client.

PREAMBLE

The **PREAMBLE** is a one-page mission statement that explains the goals and describes the overall structure of the USPAP document. USPAP addresses the ethical and performance obligations of appraisers through DEFINITIONS, Rules, Standards, Standards Rules, and Statements on Appraisal Standards. The USPAP document also includes <u>Comments</u> and **Advisory Opinions**.

<u>Comments</u> are extensions to these components of USPAP, providing interpretation, and establishing context and conditions for application. They are an integral part of USPAP and have the same weight as the component they address.

Advisory Opinions (AOs) illustrate the applicability of Standards in specific situations and offer advice for the resolution of appraisal issues and problems. Advisory Opinions are for guidance only and are not considered an integral part of USPAP. However, they are included in USPAP for convenience of reference.

Rules

The Rules address how appraisers must conduct themselves while performing appraisal practice. The current USPAP Rules are the ETHICS RULE, the RECORD KEEPING RULE, the COMPETENCY RULE, the SCOPE OF WORK RULE, and the JURISDICTIONAL EXCEPTION RULE. Regardless of the type of assignment, an appraiser must follow these rules at all times.

ETHICS RULE

The ETHICS RULE identifies the requirements for "integrity, impartiality, objectivity, independent judgment, and ethical conduct". The ETHICS RULE is divided into three sections: <u>Conduct</u>, <u>Management</u>, and <u>Confidentiality</u>.

Conduct

As its name implies, the <u>Conduct</u> section of the ETHICS RULE identifies issues regarding appraisers' conduct. This section states that appraisers must not engage in criminal conduct, must be impartial and unbiased, and cannot act as advocates. Acting as an advocate means you represent someone or have a bias toward a party or issue. This is forbidden under the <u>Conduct</u> section.

Many appraisers are also real estate salespeople, real estate brokers, lawyers, etc. and are required to be advocates as part of their non-appraisal duties. Advocacy is acceptable within those roles.

> Example: Appraiser Jane is also a licensed real estate broker. In her role as a broker, she is helping a client sell his home, and she is trying to get him the best possible price. In this situation, Jane is an advocate for her client. This would not be a violation of USPAP since Jane is acting as a broker, not an appraiser.
>
> In contrast, Jane is not an advocate for anyone when she is acting as an appraiser. Her role as an appraiser is to collect and analyze data to develop an opinion of the market value of the property.

Appraisers must not have predetermined opinions and conclusions when accepting assignments. They must not be negligent when performing appraisal assignments or knowingly prepare appraisal reports that are misleading or fraudulent.

An appraiser must not willfully or knowingly violate the requirements of the RECORD KEEPING RULE.

Management

The Management section discusses the disclosure of certain fees and commissions, identifies prohibited compensation arrangements, and discusses certain prohibited advertising and solicitation issues. For example, paying a finder's fee would qualify as something to disclose, and generally any undisclosed fees in connection with an assignment are a violation. This section also prohibits accepting an assignment where the fee is contingent on a predetermined or future result.

> Example: Bob of ZYX Loans contact Appraiser John. Bob engages John in an appraisal assignment for a property for which his company is lending $200,000. Bob tells John that he will pay John for his services as soon as the loan closes. This arrangement is not acceptable because John will have an incentive to make the loan close by providing Bob with the required property value.

Confidentiality

The Confidentiality section of the ETHICS RULE states that the appraiser must protect the confidential nature of the appraiser-client relationship and is obligated to obey all confidentiality and privacy laws. The Confidentiality section also identifies to whom confidential information may be disclosed. USPAP defines confidential information as either information that is classified as confidential or private by law or regulation, or information that is identified by the client as confidential and is not available from any other source.

RECORD KEEPING RULE

The RECORD KEEPING RULE identifies the record keeping requirements appraisers must follow. An appraiser must prepare a workfile for each appraisal, appraisal review, or appraisal consulting assignment. The appraiser's **workfile** for a particular assignment consists of all the documentation necessary to support the analyses, opinions, and conclusions conveyed in the appraisal report. Therefore, an appraiser must have a workfile prior to issuance of any report. A written summary of an oral report must be added to the workfile within a reasonable time after the issuance of an oral report.

Essential Items in a Workfile

- Name of client and identity, by name or type, of any other intended users.
- True copies of any written reports. A **true copy** is a photocopy or electronic copy of the entire report transmitted to the client.
- Summaries of all oral reports or testimony (or transcript), including the appraiser's signed and dated certification.
- All other data necessary to support the appraiser's opinions and conclusions and to show compliance with USPAP.

A workfile supporting a Restricted Use Appraisal Report must be sufficient for the appraiser to produce a Summary Appraisal Report (for assignments under STANDARDS 2 or 8) or an Appraisal Report (for assignments under STANDARD 10).

An appraiser must keep his workfiles for at least five years after preparation or two years after final disposition of any judicial proceeding involving the file, whichever period expires last. An appraiser must have custody of workfiles or be able to retrieve them.

> Example: Appraiser John works for QC Appraisals and the firm has contracted with a third party to retain all of its files. After two years, he moves on to another company but is concerned about complying with the Record Keeping section of the ETHICS RULE. He refers to USPAP. He realizes that he must continue to retain his workfiles but finds out that USPAP does not require him to have custody of the files. He makes arrangements with QC Appraisals to access his files in the future.

An appraiser who willfully or knowingly fails to comply with the obligations of this RECORD KEEPING RULE is in violation of the ETHICS RULE.

COMPETENCY RULE

Although the ETHICS RULE covers ethical behavior on the part of appraisers, the COMPETENCY RULE and the three remaining Rules cover performance standards imposed upon appraisers.

The COMPETENCY RULE identifies requirements for experience and knowledge both when completing an appraisal and prior to accepting an appraisal assignment. When an appraiser is offered an assignment he or she is not competent to handle, this rule outlines the steps an appraiser should follow, which include speaking with experienced professionals to gain education, subcontracting experienced professionals to handle the aspects of the assignment that the appraiser is not competent in, or simply declining the assignment.

> Example: A client asks John to appraise a single-family residence (SFR) in a town where he has never previously appraised property. Following the COMPTETENCY RULE, John discloses his lack of geographical knowledge to the client and explains the steps he will take in order to gain competency. The client agrees to these terms. Appraiser John then speaks to several real estate brokers in the area in order to get a better understanding of that town's market.

SCOPE OF WORK RULE

The SCOPE OF WORK requires the appraiser to do all the analysis necessary to complete the appraisal assignment and provide reliable and credible results.

Requirements of the SCOPE OF WORK RULE
- Appraisers must identify the problem to be solved,
- Appraisers must determine and perform the scope of work necessary to develop credible assignment results, and
- Appraisers must disclose the scope of work in the report.

Each of these steps has its own section in the SCOPE OF WORK RULE. The sections are titled Problem Identification, Scope of Work Acceptability, and Disclosure Obligations.

The SCOPE OF WORK RULE gives the appraiser a lot of flexibility in determining the scope of work. However, this means that responsibility rests with the appraiser to do so correctly.

JURISDICTIONAL EXCEPTION RULE

The JURISDICTIONAL EXCEPTION RULE recognizes that in some instances, portions of USPAP may be contrary to law or public policy. This rule serves as a severance clause; it voids any part of USPAP that contradicts local laws or public policy, while still preserving the remainder of USPAP. This means that the remainder of USPAP must still be followed even if one or more parts of USPAP are not valid in a particular jurisdiction.

If this is an issue in a particular assignment, the appraiser must disclose which part(s) of USPAP he or she did not follow and which legal authority justified that action. The appraiser must still follow all of USPAP's remaining requirements.

Standards and Standards Rules

The Standards are the meat of USPAP. They are essentially systematic instructions as to what to do when you are appraising something, and they give the requirements for reporting this appraisal to the client.

There are ten **Standards** within USPAP, and each Standard includes a series of Standards Rules. The **Standards Rules** specify what the appraiser must do.

The Standards cover the various appraisal disciplines and types of assignments. The type of assignment you are completing will determine which standard(s) you need to follow.

- STANDARDS 1 and 2 - Real Property Appraisal
- STANDARD 3 - Appraisal Review
- STANDARDS 4 and 5 - Appraisal Consulting
- STANDARD 6 - Mass Appraisal
- STANDARDS 7 and 8 - Personal Property Appraisal
- STANDARDS 9 and 10 - Business Appraisal

When USPAP was developed, it was designed to encompass all appraisal disciplines, but in this text, we will focus on the sections of USPAP concerning real property appraisal (Standards 1 & 2), since these are the ones that a beginning real estate appraiser will need to apply.

STANDARD 1: Real Property Appraisal, Development

STANDARD 1 covers the requirements for developing a real estate appraisal. It identifies what an appraiser needs to consider when formulating his or her opinions and conclusions. This Standard also requires the appraiser not to "commit a substantial error of omission or commission", nor to "render appraisal services in a careless or negligent manner". This covers the first part of the appraisal process.

> Example: Jane followed all of the steps in STANDARD 1 and developed an opinion of the market value of the condo she was appraising. Her supervisor says, "Great! You developed your appraisal well; now communicate it to the client." Next, Jane reviews STANDARD 2 to find the available options for reporting the appraisal development results to the client.

STANDARD 2: Real Property Appraisal, Reporting

STANDARD 2 covers the requirements for reporting a real estate appraisal. When reporting a real estate appraisal, the appraiser must, among other things, "clearly and accurately set forth the appraisal in a manner that will not be misleading", and the report must "contain sufficient information to enable the intended users of the appraisal to understand the report properly".

A signed certification is required for all reports, and it is important to note that anyone who signs the certification takes full responsibility for the report.

Report Options

In addition to the rules that govern report clarity and content, STANDARD 2 also provides three reporting options: Self-Contained, Summary, and Restricted Use. The difference between the three types of reports is the level of detail, with the Self-Contained being the most detailed and the Restricted Use being the least detailed.

None of the reporting options is superior to another; they all must produce credible and reliable results. The reporting option chosen to communicate an appraisal depends on who the client is, the intended use, etc.

> Example: After following the steps outlined in STANDARD 1, Jane knows that the property is worth $250,000. After explaining the three reporting options to the client, they agreed to go with the Summary Appraisal Report. The information that must be included in a Summary Appraisal Report is outlined in STANDARD 2. Jane

knows that she will be doing many summary appraisals in the future, so she has memorized the major things that have to be in every appraisal, such as the intended use, effective date, and date of the report.

It is also permissible to communicate a report orally. If that is done, the oral report must at least meet the requirements for a summary report.

The **Summary Appraisal Report** option is the most common as it fulfills the minimum requirements for lenders to process their loans. If the client does not specifically state the desired report format, the report should at least meet the requirements of a Summary Appraisal Report. The Uniform Residential Appraisal Report (URAR) is an example of a summary report and is probably the most widely used form.

The **Self-Contained Appraisal Report** option contains the most detailed information. An appraiser preparing this type of report would include significant details instead of just summarizing information.

The **Restricted Use Appraisal Report** option is unique, because with this option the client is the only one allowed to use the report. Because the Restricted Use Appraisal Report is for client use only, appraisers must be careful to identify accurately the client to avoid violations of the Confidentiality section of the ETHICS RULE.

STANDARD 3, Appraisal Review

STANDARD 3 establishes requirements for the development and communication of an appraisal review. **Appraisal review** is defined in USPAP as "the act or process of developing and communicating an opinion about the quality of another appraiser's work that was performed as part of an appraisal, appraisal review, or appraisal consulting assignment."

STANDARD 3 gives the review appraiser the option to develop his or her own opinion related to the subject of an appraisal. In the review of an appraisal assignment, the reviewer can provide an opinion of value for the property and of quality for the work that is the subject of the appraisal review assignment.

STANDARDS 4 and 5, Appraisal Consulting

Appraisal consulting is defined as the act or process of developing an analysis, recommendation, or opinion to solve a problem, where an opinion of value is a component of the analysis leading to the assignment results. The main type of appraisal consulting assignment is a feasibility analysis. A **feasibility analysis** is a study of the cost-benefit relationship of an economic endeavor.

> Example: Jane, a certified general appraiser, is contacted by a developer who would like to know whether he should build homes or apartments. Jane determines this is appraisal consulting because she is trying to solve a problem (whether to build single-family or multi-family dwellings). However, she realizes that in order for it to be appraisal consulting, in addition to solving a problem, an opinion of value must be part of her assignment. She goes forth with the assignment and includes two opinions of value: one for the potential homes and another for the apartments.

STANDARD 6, Mass Appraisal

A **mass appraisal** is appraising more than one property using standard computerized techniques (statistical analysis, regression, automated valuation models, etc.). This standard contains technical terminology specific to this type of appraising which the beginning appraiser will not use.

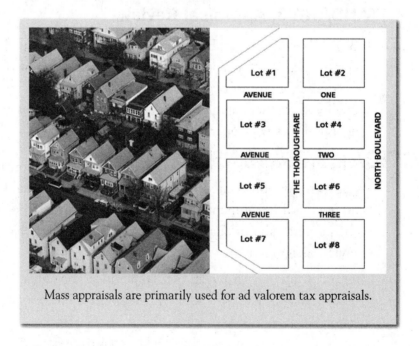

Mass appraisals are primarily used for ad valorem tax appraisals.

Mass appraisal is used primarily for *ad valorem* tax appraisals. *Ad valorem* is a Latin phrase that means "according to value". Property taxes are an example of an *ad valorem* tax since the amount of tax paid is based on the value of the property being taxed.

STANDARDS 7 and 8, Personal Property

Personal property includes all tangible assets that are not real property, such as jewelry, autos, boats, etc. A real estate appraisal license does not permit an appraiser to appraise this type of property. The appraiser must be fully competent in the type of property he or she is appraising (see the COMPETENCY RULE).

STANDARDS 9 and 10, Business Appraisal

These standards cover the appraisal of business entities including a business' intangible assets, like a logo or copyright. The rules are similar to those for real property appraisal.

Statements on Appraisal Standards

The **Statements on Appraisal Standards** (SMT) are authorized by the by-laws of The Appraisal Foundation. The purpose of the Statements on Appraisal Standards is to clarify, interpret, explain, or elaborate on a Rule or Standard. Statements have the full weight of a Standards Rule.

PRACTICAL APPLICATION

Not only is following USPAP a legal requirement, conscientious compliance with USPAP will help the appraiser avoid becoming involved in mortgage fraud or giving in to lender pressure.

Fraud is intentional deceit, the act of misleading someone in order to induce him or her to part with something of value. Historically, real estate fraud has been a white-collar crime that has gone largely unpunished. However, in recent years, the law has begun treating real estate fraud with more severity.

Appraisers most often are caught up in fraud when mortgages are involved, because **mortgage fraud** requires the help of an appraiser. The appraiser is usually not paid an additional fee and may not even be aware of the fraudulent situation.

Mortgage fraud is committed by individuals as well as organized crime rings. They operate by submitting exaggerated appraisals to lenders for inflated loan amounts. HUD has unknowingly granted many loans based on these fraudulent appraisals.

Deceptive Practices Used in Mortgage Fraud

- Falsified credit applications
- Credit reports that are cleansed, altered and/or forged
- Altered or forged verifications of employment
- Altered and forged certificates of deposit
- Appraisals that are inflated by the appraiser, lender, or borrower

These excerpts from newspaper articles illustrate the problem of fraud:

RIVERSIDE, CA - Riverside Press Enterprise, 7/14/00

"Seven Southern California residents were charged Thursday with operating a mortgage-fraud ring in the Inland Empire that resulted in losses of more than $10 million and involved more than 100 homes. The U.S. attorney's office in Los Angeles said the defendants set up an imaginary credit union and used phony names; bank statements, appraisals, employment records, and other information to obtain home loans for amounts far greater than the homes were actually worth."

SCHENECTADY, NY - Albany Times Union, 3/15/01

"A couple was renting an apartment when their landlord offered to sell the building to them. The husband and wife are both mentally retarded and unable to read or write. The wife also suffers from cerebral palsy and uses a wheelchair. Their sole income is public assistance. They signed papers and bought their house for $65,000. They subsequently lost their Medicaid because they had obtained an asset, and had to default on their loan.

According to an independent appraisal done afterwards, the property was valued at $19,000. It had been on the market for 7 years and was listed 4 years prior for $46,000. Another lawsuit claims the same landlord sold another property for $60,000, which was later appraised for $24,500.

With more frequency, appraisers are lured into committing mortgage fraud.

The lawsuits allege that the landlord conspired with an appraisal agency and a local mortgage broker to inflate the value of the properties and then teamed up with a lender to offer loans on the inflated real estate. The lender sold the loan almost immediately. The attorney said 'the bigger the appraisal, the bigger the mortgage; the bigger the mortgage, the bigger the fee for 'flipping' the loan and assigning it to another lender.'"

Common Fraud Schemes

Common fraud schemes include flipping, packed sales, and bogus sales.

Flipping

Flipping occurs when a person buys a property at one price and quickly sells it to another at an inflated price. The second sale may occur on the same day (double escrow), or take place a few days later. It is not illegal to resell a property within a short period. What makes this fraud is the inflated sales price. The second buyer is an accomplice of the seller and is in on the fraud. The sale appears to be an arm's length transaction, but the inflated sales price is designed to defraud the lender.

Many times the flipper (the first buyer) provides comparable sales for the appraisal. Many of the comparables are also fraudulent and may be properties that were also flipped. Appraisers who are hired for these deals are usually from another area and do not completely confirm the sales. Occasionally the appraiser is in on the scam, but usually the appraiser receives the regular fee and inadvertently helps in the transaction by providing an appraisal that is over value, either by not following the rules of appraisal or by inattention to detail.

Packed Sales

A **packed sale** charges excessive points, fees, and interest rates to unsuspecting buyers. Elders, minorities, and sub-prime borrowers are common targets. This fraud may be accomplished without an appraiser.

Bogus Sales

A **bogus sale** occurs when a lender asks an appraiser to inflate his or her estimate of value for a property to a certain degree, providing justification for a higher selling price.

These sales often occur between a bogus seller and another person or group conspiring with the seller. In effect, the seller is selling the property to himself/herself or his/her fellow conspirators. The increased selling price is equal to the amount that would be paid by a buyer for a down payment. The lender can then offer the buyer a zero down payment, 100% financing deal, and ultimately collect more interest from the buyer. Of course, none of this is possible without an appraisal to justify the higher price.

Lender Pressure

Pressure from lenders is an on-going problem in real estate appraisal. **Lender pressure** involves the lender directly or indirectly pressuring the appraiser to hit a certain number.

Sometimes the pressure is obvious. For example, it is not unusual for a lender to fax over an appraisal request that specifically states the desired value along with a comment like, "If the value isn't there, stop and notify us." Accepting this assignment could be a violation of USPAP, since the lender is making payment for the assignment contingent upon hitting a pre-determined value.

The pressure does not end there, however. Picture a conscientious appraiser (Bob) who accepts an assignment from a lender who "suggests" that in order for the loan to fund, the appraisal needs to reach a minimum of $335,000. The appraiser scrupulously completes the assignment and arrives at a value of $305,000. Then the appraiser receives a call strongly questioning his conclusions. The appraiser stands by his work, but realizes that it is unlikely that the lender will use him for future jobs. Appraisers feel the pressure when they begin to lose jobs because of their unwillingness to give the lenders the value they want.

In these cases, the lender is not out to explicitly defraud a buyer or seller. In fact, some lenders may actually believe they are assisting the borrowers. Most homeowners will not complain either. Homeowners love to be told that the value of their property has increased. However, inflated appraisals can lead to situations where property owners and investors discover that they are "upside-down" on their loan, that is they owe more than their property is actually worth. In fact, this practice has a ripple effect that inflates property values across the board in a neighborhood. Another appraiser could use an inflated refinance appraisal as a comparable for a sale the following day, which would inflate the sale price of the transaction.

In theory, this practice goes against the lender's best interests. If the borrower defaults, the lender needs to be able to recoup its losses, so they need to have an accurate estimate of the property value before they make a loan. However, with the practice of selling loans on the secondary mortgage market, the risk is transferred to secondary market institutions like Freddie Mac. For today's lender, it boils down to this equation: the greater quantity of loans at the highest possible loan value equals a higher profit for the mortgage lender.

Appraisers may feel as if their hands are tied because of lender pressure to meet predetermined values.

Fraud Prevention

USPAP contains several sections that can help you avoid potentially fraudulent situations. In particular, the **COMPETENCY RULE** states that an appraiser should not perform an appraisal outside of his or her market or geographic area without taking the steps necessary to learn the important nuances of the different market. **Standards Rules 1-4** and **1-5** prevent an appraiser from using a flip sale as a true comparable sale and **Standards Rule 1-2** requires the appraiser to look out for and eliminate bogus sales, whether they are the subject or the comparables.

The U.S. Department of Housing and Urban Development (HUD) also has some important guidelines in its valuation directive. HUD's valuation directive states:

> "The appraiser must verify all market and comparable information used in the appraisal process and is accountable for any information presented as 'fact' used to develop the subject property's value estimate. Verification ensures that the information is accurate and meaningful and provides the appraiser with a firm understanding of market motivations and trends. The goal of the verification process is to ensure that only information that accurately reflects current market conditions and trends is presented and that meaningful conclusions can be reached from this information.
>
> During the verification process, it is necessary for the appraiser to gain an understanding of the motivations surrounding the sale in order to determine if the sale is arm's length and not distressed, and to understand current market conditions that influence value...."

Verification involves much more than checking with two sources and providing a document number. Verification involves interviewing someone directly involved in the transaction to determine the buyer and seller's motivations, the conditions of the sale, whether there was consideration given outside of escrow, and whether the transaction was truly at arm's length.

The **HUD valuation directive** is used by lawyers in civil and criminal cases to prove the appraiser failed to exercise due diligence. (This is true even if the transaction is not for an FHA loan.) Properly verifying the sale is a time consuming step, but it is a critical part of good appraisal practice.

Common Violations - California's Office of Real Estate Appraisers
- Failure to state which reporting option was used
- Failure to address scope of work
- Failure to analyze current agreements of sale or sales history
- Failure to identify client, intended use, and intended users of a report
- Failure to incorporate license number with signature on appraisal reports
- Failure to comply with the competency rule
- Inaccurate or insufficient property descriptions

- Problems with the Cost Approach
  - » No support for cost per square foot
  - » Minimal support for depreciation estimates
- Problems with the Sales Comparison Approach
  - » Using generic discussion and minimal support for adjustments
  - » Inconsistency of adjustments among comparable sales
  - » Using out-of-neighborhood comparable sales when sales are available within
  - » Failure to use MLS as a data source
- Problems with the Income Capitalization Approach
  - » Generic discussion of rental comparables, no discussion of relative comparability
  - » Lack of due diligence in extracting GRM (Gross Rent Multiplier) and misuse of actual vs. projected rents

CASE STUDY

Reasonable care requires appraisers to meet the steps in USPAP STANDARD RULE 1, which dictates how the appraisal is performed and determines the completeness of the research. Failure to verify and investigate data breaches the duty of care when facts are present that would alert a reasonable person to possible misrepresentations.

Case Study – Fraud

Steve is a Certified Residential Appraiser who appraises single-family residences and small income properties. Most of his work is done around Fresno, California. A year ago, he wanted to diversify his business and began soliciting work from attorneys who practice estate planning. One attorney asked Steve to perform a series of estate appraisals in Riverside, California. The properties to be appraised were six duplexes and two triplexes that were all approximately 30 years old.

Steve was informed that the properties were going to be sold, and that the attorney wanted a high value for his clients. Steve stated the values could not be changed, but he would keep the request in mind, as there is considerable room in the typical range of value for a high "point estimate" of value. He agreed to perform the appraisals.

Case Study – Fraud *(continued)*

The attorney informed Steve that the property owner would meet him at the sites and would bring some recent comparable sales, because Steve did not have any sources of comps in Riverside. Steve also requested rental data for the units. The owner agreed to bring the information, but pointed out that the rents were below market because many rents had not been raised to current market rates.

The property owner furnished Steve with information on nine comparable sales, including the sales price and the recorder's document numbers. The sales prices ranged from $280,000 to $320,000 for the duplexes, and $295,000 to $330,000 for the triplexes. No rental data was supplied for the comparables.

Steve performed the appraisals primarily using the sales comparison approach. However, he did not research the sales histories of the comparables because the data was too hard to obtain. Steve did not belong to the local Multiple Listing Service (MLS) and did not know any local real estate agents. He considered the cost approach, but did not use it because the few land comparables were all over 30 years old. He also considered using the income approach, but stated in the report that he could not find many comparable rents, and those he did find were about the same as the subject. He concluded that the whole area seemed to be renting below market, and that the income approach was not a reliable indicator of value.

He valued the duplexes at an average of $310,000 and the triplexes at an average of $325,000. Steve received a good fee for the appraisals and did not give the assignment another thought for over a year. Then, to his dismay, a group of Federal Fraud Investigators who had a Certified General Appraiser on their team contacted him to talk about his appraisals.

The investigators discovered that, although the comparable sales had document numbers, they were the result of flips. The buyers purchased the properties for around $160,000 and then "sold" them to an accomplice for the higher figures, through either a

> **Case Study – Fraud** *(continued)*
>
> double escrow or an escrow a short time later. The fraud occurred when FHA loans were secured based on Steve's appraisals. After the money was taken from the FHA loans, the buyers left town and the properties went into default.
>
> Steve was eventually charged with real estate fraud and providing fraudulent appraisals. His defense was that he did not know anything about any fraud and was only doing his job as an appraiser. Unfortunately, for Steve, this defense is not adequate. Although he was not knowingly involved in the fraud, he was culpable because of his failure to exercise reasonable care and because he did not follow USPAP or verify the sales as required in the HUD valuation directive.

An appraiser cannot satisfy the duty of reasonable care by blindly relying on representations made by others. The appraiser must perform his own research and adequately verify information about comparable sales. In Steve's case, there was adequate information that he could have easily discovered, which makes his neglect even more difficult to justify.

Protect Yourself from Becoming Involved In or Suspected Of Fraud

Do not give in to lender pressures. Do your appraisals in a professional manner. Forget the idea that one has to "hit the number" if sales and other data do not support the conclusion of value.

Verify everything. According to The Appraisal Foundation, "…to ensure the reliability of value conclusions derived by applying the sales comparison approach, the appraiser must verify the market data obtained and fully understand the behavioral characteristics of the buyers and sellers involved in property transactions." In addition, Standards Rule 1-4 of USPAP states "In developing a real property appraisal, an appraiser must collect, verify, and analyze all information applicable to the appraisal problem, given the scope of work identified in accordance with SR 1-2(f)."

SUMMARY

USPAP will permeate the appraiser's professional life, as it is comprised of the minimum standards that licensed appraisers are required to follow. USPAP is not limited to real property either, but covers all aspects of professional appraising, including personal property and business assets.

As a whole, USPAP helps to ensure ethical and accurate appraisals and provides the appraiser with guidance in developing and reporting each appraisal assignment. Following USPAP conscientiously and consistently will keep the appraiser from inadvertently becoming involved in real estate fraud.

UNIT 14 REVIEW

Matching Exercise

Instructions: Write the letter of the matching term on the blank line before its definition, and then check your response with the Answer Key that immediately follows the Multiple Choice Questions.

Terms

A. appraisal consulting

B. Comments

C. COMPETENCY RULE

D. flipping

E. lender pressure

F. packed sale

G. Restricted Use Appraisal Report

H. Self-Contained Appraisal Report

I. Statements on Appraisal Standards

J. USPAP

Definitions

1. _____ Recognized and accepted standards of appraisal practice in the United States.

2. _____ Extensions of the USPAP that provide interpretation and establish context and conditions for application.

3. _____ They clarify, interpret, explain, or elaborate on a Rule or Standard.

4. _____ Report option that contains the most detailed information.

5. _____ Report option that prohibits any other user than the client.

6. _____ Act of developing an analysis, recommendation, or opinion to solve a problem, where an opinion of value is a component of the analysis leading to the assignment results.

7. _____ States that an appraiser should not perform an appraisal outside of his or her market without taking the steps necessary to learn the important nuances of the different market.

8. _____ Buying a property at one price and quickly selling it to another at an inflated price.

9. _____ Charging excessive points, fees, and interest rates to unsuspecting buyers.

10. _____ Lender directly or indirectly pressuring the appraiser to hit a certain number.

Multiple Choice Questions

Instructions: Circle your choice, and then check your response with the Answer Key that immediately follows the Multiple Choice Questions.

1. USPAP contains many sections. Which of the following is NOT technically considered part of the USPAP document?
   - a. DEFINITIONS
   - b. Advisory Opinions
   - c. Statements on Appraisal Standards
   - d. Comments

2. Which of the following illustrates the applicability of Standards in specific situations and offers advice from the ASB for the resolution of appraisal issues and problems?
   - a. Comments
   - b. Statements on Appraisal Standards
   - c. Advisory Opinions
   - d. Rules

3. The ETHICS RULE is divided into three subsections. These sections are called:
   - a. Conduct, Management, and Competency.
   - b. Conduct, Management, Capability.
   - c. Confidentiality, Management, and Competency.
   - d. Conduct, Management, and Confidentiality.

4. According to the Conduct section of the ETHICS RULE, when is advocacy acceptable?
   - a. When acting as an appraiser
   - b. When working in non-appraisal related professions
   - c. When buying or selling property for a client
   - d. Both b. and c.

5. All of the following Rules cover performance standards imposed upon appraisers, EXCEPT the:
   - a. COMPETENCY RULE.
   - b. ETHICS RULE.
   - c. JURISDICTIONAL EXCEPTION RULE.
   - d. SCOPE OF WORK RULE.

6. Every appraisal discipline encompassed within the USPAP has two Standards associated with it EXCEPT, which are:

    a. Appraisal Review and Appraisal Consulting.

    b. Mass Appraisal and Appraisal Review.

    c. Business Appraisal and Personal Property Appraisal.

    d. Real Property Appraisal and Personal Property Appraisal.

7. Regarding the Standards, which of the following statements is most correct?

    a. USPAP covers real estate appraisal only.

    b. Some standards deal with aspects of appraisal that are not real estate related.

    c. Most beginning appraisers need only concern themselves with STANDARDS 1-5.

    d. The comments found within the Standards are less important than the Standards themselves.

8. Which of the following is a requirement of STANDARD 2: Real Property Appraisal, Reporting?

    a. An appraiser must not commit a substantial error of omission or commission.

    b. An appraiser must not render appraisal services in a careless or negligent manner.

    c. An appraiser must clearly and accurately set forth the appraisal in a manner that will not be misleading.

    d. An appraiser must be impartial and unbiased, and may not act as an advocate.

9. Which of the following is NOT a report option recognized by the USPAP?

    a. Limited-Use Appraisal Report

    b. Self-Contained Appraisal Report

    c. Restricted-Use Appraisal Report

    d. Summary Appraisal Report

10. When an appraiser is contracted to develop an opinion regarding another real estate appraiser's work as well as develop his or her own value opinion of the subject property, this assignment is:

    a. a review appraisal.

    b. an appraisal consulting assignment.

    c. a mass appraisal.

    d. a review appraisal and a real estate appraisal.

11. Bill is hired to appraise a residence and all of its contents, including appliances and furniture. Which of the following is true?

    a. This appraisal assignment includes personal property.

    b. Bill should contact an experienced appraiser if Bill has never appraised furniture and appliances before.

    c. This assignment is considered a mass appraisal because it encompasses several different disciplines.

    d. Both a. and b.

12. A lender hired Nora to appraise Jim's retail store because Jim is using the store as collateral for taking out a loan to purchase a warehouse. This is an example of a:

    a. Business Appraisal.

    b. Personal Property Appraisal.

    c. Real Property Appraisal.

    d. None of the above

13. Kelly accepts an assignment that stipulates she will be paid if the appraised value comes in above $300,000. This assignment is:

    a. permitted within the context of USPAP.

    b. prohibited by the Management Section of the ETHICS RULE.

    c. permitted if the fees are disclosed properly.

    d. prohibited by the JURISDICTIONAL EXCEPTION RULE.

14. Bob completed an appraisal for Popular Bank on December 15 of 2010. According to the record keeping section, when is the soonest he will be able to dispose of the files?

    a. 12/15/2015

    b. 12/15/2012, assuming there are no judicial proceedings involving this appraisal

    c. 12/15/2017

    d. 12/15/2015, assuming there are no judicial proceedings involving this appraisal

15. Which of the following is NOT a scheme that may entangle an appraiser in mortgage fraud?

    a. Lender pressure

    b. Flipping

    c. Packaged sale

    d. Bogus sale

UNIT 14 ANSWER KEY

Answers – Matching

1. J	4. H	7. C	10. E
2. B	5. G	8. D	
3. I	6. A	9. F	

Answers – Multiple Choice

1. **(b)** Currently the USPAP document contains the Definitions, Preamble, Rules, Standards, Standards Rules, Comments, and Statements on Appraisal Standards. In addition, the USPAP document also includes the Advisory Opinions (AOs), but these are not technically part of USPAP. **Page 420**

2. **(c)** Advisory Opinions are issued to illustrate the applicability of Standards in specific situations and to offer advice from the ASB for the resolution of appraisal issues and problems; they are for guidance only and are not considered an integral part of USPAP. **Page 420**

3. **(d)** The ETHICS RULE is divided into three sections: Conduct, Management, and Confidentiality. **Page 421**

4. **(d)** The Conduct section forbids an appraiser to act as an advocate. Many appraisers are also real estate salespeople, real estate brokers, lawyers, etc. and are required to be advocates as part of their non-appraisal duties. Advocacy is acceptable within those roles. **Page 421**

5. **(b)** The ETHICS RULE covers ethical behavior on the part of appraisers. The COMPETENCY RULE, SCOPE OF WORK RULE, and the JURISDICTIONAL EXCEPTION RULE cover performance standards imposed upon appraisers. **Page 421**

6. **(b)** STANDARDS 1 and 2 (Real Property Appraisal), STANDARD 3 (Appraisal Review), STANDARDS 4 and 5 (Appraisal Consulting), STANDARD 6 (Mass Appraisal), STANDARDS 7 and 8 (Personal Property Appraisal), and STANDARDS 9 and 10 (Business Appraisal). **Page 425**

7. **(b)** When USPAP was developed, its creators decided to encompass all appraisal disciplines, but Standards 1 & 2 are the ones that a beginning real estate appraiser will need to use. **Page 425**

8. **(c)** When reporting a real estate appraisal, the appraiser must "clearly and accurately set forth the appraisal in a manner that will not be misleading". **Page 426**

9. **(a)** In addition to the rules that govern report clarity and content, Standard 2 also provides three reporting options: Self-Contained, Summary, and Restricted Use. **Page 426**

10. **(d)** Standard 3 gives the review appraiser the option to develop his or her own value opinion based on the information in the original workfile. However, once the appraiser does this, the assignment becomes two-fold: a new appraisal as well as a review assignment, producing two reports. **Page 427**

11. **(d)** Personal property includes all tangible assets that are not real property, such as jewelry, autos, boats, etc. The appraiser must be fully competent in the type of property he or she is appraising, or take the steps necessary to gain competency. **Page 429**

12. **(c)** Nora is appraising the building—not the intangible assets of the business such as a logo or copyright. This assignment is a real property appraisal. **Page 426**

13. **(b)** The Management section prohibits accepting an assignment where the fee is contingent on a predetermined or future result. **Page 422**

14. **(d)** An appraiser must keep his workfiles for at least 5 years or 2 years after final disposition of any judicial proceeding involving the file. **Page 423**

15. **(c)** Some of the most common fraud schemes include flipping, packed sales, bogus sales, and lender pressure. **Page 431**

Appraisal Math & Statistical Concepts

Unit 15

INTRODUCTION

Many people are intimidated by the word "math", but in this case, the concepts presented here are mainly a review of knowledge you already possess—and probably use in your daily life. This unit reviews the basic mathematical procedures needed to solve common real estate appraisal problems. Additionally, it presents an introduction to statistics.

Learning Objectives

After reading this unit, you should be able to:

- recall how to work with percentages, fractions, and decimals.
- compute basic and algebraic problems.
- calculate perimeter and area.
- calculate volume of odd shapes.
- compute measures of central tendency.
- determine the components of dispersion.

BASIC MATH REVIEW

It is important to review math basics including decimals, fractions, percentages, rounding, and formulas before starting our study of how to solve various appraisal problems.

For most appraisal math, a basic four-function calculator is recommended. The functions on a basic calculator are add (+), subtract (–), multiply (×), divide (÷), percent (%), and square root (√). However, once you begin to work more with income producing properties, you may want to purchase a financial calculator. A financial calculator provides many benefits, including the Six Functions of 1 Dollar tables at a touch of a button. For now, a basic calculator is sufficient for these problems, so it is not necessary to purchase a financial calculator.

Decimals, Fractions, and Percentages

Before starting to study various mathematical problems, a review of decimals is helpful. The period that sets apart a whole number from a fractional part of that number is called a **decimal point**. The position of the decimal point determines the value of the number.

Any numerals to the right of the decimal point are less than one. The 10th position is the first position to the right of the decimal point, the 100th position is the second to the right of the decimal point, the 1,000th position is the third to the right of the decimal point, and so forth.

The whole numerals are to the left of the decimal point. The ones are in the first position to the left of the decimal point, the 10s in the second position to the left of the decimal point, the 100s in the third position to the left of the decimal point, the 1,000s in the fourth position to the left of the decimal point, and so forth.

Equivalent Amounts		
Decimal	**Fraction**	**Percentage**
0.045	1/22	4 ½%
0.0667	1/15	6 ⅔%
0.10	1/10	10%
0.125	1/8	12 ½%
0.1667	1/6	16 ⅔%
0.25	1/3	33⅓%
0.33	1/3	25%
0.5	1/2	50%
0.667	2/3	66 ⅔%
0.75	3/4	75%
1.00	1/1	100%

Converting Fractions into Decimals

Fractions are always composed of two numbers, one on top, and one on bottom. The top number is the **numerator**, and the bottom number is the **denominator**. These numbers are related as a part to the whole, where the numerator (top) is the part of the denominator (bottom) whole.

To convert the fraction into a decimal, simply divide the top number (numerator) by the bottom number (denominator).

Example:

To convert 1/2,	$1 \div 2 = 0.5$
To convert 3/4,	$3 \div 4 = 0.75$
To convert 3/10,	$3 \div 10 = 0.3$

Converting Decimals to Percentages

To convert a decimal to a percentage move the decimal point two places to the right and add a percent symbol. When no decimal is present (in whole numbers), assume the decimal is to the very right of the number (for example, 10 is the same as 10.0).

Example:

0.02	becomes	2.0%
0.57	becomes	57.0%
0.058	becomes	5.8%
9.02	becomes	902.0%

Converting Percentages to Decimals

Reverse the above process to convert a number expressed as a percentage to a decimal. Again, when working with numbers like 10% or 20%, the decimal point is assumed to be on the right side of the number. Move the decimal point two places to the left and remove the percentage sign.

Example:

6.0%	becomes	0.06
30.0%	becomes	0.30
2.3%	becomes	0.023
210.0%	becomes	2.10

Rounding

Rounding a number means making it the closest whole number or other designated position, i.e., making 5.8 up to 6 or rounding $392 to the nearest hundred ($400). A few rules of thumb are in order when rounding numbers.

If the number is greater than or equal to half of the place you are rounding to, round up; if it is lower, round down. This depends on the position to which you are rounding. For example, if rounding to the nearest hundred, when the number is 50 or above round up; if it is below 50 round down.

Examples:

0.66666	Rounded to hundredth	0.67
10,550.0	Rounded to hundred	10,600.0
24.0	Rounded to ten	20.0
5.167	Rounded to tenth	5.2
321.568	Rounded to whole	322.0
321.444	Rounded to whole	321.0

Typically, appraisers work with large monetary figures as well as miniscule percentages. The second rounding rule is DO NOT round until you get to the final answer.

The exception to this rule is percentages. Generally, percentages do not need to exceed the hundredth place, but be sure not to over-round to the tenths or a whole percentage, as the result will vary.

No rounding

$$\frac{\$39,956}{8.5699\%} = \$466,236.47$$

Rounding 100ths

$$\frac{\$39,956}{8.57\%} = \$466,231.0$$

When the rules above are followed, the rounded final answer (to the closest hundred) is the same, $466,200. However, if you over-round, the final answer can change significantly.

$$\frac{\$40,000}{9\%} = \$444,444.44$$

When tallying multiple figures, the rounding principle becomes more important because combining the disparities caused by over-rounded figures significantly affects the analysis. In the above example, the disparity was a couple hundred dollars. Imagine if five samples were added together and each had a disparity of $200 to $300. The final answer could be off by $1,000 or more. Moreover, if you had to apply that answer elsewhere, the result of that calculation would be affected even more. The possibility of the snowball effect due to excessive rounding is clear.

FORMULAS

The following formulas can help the beginning appraiser solve for an unknown variable, whether working with percentages (usually capitalization rates or interest rates), dollar figures, or both.

There are usually only three variables in any real estate problem—two things that are known and one that is unknown. Problems that are more complex really are just comprised of multiple smaller problems and merely need to be broken down into their components.

Basic Formulas

An easy way to solve most appraisal math problems is to use the Whole-Part formula, which has three variations.

Part = Whole x Rate
Whole = Part ÷ Rate
Rate = Part ÷ Whole

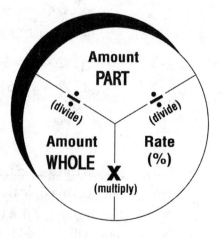

Whenever you have a math problem, one of these formulas probably can be used. You will always know two of the quantities and will be asked to find the third. From the information given in the problem, you must decide whether to multiply or divide the two numbers that you know in order to find the unknown third number.

Working with Algebra

The basic algebraic formula is: **x (± or ×/÷) y = z**. And, anyone with a basic understanding of algebra can manipulate the basic formula to calculate the unknown.

The key to this principle is that whichever operation is in the formula, whether it be +, −, ×, or ÷, use the opposing operation and perform it to both sides of the equals sign (=).

Example 1

If x = 4 and y = 3; solve for z.

x + y = z

4 + 3 = 7

However, in instances where the unknown variable is not isolated on one side of the equals sign, steps can be taken to isolate it.

Example 2

If $x = 2$ and $z = 5$; solve for y

x + y = z

2 + y = 5

To calculate the value of y, isolate the unknown variable (y) by applying the opposing operation (+/− or ×/÷) to the numeral that accompanies the unknown variable. Then, subtract 2 from both sides of the equation (=).

2 (− 2) + y = 5 (− 2)

[2 − 2] + y = 5 − 2

y = 5 − 2

y = 3

As you can see, on the left side of the equation the +2 and − 2 cancel each other out, leaving only the unknown variable. On the right side of the equation, the negative 2 is added to the 5 (or subtract 2 from 5). and the result is 3. This will work with subtraction, multiplication, and division problems as well. Remember, though, that you need to apply the opposing operation.

Example 3, Multiplication

Formula: x × y = z

Solve for y when x = 25 and z = 100

25 × y = 100

25 (÷ 25) × y = 100 (÷ 25)

[25 ÷ 25] × y = 100 ÷ 25

y = 4

(handwritten:)
$x = 25$
$z = 100$
$x \times y = z$
$25 \times y = 100$
$y = 4$

In the above multiplication problem, the opposing operation is division, and the 25 divided by itself cancels itself. The same occurs in reverse when working with division problems.

Example 4, Division

Formula: x ÷ y = z

Solve for x when y = $400 and z = 8%

x ÷ $400 = 8%

x ÷ $400 (× $400) = 8% (× $400)

x [÷ $400 × $400] = 8% × $400

x = $32

(handwritten:)
$x \div y = z$
$x \div \$400 = 8\%$
$x \div \$400 = 8\%$
$x \div 400 (x\,400) = 8\% (x\,400)$
$x = 8\% \times \$400$

Practice Problems

There are several ways any of the following examples may be solved. Some students will use algebra, whereas others will use the Whole-Part formula or their own techniques to solve the problems.

$$\text{Formula} \quad \frac{\text{Whole}}{\text{(x)}} \quad \times \quad \frac{\text{Rate}}{\text{(y)}} \quad = \quad \frac{\text{Part}}{\text{(z)}}$$

The key to word problems is knowing where the variables fit into the formula. The most important thing regarding word problems is to read the problem carefully and know what is being asked. Often, extra information is included. Other times all the variables are not included, rather information is included that will allow you to determine the needed variables.

(handwritten:) $P = W \times R.$

Dollar-Off Problem

A freeway was constructed next to a home that was previously valued at $500,000. Since the construction of the freeway, the property's value has dropped by 35%. How much value did the property lose?

Formula: Part = Whole x Rate

Solution: By plugging the factors into the formula, this word problem is relatively uncomplicated to solve.

      Part = $500,000 x 0.35 (35%)

      Part = $175,000 (the dollar amount of value lost due to the freeway)

Percentage-Off Problem

Sometimes, instead of wanting to know the sales price, the problem asks how much the percentage-off is.

Barbara's parents just sold their home to her for $300,000. An appraiser concludes that it was not an arm's-length transaction and determines its actual market value is $400,000. What was Barbara's percentage of savings?

Formula: Rate = Part ÷ Whole

Solution: In this problem, in order to solve for the percentage of savings, the Part used must be the dollar amount saved, which is not provided but can easily be calculated ($400,000 − $300,000 = $100,000).

      Rate = $100,000 ÷ $400,000

      Rate = 0.25 or 25%

However, if you use the below market value (which is a common mistake), you are solving for the percentage below-market that the daughter paid. $300,000 ÷ $400,000 = 0.75 or 75%

As you can see each result is complementary to the other (25% and 75%), and added together, they equal 1 or 100%.

Investment Problem

Mitch bought a house for $145,000. The house was later sold for $165,000. What is the rate of profit Mitch made on this sale?

Formula: Rate = Part ÷ Whole

Solution: The problem is asking you to solve for something that is not included in the problem, the profit. However, it is easily calculated by subtracting the price paid from the price sold, $165,000 – $145,000 = $20,000.

Rate = $20,000 ÷ $145,000

Rate = 0.138 or 13.8%

Capitalization Problems

Problem 1

If the sales price for a property is $200,000 and the monthly potential rental income for a property is $2,500, what is the GRM?

Formula: GRM = Sales Price ÷ PGI

Solution: GRM = $200,000 ÷ $2,500

GRM = 80

Problem 2

A market GRM can provide a rough estimate of value. An appraiser analyzed several similar properties that sold recently in the same area to determine that their average monthly GRM is 80. If the subject property has $3,000 monthly potential gross income, what is its estimated value?

Formula: Estimated Market Value = PGI x GRM

Solution: Estimated Market Value = $3,000 x 80

Estimated Market Value = $240,000

Problem 3

A property has a NOI of $29,250 and the sales price is $325,000. What is the capitalization rate?

Formula: Rate = Part ÷ Whole

Cap Rate = NOI ÷ Sales Price

Solution: Cap Rate = $29,250 ÷ $325,000

Cap Rate = 0.09 or 9%

Problem 4

A property has $50,000 EGI and $20,000 in operating expenses. If the capitalization rate for this type of property in this neighborhood is 8%, what is the estimated value of the property?

Formula:	Whole = Part ÷ Rate
	Estimated Value = NOI ÷ Rate
Solution:	The first step is to determine the net operating income, which is $30,000 ($50,000 - $20,000).
	Estimated Value = $30,000 ÷ .08
	Estimated Value = $375,000

Interest and Loan Problems

The charge for the use of money is called **interest**. The rate of interest that is charged determines the total dollar amount of the payments. When money is borrowed, both the principal and interest must be paid back according to the agreement between the borrower and lender.

The formula for interest and loan problems is a variation of the *xyz* formula introduced earlier in the unit. However, this one contains a fourth variable. It is treated the same, but there is one more step to isolate the unknown, which is time.

Formula: $I = P \times R \times T$

I - Interest	amount charged for the use of money (*part*)
P - Principal	dollar amount of money borrowed (*whole*)
R - Rate	percentage of interest charged (*percentage*)
T - Time	duration of loan in years (*time*)

Problem 1

Andrea borrowed $6,000 for two years and paid $520 interest. What interest rate did she pay?

Formula:	Rate = Part ÷ (Whole x Time)
	R = I ÷ (P x T)
Solution:	R = $520 ÷ ($6,000 x 2)
	R = $520 ÷ $12,000
	R = 4.33%

Problem 2

If one month's interest is $50 on a five-year, straight, interest-only note, and the interest rate on the note is 10% per year, what is the amount of the loan?

Formula: Whole = Part ÷ (Rate x Time)
             P = I ÷ (R x T)

Solution: When you are asked to find an amount resulting from an interest rate, it will usually be an annual number. If not otherwise specified, make sure you annualize, that is convert any monthly figures to annual or yearly figures by multiplying the monthly figures by 12. The annual interest is $600 ($50 x 12 months)
             P = $600 ÷ (0.10 x 1)
             P = $600 ÷ 0.10
             P = $6,000

AREA AND VOLUME CALCULATIONS

In actual practice, appraisers calculate the area of lots, buildings, and garages, and the volume of structures like warehouses. Fortunately, computer programs and specialized measuring devices do most of the work when it comes to determining area and volume. However, it is always good to know the basics. That way, you can check the computer-generated answers and make sure they are reasonable.

Before areas and volumes are further explored, certain clarifications need to be addressed. We live in a three dimensional universe, and as such, these dimensions are reflected in an appraiser's measurements and calculations.

Linear Measurement

A **linear measurement** is a measurement of distance and can be straight, curved, or angled. Examples of linear measurements include the length of the property's front boundary or the perimeter (or distance around) a grain silo. This measurement is expressed in linear terms, i.e. an inch long, a foot deep, or a mile wide.

Area Measurement

When a second dimension is included, the measurement becomes an **area measurement** instead of a linear one. **Area** articulates the amount of space covered, whether by a real object or theoretical shape, and is always expressed in terms of square measurements. This is because the most basic area measurement is a square, but this does not preclude other shapes. Typical area measurements include the floor area of a bedroom, a lot size, and the area of a wall the window occupies. To compute a square measurement, one simply needs to multiply two linear measurements together. Examine the following for clarification:

Volume Measurement

When a third dimension is added, **volume** is being quantified, that is the amount of space being occupied. When a three dimensional object is measured in terms of volume, like an Olympic sized swimming pool for instance, it consists of three measurements: the width, the length, and the depth (or height). When these three measurements are multiplied, the resulting figure is a cubic measurement.

Example: According to the Olympic committee, an Olympic sized pool must measure 50 meters in length, 25 meters in width, and must be at least 2 meters deep. Using the formula for a cube, the volume of the pool is calculated at 2500 cubic meters (50m × 25m × 2m).

These types of calculations require a basic understanding of geometry. The following chart summarizes the formulas an appraiser may need:

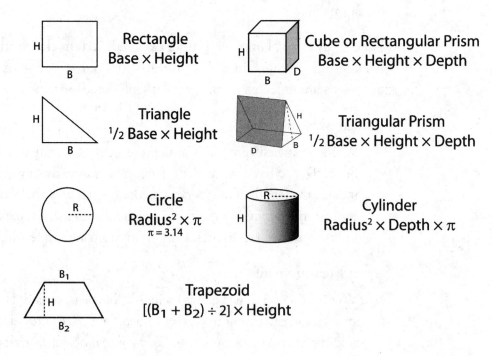

Rectangle
Base × Height

Cube or Rectangular Prism
Base × Height × Depth

Triangle
$\frac{1}{2}$ Base × Height

Triangular Prism
$\frac{1}{2}$ Base × Height × Depth

Circle
Radius^2 × π
π = 3.14

Cylinder
Radius^2 × Depth × π

Trapezoid
[(B$_1$ + B$_2$) ÷ 2] × Height

Conversions

Often figures are not presented to you in like measurements, so knowing how to convert inches to feet, and feet to yards, and yards to miles or acres is invaluable. It is very important to use like measurements when working through computations or else answers will be wrong.

Linear	Square	Cubic
12 inches = 1 foot	144 square inches = 1 square foot	1,728 cubic inches = 1 cubic foot
3 feet = 1 yard	9 square feet = 1 square yard	27 cubic feet = 1 cubic yard
1,760 yards = 1 mile	36 sections = 36 square miles	46,565 cubic inches = 1 cubic yard
1 mile = 5,280 feet	23,040 acres = 36 square miles	1 board foot = 144 cubic inches
1 mile = 63,360 inches	640 acres = 1 section	
1 yard = 36 inches	43,560 square feet = 1 acre	
1 section's perimeter = 21,120 feet	1 township = 36 square miles	

An acre is not a particular shape. Rather, an **acre** is a measure of area that covers 43,560 square feet, no matter the form. Therefore, an acre could be a perfect square with sides measuring 208.71 feet or it could be a narrow rectangle measuring one foot wide and 43,560 feet long. As long as a shape contains 43,560 square feet, it is an acre, or portion thereof.

A similar, but less frequently used, cubic measurement is the board foot. A **board foot** always measures 144 cubic inches; any measure of volume containing 144 in^3 is considered a board foot. A piece of lumber that is 2 inches by 6 inches by 12 inches long contains a board foot, just as a box that measures 6 inches by 6 inches by four inches contains a board foot.

Area of Odd Shapes

Unfortunately, lots and rooms are not always perfect rectangles, and warehouses and other industrial buildings are not always perfect cubes or rectangles. When you have to calculate area for an irregular lot or building, break it down into its component parts.

Break the floorplan into smaller shapes that are easier to compute. Then add all of the figures together to achieve the final answer. There is no one right way to divide this shape into several smaller shapes. Ideally, make it as uncomplicated as possible. The fewer shapes you must calculate, the less potential for mistakes.

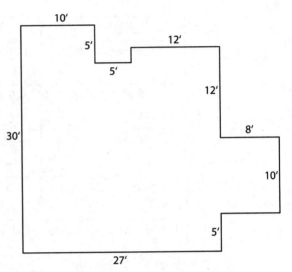

Once it is broken into smaller, more manageable rectangles, the area becomes much easier to compute.

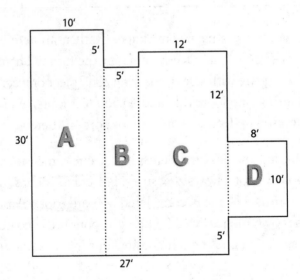

Rectangle A	10' × 30'	=	300 sq ft
Rectangle B	5' × 25'	=	125 sq ft
Rectangle C	12' × 27'	=	324 sq ft
Rectangle D	8' × 10'	=	80 sq ft
Floorplan total area		=	829 sq ft

Volume of Odd Shapes

When measuring volume, a similar instance may occur. Some warehouses may have a gable roof, or some other feature that complicates the calculations. Again, break the object into its simpler component parts and determine the volumes separately before you add them all together for a final computation.

In the following figure, the industrial building pictured is 80' × 100' × 30'. The height of the eaves is measured at 18'.

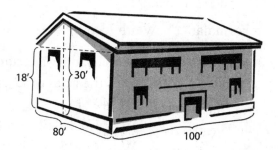

To solve for the volume of this building, divide the shape into a rectangular prism that measures 80' × 100' × 18' and a triangular prism that measures 100' × 80' × 12'. Then calculate the volume for each and add the two figures together for the entire building's volume.

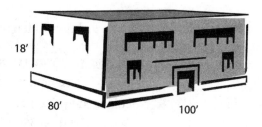

Rectangle	80' × 100' × 18'	=	144,000 cu. ft.
Triangle	100' × 80' × 12' ÷ 2	=	+ <u>48,000 cu. ft.</u>
Warehouse total area		=	192,000 cu. ft.

Practice Problems

The following problems combine elements of the preceding unit into semi-complex problems. Read each carefully and learn how to decipher the word problems and break the equations into smaller, manageable steps.

Problem 1

Felix owned 4 acres of land with a front footage of 500 feet along Old Bucket Country Road. What is the depth of the land?

> **Formula:**   Width (depth) = Area ÷ Height
>
> **Solution:**   If necessary, draw a rectangle representing the land.
> Convert the acres to square feet. (43,560 SF × 4 acres
> = 174,240 SF).
> W = 174,240 SF ÷ 500 feet
> W = 348.48, or 350 ft (rounded).

Problem 2

Tom bought a triangular lot for $800,000 that measures 450 feet at its widest point and 350 feet at its longest point. How much did Tom pay for his property per acre?

> **Formula:**   Area = ½ Base x Height
>
> **Solution:**   If necessary, draw a triangle representing the lot. The
> first step is to calculate the number of acres. Then,
> calculate the price per acre.
> A = (450 ft × 350 ft) ÷ 2
> A = 78,750 SF

78,750 SF ÷ 43,560 SF = 1.81 acres
$800,000 ÷ 1.81 acres = $441,988 or $442,000 per acre (rounded)

Problem 3

Cliff owns a four-acre lot that is 80 feet deep. He originally paid $1,000 per acre 2 years ago. He is in the process of purchasing a neighboring lot that contains two more acres with the same depth for $3,300. He wants to assemble the lots and then subdivide them into 27 equal neighboring lots so he can sell them. His appraiser notified him that he could expect to make $5 per front foot per lot. How much can he expect to make in profit?

Solution: First, determine the size and dimensions of the four-acre and two-acre lot combined before subdivision. Six acres is 261,360 square feet (6 acres x 43,560 ft per acre).

Formula: Width = Area ÷ Depth
Width = 261,360 square feet ÷ 80 foot depth
Width = 3,267 feet

The size and shape of the lot is known – a rectangle that measures 80 by 3,267 feet, and covers an area of 261,360 square feet. Next, figure out the front footage of the individual lots once subdivided for sale.

3,267 feet ÷ 27 lots = 121 front feet

Once divided, he will have 27 lots for sale that are 121 feet wide and 80 feet deep. To finish the problem, compute the gross sales then subtract the amount he paid for the properties.

Gross Sales = $16,335 (121 × $5 = $605 per lot × 27 lots)
Cost of lots = $7,300 ($4,000 + $3,300)
Profit = $16,335 – $7,300
Profit = $9,035

STATISTICS

Statistics is the science of gathering, categorizing and interpreting data. Although appraisers use statistical analysis, it should never be solely relied on for value conclusions. Rather, statistical analysis should outline parameters and assist appraisers in developing an opinion. This unit covers the basest statistical concepts.

> **Terminology**
>
> **Population**—the entire group (aggregate) of items from which samples are drawn.
>
> **Parameter**—a single number or attribute of the individual things, persons, or other entities in a population.
>
> **Sample**—a subset of a population.
>
> **Variate**—a single item in the group.
>
> **Aggregate**—the sum of all individual variates.

Assume that you are appraising a 3-bedroom 2-bath house. After market research, you pull a list of ten sales comps that are nearly identical in size and amenities. When analyzing statistical data, the numbers (sales prices) are the most important. For illustrative purposes, we will use a small sample for all of the following demonstrations.

Sales Prices of Comps for 3-bed, 2-bath Subject Property

560 Willow Place	$320,000
211 Willow Place	$305,000
1010 Rose Avenue	$299,500
1099 Rose Avenue	$305,000
4256 Rose Avenue	$310,000
14 Oak Street	$300,000
27 Oak Street	$305,500
898 Walnut Court	$312,000
787 Magnolia	$308,500
2 Palm Court	$301,000

Once the data is gathered, the first step is to organize the sales prices into an array by sorting the list from lowest to highest or highest to lowest.

Sales Prices from Lowest to Highest

1010 Rose Avenue	$299,500
14 Oak Street	$300,000
2 Palm Court	$301,000
1099 Rose Avenue	$305,000
211 Willow Place	$305,000
27 Oak Street	$305,500
787 Magnolia	$308,500
4256 Rose Avenue	$310,000
898 Walnut Court	$312,000
560 Willow Place	$320,000

The sales prices vary from $299,500 up to $320,000, which is not a huge disparity, but the sales are not identical either. To analyze this sample further, appraisers apply what are known as the measures of central tendency.

Measures of Central Tendency

Central tendency is the numeric value that is suggested as a typical value in a statistical sample. The three common statistical measures are the mean, the median, and the mode. They are used to measure central tendency and to identify the typical variate in a sample or population.

Mean

The **mean**, commonly known as the average, is calculated by adding all of the variates together and then dividing that by the number of variates. The result provides a single figure that accounts for all variates, even ones that are significantly lower or higher than the majority.

Steps to Calculate Mean
- Array the numbers.
- Add all of the numbers.
- Divide the total by how many numbers are in the array.

Mean of the Sales Prices Sample

1010 Rose Avenue	$299,500
14 Oak Street	$300,000
2 Palm Court	$301,000
1099 Rose Avenue	$305,000
211 Willow Place	$305,000
27 Oak Street	$305,500
787 Magnolia	$308,500
4256 Rose Avenue	$310,000
898 Walnut Court	$312,000
560 Willow Place	+$320,000
Total	$3,066,500
Mean ($3,066,500 ÷ 10)	$306,650

Therefore, although the sample ranges from $299,500 to $320,000, the average or mean house price for this sample is $306,500.

Median

The second measure of central tendency is called the **median**, which provides a figure that is directly in the middle of the population. Unlike the mean, the median is not significantly affected by one unusually high or low number. Finding the median is like lining up all of your favorite photos in order of favorite to least favorite, and then picking the photo in the middle of the line.

To do this, divide a sampling into two equal groups. The number in the middle is the median is the midpoint.

> Example: With a sampling of 12, 3, 6, 15, and 9, first place the numbers into an array: 3, 6, 9, 12, 15, and then divide them into equal groups: (3, 6) 9 (12, 15). Since 9 is in the middle of the list, it is the median.

If the number of variates is an even number, as is the sales price sample with which we have been working, there will not be a single variate directly in the middle. In situations with an even number of variates, find the mean of the two numbers on either side of the midpoint.

Median of the Sales Prices Sample

1010 Rose Avenue	$299,500
14 Oak Street	$300,000
2 Palm Court	$301,000
1099 Rose Avenue	$305,000
211 Willow Place	$305,000

The middle – add these two and divide by 2 ↕

27 Oak Street	$305,500
787 Magnolia	$308,500
4256 Rose Avenue	$310,000
898 Walnut Court	$312,000
560 Willow Place	$320,000

$305,000 + $305,500 = $610,500. $610,500 ÷ 2 = $305,250

$305,250 is the median in this sample.

Mode

The final measure of central tendency is called the mode. This **mode** is the number that occurs the most frequently, and when analyzing comparable sales, the most frequently occurring sales price definitely warrants consideration.

Mode of the Sales Prices Sample

Once	$299,500
Once	$300,000
Once	$301,000
Twice	$305,000
Once	$305,500
Once	$308,500
Once	$310,000
Once	$312,000
Once	$320,000

From the array above, the most frequently occurring variate is $305,000.

In analyzing this sample of comparable sales, the sale prices range from $299,500 to $320,000 with a mean of $306,650, a median of $305,250, and a mode of $305,000. An appraiser could make an argument for any value within the range. However, after further analysis, there is a better argument for a value that fits the central tendencies.

Measures of Dispersion

Sometimes, the measures of central tendency are not adequate for the statistical analysis. In order to determine if the variates of the sample are clustered together or spread out, appraisers apply three measures of dispersion—range, average deviation, and standard deviation.

Range

The **range** is simply the difference between the highest and lowest variate. The lower the range, the more clustered the grouping, and conversely, the higher the range, the more spread out they are. The range for the sales prices sample that we have used through this section can be found by subtracting $299,500 from $320,000. The range equals $20,500. Although this certainly is a lot of money, it is not a huge difference when put into the context of the housing market.

Average Deviation

All of these variates differ from the central tendency to some degree; and **average deviation** measures their combined average dispersion. For this, the mean is needed. Once the mean of the sample is known, add the difference of each variate in relation to the mean together and then divide the sum by the number of variates in the sample.

For this, it may help to imagine a numberline, which is a line with equally spaced tick marks representing a different sequential number.

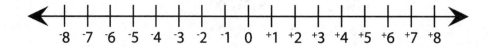

In the above numberline, both +1 and –1 are the same number of positions, one, from the mean of 0. When counting deviation, it is important to disregard the positive or negative attributes of the deviations because, whether positive or negative, they are a certain measure from the mean. If the average income is $50,000 and Joe makes $45,000 and Jane makes $55,000, both are $5,000 from the mean.

Before this is applied to the sample of houses, examine this demonstration on a smaller scale. If the sample is 14, 5, 26, 7, 38, 9, 1, and 4, the mean is 13. To calculate the average deviation, find the number of places that each variate is different from the mean, like so:

Mean	Variate	Difference +/-	Difference
13	1	-12	12
13	6	-7	7
13	5	-8	8
13	7	-6	6
13	9	-4	4
13	14	1	1
13	26	13	13
13	38	25	25
Sum of differences			76

Finally, divide the sum of differences by the number of variates. The average deviation is 9.5. Again, as with the measure of range, the more spread out the sample is the higher the deviation figure will be.

Apply this concept to the sales price list of 10 variates.

Mean	Variates	Diff +/−	Difference
$306,650	$299,500	$7,150	$7,150
$306,650	$300,000	$6,650	$6,650
$306,650	$301,000	$5,650	$5,650
$306,650	$305,000	$1,650	$1,650
$306,650	$305,000	$1,650	$1,650
$306,650	$305,500	$1,150	$1,150
$306,650	$308,500	−$1,850	$1,850
$306,650	$310,000	−$3,350	$3,350
$306,650	$312,000	−$5,350	$5,350
$306,650	$320,000	−$13,350	$13,350
Sum of differences			$47,800

The average deviation for the price list sample is $4,780 ($47,800 ÷ 10).

Standard Deviation

Standard deviation is even more complex than average deviation, but produces a useful and credible analysis by statistical means. With this method, before adding the deviations from the mean, they must be squared.

Squaring a number means multiplying the figure by itself. Once the deviations are squared, the square root ($\sqrt{}$) of their mean is taken, and that figure represents the standard deviation of the sample.

A **square root** is, it is the inverse of squaring. If squaring 3 equals 9 (3 × 3 is 9), then the square root of 9 is 3. You do not have to figure this out by hand. Simply punch into your calculator whatever number you need to find the square root of and hit the [$\sqrt{}$] button.

Perhaps a visual illustration will help. Using the same practice sample as we did in average deviation:

Mean	Variates	Difference	Diff Square
13	1	12	(12 × 12) 144
13	6	7	(7 × 7) 49
13	5	8	(8 × 8) 64
13	7	6	(6 × 6) 36
13	9	4	(4 × 4) 16
13	14	1	(1 × 1) 1
13	26	13	(13 × 13) 169
13	38	25	(25 × 25) <u>625</u>

Sum of differences squared	1104
Mean of differences squared	(1104 ÷ 8) 138
Square root of mean	($\sqrt{138}$) 11.75

The standard deviation is 11.75.

In our final example, we will calculate the standard deviation for the list of comparables.

Mean	Variates	Difference	Diff Squared
$306,650	$299,500	$7,150	$ 51,122,500
$306,650	$300,000	$6,650	$ 44,222,500
$306,650	$301,000	$5,650	$ 31,922,500
$306,650	$305,000	$1,650	$ 2,722,500
$306,650	$305,000	$1,650	$ 2,722,500
$306,650	$305,500	$1,150	$ 1,322,500
$306,650	$308,500	$1,850	$ 3,422,500
$306,650	$310,000	$3,350	$ 11,222,500
$306,650	$312,000	$5,350	$ 28,622,500
$306,650	$320,000	$13,350	<u>$178,222,500</u>

Sum of differences squared	$355,525,000
Mean of differences squared	$ 35,552,500
Square root of mean	$ 5,963

The measures of dispersion may seem convoluted, but they convey useful information. Consider our list of comparables. If an appraiser were using this list to develop an opinion of the subject's value, he or she would certainly want to make sure that the indicated value fell within the range. In addition, a good value check is to make certain that the chosen value does not deviate from the mean by being greater than the standard and average deviations, at least not without reasonable explanation.

Statistical analysis cannot be the sole indicator of value. For instance, with the list we have been using, the data indicates that the subject's value should be around $305,000 and no more than $6,000 higher or lower than that number. This analysis of the numbers does not take into account any non-quantifiable characteristics of the subject or comparables like condition, quality, and other amenities like landscaping or customization. This is where appraising becomes more than just number crunching; it becomes an art.

However, if an appraiser does choose a value outside of the range supported by a statistical analysis, he or she may need to go back and verify the information and be certain that he or she is using appropriate comparables.

SUMMARY

Math is a major component of the appraisal process. Appraisers need to know how to **calculate areas and volumes** as well as **interest** and **capitalization rates,** among others. It will be of tremendous use both in the practical world and in testing conditions to know when to **round,** how to **convert percentages to decimals,** and **units of measurement**.

Knowing how to analyze statistical data will be very practical as well. Though appraisers cannot rely solely on **statistical analysis,** it is a good tool to add greater support to or assist an appraiser in his or her analysis.

UNIT 15 REVIEW

Matching Exercise

Instructions: Write the letter of the matching term on the blank line before its definition, and then check your response with the Answer Key that immediately follows the Multiple Choice Questions.

Terms

A. acre

B. aggregate

C. area

D. average deviation

E. decimal point

F. interest

G. mean

H. median

I. mode

J. parameter

K. range

L. square root

M. squaring

N. standard deviation

O. statistics

P. variate

Q. volume

Definitions

1. _____ Amount of space covered in two dimensions.

2. _____ Amount of space being occupied in three dimensions.

3. _____ 43,560 square feet.

4. _____ Science of gathering, categorizing, and interpreting data.

5. _____ Single item in the group, statistically.

6. _____ Charge for the use of money.

7. _____ Statistical total.

8. _____ Average.

9. _____ Figure that is directly in the middle of the population.

10. _____ Most frequently occurring number.

11. _____ Difference between the highest and lowest variate.

12. _____ Measure of combined average dispersion.

13. _____ Measure of the dispersion or variation in a distribution using the squares of the mean.

14. _____ Multiplying a number by itself.

15. _____ Number that, when multiplied by itself, will result in a given number.

Multiple Choice Questions

Instructions: Circle your choice, and then check your response with the Answer Key that immediately follows the Multiple Choice Questions.

1. The dot in 425.9056 is called a:
    a. period.
    b. point.
    c. decimal point.
    d. decibel point.

2. In the number 425.9056, the 9 is in which position?
    a. 10
    b. 1
    c. 10th
    d. 100th

3. 240% expressed as a decimal is:
    a. 2,400.
    b. 2.4.
    c. 0.24.
    d. 240.

4. 5/2 expressed a percentage is:
    a. 10%.
    b. 250%.
    c. 4%.
    d. 400%.

5. Meagan found three comps that recently sold. After applying a market derived cap rate, the market value for these comps is as follows: $574,511; $499,996; and $525,444. Rounded to the nearest thousand, the final comparable values are:
   a. $500,000; $525,000; $575,000.
   b. $499,000; $525,000; $574,500.
   c. $500,000; $526,000; $575,000.
   d. $500,000; $524,500; $570,000.

6. Since Rebecca purchased her home one-year ago, property values in the area have increased by 30%. Her property is currently valued at $390,000. How much equity has accrued in the last year?
   a. $117,000
   b. $90,000
   c. $113,000
   d. $11,700

7. Melissa found a property selling for $210,000 that she really liked but could not afford. After the property was on the market for 45-days, the seller offered a $30,000 rebate to facilitate the sale. At that time Melissa decide to purchase the property. What percentage of savings is she receiving?
   a. 85.7%
   b. 63%
   c. 14.3%
   d. 16.7%

8. Sherri is considering buying two adjoining lots and assembling them and then reselling the single lot for a profit. Lot 1 is priced at $30,000 and Lot 2 is priced at $55,000. A contractor estimates the cost to demolish the structures on the sites at $15,000 and Sherri's appraiser estimates the value of the combined lot at $115,000. What would Sherri's rate of return be if she goes forward with this?
   a. 10%
   b. 13%
   c. 15%
   d. 30%

9. Ramon took out a one-year interest only loan of $10,000 at 9%. If his final monthly payment must include the last interest payment and the loan balance, how much will it be?
   a. $10,900
   b. $10,075
   c. $908.33
   d. $874.51

10. Which type of measurement is produced when you multiply width by depth?

    a. Inches

    b. Area

    c. Volume

    d. Feet

Use the following figure for questions 11-13.

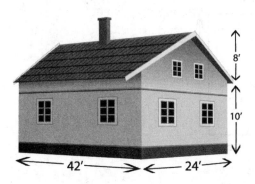

11. What is the perimeter of the house?

    a. 1,008 feet

    b. 132 square feet

    c. 1,008 square feet

    d. 132 feet

12. What is the square footage of the first floor of the house?

    a. 1,008 square feet

    b. 1,008 feet

    c. 132 square feet

    d. 18,144 feet

13. What is the volume of the house?

    a. 18,144 feet

    b. 14,112 cubic feet

    c. 18,144 cubic feet

    d. 9,072 square feet

14. What is the GLA of the following floorplan?

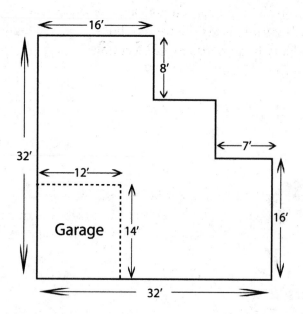

   a. 816 feet
   b. 137 square feet
   c. 672 square feet
   d. 616 feet

15. Which of the following is a larger measurement?

   a. 3 acres
   b. 15 square yards
   c. 1/128 of a section
   d. 1/2 mile square

16. Sue owns a 6-acre parcel that is 396 feet deep that she would like to subdivide and sell off as separate lots. If she creates lots that are 60' × 44' and sells them for $20,000 apiece, how much money will she make?

   a. $1,980,000
   b. $5,280,000
   c. $180,000
   d. $133,333

17. A rural lot starts at the southwest corner of the intersection of Rural Route 8 and Old County Road. The northern property line follows RR-8 100 yards west, thence southeasterly 175 yards until it meets the western border of Old County Road, thence follows Old County Road northerly 432 feet until it meets the point of origin. How many acres is this parcel?

    a. 105

    b. 87

    c. 1.5

    d. 0.6

18. Beth is using the unit-in-place method on a newer home. She measures the foundation at 36'4" by 38'10". A contractor tells her that the cost of a foundation in the subject neighborhood is $18.63 per linear foot. What is the total cost of the foundation?

    a. $26,280

    b. $2,800

    c. $1,397

    d. $25,837

19. As part of his first farm appraisal, Sal must appraise a grain silo. After inspection, Sal concludes the following: It measures 41 feet tall and has a radius of 9 feet. The comparative unit is $15.00 per cubic foot, with a regional multiplier of 0.98. The silo has 90 years of economic life remaining on an expected life of 100 years. What is Sal's opinion of value for the silo?

    a. $138,000

    b. $48,800

    c. $44,000

    d. $15,300

For questions 20-26, use the following 3 bedroom/2 bath sample from Riverside.

8181 High St.	$15,000
122 Kenny St.	$103,000
211 Road Blvd.	$99,900
214 Burk Ln.	$67,500
706 Hazelnut Hwy.	$95,000
743 Eicher Way	$95,000
1031 N 26th Ave.	$66,000
2050 7th Ave.	$33,000
7107 Oceans Ave.	$74,900

20. What is the mean house price for a 3br/2ba home in Riverside?
   a. $72,144
   b. $74,900
   c. $88,000
   d. $95,000

21. What is the median house price for a 3br/2ba home in Riverside?
   a. $72,144
   b. $74,900
   c. $88,000
   d. $95,000

22. What is the mode for this sample of 3br/2ba homes in Riverside?
   a. $72,144
   b. $74,900
   c. $88,000
   d. $95,000

23. What is the range of the sample of 3br/2ba homes in Riverside?
   a. $72,144
   b. $74,900
   c. $88,000
   d. $95,000

24. What is the average deviation of the sample population of 3br/2ba homes in Riverside?

    a. $29,120

    b. $103,000

    c. $23,795

    d. $87,361

25. What is the standard deviation of the sample population of 3br/2ba homes in Riverside?

    a. $649,300

    b. $30,886

    c. $23,795

    d. $29,120

UNIT 15 ANSWER KEY

Answers – Matching

1.	C	5.	P	9.	H	13.	N
2.	Q	6.	F	10.	I	14.	M
3.	A	7.	B	11.	K	15.	L
4.	O	8.	G	12.	D		

Answers – Multiple Choice

1. **(c)** The period that sets apart a whole number from a fractional part of that number is called a decimal point. **Page 446**

2. **(c)** Any numerals to the right of the decimal point are less than one and the 10th position is the first position to the right of the decimal point. **Page 446**

3. **(b)** To convert a percentage to a decimal, move the decimal point two places to the left and remove the percentage sign. **Page 447**

4. **(b)** To convert a fraction into a percentage is a two step process. First, divide the numerator (top) by the denominator: $5 \div 2 = 2.5$. Then, convert the resulting decimal into a percentage by moving the decimal two places to the right and adding a percent sign. **Page 447**

5. **(a)** If the number is greater than or equal to half of the place you are rounding to, round up; if it is lower, round down. Since the thousand place is being rounded to, $574,511 is rounded up to $575,000; $499,996 is rounded up to $500,000; and $525,444 is rounded down to $525,000. **Page 448**

6. **(b)** The problem states that the unknown original price plus 30% is equal to the current price of $390,000. It asks you to solve for 30% of the unknown price. Using the Whole $\times$ Rate = Part problem, the calculations are as follows:

   x **x** 1.3 (100% original price + 30% rise in value) = $390,000
   x = $390,000 $\div$ 1.3
   x = $300,000 (price one year ago)
   $390,000 – $300,000 = $90,000 accrued equity
   Page 453

7. **(c)** The problem is asking what percentage of the original price is the rebate. Using the Whole $\times$ Rate = Part problem, the calculations are as follows:

   $210,000 **x** y = $30,000
   y = $30,000 $\div$ $210,000
   y = 0.1428 or 14.3%
   Page 452

8. **(c)**   Sherri's total expenditure for the investment would be $100,000: Lot 1 + Lot 2 + Cost to Demolish ($30,000 + $55,000 + $15,000) Sherri would earn $15,000 in profit ($115,000 – $100,000) once the project was sold. Using the Whole × Rate = Part problem, the calculations are as follows:

   $100,000 × y = $15,000
   y = $15,000 ÷ $100,000
   y = 15%.
   Page 452

9. **(b)**   Since it is an interest only loan, all the payments up to the final one were only interest payments. Using the I = P × R × T formula, the solution is as follows:

   I = $10,000 × 9% × 1
   I = $900 a year, $75 a month ($900 ÷ 12)
   11 payments of $75, 1 payment of $10,075 (loan balance + last month of interest)
   Page 454

10. **(b)**   To compute an area or square measurement, one simply needs to multiply two linear measurements together. **Page 456**

11. **(d)**   The perimeter is the linear measurement around a shape. Add the linear measurements that compose four sides of the rectangular house (42' + 42' + 24' + 24' = 132 feet). A linear measurement cannot be square. **Page 455**

12. **(a)**   To compute an area measurement, one simply needs to multiply two linear measurements together: 24' × 42' = 1,008 square feet. **Pages 455-456**

13. **(b)**   To properly calculate the volume for this structure it must be separated into two separate geometric shapes: the rectangular prism that makes up the bottom floor and the triangular prism that is the second floor. Once these two volumes are calculated separately, add them together to compute the total volume.

Rectangular Prism:	24' × 42' × 10'	= 10,080 cubic feet
Triangular Prism:	½ × 24' × 42' x 8'	= 4,032 cubic feet
Total volume:	10,080 + 4,032	= 14,112 cubic feet

   Page 456

14. **(c)** Make the figure a rectangle then subtract the dotted-line sections:

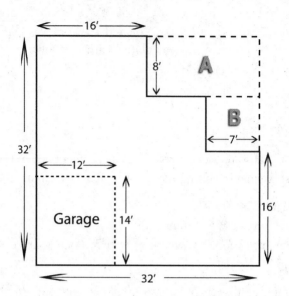

Square:	32' × 32'	= 1,024 square feet
Section A:	8' × 16'	= − 128 square feet
Section B:	7' × 8'	= − 56 square feet
Garage:	12' × 14'	= − 168 square feet
Floor plan square footage:		672 square feet

Page 458

15. **(d)** To solve this problem, convert all of the measurements to the same unit of comparison. Once all the measurements have been converted to square feet, they can be easily compared. Choice d is clearly the largest.

   a. **There** are 43,560 sq ft in 1 acre. 3 × 43,560 = 130,680, so 3 acres equals 130,680 square feet.

   b. **There** are 9 sq ft in 1 sq yd. (9 sq. ft × 15 sq. yds. = 135 sq. ft.) 15 square yards equals 135 square feet.

   c. **We** have to apply two conversion factors. First, there are 640 acres in 1 section. 640 acres divided by 128 = 5 acres. Second, there are 43,560 sq ft in 1 acre. 5 acres × 43,560 sq. ft. = 217,800 square feet.

   d. **Pay** careful attention to the wording here. "A 1/2 mile square" means a square that is 1/2 mile on each side. One mile is 5,280 feet, therefore 1/2 mile equals 2,640 ft. (5,280 × 1/2 = 2,640 ft.) To find the square feet, multiply length times width: 2,640 ft. × 2,640 ft. = 6,969,600 square feet.
   Page 457

16. **(a)**   6 acres equals 261,360 square feet. If her lots are 2,640 square feet each (60 feet × 44 feet), then she can subdivide the parcel into 99 equal lots: 261,360 sq, ft, ÷ 2,640 sq,ft, = 99. The lots sell for $20,000 each or $1,980,000 total: 99 × $20,000 = $1,980,000. **Page 460**

17. **(c)**   First, convert measurements to feet (300 ft W, 525 ft SE, and 432 ft N). Then, draw the figure from the description.

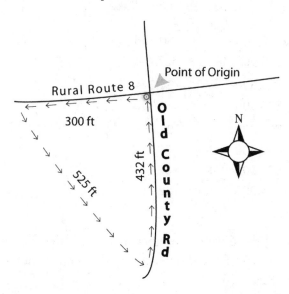

The **formula** for a triangular shape is ½ × base × height, so the area for this lot is ½ × 300 × 432, which equals 64,800 square feet. The question wants it converted into acreage, so divide this number by 43,560. This gives an answer of 1.49 acres, or 1.5 rounded. **Page 456**

18. **(b)**   First, calculate the perimeter of the home. The cost of a foundation is typically measured in linear feet, so add the four sides of the rectangle 36.33 feet + 38.83 feet + 36.33 feet + 38.83 feet to get the linear measurement of 150.32 feet. Multiply 150.32 linear feet by the cost per linear foot. 150.32 times $18.63 equals $2,800.46 for the cost of the foundation. **Page 457**

19. **(a)**   Use the formula for a cylinder and plug in the provided dimensions. The formula is $R^2 \times \pi \times H$, so 81 square feet × 3.14 × 41 feet = 10,428 cubic feet. At $15.00 per cubic foot with a regional multiplier of 0.98 the cost-new for the silo will be $153,291. Using the time age/life method (90 ÷100), the structure has approximately 90% of its life remaining, so apply that percentage to the cost-new to get $138,000 rounded. **Page 456**

20. **(a)**   Add all the variates together and divide by the number of variates. 649,300 ÷ 9 = $72,144. **Page 463**

21. **(b)**   Organize the figures into an array from lowest priced to highest priced and then find the variate in the middle. Since there are nine variates in this sample, the fifth variate in the array will be the median. **Page 464**

22. **(d)** The most frequently occurring variate is $95,000. **Page 465**

23. **(c)** Subtract the lowest-priced home from the highest-priced home to calculate the range of the sample. $103,000 – $15,000 = $88,000. **Page 465**

24. **(c)** Subtract each variate from the population's mean.

Variate	Deviation
$15,000	$57,144
$103,000	$30,856
$99,900	$27,756
$67,500	$4,644
$95,000	$22,856
$95,000	$22,856
$66,000	$6,144
$33,000	$39,144
$74,900	$2,756

Then, **add** those figures together (ignoring if they are positive or negative), and divide the sum of the differences by the number of variates: $214,156 ÷ 9 = $23,795. **Page 466**

25. **(d)** Subtract each variate from the population's mean and then square them.

Variate	Difference Squared
$15,000	$3,265,436,736
$103,000	$952,092,736
$99,900	$770,395,536
$67,500	$21,566,736
$95,000	$522,396,736
$95,000	$522,396,736
$66,000	$37,748,736
$33,000	$1,532,252,736
$74,900	$7,595,536

Find **the** total of the squared differences ($7,631,882,224), divide by 9 ($847,986,914), and then take the square root of this figure ($29,120). **Page 467**

GLOSSARY

A

absorption analysis

A study of the number of units of residential or nonresidential property that can be sold or leased over a given period of time in a defined location.

absorption period

The estimated time period required to sell, lease, place in use, or trade the subject property in its marketing area at prevailing prices or rental rates.

abstraction method

See extraction method.

abut

To border on, touch, as contiguous lots along a border or with a projecting part.

abutter's rights

The reasonable right to light, air, and visibility that a property enjoys from another.

access right

The right of an owner to have ingress to and egress from owner's property over adjoining property.

accession

An addition to property through the efforts of man or by natural forces.

accessory building

A building separate from the main structure on a property.

accretion

Accession by natural forces, e.g., alluvium.

accrued depreciation

Depreciation that has already occurred. It is the difference between the cost to replace the property and the property's current market value.

acquisition appraisal

A market value appraisal of property condemned or otherwise acquired for public use, to establish the compensation to be paid to the owner.

actual age

The number of years elapsed since a structure's construction. Also called physical age, real age, or chronological age.

actual depreciation

The depreciation occurring as a result of physical, functional, or economic forces, causing loss in value to a building.

adjacent

Lying near, close, contiguous, neighboring, bordering, or juxtaposed.

adjoining

In contact with, abutting on, or lying next to, especially in actual contact along a line.

adjustment

In the sales comparison approach, a dollar or percentage amount that is added to or subtracted from the sale price of a comparable property, to account for a feature that the property has or does not have which differentiates it from the subject property.

adjustment grid

Lists important items affecting value such as site area, location, design and appeal, quality, condition, gross building area, basement area, room count, view, age, amenities, etc. Also known as a matrix.

adjustment guidelines

Per Fannie Mae, state that a single line item adjustment should not exceed 10% of the sales price of the comparable.

administrative expense

The cost of direct management and services related to the management of property.

Advisory Opinions

The Appraisal Standards Board (ASB) issues Advisory Opinions to illustrate the applicability of USPAP in specific situations and offers advice for the resolution of appraisal issues and problems.

aesthetic value

Relating to beauty, rather than to functional considerations.

aesthetic zoning

Regulates the appearance of buildings in the area.

A-frame roof

A roof whose two sides slope upward at a steep pitch and meet at the top.

age/life method

A method of computing accrued depreciation in which the cost of a building is depreciated at a fixed annual percentage rate. This is the method most frequently used by residential appraisers. Also known as the straight-line method.

agents of production
Land, labor, capital, and management. See principle of increasing and decreasing returns and principle of surplus productivity.

air rights
The rights in real property for the reasonable use of the air space above the surface of the land.

airspace
The interior area which an apartment, office, or condominium occupies. Airspace is considered real property to a reasonable height. For example, an owner or developer of condominiums may sell the airspace as real property.

allocation method
The allocation of the appraised total value between land and improvements. Allocation may be made using a ratio comparing building value to the total price (or value).

allowance for vacancy and collection losses
The percentage of potential gross income that will be lost due to vacant units, collection losses, or both.

amenities
Features that add value to a property.

amenity value
That value, difficult to measure in monetary terms, that is attributable to a property because of pleasant surroundings, such as a pretty view, quiet area, or ideal climate.

annuity method
A method of capitalization that treats income from real property as a fixed, regular return on an investment. For the annuity method to be applied the lessee must be reliable and the lease must be long term.

appraisal
An unbiased estimate or opinion of the property value on a given date.

appraisal process
An orderly systematic method to arrive at an estimate of value.

appraisal report
A written statement in which an appraiser gives his or her opinion of value.

appraisal review
The review of an appraiser's analysis, research, and conclusions by another appraiser.

Appraisal Standards Board (ASB)
Part of The Appraisal Foundation, the ASB develops, interprets, and amends USPAP.

appraised value
An appraiser's estimate of the amount of a particular value, such as assessed value, insurable value, or market value, based on the particular assignment.

appraiser
A person qualified by education, training, and experience who is hired to estimate the value of real and personal property based on experience, judgment, facts, and use of formal appraisal processes.

Appraiser Qualification Board (AQB)
Part of The Appraisal Foundation and responsible for establishing minimum requirements for licensed and certified appraisers and for licensing and certifying examinations.

appreciation
An increase in the worth or value of property over time.

approaches to value
Any of the following three methods used to estimate the value of real estate: sales comparison approach, cost approach, and income capitalization approach.

area
The space or size of a surface that is defined by a set of boundaries.

arm's-length transaction
A transaction, such as a sale of property, in which all parties involved are acting in their own self-interest and are under no undue influence or pressure from other parties.

aseptic system
The clean water system.

assemblage
The process of putting several smaller, less valuable lots together under a single ownership.

assessed value
Value placed on land and buildings by a public tax assessor as a basis for use in levying annual real estate taxes.

assessment roll
A list of all taxable property showing the assessed value of each parcel, establishing the tax base.

assessor
The official who has the responsibility of determining assessed values.

association agreement
Set of conditions and restrictions applying to all properties in a planned unit development, condominium, or other community project.

attached housing
Any number of houses or other dwellings, which are physically attached to one another.

automated valuation models (AVM)
Computer software programs that analyze data using automated systems, such as regression analysis and/or so-called artificial intelligence.

average deviation
In statistics, the measure of how far the average variate differs from the mean of all variates.

avigation easement
An easement over private property near an airport that limits the height of structures and trees in order to keep the take off and landing paths of airports clear.

avulsion
A sudden and perceptible loss of land by the action of water, as by a sudden change in the course of a river.

band of investment technique
Method of estimating interest and capitalization rates, based on a weighted average of the mortgage interest rate (or other cost of borrowed funds) and the rate of return on equity required.

bargain and sale deed
Any deed that recites a consideration and purports to convey the real estate.

baseline
A survey line running east and west, used as a reference when mapping land.

basement
A building's lowest story, which is partially or entirely below ground.

bearing wall
A wall or partition that supports a part of a building, usually a roof or floor above.

benchmark
Definite identification characteristics familiar to the appraiser and relied upon in his or her further analysis of a property. A location indicated on a durable marker by surveyors.

betterment
The enhanced value of real property from improvements.

bias
A preference or inclination that precludes an appraiser's impartiality, independence, or objectivity in an assignment.

blighted area
A district affected by extensive or numerous detrimental influences that have caused real property values to seriously decline.

blockbusting
The unscrupulous practice of inducing panic selling of homes at prices below market value, particularly by exploiting neighborhoods in which the racial makeup is or appears to be changing.

book depreciation
An accounting concept referring to an allowance taken to provide for recovery of invested capital.

book value
The current value, for accounting purposes, of an asset expressed as original cost plus capital additions minus accumulated depreciation.

bracketing
When using the sales comparison approach, selection of market data so that the subject is contained within a range of data.

breakdown method
A method of computing depreciation in which the appraiser estimates the loss in value for each type of depreciation separately. Also known as observed condition method.

breezeway
A covered porch or passage, open on two sides and connecting house and garage or two parts of the house.

brownfield
An abandoned commercial or industrial site or under-utilized neighborhood where redevelopment is complicated by actual or perceived contamination.

buffer zone
A segment of land between two disparate municipal zones acting as a shield to keep one zone from encroaching upon the other. Often used to separate residential districts from commercial areas.

building capitalization rate
The sum of the discount and capital recapture rates for a building.

building code
Municipal ordinance that regulates the type and quality of building materials and methods of construction permitted.

building components
Parts of a building.

building residual technique
Technique of income capitalization in which the net income to the building (after deducting the income required for the land) is capitalized into an estimated value for the building.

building restrictions
Restrictions that limit the way a property can be used. They may appear in building codes or title documents.

built-ins
Cabinets or similar features built as part of the house.

bulk zoning
Controls density and prevents overcrowding. Bulk zoning regulates setbacks, building height, and percentage of open area.

buyer's market
A market containing more supply than demand.

capital
Money and/or property owned or used by a person or business to acquire goods or services.

capital assets
Assets of a permanent nature used in the production of an income, such as land, buildings, machinery, and equipment. Under income tax law, these are usually distinguished from inventory, which are assets held for sale to customers in the ordinary course of the taxpayer's trade or business.

capital gain
At resale of a capital item, the amount by which the net sale proceeds exceed the adjusted cost basis (book value).

capital improvement
Any permanent improvement made to real estate for the purpose of increasing the useful life of the property or increasing the property's value.

capital recapture
The return of an investment.

capitalization
The process that can be employed to convert income to value.

capitalization method
See income capitalization method.

capitalization rate
The rate of interest, which is considered a reasonable return on the investment, and used in the process of determining value, based upon net income. It may also be described as the yield rate that is necessary to attract the money of the average investor to a particular type of investment.

carport
A roofed space having at least one side open to the weather.

cash equivalency technique
Method of adjusting a sales price downward to reflect the increase in price due to assumption or procurement by buyers of a loan at an interest rate lower than the prevailing market rate.

central tendency
The numeric value that is suggested as a typical value in a statistical sample.

certification
A signed and dated statement included in an appraisal report that the appraiser has performed an appraisal in an unbiased and professional manner and that all assumptions and limiting conditions are set forth in the report.

Certified General Appraiser
An individual who has met specific education, experience, and examination requirements. May appraise any property.

Certified Residential Appraiser
An individual who has met specific education, experience, and examination requirements. May appraise any 1-4 unit residential properties without regard to complexity.

characteristics
Distinguishing features of a property.

chronological age
The number of years elapsed since a structure was built. Also known as actual or physical age.

client
The person who employs an agent to perform a service for a fee.

closing costs
The numerous expenses buyers and sellers normally incur in the transfer of ownership of real property.

cloud on title
A claim, encumbrance, or condition that impairs the title to real property until disproved or eliminated as, for example, through a quitclaim deed or a quiet title legal action.

code of ethics
A set of rules and principles expressing a standard of accepted conduct for a professional group and governing the relationship of members to each other and to the organization.

collateral
(1) The property subject to the security interest. (2) Anything of value a borrower pledges as security.

collection loss
A loss incurred if tenants do not pay their agreed-upon rents.

collusion
An agreement between two or more persons to defraud another of rights by the forms of law or to obtain an object forbidden by law.

color of title
That which appears to be good title but is not title in fact.

Comments
Extensions of USPAP DEFINITIONS, Rules, and Standards Rules that provide interpretation, and establish context and conditions for application.

common area
An entire common interest subdivision except the separate interests therein.

common interest development (CID)
A common-interest development combining the individual ownership of private dwellings with the shared ownership of common facilities of the entire project. The common areas are usually governed by a homeowners' association. Also known as common interest subdivision.

community
Part of a metropolitan area, a number of neighborhoods that tend toward common interests and problems.

community property
All property acquired by a husband and wife during a valid marriage (excluding certain separate property).

comparable sales (comps)
Sales that have similar characteristics to the subject property and are used for analysis in the appraisal process. Commonly called "comps", they are recently sold properties similarly situated in a similar market.

comparative market analysis (CMA)
A comparison analysis that real estate brokers use, while working with a seller, to determine an appropriate listing price for the seller's house.

comparative unit method
A method for estimating reproduction or replacement cost, using typical per unit costs for the type of construction being estimated. See square-foot method.

comparison approach
A real estate appraisal method, which compares a given property with similar or comparable surrounding properties. Also known as sales comparison approach or market comparison approach.

COMPETENCY RULE
Per USPAP, identifies requirements for experience and knowledge both when completing an appraisal and prior to accepting an appraisal assignment.

complete appraisal
The act or process of estimating value or an estimate of value, performed without invoking the Departure Rule of the Uniform Standards of Professional Appraisal Practice.

component
One of the features making up the whole property.

composite rate
A capitalization rate composed of interest and recapture in separately determined amounts.

comps
See comparable sales.

concessions
Additional value granted by a buyer or seller to entice another party to complete a transaction.

conclusion
(1) The final estimate of value, realized from facts, data, experience, and judgment, set out in an appraisal. (2) An appraiser's certified conclusion.

condemnation
The process to exercise the power of the government to take private property from an owner for the public good, paying fair market value.

conditional use
A use that does not meet the current use requirements but may be allowed by obtaining a special permit.

conditions of sale
Circumstances of the sale such as exposure time, marketing process, and buyer motivation. Unusual conditions may affect the final purchase price of a comparable sale and cause the sales price to reflect the market improperly.

condominium
A housing unit consisting of a separate fee interest in a particular specific space, plus an undivided interest in all common or public areas of the development. Each unit owner has a deed, separate financing and pays the property taxes for the unit.

Conduct
The section of the USPAP ETHICS RULE that identifies issues regarding appraisers' conduct.

Confidentiality
Per USPAP, the section of the ETHICS RULE which states that the appraiser must protect the confidential nature of the appraiser-client relationship and is obligated to obey all confidentiality and privacy laws.

conforming loans
Loans which conform to Fannie Mae guidelines, which set loan limits to a certain amount.

construction classification
A system that rates fireproofing of structures according to the relative fire resistance of the structures, taking into account the type of frame, walls, and roof. Class A is the most fireproof, descending to Class D, the least fire resistant.

contiguous
In actual contact, touching.

contingent
Conditional, uncertain, conditioned upon the occurrence or nonoccurrence of some future event.

contingent valuation methodology (CVM)
A method used to identify how a particular feature affects the value of a property by asking those who are knowledgeable about that market (other appraisers and agents) when no sales data is available.

contour
The surface configuration of land. Shown on maps as a line through points of equal elevation.

contract rent
The rent established by agreement or contract.

contributory value
Value given by appraisers to site improvements after identifying them.

conventional loan
Any loan made by lenders without any governmental guarantees (FHA-insured or VA-guaranteed).

conversion
Change from one character or use to another, as converting an apartment building to condominium use.

cooperative (co-op)
(1) A form of legal ownership with each owner holding a stated ownership percentage in the cooperative association. The association owns the land and buildings, and grants each owner the permanent right to occupy the specific dwelling unit, as well as the right to the joint use of the common areas. (2) A residential multifamily building.

coordination
As an agent of production, it is management.

corner influence
The effect on a property's value due to its location on or near a corner.

corner lot
A lot at the confluence or convergence of two streets.

cost
The expenses in money, labor, material, or sacrifices in acquiring or producing something.

cost approach
An approach to value in which a value estimate of a property is derived by estimating the replacement cost of the improvements, deducting the estimated accrued depreciation, and then adding the market value of the land. Also known as the summation method.

cost basis
Original price paid for a property.

cost index
Figure representing construction cost at a particular time in relation to construction cost at an earlier time, prepared by a cost reporting or indexing service.

cost multiplier
Regional or local factor used in adjusting published construction cost figures to estimate local costs.

cost services
Companies who collect and provide information regarding cost trends.

cost-to-cure method of depreciation
Method of estimating accrued depreciation based on the cost to cure or repair observed building defects.

courtyard home
A zero-lot-line home.

crawlspace
An unfinished accessible space below the first floor of a building with no basement.

credible
Something worthy of belief.

credit
A bookkeeping entry on the right side of an account, recording the reduction or elimination of an asset or an expense or the creation of or addition to a liability or item of equity or revenue.

cubic-foot method
Similar to the square-foot method, except that it takes height as well as area into consideration. The cubic contents of buildings are compared instead of just the square footage.

cul-de-sac lot
A lot situated at the end of a dead-end street that has a turn-around area.

cumulative zoning
Zoning laws that allow so-called higher uses (residential) to exist in lower use zones (industrial), but not vice versa.

curable depreciation
Items of physical deterioration and functional obsolescence which are economically feasible to repair or replace.

curb appeal
A phrase implying an informal valuation of a property based on observation and experience.

cut
The level building site or the space created in areas of sloping land when earth is removed. Unlike fill material, which can be unstable, a building site from a cut is generally a more solid base for structures.

cyclical movement
The sequential and recurring changes in economic activity of a business cycle, moving from prosperity through recession, depression, recovery, and back again to prosperity.

data
Information pertinent to a specific appraisal assignment. Data may be general (relating to the economic background and the region), local (relating to the city and the neighborhood), or specific (relating to the subject property and comparable properties in the market).

data services
The numerous companies engaged in the business of selling data to real estate appraisers.

data sources
Any of a variety of sources used by appraisers when collecting general, local, and specific information.

date of appraisal
The specific point in time when an appraiser designates the value of a home. Often stipulated as the date of inspection.

debit
A bookkeeping entry on the left side of an account, recording the creation of or addition to an asset or an expense or the reduction or elimination of a liability or item of equity or revenue.

debt capital
The amount borrowed by the buyer to purchase a property.

decline phase
Third phase in the cycle of a neighborhood, generally marked by delayed repairs and deterioration of buildings.

deed
A formal legal document used to transfer title from one person to another.

deed in lieu of foreclosure
A deed to real property accepted by a lender from a defaulting borrower to avoid the necessity of foreclosure proceedings by the lender.

deed of reconveyance
Document used to transfer legal title from the trustee back to the borrower after a debt secured by a trust deed has been paid to the lender.

deed of trust
A security instrument that conveys naked legal title of real property.

deed restrictions
Limitations in the deed to a property that dictate certain uses that may or may not be made of the property.

deferred maintenance
Building maintenance that has been postponed or neglected. A type of physical deterioration.

define the problem
Part of the appraisal process, includes identifying the client and other intended users, the intended use of the appraiser's opinions and conclusions, the type and definition of the value sought, and the effective date of the appraiser's opinions and conclusions.

DEFINITIONS section
The first section of USPAP containing definitions of terms specific to USPAP.

demand
The desire to possess plus the ability to buy.

demographic profile
A profile of a specific area that contains general demographic information such as employment, education, average age, average salary ranges, gender, occupation, number of children, etc.

demographics
The statistical characteristics of human population studies.

Department of Housing and Urban Development (HUD)
A federal department active in national housing programs, including but not limited to urban renewal, public housing, and FHA subsidy programs. HUD oversees FHA, Fannie Mae, Ginnie Mae, and FMIC, among others.

Department of Veteran Affairs (VA)
Functions to guarantee loans to purchase and construct homes for eligible veterans and their spouses.

DEPARTURE RULE
This USPAP rule allows appraisers to "depart" from certain Standards Rules in particular situations. Replaced by the SCOPE OF WORK RULE in 2006 USPAP.

depreciated cost method
Method for adjusting comparable sales in which adjustments are calculated from an analysis of the depreciated replacement cost for each differentiating feature.

depreciation
(1) In appraisal, a loss in value from any cause. (2) A tax advantage of ownership of income property.

depreciation rate
The degree of lessening in value of an object or property, usually applied on an annual scale.

depression
A phase of the business cycle marked by industrial and commercial stagnation, scarcity of goods and money, low prices, and mass unemployment.

depth
Distance from the front lot line to the rear lot line.

depth table
A statistical table that may be used to estimate the value of the added depth of a lot.

detached house
A house surrounded by permanent open spaces.

deterioration
A worsening, impairment, or degeneration.

development method (land development method)
Method of vacant land valuation in which development costs and developer's profits are subtracted from estimated gross sales, resulting in a raw land value estimate.

development phase
First phase of the life cycle of a neighborhood, consisting of initial construction of improvements on vacant land.

diminished utility
A loss in the usefulness of a property resulting in a loss in property value.

direct capitalization method
Income capitalization technique in which value is estimated by dividing net operating income by the overall capitalization rate.

direct costs
All of the costs directly involved with the construction of a structure, including labor, materials, equipment, design and engineering, and subcontractors' fees.

direct lender
Lends their own funds and handles the entire loan process from origination to funding.

direct market comparison approach
See sales comparison approach.

discount rate
The interest rate that is charged by the Federal Reserve Bank to its member banks for loans.

discounted cash flow
Estimated future investment returns mathematically discounted to their present value.

distressed property
Property foreclosed on by the lender.

documents
Legal instruments, such as mortgages, contracts, deeds, options, wills, and bills of sale.

downzoning
A zone change from a high-density use to a lower density use. For example, a commercial zone to a light industrial zone.

drainage
The removal of excess surface water or groundwater from land by means of ditches or drains.

dry rot
A wood fungus that thrives in damp conditions and turns wood fibers into powder.

duress
The use of force to get agreement in accepting a contract.

easement

A non-possessory right to enter or use someone else's land for a specified purpose.

easement appurtenant

An easement that is connected to a particular property and is transferred along with that property. Each easement appurtenant involves two properties—the servient tenement and the dominant tenement.

easement in gross

An easement that is not appurtenant to any one parcel. For example, public utilities to install power lines.

ecology

The relationship between organisms and their environment.

economic age

Estimated age of a building based on its condition and usefulness.

economically feasible

Financially possible, reasonable, or likely. One of the tests of highest and best use.

economic base

The companies that provide jobs for a community or defined geographic area.

economic life

The estimated period over which a building may be profitably used. Also known as useful life.

economic obsolescence

Depreciation caused by changes in the economy that negatively affects the subject property's value.

economic rent

What a leased property would be expected to rent for under current market conditions if the property were vacant and available for rent. Also known as market rent.

economics

The science that studies the production, distribution, and consumption of wealth.

economic trend

Pattern of related changes in some aspect of the economy.

effective age

The age of a building based on its condition and usefulness. The apparent age based on the condition of the structure, instead of the chronological age.

effective date

The specific day the conclusion of value applies whether it is a present, past, or future date.

effective demand

Demand or desire coupled with purchasing power.

effective gross income (EGI)

The amount of income that remains after vacancy and credit losses are deducted from gross income.

egress

A way to exit a property.

element of comparison

Any aspect of a real estate transaction or any characteristic of the property that may affect the property's sales price.

elements of value

Four prerequisites that must be present for an object to have value: demand, utility, scarcity, and transferability.

elevation sheet

A labeled diagram or cutaway of a home detailing its features and building components, both interior and exterior.

Ellwood technique

A mortgage/equity method of capitalization, expressed in tables.

eminent domain

The right of the government to take private property from an owner, for the public good, paying fair market value.

encroachment

The unauthorized placement of permanent improvements that intrude on adjacent property owned by another.

encumbrance

An interest in real property that is held by someone who is not the property owner.

entrepreneur

One who assumes the risk and management of business.

entrepreneurial profit

A market-derived figure that represents the compensation the owner or developer actually receives from developing the property.

entry-level home

A type of home for first-time buyers.

environment surroundings

All the external conditions and influences affecting the life and development of an organism, for example, human behavior, society.

Environmental Impact Report (EIR)

A formal report assessing the results or impact of a proposed activity or development upon the environment.

environmental obsolescence
See economic obsolescence.

equity
The difference between the market value of a home and the loan amount.

equity build-up
The gradual increase of the borrower's equity in a property caused by amortization of loan principal.

equity capital
The amount a buyer invests into a property.

equity capitalization rate
(1) Factor used to estimate the value of the equity in the band of investment method of capitalization and other mortgage and equity techniques. (2) The equity cash flow divided by the equity value.

equity investors
Investors using venture capital to take an unsecured and thus relatively risky part in an investment.

erosion
The gradual wearing away of land by natural processes.

escrow
A small and short-lived trust arrangement used to close real estate transactions.

estate
The ownership interest or claim a person has in real property. It defines the nature, degree, extent, and duration of a person's ownership in land.

estate at sufferance
A tenancy created when one is in wrongful possession of real estate even though the original possession may have been legal.

estate at will
A tenancy that may be ended by the unilateral decision of either party. There is no agreed-upon termination date, and either party must give 30 days notice before ending the tenancy.

estate for years
A leasehold estate with a definite end date. The lease must be renegotiated.

estate from period to period
A leasehold estate that does not need to be renegotiated upon each renewal.

estimate
(1) A preliminary opinion of value. (2) To appraise or determine value.

estimated remaining life
The period of time (years) it takes for improvements to become valueless.

ETHICS RULE
Per USPAP, identifies the requirements for "integrity, impartiality, objectivity, independent judgment, and ethical conduct."

evaluation
An analysis of a property and/or its attributes in which a value estimate is not required.

excess land
Surplus land beyond that which is needed to support the property's highest and best use.

excess rent
The amount by which the total contract rent exceeds market rent.

execute
(1) To perform or complete. (2) To sign.

execution sale
The forced sale of a property to satisfy a money judgment.

expansible house
Home designed for further expansion and additions in the future.

expenditures
Money laid out, disbursed, or expended.

expense ratio
See operating expense ratio.

expenses
The costs incurred in an enterprise. In appraisal, expenses are estimated on an annual basis regardless of the period in which they are incurred or paid.

expert testimony
Testimony given in a court trial by a person qualified by the court as an expert on a particular subject, for example, as an expert witness on real estate values.

expert witness
One qualified to give expert testimony in a court of law on a particular subject, such as medicine, engineering, or real estate appraising.

external obsolescence
A type of depreciation occurring because of negative influences outside of the specific property site (i.e. an airport flight pattern). See economic obsolescence.

externalities

Outside influences that may have a positive or negative effect on property value.

extraction method

A method of determining the land value of a comparable property by deducting the depreciated costs of the improvements on that property from the property's known sale price. The remaining value represents value attributable to the land. This method is a variation on the allocation method and is based on the same principles. Also known as abstraction method.

extraordinary assumption

Per USPAP, "an assumption, directly related to a specific assignment, which, if found to be false, could alter the appraiser's opinions or conclusions."

facade

The face of a building, especially the front face.

factory-built housing

Housing built in a factory instead of on site. Includes manufactured, modular, panelized, and precut homes.

fair market value

See market value.

fair rental value

See rent, economic.

feasibility study

An analysis of a proposed subject or property with emphasis on the attainable income, probable expenses, and most advantageous use and design. The purpose of such a study is to ascertain the probable success or failure of the project under consideration. A study of the cost-benefit relationship of an economic endeavor.

Federal Emergency Management Agency (FEMA)

A government agency involved with all the different aspects of emergency management from preparation to recovery and prevention.

Federal Housing Administration (FHA)

A government agency that insures private mortgage loans for financing of homes and home repairs.

federally related transaction

Any real estate transaction involving federal insurance or assistance.

fee simple absolute

An estate in fee with no restrictions on its use. It is the largest, most complete ownership recognized by law.

fee simple estate

The most complete form of ownership of real property, which can be passed by descent or by will after the owner's death. Also known as estate of inheritance or estate in fee.

fiduciary duty

The duty owed by an agent to act in the highest good faith toward the principal and not to obtain any advantage over the latter by the slightest misrepresentation, concealment, duress, or pressure.

fill

(1) Earth used to raise the existing ground level. (2) In residential real estate, base material that is borrowed from another source and is not generally as stable as a cut.

filtering

The process whereby higher priced properties become available to lower income buyers.

final value estimate

The appraiser's estimate of the defined value of the subject property, arrived at by reconciling the estimates of value, derived from the sales comparison, cost, and income approaches.

Financial Institutions Reform, Recovery, and Enforcement Act (FIRREA)

A federal law passed in 1989 to provide guidelines for the regulation of financial institutions. One part of the law requires a state license or certification for the performance of federally related real estate transactions (with de minimus exceptions).

finished area

The enclosed area in a home that is suitable for year-round use.

fire door

A door of fire-resistant material to prevent or retard the spread of fire.

firewall

A wall of fire-resistant material to prevent or retard the spread of fire.

FIRREA

See Financial Institutions Reform, Recovery, and Enforcement Act.

fiscal year

A 12-month accounting period not related to the actual calendar year.

fixed expenses

Operating costs that are more or less permanent and that vary little from year to year regardless of occupancy.

fixity of location
The physical characteristic of real estate that subjects it to the influence of its surroundings.

fixture
Personal property that has become affixed to real estate.

flag lot
A lot located so that access can be had only at the side of another lot.

flipping
Buying a property at one price and quickly selling it to another at an inflated price.

flood plain
An area that is adjacent to a river or watercourse and is subject to periodic flooding.

floor plan
A depiction of the floor layout including each room's size and connection with other rooms.

foreclosure
The legal procedure by which mortgaged property is sold to satisfy a debt when the borrower has defaulted on the loan.

form report
Written appraisal report, presented on a standardized form or checklist.

fraud
An act meant to deceive in order to get someone to part with something of value.

freehold estate
An estate in real property which continues for an indefinite period of time. It differs from a leasehold estate, which allows possession for a limited time.

frequency distribution
The arrangement of data into groups according to the frequency with which they appear in the data set.

front foot
Measurement in feet of the width of a property on the side facing the street.

frontage
The width of a property on the side facing a street.

frostline
The depth of frost penetration in the soil. Varies in different parts of the country. Footings should be placed below this depth to prevent movement.

fully amortized note
The most common type of loan with institutional lenders. Interest is charged on the outstanding principal balance at the rate and term agreed upon by the lender and borrower in a loan.

functional obsolescence
A type of depreciation stemming from poor architectural design, lack of modern facilities, out-of-date equipment, changes in styles of construction or in utility demand.

functional utility
The combined factors of usefulness with desirability.

future benefits
The anticipated benefits the present owner will receive from the property in the future.

future interest
An interest in real property that will take effect at a future time.

future value
The estimated lump-sum value of money or property at a date in the future.

gable roof
A roof with two sides sloping upward and meeting at the top.

gambrel roof
A curb roof, having a steep lower slope with a flatter upper slope above.

garage
A building or enclosure primarily designed or used for motor vehicles.

general warranty deed
A deed which conveys not only all the grantor's interests in and title to the property to the grantee, but also warrants that if the title is defective or has a cloud, the grantee may hold the grantor liable.

gentrification
A form of revitalization that occurs when run down properties are renovated or rehabilitated.

geodetic survey
A U.S. government survey generally used in identifying government lands and coastal areas.

gift deed
Used to make a gift of property to a grantee, usually a close friend or relative.

going concern value

The value existing in an established business property compared with the value of selling the real estate and other assets of a concern whose business is not yet established. The term takes into account the goodwill and earning capacity of a business.

goodwill

An intangible, but salable, asset of a business derived from the expectation of continued public patronage.

Government National Mortgage Association

An agency of HUD, called Ginnie Mae, that functions in the secondary mortgage market.

government survey system

See rectangular survey system.

grade

Ground level at the perimeter of the building.

grading

A process used when the level or elevation of the ground has to be changed or altered using bladed machines that scrape the earth.

graduated lease

A long-term lease that provides for adjustments in the rental rate on the basis of some future determination.

graphic analysis

A technique used to identify and measure adjustments to the sale prices of comparable properties.

grandfather clause

A legal clause that keeps a law from being retroactive. For example, a grandfather clause in a zoning law would allow the continuation of a previously legal use even if the new zoning law does not permit such use.

grant deed

A deed in which the grantor warrants that he or she has not previously conveyed the property being granted, has not encumbered the property except as disclosed, and will convey to the grantee any title he or she may acquire afterwards.

gross building area (GBA)

All enclosed floor areas, as measured along a building's outside perimeter.

gross income

Total income from property before any expenses are deducted.

gross income multiplier (GIM)

A figure which, when multiplied by the annual gross income, will equal the property's market value. The amount of the GIM must be obtained from recent comparable sales since it varies with specific properties and areas.

gross leasable area

Total space designed for occupancy and exclusive use of tenants, measured from outside wall surfaces to the center of shared interior walls.

gross lease

A lease agreement in which the tenant pays an agreed-upon sum as rent and the landlord pays any other expenses such as taxes, maintenance, or insurance. Also known as a flat, fixed, or straight lease.

gross living area (GLA)

The total finished, habitable, above-grade space, measured along the building's outside perimeter. This generally excludes garages and screened patios or porches ("Florida rooms").

gross rent

Income (calculated annually or monthly) received from rental units before any expenses are deducted.

gross rent multiplier (GRM)

A figure which, when multiplied by the monthly rental income, will equal the property's market value. The amount of the GRM must be obtained from recent comparable sales since it varies with specific properties and areas.

ground lease

A lease of land only on which the lessee usually owns the building or is required to build as specified by the lease. Such leases are usually long-term net leases.

ground rent

Earnings of improved property credited to earnings of the ground itself after allowance has been made for earnings of improvements.

hidden amenities

Assets of a property that contribute to its value, but are not readily apparent. Examples might include upgraded or premium building materials.

highest and best use (HBU)

The use, from among reasonably probable and adequately supported alternative uses, that is physically possible, legally permitted, economically feasible, and maximally productive. This is the starting point for appraisal.

hip roof

A roof with four sides sloping upward to meet at a ridge.

historic cost

Cost of a property at the time it was constructed or purchased.

holding period
The length of time the property will be used as an investment.

homogeneous
Of the same kind or nature.

house
A single-family detached residence.

houseboat
Essentially a barge designed and equipped for use as a dwelling.

HUD
See Department of Housing and Urban Development.

HUD-1 Statement
A standardized, itemized list, published by the U.S. Department of Housing and Urban Development (HUD), of all anticipated CLOSING COSTS connected with a particular property purchase.

hypothetical condition
Defined in USPAP as "that which is contrary to what exists but is supposed for the purpose of analysis."

improved value
A value placed upon a property when proposed improvements have been completed.

improvements
Additions made to property to enhance value or extend useful life. This term is typically used to refer to buildings and other structures that are permanently attached to the land.

incentive zoning
Allows a developer to exceed the limitations set by a zoning law if the developer agrees to fulfill conditions specified in the law.

income approach
An appraisal method that estimates the present worth of future benefits from ownership of a property to determine that property's value. Also known as income capitalization approach.

income capitalization method
Method for estimating depreciation by comparing the subject's capitalized value to its replacement cost new or by determining loss in rental income attributable to a depreciated item and applying a gross rent multiplier to that figure.

income forecast
Gross or net income estimate.

income property
Property that is purchased for its income-producing capabilities.

income stream
Actual or estimated flow of net earnings over time.

increment
An increase. Most frequently used to refer to the increase of value of land that accompanies population growth and increasing wealth in the community. The term unearned increment is used in this connection, since values are supposed to have increased without effort on the part of the owner.

incurable depreciation
Building defects or problems that would cost more to repair than the anticipated value increase from such repair.

index method
Method for estimating construction costs that adjusts the original costs to the current cost level by a multiplier obtained from a published cost index.

indicated value
Value estimate calculated or produced by an appraisal approach.

indirect costs
All of the time and money costs involved in a construction project that are not directly involved with construction itself. Examples are loan fees, interest, legal fees, and marketing costs.

industrial property
Land and/or improvements adapted for industrial use.

inflation
The increase in the general price level of goods and services.

inspection
The examination of a property, its buildings or other amenities.

instrument
A formal legal document such as a contract, deed, or will.

insurable value
The highest reasonable value that can be placed on property for insurance purposes.

intangible property
Property that lacks a physical form.

intangible value
That value attributable to a property that is difficult to determine precisely.

intellectual property (IP)

A general term for various legal rights, which attach to certain types of information, ideas, or other intangibles.

intended users

Per USPAP, parties intending to use an appraisal.

interest

(1) The charge for the use of money. (2) A legal share of ownership in property.

interest rate

The percentage of interest charged on the principal.

interim use

A short-term and temporary use of a property until it is ready for a more productive highest and best use. Occurs when the highest and best use is expected to change.

interior lot

A lot situated so that its boundaries touch no more than five lots. Generally, it is surrounded by three lots.

internal rate of return

The rate of return generated by an investment over the holding period, considering all future benefits, and discounting them to equal the present value.

intrinsic value

The value inherent in the property itself.

inverse condemnation

An action brought by a private party to force the government to pay just compensation for diminishing the value or use of his or her property.

investment property

Property purchased for expected future return.

investment value

The value of a particular property to a particular investor.

joint appraisal

An appraisal made by two or more appraisers working together.

joint tenancy

A type of ownership interest in which two or more parties own real property as co-owners, with the right of survivorship.

jumbo loans

Loans that exceed the maximum loan limit set by Fannie Mae and Freddie Mac.

junior mortgage

A mortgage recorded subsequently to another mortgage on the same property or made subordinate by agreement to a later-recorded mortgage.

jurisdiction

(1) The authority by which judicial officers take cognizance of and decide causes. (2) The power to hear and determine a cause.

JURISDICTIONAL EXCEPTION RULE

Part of USPAP, preserves the remainder of USPAP if one portion is contrary to a jurisdiction's law or public policy.

just compensation

Fair and reasonable payment due to a private property owner when his or her property is condemned under eminent domain.

key lot

A lot situated so that it is surrounded by the backyards of other lots.

labor

As an agent of production, it is the cost of all operating expenses and wages except management costs.

land

The surface of the earth including airspace, surface rights, mineral rights, and water rights.

land capitalization rate

The rate of return in investment and return of investment for the land only.

land residual technique

Income capitalization technique in which the net income remaining to the land (after income attributable to the building has been deducted) is capitalized into an estimate of value for the land.

landlocked

Property surrounded by other property with no access to a public road or street.

landlord

One who rents property to another. The lessor under a lease.

landscaping

The art of arranging plants, rocks, and lumber around the outside of a property for aesthetic or practical purposes, such as to prevent erosion or provide parking areas.

latent defects

Any defect in a property which is not readily apparent, but which has an impact on the value. Structural damage or termite infestation would be examples of latent defects.

lateral support

The support the soil of an adjoining owner gives to a neighbor's land.

lean-to

A temporary structure for protection from the elements.

lease

A contract between landlord (owner/lessor) and tenant (lessee) which gives the tenant an interest in the property. Also known as a rental agreement.

leased-fee estate

The property owner's interest in the leased property.

leasehold estate

The tenant's interest in the leased property during the term of the lease. This type of estate only has value if the agreed-on rent is less than the market rent. Also known as a less-than-freehold estate.

leasehold value

Market value of the excess of economic rent over contract rent

legal description

A land description recognized by law which can be used to locate a particular piece of property. Lot, block, and tract, government survey, and metes and bounds are types of legal descriptions.

legally permitted

Land uses that are allowed under current zoning and other land use regulations. One of the tests of highest and best use.

lender pressure

A lender directly or indirectly pressuring an appraiser to estimate a property's value at a certain amount.

lessee

Tenant or renter.

lessor

The person (landlord or property owner) who signs the lease to give possession and use to the tenant.

less-than-freehold estate

See leasehold estate.

lien

A claim on the property of another for the payment of a debt. A type of encumbrance.

life estate

An estate that is limited in duration to the life of its owner or the life of another designated person.

limited appraisal

An appraisal developed under and resulting from invoking USPAP's Departure Rule.

linear regression

Statistical technique used to calculate adjustment value or estimate sales price.

liquid assets

Assets that can be promptly converted into cash.

liquidation value

The value that can be received from the marketplace when the property has to be sold immediately.

liquidity

Holdings in or the ability to convert assets to cash or its equivalent. The ease with which a person is able to pay maturing obligations.

littoral

Land bordering a lake, ocean, or sea—as opposed to land bordering a stream or river (running water).

living units

A house or portion thereof providing complete living facilities for one family, including provisions for living, sleeping, eating, cooking, and sanitation.

loan closing

When all conditions have been met, the loan officer authorizes the recording of the trust deed or mortgage.

loan-to-value ratio (LTV)

The ratio of debt to the value of the property.

location

The site, setting, or position of a property or object in relation to other properties or objects.

locational obsolescence

Depreciation caused by the physical location of the subject property and its proximity to a negative influence. See external obsolescence.

long-lived

Structural components that need replacement infrequently, and sometimes never.

lot

A plot of ground.

lot, block, and tract system

A type of legal description that is created when developers divide parcels of land into lots. Each lot in a subdivision is indentified by number, as is the block in which it is located, and each lot and block is in a referenced tract. Also known as lot and block system, subdivision system, or recorded map system.

maintenance expenses
Costs incurred for day-to-day-upkeep, such as management, employee wages and benefits, fuel, utility services, decorating, and repairs.

management
The section of USPAP that discusses the disclosure of certain fees and commissions, identifies prohibited compensation arrangements, and discusses certain prohibited advertising and solicitation issues.

mansard roof
A roof with four sides sloping upward but stopping short of meeting, so that the top of the roof is flat.

margin of security
The difference between the amount of the mortgage loan(s) and the appraised value of the property.

manufactured home
A home built in a factory after June 15, 1976 which must conform to the U.S. government's Manufactured Home Construction and Safety Standards.

marginal land
Land whose value has been diminished due to some internal defect or external condition. In most cases, the cost to correct the flaw or condition is as much or more than the expected return from the property.

marital property
A general term for property owned by married people. Forms of ownership vary from state-to-state.

market
A place or condition suitable for selling and buying.

marketable title
Title that a reasonable purchaser, informed as to the facts and their legal importance and acting with reasonable care, would be willing, and ought, to accept.

market analysis
To identify, research, and analyze the particular market in which the appraised property operates.

market area
A geographic area in which similar property types compete for potential buyers or customers.

market exposure
Making a reasonable number of potential buyers of a property aware that the property is available.

market extraction
(1) General term for collecting information from the market. (2) Method of estimating depreciation in which building values abstracted from sales are compared to current costs new.

market price
The price paid regardless of pressures, motives, or intelligence.

market rent
The rent a property should bring in the open market as determined by current rents on comparable properties.

market segmentation
The process of identifying and analyzing submarkets within larger markets.

market value
The price a property would bring if freely offered on the open market, with both a willing buyer and a willing seller. Also known as objective value or value in exchange.

mass appraisal
Appraising more than one property using standard computerized techniques (statistical analysis, regression, automated valuation models, etc.).

master plan
A city or county's overall plan for physical development.

matched pair method
See paired sales method.

matrix
See adjustment grid.

mature phase
Second phase in the cycle of a neighborhood, marked by the stability of the existing buildings and occupants.

maximally productive
The property use that produces the greatest return on investment. One of the tests of highest and best use.

mean
A measure of central tendency which is calculated by adding the average prices or numeric values of a statistical sample and dividing that by the number of values in the sample. Also known as the average.

median
A measure of central tendency that equals the middle value in a statistical sample. The middle value in a statistical sample.

metes and bounds
A type of legal description that delineates boundaries and measures distances between landmarks to identify property.

mile
A linear measurement of distance. Equals 5,280 feet.

mill
Equals one-thousandth of a dollar and is numerically expressed as $0.001

millage rate
Expresses the property tax rate in terms of tenths of a cent per dollar of property value. The rate varies from district to district and county to county.

mineral rights
The legal interest in the valuable items found below the surface of a property (i.e., gold and coal).

minimum rent
The fixed minimum rent amount paid under a percentage lease. Also known as base rent.

minor
All persons under 18 years of age.

misplaced improvements
Improvements on land that do not conform to the most profitable use of the site.

mobile home
A factory-built home manufactured prior to June 15, 1976, constructed on a chassis and wheels, and designed for permanent or semi-attachment to land.

mode
A measure of central tendency that equals the most frequently occurring price or value in a statistical sample.

modified age/life method
A method of calculating depreciation. Curable physical and functional items of accrued depreciation are identified. The cost to cure all these items is deducted from the reproduction or replacement cost of the improvements. The ratio derived from the age/life method is then multiplied by the remaining cost to arrive at an estimate of accrued depreciation from all other causes.

modified gross lease
Tenant and landlord share expenses in accordance to the provisions of the lease.

modular home
Building composed of modules constructed on an assembly line in a factory.

monument
A fixed landmark used in a metes and bounds land description.

moratorium
The temporary suspension, usually by statute, of the enforcement of liability of debt.

mortgage
A legal document used as security for a debt. The mortgage is the instrument which secures the promissory note.

mortgage constant or mortgage capitalization rate (RM)
The capitalization rate of the debt. It is the ratio of annual debt service to the principal amount of the mortgage loan.

mortgage yield
The amount received or returned from an investment expressed as a percentage.

multiple listing service (MLS)
A cooperative listing service conducted by a group of brokers (usually members of a real estate association) to provide an inventory of all available properties in an area.

multiple regression analysis
A statistical technique for estimating a particular variable, such as probable sales price, using more than one other known variable.

multiplier
A number that, when multiplied by the income, gives an estimate of value. Also known as gross income multiplier or gross rent multiplier.

narrative appraisal report
A detailed, formal written report of the appraisal and the value conclusion.

negative cash flow
When monies will flow from the investor toward the investment.

negative easement
Prohibits a property owner from doing something on his or her estate because of the effect it would have on the dominant estate.

neighborhood
An area whose occupants and users share some common ties or characteristics. A neighborhood may be defined by physical boundaries, a change in land use, or intangible factors like school district boundaries.

neighborhood life-cycle
The process of neighborhood change, including four phases of change: development, maturity, decline, and renaissance.

net income
Gross annual income, less income lost due to vacancies and uncollectible rents, less all operating expenses.

net income ratio (NIR)
Net income divided by the effective gross income.

net lease
The tenant pays an agreed-upon sum as rent, plus certain agreed upon expenses per month (e.g., taxes and insurance).

net operating income (NOI)
The income remaining after deducting operating expenses from effective gross income.

net operating income ratio
The ratio between the net operating income of a property and its effective gross income (EGI).

net worth
The surplus of assets over liabilities.

non-conforming building
An existing building that does not conform to the latest building or zoning codes.

non-conforming loan
A loan that does not meet the standards of Fannie Mae and Freddie Mac. Jumbo loans and sub-prime loans are types of non-conforming loans.

non-conforming use
Legal use of property that was established and maintained at the time of its original construction but no longer conforms to the current zoning law.

non-economic highest and best use
A type of highest and best use that focuses on contribution to the community and community developmental goals rather than income-production.

nuisance value
The value reflected in the price that a buyer would be willing to pay to eliminate an objectionable situation.

observed condition method
See breakdown method.

observed conditions
The condition of a property, determined by observation.

obsolescence
Loss in value due to reduced desirability and usefulness of a structure because its design and construction became obsolete or due to factors outside the property itself. May be functional or economic.

occupancy
An act of taking or holding possession of an owned thing.

occupancy rate
The percentage of total rental units occupied and producing income.

off-site improvements
Improvements not directly on the site that add to the site's utility.

off-street parking
Designated parking spaces associated with a particular building or other structure that are not located on public streets.

on-site improvements
Buildings, structures or other amenities that are erected on a property and contribute to its value.

open housing law
A law passed by Congress in April 1968 that prohibits discrimination in the sale of real estate because of race, color, or religion of buyers.

operating expense ratio
Relationship of a property's expenses to income, found by dividing total operating expenses by effective gross income.

operating expenses
Expenses required to run a property (i.e., to maintain its income). Includes fixed, variable, and reserves for replacement.

operating statement
Written record of a property's gross income, expenses, and resultant net income for a given period of time.

optimum use
See highest and best use.

oral report
An appraisal report that is communicated to the client verbally, rather than in writing.

orientation
The placement of a building on its lot in relation to exposure to sun, prevailing wind, traffic, and accessibility from the street.

overage rent
The amount paid over and above the base rent, under a percentage lease.

overall rate
A capitalization rate that measures income attributable to both land and improvements, that is, to the whole property.

over-improvement
An improvement which is not the highest and best use for the site on which it is placed by reason of excess size or cost. Also called superadequacy.

ownership
(1) The right of one or more persons to possess and use property to the exclusion of all others. (2) A collection of rights to the use and enjoyment of property.

ownership in severalty
Property owned by one person or entity.

paired sales analysis
A method of estimating the amount of adjustment for the presence or absence of any feature by pairing the sales prices of otherwise identical properties with and without that feature. Also known as paired data set analysis, matched pairs analysis, and direct market method.

panelized home
A type of factory-built housing. A panelized home arrives at the construction site in small units, usually as completed walls with all the wiring and plumbing intact.

par value
Market value, nominal value.

parameter
A statistical term for a single number or attribute of the individual things, persons, or other entities in a population.

parcel
(1) A tract or an extended area of land. (2) A part, as in a certain piece of land is part and parcel of another piece.

parcel map
Map showing a parcel of land that will be subdivided into less than five parcels or units, and shows land boundaries, streets, and parcel numbers.

partial interest
An interest in real estate that represents less than the fee simple estate (i.e., a leased fee or leasehold estate).

partial taking
The process by which a governmental agency acquires only a portion of a property through condemnation.

partition action
A court action to divide a property held by co-owners.

party wall
A wall erected on the line between two adjoining properties that are under different ownership, for the use at both properties.

percentage adjustment
Type of sales adjustment in which the estimated difference between the comparable sale and the subject is first calculated as a percentage of the sale price of the comparable, and then applied as an upward or downward adjustment to the price.

percentage lease
A type of lease in which the tenant pays a percentage of gross monthly receipts in addition to a base rent.

percolation
The draining or permeating of water through soil.

personal property
Anything movable that is not real property.

physical deterioration
Depreciation that comes from wear and tear, negligent care, damage by dry rot or termites, or severe changes in temperature. Also known as deferred maintenance.

physical life
The length of time a structure can be considered habitable, without regard to its economic use.

physically possible
A use for the property that is not prevented by any physical issues such as poor access, steep topography, or unusable soil. The first test for highest and best use.

planned development
A planning and zoning term describing land not subject to conventional zoning to permit clustering of residences or other characteristics of the project which differ from normal zoning.

planning commission
An agency of local government charged with planning the development, redevelopment, or preservation of an area.

plat
An illustration, plan, or map of a plot of ground or a town site.

plat map
Map of a subdivision indicating the location and boundaries of individual lots.

plottage
The value added by combining two or more parcels together into one large parcel.

plottage increment
The appreciation in unit value created by joining smaller ownerships into one large single ownership.

plottage value

The increase in value brought about by the combining of two or more parcels of land with the result that the total value of the combined parcels in the "after" situation exceeds the value of the sum of the individual parcels in the "before" situation.

point of beginning

Starting place for a legal description of land using the metes and bounds method.

point estimate of value

The final value indication reported as a single dollar amount.

police power

The power of the state to enact laws within constitutional limits to promote the order, safety, health, morals, and general welfare of our society.

population

(1) The total number of people inhabiting a specific area. (2) In statistics, the entire set of data from which a statistical sample is drawn.

positive cash flow

When income generated by the property flows toward the owner.

potential gross income

A property's total potential income from all sources during a specified period of time.

potential value

The value that can reasonably be foreseen in the future.

precut home

A type of factory-built housing. A precut home is like a house in a box. All the materials are delivered to the construction site unassembled, but precut to fit exactly in place.

prefabricated

Any building or portion thereof, which is manufactured and assembled off site, then erected on a property.

pride of ownership

The pride of the owner in his or her property, reflected in the care and maintenance of the property.

primary mortgage market

The term for the market made up of lenders who make mortgage loans by lending directly to borrowers.

prime rate

The rate the bank charges its strongest customers (those with the highest credit ratings), is heavily influenced by the discount rate.

principal

(1) In a real estate transaction, the one who hires the broker to represent him or her in the sale of the property. (2) The amount of money borrowed.

principal meridian

One of 35 north and south survey lines established and defined as part of the U.S. government survey system.

principle(s) of:

anticipation

States that value is created by the anticipation of benefits derived in the future.

balance

States that the greatest value of a property will occur when the type and size of the improvements are proportional to each other as well as to the land.

change

Holds that it is the future, not the past, which is of prime importance in estimating value. Real estate values are constantly changed by environmental, economic, political, and social forces.

competition

States that real estate values are affected by supply and demand because of competition. Typically follows three steps: (1) market demand generates profits, (2) profits generate competition, and (3) competition stabilizes profits.

conformity

States that maximum value results when properties in a neighborhood are relatively similar in size, style, quality, use, and/or type.

consistent use

Requires that land and improvements be appraised on the basis of the same use.

contribution

Calculates the worth of a particular component in terms of its contribution to the value of the whole property, or an item's worth is calculated as the amount that its absence would detract from the value of the whole.

increasing and decreasing returns

The idea that income and other benefits available from real estate may be increased by adding capital improvements only up to the point of balance in the agents of production, beyond which the increase in value tends to be less than the increase in costs. Also known as law of increasing and decreasing returns.

opportunity cost
The economic principle that recognizes competing investments, usually in different industries, that may have a greater return.

progression
States that the worth of a lesser valued residence tends to be enhanced by association with higher valued residences in the same area.

regression
States that higher-valued properties tend to suffer when placed in close proximity with lower-valued properties.

substitution
Affirms that the maximum value of a property tends to be set by the cost of acquiring an equally desirable and valuable substitute property, assuming no cost delay is encountered in making the substitution. The foundation for the appraisal process.

supply and demand
States that market value is affected by the intersection of supply and demand forces in the market as of the appraisal date. Prices and rent levels tend to increase when demand is greater than supply and tend to decrease when supply exceeds demand.

surplus productivity
States that the net income that remains after the ownership expenses of labor, capital, and management have been paid is surplus income that is attributable to the land. This is also known as land rent and is used as the basis for the residual land valuation techniques.

private restrictions
Created at the time of sale or in the general plan of a subdivision.

pro rata
According to a certain percentage or proportion of a whole.

profits
The excess of returns over expenditures in a given transaction or series of transactions. Also, the excess of income over expenditure, as in a business, during a given period of time.

progress payments
Scheduled, periodic, and partial payment of construction loan funds to a builder as each construction stage is completed.

promissory note
The evidence of the debt, which states the amount of the money borrowed and the terms of repayment.

property
Anything that may be owned and gained lawfully.

property residual technique
A method of value estimation by capitalizing the income to the whole property.

proprietary lease
The lease used in co-op apartment buildings.

proration
Adjustments of interest, taxes, and insurance, etc., on a pro rata basis as of the closing or an agreed-upon date.

public record
A document disclosing all-important facts about the property.

qualitative analysis
Compares data on properties to obtain relative comparisons between properties in the same market.

quantitative analysis
Compares data on properties to obtain results that are then applied to other properties in the same market.

quantity survey method
The most in-depth and detailed method used to estimate reproduction or replacement cost. This method requires a detailed estimate of all labor and materials used in the components of a building. Items such as overhead, insurance, and contractor's profit are added to direct costs of building. This method is time consuming but very accurate.

quitclaim deed
Transfers any interest the grantor may have at the time the deed is signed with no warranties of clear title.

radon
Colorless, odorless, gas that is a carcinogen detected by a spectrometer.

range of value
The difference between the highest and lowest variant.

rate

(1) A fixed ratio, proportion. (2) A charge, payment, or price fixed according to a ratio, scale, or standard. (3) To appraise or assess value for tax assessment purposes.

ratio

Fixed or approximate relation, as between things, in number, quantity, degree, rate, or proportion.

ratio capitalization

Describes any capitalization method that uses the typical ratio of income to value to convert projected income into a value estimate for the property (or property component) under appraisal. Includes direct capitalization, as well as land, building, and equity residual capitalization methods when sales price-income ratios are used.

real estate

An identified parcel or tract of land, including any improvements.

Real Estate Settlement Procedures Act (RESPA)

A federal law requiring the disclosure to borrowers of settlement (closing) procedures and costs by means of a pamphlet and forms prescribed by the United States Department of Housing and Urban Development.

real property

Land (air, surface, mineral, water rights), appurtenances, and anything attached, and immovable by law. Also included are the interests, benefits, and rights inherent in owning real estate, i.e., the "bundle of rights". Current usage makes the term real property synonymous with real estate.

recapture

The recovery by an owner of money invested. Known as return of investment, not to be confused with interest, which is a return on investment. Also known as capital recapture.

reconciliation

The adjustment process of weighing results of all three appraisal methods to arrive at a final estimate of the subject property's market value. Also known as correlation.

reconstructed operating statement

One that eliminates the inapplicable expense items for appraisal purposes and adjusts the remaining valid expenses, if necessary.

Record Keeping

Per USPAP, this section of the ETHICS RULE identifies the record keeping requirements appraisers must follow.

rectangular survey system

A method of specifying the location of a parcel of land using prime meridians, base lines, standard parallels, guide meridians, townships, and sections. Also known as the rectangular survey system, or the U.S. Government Section and Township Survey.

redlining

An illegal lending policy, which denies real estate loans on properties in older, changing urban areas, usually with large minority populations, because of alleged higher lending risks and without due consideration being given by the lending institution to the creditworthiness of the individual loan applicant.

refinancing

The paying-off of an existing obligation and assuming a new obligation in its place. To finance anew, or to extend or renew existing financing.

region

Generally a segment of the nation set apart from other areas by geographical boundaries.

regression analysis

Statistical technique for calculating sales price or adjustments, or for estimating probable sales prices or other variables.

rehabilitation

The restoration of a property to its former or improved condition without changing the basic design or plan.

remainder depreciation

The possible future loss in value of an improvement to real property.

remaining economic life

The number of years between the structure's estimated economic life and its effective age.

remodel

An activity designed to improve the value or desirability of a property through rebuilding, refurbishing, redecorating or adding on to it.

renaissance

Fourth phase in the cycle of a neighborhood. The transition to a new cycle through the demolition, relocation, or major renovation of existing buildings.

renovation

Renewal, repair, or restoration to life.

rent

Payment for the use of a property, generally under a lease agreement.

rent roll

Total of all scheduled rental amounts for tenant space, services, and parking.

rental income

The total of the economic, or fair, rent for each of the units.

rental survey

An analysis of competitive rents used to identify the amount of income the subject property might generate.

replacement cost

Cost of constructing a building or structure that would have a similar utility to the subject improvement, but constructed with modern materials and according to current standards, design, and layout.

replacement reserves

Funds set aside by the property owner to pay for the replacement of certain building components and fixtures that periodically wear out. Also known as reserves for replacement.

replacement value

The amount of money required to replace any improvements that have been lost to fire, flood, wind, or other natural disasters.

reproduction cost

The current cost of building a replica of the subject structure, using similar quality materials.

residential lease

A lease used for single-family homes and duplexes.

RESPA

See Real Estate Settlement Procedures Act.

Restricted Use Appraisal Report

This is the briefest presentation of an appraisal and contains the least detail. Also known as restricted use because the client is the only intended user of the report.

restriction

A limitation placed on the use of property. A restriction may be placed by a private owner, a developer, or the government.

retaining walls

Walls constructed to hold back soil and prevent erosion.

retrospective appraisal

An appraisal that looks at the value of a property at a point of time in the past.

return of investment

Recapture or conversion of the investment in real estate to cash or other valuable assets.

return on investment

The interest earned by an investor on an investment. Also known as return or yield.

reversion

The right to future possession or enjoyment by a person, or the person's heirs, creating the proceeding estate.

reversionary interest

A future interest. For example, the right of a landlord to reclaim the property at the end of the lease.

right-of-way

A right of passage on, over, or under another person's land.

riparian rights

The rights of a landowner whose land is next to a natural watercourse to reasonable use of whatever water flows past the property.

risk analysis

A study made, usually by a lender, of the various factors that might affect the repayment of a loan.

risk rating

A process used by the lender to decide on the soundness of making a loan and to reduce all the various factors affecting the repayment of the loan to a qualified rating of some kind.

room

Space that is enclosed or set apart by a partition.

rounding

Expressing an amount as an approximate number.

row house

A single-family residence, much like a townhouse, with sidewalls that are common with adjoining row houses. Differs from a townhouse in that the tandem garage and utility area usually occupy the ground floor or basement level and there are generally no common areas of ownership.

RULES

The rules in USPAP: the ETHICS RULE, the COMPETENCY RULE, the DEPARTURE RULE (or SCOPE OF WORK RULE), and the JURISDICTIONAL EXCEPTION RULE.

rural

An area outside of an established urban area or metropolitan district.

R-value

A rating that measures how well insulation resists heat.

sale-leaseback-buyback

A sale and leaseback transaction in which the leaseholder has the option to buy back the original property after a specified period of time.

sale-resale analysis
A method for determining adjustment or depreciation amounts that is useful when a property sells and is resold in a relatively short period of time. Assuming both sales are arm's-length, open market transactions, and assuming that there have been no significant changes to the property during the time between the two sales, the difference in price could be a basis for a time adjustment.

sales price
The actual price that a buyer pays for a property.

salvage value
(1) For income tax purposes, the anticipated fair market value of the property at the end of its useful life. (2) The value imputable to a house, structure, or object if it were to be moved to another location.

sample
A defined group within the whole that appraisers work with when analyzing statistical data.

sandwich lease
A lease agreement in which a tenant sublets the property to another person, thus creating a sublessor-sublessee relationship.

scarcity
A lack of supply of some type of real property resulting in increased value when demand exceeds supply.

scheduled rent
Rent paid by agreement between lessor and lessee. Also known as contract rent.

scope of work
The type and extent of research done and the type and extent of analysis applied.

scrap value
The value imputable to components of a structure, such as lumber, copper, roofing materials, or bricks, if they are removed from the existing premises for use elsewhere.

secondary mortgage market
The market involved in the buying and selling of existing mortgage loans from the primary mortgage market or from each other.

section
An area of land that is one square mile, 640 acres, or 1/36 of a township.

Self-Contained Appraisal Report
Contains the most detailed information. Self-contained means that everything the user of the report needs to fully understand it is contained within the report.

seller's market
The market condition in which demand exceeds supply.

semi-detached house
A house with one side a party or lot-line wall.

sentimental value
The value imputable to a property because of a close personal interest or relationship by the owner or potential owner.

separate property
Property owned by a married person in his or her own right outside of the community interest including property acquired by the spouse before marriage or by gift or inheritance.

septic system
The waste removal system.

septic tank
A watertight sewage-settling tank designed to accommodate liquid and solid waste.

service income
Includes receipts from laundry facilities, vending machines, and selling of utility services to tenants.

setback
The distance a building must be set back from the lot line. It is usually a front, back, or side setback.

setback line
A line set by an ordinance that determines how close to a property line a structure can be erected or installed.

setback ordinance
An ordinance requiring improvements built on property to be a specified distance from the property line, street, or curb.

severance damage
In eminent domain actions, the damage to the remainder of a property resulting from a part take of the whole property and the construction of the improvements as proposed.

shed roof
A lean-to type roof with one sloping side and one vertical side meeting at a ridge.

shopping center, regional
A large shopping center with 250,000 to 1,000,000 square feet of store area and serving 200,000 or more people.

short-lived
Structural components that are expected to be replaced or repaired on a consistent basis throughout the life of the structure.

significant digits
Those that go from the first numeral on the left over to the last numeral on the right that is not a zero.

single-family residence
Any improvement used as a dwelling for one related family group.

sinking fund
A fund set aside from a property's income which, with accrued interest, will eventually pay for replacement of the improvements.

site
(1) Land that has been prepared for use with grading, utilities, and access. (2) The position, situation, or location of a piece of land in a neighborhood.

skylight
An opaque window in the roof.

slab-on-grade
A type of foundation in which the structure sits directly on the ground. Monolithic slabs, floating slabs, screeded slabs, and post-tensioned slabs are all types of slab-on-grade foundations.

slum area
An area of generally run-down, overcrowded residences, usually multiple-family, whose inhabitants are usually economically deprived.

solar panels
Gather the sun's heat for use in a solar water heater, solar heating system, and even as a source of electricity in the residence.

special flood hazard area
Flood-prone area identified by FEMA. If the subject property is within a flood hazard zone, it needs to be noted in the appraisal report.

special warranty deed
A deed in which the grantor warrants or guarantees the title only against defects arising during the grantor's ownership of the property and not against defects existing before the time of the grantor's ownership.

special-purpose property
Property that has unique usage requirements, such as a church or a museum, making it difficult to convert to other uses.

square foot cost
The cost per square foot of area of land or a building found by dividing the number of square feet of area into the total cost of the structure or land.

special-use permit
See conditional-use permit.

square-foot method
A method for calculating reproduction or replacement cost by multiplying the cost per square foot by the building's area in square feet. The most common method used by appraisers and real estate agents to estimate the cost of construction.

squatter's rights
The right of use and enjoyment by reason of a long and uncontested possession of a parcel of real property.

stable phase
Second phase in the cycle a neighborhood, marked by stability of the existing buildings and occupants.

standard depth
The most typical lot depth in the neighborhood.

standard deviation
A measure of the extent of variability in a sample, that is, whether the observations are clustered near the mean or scattered throughout the range.

Standards Rules
A series of rules within USPAP that specify what the appraiser must do.

Statements on Appraisal Standards
Part of USPAP, they clarify, interpret, explain, or elaborate on a Rule or Standard.

statistics
The science of collecting, classifying, and interpreting information based on the number of things.

stigmatized property
Property which buyers or tenants may avoid for reasons which are unrelated to its physical conditions or features. Also known as psychologically impacted property.

straight lease
Lease agreement in which rent is a fixed amount that stays the same over the entire lease term.

straight-line method
See economic age/life method.

structure
Anything constructed or erected from an assembly of materials (for example, a house or garage).

subdivision
A tract of land divided by the owner into building lots and streets by a recorded subdivision plat.

subdivision development method
A method of valuing land used for subdivision development. Also known as the land development method.

subdivision system

See lot, block, and tract system.

subject property

The property that is being appraised.

subjective value

Value based on personal reasons.

sublease

A lease given by a lessee.

sub-marginal land

Land from which the return or income falls short of paying all expenses.

subprime loans

loans that do not meet the borrower credit requirements of Fannie Mae and Freddie Mac. Also known as "B" and "C" paper loans as opposed to "A" paper conforming loans.

substructure

Refers to all the below grade improvements.

subsurface

That which lies below the surface.

subsurface rights

Rights in property (oil, water, minerals) found below the surface.

Summary Appraisal Report

The most commonly used report option. It fulfills the minimum requirements for lenders to process their loans.

summation method

Establishes a safe rate for an investment and adds or subtracts from this basic rate according to the proper interest rate for the subject property. Another name for the cost approach to estimating value.

superadequacy

A feature that is too large or of a higher quality than needed for a property. Also known as an over-improvement.

superstructure

Refers to all the above-grade improvements.

supply

The total amount of a given type of property for sale or lease, at various prices, at any given point in time.

surface rights

The rights to use the surface of land, including the right to drill or mine through the surface when subsurface rights are involved.

survey

The process by which a parcel of land is measured and its area is ascertained.

tangible property

Property that has a physical form. Physical objects and/or the rights thereto.

tax rate

The ratio of the tax to the tax base. The rate to be applied to assessed value of real property, which determines the amount of ad valorem tax to be paid.

tenancy by the entirety

The joint ownership, recognized in some states, of property acquired by husband and wife during marriage. On the death of one spouse the survivor becomes the owner of the property.

tenancy in common

When two or more persons, whose interests are not necessarily equal, are owners of undivided interests in a single estate.

tenancy in partnership

Ownership by two or more persons who form a partnership for business purposes.

tenant

The party who has legal possession and use of real property belonging to another.

The Appraisal Foundation

An entity created by the appraisal profession to regulate its own industry. Empowered by the Financial Institutions Reform, Recovery, and Enforcement Act of 1989 to set minimum standards and qualifications for performing appraisals in federally related financial transactions.

tidelands

Lands that are covered and uncovered by the ebb and flow of the tide.

time adjustment

A term usually applied to adjustments made because of changing market conditions.

time value of money

The financial principle that a dollar in the present is worth more than a promised dollar in the future because of the present dollar's interest earning capability.

timeshare

A real estate development in which a buyer can purchase the exclusive right to occupy a unit for a specified period each year.

T-intersection lot
A lot that is fronted head-on by a street.

title
Evidence that the owner of land is in lawful possession.

title plant
The storage facility of a title company in which it has accumulated complete title records of properties in its area.

topography
Nature of the surface of land.

townhouse
One of a row of houses usually of the same or similar design with common side walls or with a very narrow space between adjacent side walls. Also known as a row house.

township
Used in the government survey system, an area six miles by six miles (36 square miles) described by its location relative to the intersection of the baseline and meridian.

tract
A piece of land in an unimproved state – it does not have utilities, sewer lines, etc.

trade fixture
An item of personal property, such as a shelf, cash register, room partition or wall mirror, used to conduct a business.

Trainee License
In some states, this is the beginning level of appraisal license. The education, experience, and exam requirements to obtain a trainee license vary widely by state. Trainees must be supervised.

transferability
The ability to transfer ownership of an item from one person or entity to another.

transition
Change in use, such as farm to residential to commercial.

trend
A particular direction of movement.

trend analysis
Analysis that uses an arrangement of statistical data in accordance with its time of occurrence, usually over a period of years.

trust deed
See deed of trust.

turnkey costs
Costs that include all of the charges to the consumer, not just the costs to the developer or builder.

under-improvement
An improvement which, because of a deficiency in size or cost, is not the highest and best use of the site.

underwriting
Insuring something against loss.

unearned increment
An increase in real estate value that comes about from forces outside the control of the owner(s), such as a favorable shift in population.

unfinished areas
The areas of a home that do not have flooring, insulation, etc., that is similar to the rest of the house.

Uniform Residential Appraisal Report (URAR)
An example of a summary report. It is probably the most widely used form.

Uniform Standards of Professional Appraisal Practice (USPAP)
A set of standards and ethics, originally developed by nine appraisal associations to guide members in the development and reporting of appraisals. Now developed, published, interpreted, and amended by the Appraisal Standards Board of the Appraisal Foundation.

unimproved
Not improved, as not used, tilled, cultivated, or built upon.

unit
(1) A single object. (2) A standard of measure by which other quantities are evaluated.

unit cost
The cost in money of a standard quantity (for example, a square foot or a cubic yard) of a particular item.

unit-in-place method
A method of determining reproduction or replacement cost. Also known as the segregated cost method.

unit-of-comparison adjustment
Sales analysis tool, wherein the sales prices of the comparables are converted to price per physical or economic unit that is found to be closely related to selling price or value.

unit of measurement
The particular measurement being used. The two most commonly used are square foot (area) and cubic foot (volume).

urban property
City property.

urban sprawl
The unplanned and often haphazard growth of an urban area into adjoining areas.

usable area
That portion of the gross area of a site that can be built on or developed. Also known as useful area.

useful life
See economic life.

utility
The ability of a property to satisfy a need or desire, such as for shelter or income.

vacancy factor
The percentage of a building's space that is unrented over a given period.

vacancy loss
Loss of potential income because of a vacant unit.

vacant land
Land or site that is unimproved and that does not have any structures.

valuation
The process of estimating value.

value
The present and future anticipated enjoyment or profit from the ownership of property. Also known as worth.

value conclusion
See final value estimate.

value in exchange
See market value.

value-in-use
(1) The subjective value of an item or object to a particular user. (2) The value of a property under a given use. Also known as use value.

variable expenses
Operating expenses that vary with occupancy level or intensity of use of a property (e.g., utility costs and maintenance).

variance
An exception granted to existing zoning regulations for special reasons.

verification
An inquiry into the circumstances surrounding and affecting a sale.

warranty deed
A deed used to transfer title to property, guaranteeing that the title is clear and the grantor has the right to transfer it.

waste
The destruction, or material alteration of, or injury to, premises by a tenant.

water rights
(1) The right to draw water from a water course. (2) The right to use water, as water on a lake, for recreation.

water table
The depth below the land surface at which water is found.

wear and tear
Depreciation of an asset due to ordinary usage.

workfile
Appraiser's records that contain all the documentation necessary to support the appraiser's analyses, opinions, and conclusions conveyed in the appraisal report.

xeriscape
A patented name for landscaping that conserves water by using a wide variety of plants appropriate for the natural environment.

yield
The interest earned by an investor on an investment (or by a bank on the money it has loaned). Also known as return or profit.

yield capitalization
A method that discounts future benefits at appropriate yield rates, producing a value that reflects the income pattern, value change, and yield-rate characteristics of the investment.

yield rate
The yield expressed as a percentage of the total investment. Also known as rate of return.

zero lot line
A municipal zoning category wherein a building or other fixture may abut the property line.

zeroscaping
The use of rock and hardscape with only a few sparse plants to create low water landscaping.

zone
An area subject to certain restrictions or restraints.

zoning
The regulation of structures and uses of property within selected districts.

zoning law
Type of law used to execute master plans and control the mix of properties in a particular area.

zoning variance
An exemption from a zoning ordinance or regulation permitting a structure or use that would not otherwise be allowed.

INDEX